Cuban Foreign Policy

Transformation under Raúl Castro

Edited by

H. Michael Erisman
Indiana State University

John M. Kirk
Dalhousie University

ROWMAN & LITTLEFIELD
Lanham • Boulder • New York • London

Executive Editor: Susan McEachern
Editorial Assistant: Katelyn Turner
Senior Marketing Manager: Kim Lyons

Credits and acknowledgments for material borrowed from other sources, and reproduced with permission, appear on the appropriate page within the text.

Published by Rowman & Littlefield
A wholly owned subsidiary of The Rowman & Littlefield Publishing Group, Inc.
4501 Forbes Boulevard, Suite 200, Lanham, Maryland 20706
www.rowman.com

Unit A, Whitacre Mews, 26-34 Stannary Street, London SE11 4AB, United Kingdom

British Library Cataloguing in Publication Information Available

Library of Congress Cataloging-in-Publication Data

Names: Erisman, H. Michael, editor. | Kirk, John M., 1951– editor.
Title: Cuban foreign policy : transformation under Raúl Castro / edited by H. Michael Erisman, Indiana State University; John M. Kirk, Dalhousie University.
Description: Lanham : Rowman & Littlefield, 2018. | Includes bibliographical references and index.
Identifiers: LCCN 2017060471 (print) | LCCN 2018000317 (ebook) | ISBN 9781442270947 (electronic) | ISBN 9781442270923 (cloth : alk. paper) | ISBN 9781442270930 (pbk. : alk. paper)
Subjects: LCSH: Cuba—Foreign relations—21st century. | Castro, Raúl, 1930-
Classification: LCC F1788 (ebook) | LCC F1788 .C8273 2018 (print) | DDC 327.7291009/05—dc23
LC record available at https://lccn.loc.gov/2017060471

™ The paper used in this publication meets the minimum requirements of American National Standard for Information Sciences—Permanence of Paper for Printed Library Materials, ANSI/NISO Z39.48-1992.

Printed in the United States of America

Contents

List of Figures and Tables v

1 Historical Introduction to Foreign Policy under Raúl Castro 1
John M. Kirk

Part I: Key Issue Areas

2 The Defense Contribution to Foreign Policy: Crucial in the Past, Crucial Today 25
Hal Klepak

3 Cuba's International Economic Relations: A Macroperspective on Performance and Challenges 43
H. Michael Erisman

4 The Evolution of Cuban Medical Internationalism 59
John M. Kirk

Part II: Cuba's Regional Relations

5 Cuba and Latin America and the Caribbean 77
Andrés Serbin

6 Cuba and Africa: Recasting Old Relations in New but Familiar Ways 95
Isaac Saney

7 Cuba and Asia and Oceania 113
Pedro Monzón and Eduardo Regalado Florido

8 Cuba and the European Union 125
Susanne Gratius

9 Cuba, Oceania, and a "Canberra Spring" 141
Tim Anderson

Part III: Cuba's Key Bilateral Relations

10 The United States and Cuba 161
William M. LeoGrande

11 Canada and Cuba 183
John M. Kirk and Raúl Rodríguez

12 Spain and Cuba 197
Joaquín Roy

13 Venezuela and Cuba 209
Carlos A. Romero

14 Brazil and Cuba 225
Regiane Nitsch Bressan

15 Russia and Cuba 237
Mervyn Bain

16 China and Cuba 255
Adrian H. Hearn and Rafael Hernández

Part IV: Retrospective and Prospective Views

17 Conclusion 271
H. Michael Erisman and John M. Kirk

Index 291

About the Contributors 305

Figures and Tables

FIGURES

3.1 Cuban-Venezuelan total trade. 50
3.2 Cuban exports/imports with Venezuela. 50
3.3 Cuban trade with China. 51
3.4 Cuban trade with Brazil. 53
14.1 Brazilian exports to Cuba. 231
14.2 Brazilian imports from Cuba. 231
14.3 Brazil-Cuba trade balance. 232
16.1 Cuba's trade with China. 258

TABLES

3.1 Cuban GDP Growth Rates 44
3.2 Cuba's Balance of Trade 44
3.3 Cuba: External Debt by Creditor 45
3.4 Cuba's Regional Trade Profile, 2016 46
3.5 Cuba's Export Profile 47
3.6 Cuban Medical Aid Personnel 47
3.7 Tourism Revenues 48
3.8 Tourism Revenue Leakage, 2016 48
3.9 Cuba's Primary Trading Partners 49
3.10 Cuban-American Remittances 52
4.1 Cuban Health Collaborators around the World (as of May 31, 2016) 64

9.1 Cuban Services, 2006–2014 143
9.2 East Timorese and Pacific Students in Cuban Medical Training, 2016 148
9.3 "Yes I Can" Australian Aboriginal Literacy Statistics, 2012–2014 152
13.1 Venezuela: Foreign Trade with Cuba, 1988–2014 213
17.1 U.S. Agricultural Exports to Cuba, 2005–2016 275

1

Historical Introduction to Foreign Policy under Raúl Castro

John M. Kirk

> "The Cuban dictatorship remains a danger, especially to its own people, even in its twilight. It still seeks to frustrate the democratic governance in the region and to actively undermine United States interests. Cubans endure the grim reality of life in their country. Living under a dictatorship means a daily struggle to satisfy needs and wants, with immorality, and, above all, with hopelessness. . . . Only Cubans can chart a path to liberty, prosperity and reconciliation. It is they who will ensure that the dictatorship which advocated nuclear war against our nation will end."
>
> —Commission for Assistance to a Free Cuba, Report to the President, July 2006

> "I've come to Cuba to extend the hand of friendship to the Cuban people. I'm here to bury the last vestige of the Cold War in the Americas and to forge a new era of understanding to help improve the daily lives of Cubans."
>
> —President Barack Obama, March 20, 2016

Within the realm of Cuban-U.S. relations, things have changed dramatically in the past decade. Moreover, under President Donald Trump, and with the retirement from public office of Raúl Castro in 2018, we are about to witness further twists and turns in this, the most significant facet of Cuba's foreign relations. (At the time of writing the claims about "acoustic attacks" on U.S. diplomats at the embassy in Havana have not been resolved, and American tourists have been warned by Washington about the dangers of traveling to Cuba. Meanwhile all indications are that the Trump administration is seeking to reverse most of the key initiatives undertaken by his predecessor.) To a lesser extent there have also been major developments in Cuba's relations with many other countries, resulting in both positive and negative impacts. This collection of essays by leading scholars (from Europe, the United States,

Canada, South America, Australia, and Cuba) seeks to analyze the development of Cuba's foreign relations under Raúl Castro (2006–2018) and, where possible, to offer suggestions on probable future developments.

The death of Fidel Castro in November 2016 led to weeks of introspection about his role in contemporary Cuban history. It was also accompanied by many analyses of how Cuba had changed under Raúl since Fidel ceded power, first on an interim basis in 2006 following surgery, then definitively in 2008, when Raúl was elected president. Cuba has indeed changed dramatically over the past decade, in terms of both domestic events and international relations. This needs to be emphasized since our media often present Cuba in a one-dimensional, overly simplistic caricature, usually as a place caught in a time warp—complete with 1950s cars, cheap rum, salsa, and cigars. One American observer articulated well this impression: "In the decade that I've spent in and out of Cuba, I've observed that Americans tend to believe the country has been frozen in time ever since our embassy closed up shop during the Cold War. . . . The U.S. media insist on using the same tired language to discuss a country that's been undergoing drastic change for the last 20 years."[1]

Before addressing the evolution of Cuban foreign policy, however, it might be important to reflect briefly on some of the domestic developments that have occurred in Cuba in recent years to illustrate the degree of change which has occurred (mainly before the rapprochement with Washington). The growth in the numbers of the self-employed (now approximately 580,000) is noticeable throughout the island, and there are now over four hundred urban-based cooperatives (apart from hundreds more agricultural models). Some two hundred thousand Cubans work in rural areas, independent farmers working on plots provided them by the state. Particularly significant during these years is the development of tourism and the surge in *casas particulares* (bed-and-breakfast operations) and *paladares* (private restaurants). Recent estimates reveal that there are over seventeen thousand rooms in *casas* (representing fully a quarter of all tourist accommodation in Cuba) and hundreds of *paladares* in Havana alone. In 2016 over 4 million tourists visited the island, and nine U.S. airlines began regular air service. In economic terms the main sources of hard currency are now the exportation of medical services, remittances from families abroad, and tourism, all of which have come to the fore in the last decade. There are significant challenges facing the Cuban economy, however. It remains to be seen how quickly the Cuban tourist infrastructure can recover from the devastation caused by Hurricane Irma in September 2017, while it is unclear how the hardening of Cuban policy under the Trump administration will affect the large U.S. tourist market.

Cubans have witnessed many changes during the years when Raúl Castro has been president. They no longer need special exit visas to leave the island and are free to do so—provided that they can obtain entry visas elsewhere. They can stay in the same hotels as foreign tourists and buy computers and cell phones—all severely limited before. Internet access, which traditionally has been tightly controlled, is now growing rapidly. Cuban culture has also evolved, with far greater international exposure. Among the top forty series on Cuban TV, for instance, many are from the United

States (e.g., *Deadwood, The Good Wife, Game of Thrones, House of Cards, Homeland*, and *The Sopranos*). Some would argue that the latter is not necessarily good news; nevertheless it illustrates how the revolution continues to evolve in unexpected ways.[2]

To put this process of evolution into international perspective, when Fidel Castro left the presidency in 2006, the international scene was very different. War was raging in Lebanon, Tony Blair was soon to be rejected as British prime minister because of his role in the Iraq War and the alleged "weapons of mass destruction," Saddam Hussein was executed that year, and at the United Nations General Assembly Hugo Chávez melodramatically referred to President George W. Bush as "the devil." In the United States the midterm elections resulted in the Democrats controlling both houses of Congress, construction had begun on the Freedom Tower in the new World Trade Center in New York, and New Orleans was slowly recovering from Hurricane Katrina. In terms of popular culture, Al Gore's documentary on global warming, *An Inconvenient Truth*, was launched (and immediately condemned by climate change deniers), Barry Bonds of the San Francisco Giants broke Babe Ruth's home run record (715), and in July of that year, Twitter, so frequently employed by President Donald Trump, was launched.

Clearly, the world was very different then—as was Cuba at that time, when the twelve-year presidency of Raúl Castro began. Many outside Cuba wondered how Raúl, long considered the quiet, unassuming Castro brother, would fare in directing foreign policy. Some critics posited that he would not last long as president, given the overwhelming charisma and legacy of his brother. While he was highly regarded in domestic political and military circles, his quieter, lower-key approach was not widely acknowledged—and was certainly different from that of the *comandante en jefe*, who had been in power for so long. Many in Cuba at the time wondered whether there would be an orderly transition or if the tradition of Fidel's charismatic approach would prove too great a challenge for his brother to follow. Those who had worked with him in Cuba expected that he would continue the fundamental planks of domestic and foreign policy initiated under Fidel Castro, but with an ability to develop a more pragmatic and less spontaneous approach. They were proven correct.

THE EVOLUTION OF CUBA'S INTERNATIONAL RELATIONS SINCE 2006

Cuba's foreign relations in 2006, as Raúl Castro assumed power, were marked by two major constants: ongoing tensions with the United States and a notable strengthening of the country's relations with the developing world, assisted greatly by rapidly developing ties with oil-rich Venezuela under President Hugo Chávez. In terms of ideological convergence and close economic ties, no relationship was more significant than that established between Venezuela and Cuba, particularly while Chávez was alive. Also significant was the rather difficult relationship with the European Union, which had maintained an extremely critical "Common Position" (designed to pressure Cuba to improve its human rights record) for almost a decade. It is worth noting how these four themes had evolved by the end of Raúl Castro's tenure.

During the years of the two administrations headed by George W. Bush (2001–2009), relations between Havana and Washington had been badly strained. In May 2004 Bush had announced significant new measures designed to bring "democratic change" to the island. Family visits for Cuban Americans returning to the island were limited to one every three years. The maximum amount that could be sent to Cuba annually as family remittances was $1,200. Educational licenses for U.S. universities seeking to undertake research in Cuba or develop study-abroad programs there were severely limited. Substantial financial support was available from the Bush administration for activities designed to promote regime change—$36 million for "democracy-promoting" activities on the island, $18 million for broadcasts by Radio and TV Martí, and $5 million for "public diplomacy efforts," disseminating information critical about Cuba. Despite the threat of terrorism from groups in the Middle East, the Office of Foreign Assets Control in the Department of Treasury had far more officials working on the Cuba file than on the financial transactions of terrorist organizations. The desire to bring about significant change in Cuba was undoubtedly a major initiative of the Bush administration.

Tensions between the two countries were illustrated in 2006 by the battle of signs around the U.S. Special Interests Section in Havana, where five-foot-high critical electronic ticker messages were flashed along the top of the building, criticizing the revolution. The Cuban government retaliated with the "Plaza de las Banderas," as scores of hundred-foot flagpoles were set up in front, obscuring the provocative messages. In addition large billboards were erected around the U.S. building, condemning the Bush policy toward Cuba and pouring scorn on the administration. In October 2007 Bush referred to Cuba as a "tropical gulag" and noted that the government there was "a failed regime" that was emitting its "dying gasps."[3] To put it simply, bilateral relations were a diplomatic disaster, without any apparent hope for improvement.

Yet, in the international arena, particularly in developing countries, Cuba continued to be widely respected. In 2006 it was elected as a member of the initial UN Human Rights Council (and was subsequently reelected in 2009, 2014, and 2016). At the most recent election for the council, Cuba had the support of 160 nations. In 2006, 183 countries supported the annual motion of Havana condemning the U.S. embargo at the United Nations General Assembly (in 2017, 191 did so, with none voting against the Cuban motion and only 2 countries—the United States and Israel—abstaining). Chapters by Isaac Saney (on Cuba's role in Africa), Pedro Monzón and Eduardo Regalado Florido (Asia), and Tim Anderson (Oceania) illustrate the rapid growth in Cuba's ties with these areas.

Furthermore, during the first year of Raúl Castro's presidency, the fourteenth summit of the 120-nation Non-Aligned Movement (NAM) met in Havana, and Cuba was chosen to lead the NAM for the following three years, the second time that it had been accorded this honor. Some fifty-eight heads of state attended (including the leaders of Pakistan, India, Iran, and Malaysia). Several Latin American presidents chose not to do so (including the presidents of Mexico, Brazil, Chile, Colombia, and Peru)—a reality which was soon to change with the election of more liberal leaders in those countries. Since that time presidents from all these countries have visited Cuba, illustrating the increasing level of international respect for the country.

The basic principles of Cuban foreign policy, both before and during the presidency of Raúl Castro, have not changed much over the decades—although there have been some significant initiatives undertaken since he assumed the presidency. Writing in 2013, William LeoGrande noted three basic components that, up to that point, had formed the basis of Cuban foreign policy under Raúl Castro: the diversification of economic relations, the strengthening of diplomatic support (regionally and globally) through an active role in international organizations, and the pursuit of normal relations with the United States.[4] This steady policy approach has continued and indeed been strengthened under the leadership of Raúl Castro. Moreover, the basic claim made in 1978 by Jorge Domínguez that Cuba was a small country but possessed a "big country's foreign policy"[5] is still correct fully four decades later—although for different reasons than was in the case in that year, when Cuba had thirty-five thousand troops in Africa. Now it has over fifty thousand medical personnel dispatched over vast stretches of the globe.

CUBAN-U.S. RELATIONS

LeoGrande is correct in highlighting the importance of seeking normal, principled relations with the United States as a fundamental goal of Cuban foreign policy, as he illustrates in his chapter. For decades Havana had insisted that it was fully prepared to negotiate in an open, transparent manner with Washington but insisted that these negotiations be carried out in a respectful manner, without preconditions and above all respecting each country's sovereign independence. During most of that time various U.S. administrations rejected these principles and preferred to pursue a policy of regime change, refusing to accept Cuba as an equal partner at the negotiating table. With few exceptions (the Jimmy Carter presidency being one), this had been the case since January 1961, when Washington officially broke off relations with Cuba.

Indeed, while the fundamental principles of Cuban foreign policy had basically remained the same throughout the revolutionary process (and largely continue to do so), so too had the program of enmity emanating from Washington. As Raúl Castro took power in 2006, the likelihood of working toward a normal, respectful relationship looked as distant as ever. The embargo, introduced in 1960, continued as official policy, supporting the "Trading with the Enemy Act," which remained (and remains) in place. Likewise it had been strengthened by two bills also still in effect—the 1992 Cuban Democracy Act (known as the Torricelli Bill) and the 1996 Cuban Liberty and Democratic Solidarity Act (known as the Helms-Burton law). Both were intended to contribute to the collapse of the Cuban economy.

Funding was still provided to dissident groups (although most remained with Cuban American exile groups in Miami instead of the opposition groups who needed it most). Radio and TV Martí continued to broadcast (illegally) signals to Havana (although the latter were almost completely blocked). Cuban Americans still faced strict limitations on visiting their families on the island and sending them remittances. Bilateral trade was nonexistent; nor were there any regular flights or cruise ship visits to Cuba. American citizens were denied the right to travel to Cuba unless they fell within specific categories (such as journalism, religious delegations, or official government missions), and there was a strict process in place to ensure that American citizens complied with the law. Indeed there were several well-publicized cases of Americans being fined thousands of dollars for having had the temerity to travel to Cuba.

In 2004, and subsequently in 2006, the administration of George W. Bush sought to justify its promotion of regime change in Havana through the establishment of a Commission for Assistance to a Free Cuba. The 2006 report of the commission was issued by Secretary of State Condoleezza Rice, Commerce Secretary Carlos Gutiérrez, and "Transition Coordinator" Caleb McCarry. It recommended an $80 million fund (the Cuba Fund for a Democratic Future) "to increase support for Cuban civil society" and offered a detailed report of how a U.S. occupation could totally reorganize the political, social, and economic structure of the island.[6] It emphasized the responsibility of the United States "to acknowledge and honor the courage of Cuban democracy activists by supporting their efforts to recapture their sovereignty for their fellow Cubans." The report was replete with such poor analysis, incorrect assumptions, and misinformation that it was a diplomatic embarrassment. Wayne Smith, a career State Department employee and former head of the U.S. Special Interests Section in Havana, wrote a scathing denunciation, pointing out that its basic premises were mistaken and claiming that its intentions would prove counterproductive. In its place he offered the one solution that had not seemingly been considered until then—honest negotiations.

The approach the United States should take toward Cuba, rather than the dead-end policy it is now following, is also obvious. The Cold War is over. Cuba poses no threat whatsoever to the United States. We have normal trade and diplomatic relations with China and Vietnam, two other communist states, so why not with Cuba? We have disagreements with Cuba to be sure, but surely it would be better to discuss these disagreements through normal diplomatic dialogue rather than to refuse to talk. And that diplomatic dialogue should begin immediately.[7]

How distant the narrow, erroneous analysis presented by these high-ranking officials in 2006 seems in comparison with the initiatives taken by the Barack Obama administration. By contrast those brought about a significant change in perspective, culminating in the historic December 17, 2014, declarations by Presidents Obama and Castro that they intended to reopen diplomatic relations between the two countries. While many in both the United States and Cuba have expressed disappointment at the slow progress in improving bilateral relations, in fact—given the forty-three years of enmity following Washington's breaking of diplomatic relations on January 3, 1961—there has been substantial progress. It is important to bear in mind that this came about after a lengthy process—with initiatives taken by both Washington and Havana. Secret meetings in Canada and even the involvement of Pope Francis were important factors that finally resulted in this groundbreaking agreement.

Under the Obama administration there were many improvements in the bilateral relationship. These ranged from the release and exchange of prisoners (e.g., the case of the Cuban Five and of Alan Gross in 2014) to the reduction in restrictions on travel and remittances. More American citizens could now legally visit the island, and the twelve categories of "people-to-people" meetings were significantly loosened. Diplomatic contacts increased dramatically, with regularly scheduled meetings, dealing with a myriad of bilateral interests, held in Washington and Havana. In all there were "23 high-level visits, 51 technical meetings and 12 agreements signed in areas ranging from co-operation on the environment and air-travel to health and the fight against drug trafficking. 12 more were in the pipeline."[8] (Eventually twenty-two would be signed.) Cuba was removed from the list of countries sponsoring terrorism, a claim which had long been considered spurious by the international community. Direct mail service was normalized after decades of having letters rerouted through third countries. Scores of cultural and sports exchanges were organized, ranging from professional baseball teams to local junior ones, while singers and dancers, actors and orchestras toured extensively on both sides of the Florida Strait. There was also a substantial increase in U.S. citizens traveling to Cuba—an estimated seven hundred thousand passengers flew to Cuba from the United States (including five hundred thousand Cuban Americans) in 2016.[9] During the first six months of 2017, these figures doubled.

Presidents Obama and Castro met on several occasions, and embassies were established in both countries (although, in an example of narrow politics, Republican-controlled congressional committees refused to promote the eminently qualified head of the U.S. Special Interests Section to the position of ambassador). In January 2017 Obama repealed both the wet foot/dry foot policy, which provided exclusive immigration rights to Cubans landing on U.S. soil, and the 2005 Medical Parole Program, which allowed any Cuban medical personnel who defected on international soil to enter the United States. These were two long-standing issues that had been particularly troublesome for the Cuban government. All of this would have been unthinkable just a couple of years earlier, so deep was the tradition of discord that had been festering for decades.

The decision on December 17, 2014, to move toward normalizing diplomatic relations, made simultaneously on television by both presidents, dramatically changed the situation. In addition the March 2016 mission of Barack Obama to Cuba (the first presidential visit since that of Calvin Coolidge in 1928) was particularly significant. In many ways it was the culmination of all that had been accomplished over the previous fifteen months. There were extensive bilateral meetings between the two presidents, who also attended a baseball game between the Cuban national team and the Tampa Bay Rays. President Obama gave a speech to representatives of Cuban civil society, which was carried live on national television. Soon, other initiatives followed. In May the Carnival Corporation cruise ship *Adonia* arrived in Havana, the first U.S. cruise ship to visit Cuba in over fifty years. American hotel chains signed agreements to manage three hotels on the island, and in August a Jet Blue plane arrived in Santa Clara, the first regularly scheduled flight from the United States to Cuba in decades, soon to be followed by flights by several other American airlines. In the annual debate at the United Nations General Assembly on the U.S. embargo, for the first time in twenty-five years the United States abstained.[10]

But many challenges remained, and Obama's visit also revealed ongoing tensions between the two countries. Fidel Castro published a bitter denunciation of Obama's comments to an audience of Cuban entrepreneurs ("El hermano Obama" or "Brother Obama") in the Cuban daily *Granma*. Moreover, in September the president again renewed the "Trading with the Enemy Act" regarding Cuba. A report revealed that Cuban dissident organizations had received $4 million from the National Endowment for Democracy, supporting the activities of opposition groups and ultimately seeking to bring about regime change. Despite claiming early in his first presidency that he would close the Guantánamo detention center, Obama had not been able to do so. The embargo remained in effect, although in January 2017 the first Cuban exports left for the United States—two tons of artisanal charcoal. Republican opposition in Congress had still not confirmed a U.S. ambassador for Cuba—and at the time of writing still has not done so.

For many years much of the hard-line support for the policy of regime change in Cuba had come from Cuban exiles in the strategically important state of Florida. Yet, by the time Obama was inaugurated as president in 2009, a majority of Cuban exiles were opposed to the approach of the Bush administration, particularly with regard to limitations on family visits to Cuba as well as on sending of remittances to the island. Almost five hundred thousand Cuban American "exiles" traveled to the island in 2016 alone, visiting family members, bringing billions of dollars in gifts, and sending over $3 billion in remittances.

In sum, as far as the relationship between Cuba and the United States is concerned, during the Obama administrations much was accomplished in terms of working toward reducing substantially the climate of fear and hostility that had permeated bilateral ties for decades. Yet, even with the initiatives realized between 2014 and 2016, normalization was still a distant goal. The thorny issue of property rights had not been successfully addressed—with many Cuban Americans and U.S. citizens wanting redress for properties nationalized by the revolutionary government (with interest, some $6 billion to $8 billion), while Havana insisted upon several hundred billion dollars in financial compensation for the decades-long embargo, which had badly distorted the national economy. Also forgotten in the diplomatic shuffle were the thirty-four hundred Cubans killed during the 1960s and 1970s in acts of terrorism, many funded by the U.S. government and right-wing exile groups.

And the emotional issue of the U.S. military base at Guantánamo remained off the negotiating table, with extremely strong feelings on both sides of the argument.

Revolutionary Cuba had survived decades of hostility emanating from the north. It had paid dearly for that survival: over a million of its citizens had left, its society had been polarized, its economy had become distorted as a result of its thirty-year dependency upon the Soviet Union, and all had been adversely affected by the "Special Period" resulting from the implosion of the Soviet Union.

The elephant in the room, of course, was the 2016 election of Donald Trump, since it was unclear precisely what kind of policy he intended (and intends) to implement regarding the Cuban question. LeoGrande in his chapter deals with the complexities of this relationship. Prior to his election Trump moved between three contradictory positions: condemning the errors of the traditional U.S. approach to Cuba and calling for a pragmatic solution; committing himself in Miami to overturning all the executive actions of Barack Obama; and finally calling for a better "deal" to be worked out between the Cuban government and its people and between Havana and Washington. "Highly unpredictable" would appear an appropriate description of the position of the Trump administration in this regard.

CUBAN-VENEZUELAN RELATIONS

One of the greatest challenges facing Cuba at the end of Raúl Castro's term in office was how to maintain the close relationship with Venezuela. At the start of his tenure (1999), Hugo Chávez was firmly in control in Caracas, and bilateral ties were well established, with leaders of both countries frequently asserting that they were in essence defending the same revolutionary ethos.[11] Venezuela was also Cuba's largest trading partner, with over one hundred thousand barrels of oil arriving daily, while at its peak some sixty thousand Cuban medical personnel were working in Venezuela. Although the personal ties between Raúl Castro and Chávez were not as warm as they had been under Fidel, both countries were still remarkably close. In his chapter Carlos A. Romero analyzes this stage of the relationship in great detail.

One particularly significant aspect of the steadily increasing ties between Cuba and Venezuela was the emergence of the Bolivarian Alliance for the Peoples of Our America (Alianza Bolivariana para los Pueblos de Nuestra América, or ALBA), founded by Presidents Fidel Castro and Hugo Chávez on December 14, 2004. Originally intended as an alternative to the Free Trade Area of the Americas (FTAA), promoted heavily by Washington, ALBA represented a distinctive opposition to the neoliberal policies of the FTAA, but soon branched out—using Venezuelan petrodollars and Cuban human capital—to develop a number of social programs in ALBA member countries, which grew to include Bolivia, Nicaragua, Dominica, Ecuador, Antigua and Barbuda, Saint Vincent and the Grenadines, Saint Lucia, Grenada, and Saint Kitts and Nevis. It had spectacular success in social programs, particularly during the early years of its development, and also managed to provide substantial assistance to member nations through the delivery of subsidized oil.[12] Cuba's role in ALBA was a very personal initiative of its two founding presidents, and while Raúl Castro continues to support the alliance, the deterioration of the Venezuelan economy has had a significant negative impact on its outreach programs.

By 2017, the "special relationship" had been severely debilitated, largely because of the massive economic difficulties being faced in Venezuela, particularly since the death of Chávez in 2013. Oil shipments had dropped by half, and the number of Cuban medical personnel in Venezuela was reduced to thirty-eight thousand. As a result, Cuba was now buying oil on the international market from a variety of countries. It was also claimed that Venezuela "had to resort to buying oil abroad to meet its minimum obligations to Cuba for December 2016 and January."[13] The hard currency that Cuba had obtained by reexporting Venezuelan petroleum was long gone.

Venezuela's difficulties continued to mount, with rampant inflation, increasing political opposition, a shortage of basic necessities, manipulation of prices, hoarding, negative media coverage, social polarization, and pressure from both Washington and right-wing governments in Latin America. While Cuba's political support for the Nicolás Maduro government remained strong, bilateral trade continued to slide, with no apparent end in sight. To put this in context, by the summer of 2017, Cuban trade with Venezuela had fallen 70 percent since 2014. According to Reuters correspondent Marc Frank, merchandise trade had fallen from $7.4 billion to $2.2 billion in 2016, and Venezuelan exports to Cuba (mainly oil-related products) fell by 40 percent.[14] Havana wisely made contingency plans in case the Maduro government failed. This concern about how to support and maintain strong bilateral ties with Caracas, at a time when developments in Venezuela were making this increasingly difficult, in many ways mirrors the challenges facing Cuba's traditional ties with other allies in the region.

EU-CUBA RELATIONS

While not carrying the same economic weight as the ties with Venezuela, the relationship between Cuba and the European Union was also a major issue for both Havana and Brussels. As such, the discussions over normalizing relations continued for a decade. Both Susanne Gratius and Joaquín Roy analyze the significant ties between Cuba and the European Union, particularly with Spain, given the deep and historical ties involved. EU High Representative for Foreign Affairs and Security Policy Federica Mogherini played a key role in promoting closer ties with Cuba and was one of the signatories of the Political Dialogue and Cooperation Agreement between the EU and Cuba in December 2016. Photographs of smiling diplomats, with effusive praise for the agreement, have been widely distributed. But this marks a significant departure from the earlier EU position on Cuba and illustrates how ties have improved since the EU introduced the Common Position in 1996. At that time the role of extremely conservative Spanish prime minister José María Aznar was particularly crucial in introducing the Common Position, designed to bring about regime change in Cuba.

The Common Position, according to the EU press release, was "to encourage transition to pluralist democracy and respect for human rights and fundamental freedoms, as well as sustainable recovery and improvement in the living standards of the Cuban people."[15] The original document, issued on December 2, 1996, was rather presumptuous in tone and clearly indicated that the EU believed it could bring its influence to bear to pressure Cuba to change drastically. It lectured Havana about the need to seek reform, stating in Article 2 that "full cooperation with Cuba will depend upon improvements in human rights and political freedom, as indicated by the European Council in Florence." The subsequent article went further, noting that the EU intended to "intensify the present dialogue with the Cuban authorities and with all sectors of Cuban society in order to promote respect for human rights and real progress towards pluralist democracy."[16] Needless to say, Havana was not impressed—although the Cuban government retained some satisfaction in the knowledge that several of the EU members continued to trade actively with the island and to invest in its tourist industry despite the official rhetoric.

As a result, regardless of changes that the European Council in Florence might have desired from Cuba, the government in Havana paid little heed. The Common Position was reviewed every six months, with little meaningful change taking place. In actual fact the Common Position was anything but "common." While several former socialist allies of Cuba (particularly the Czech Republic, Hungary, and Poland) condemned Cuba, many of the Western capitalist countries ignored the overall objectives, instead trading actively with Cuba. Indeed Spain was one of Cuba's leading trading partners and, while paying lip service to the Common Position, continued to trade with and invest in the island. Moreover, more than half of tourists traveling to Cuba in the early 2000s were from EU countries, and the EU was Cuba's principal trading partner.

To appreciate how Cuban-EU relations have improved under Raúl Castro, one only has to look at the tense situation when he assumed the presidency in 2006. The low point had come in 2003 when seventy-five dissidents were arrested and three men were executed after violently hijacking a ferry in order to escape to Florida. The EU retaliated by inviting Cuban dissidents to national celebrations at the missions of member nations, while at the same time limiting high-level government visits by European diplomats and reducing their visibility at Cuban government functions. The situation became worse in 2005 when Cuba expelled several European journalists and politicians who had been planning to attend a conference organized by dissidents. That same year Fidel Castro "labeled EU nations as 'hypocrites,' and in the service of the United States, after the European Parliament granted the *Damas de Blanco*, a group of wives, mothers and sisters of jailed Cuban dissidents, the Sakharov Prize for Freedom of Thought."[17] For its part Cuba refused direct aid from the EU and continued to arrest dissidents, claiming that they were externally funded. Not surprisingly, until the 2016 decision to drop the Common Position, Cuba was the only country in the region without an EU cooperation agreement. In early February 2006 a key resolution on Cuba was adopted by the EU, calling on Havana to respect basic freedoms and to cease repression against human rights activists. This was the context when Raúl Castro took over.

After a decade of EU pressure on Cuba, with a series of diplomatic carrots and sticks intended to convince Cuba to accept European demands on democratic change and human rights, it finally became clear that this was not about to happen. Cuba could resist any (rather empty) threats that the EU could pose, while at the same time the consensus was reached in Europe that, given Cuba's obduracy on the one hand and the lack of EU influence on the other, no significant results could be expected from the EU position. As one astute commentator has noted, "The EU concluded that the Common Position failed to achieve its purpose, and that neither American toughness nor European flexibility does the Cuban people or its member countries much good. It also concluded that Raúl Castro's leadership has changed in some fundamental ways the circumstances in which Cuban citizens live and work."[18] Sarah Stephens puts this more succinctly, quoting a European source: "Cuba wants capital, and the European Union wants influence."

On December 6, 2016, the diplomatic wheel turned full circle when the EU Council decided to sign a Political Dialogue and Cooperation Agreement between the EU and Cuba, which was signed the following week by EU foreign ministers, EU High Representative for Foreign Affairs and Security Policy Federica Mogherini, and Cuban foreign minister Bruno Rodríguez Parrilla. A press release from the EU Council stated that the agreement sought to "support the transition process of the Cuban economy and society. It promotes dialogue and cooperation to encourage sustainable development, democracy and human rights, and find shared solutions to global challenges."[19] It also stated that the 1996 Common Position on Cuba had been repealed, diplomatically skating around the fact that it had brought little influence to bear after a decade of EU pressure.

CUBA'S INTERNATIONAL STANDING

Perhaps one clear illustration of the success of Raúl Castro's foreign policy can be seen in the extremely active agenda of the revolutionary government, both with industrialized countries in the North and developing nations in the Global South.[20] This was an extremely important component of Cuban foreign policy, since for many years Washington had attempted to isolate Havana. Indeed by the end of 1962, all countries of the Western Hemisphere—with the exception of Canada and Mexico—had broken off diplomatic relations with revolutionary Cuba. Yet the Cuban government assiduously sought to improve relations, first with the Global South and later with the developed countries. Under Raúl Castro's leadership, this tendency increased noticeably. In 2016, for example, there was an impressive list of foreign leaders who visited Havana.[21]

Several European ministers, aware that the Common Position was soon to disappear, traveled to Havana. These included Sigmar Gabriel (vice chancellor of Germany), Lilianne Ploumen (Dutch minister of trade), Heinz Fischer (Austrian president), Pirkko Hamalainen (Finnish foreign minister), Philip Hammond (British foreign secretary, the first British minister of foreign affairs to visit Cuba since 1959), Didier Reynders (foreign minister and deputy prime minister of Belgium), Mark Rutte (prime minister of the Netherlands), Augusto Ernesto Santos Silva (foreign minister of Portugal), Peter Kazimir (Slovakian finance minister), Mario Giro and Ivan Scalfaratto (deputy minister of foreign affairs and undersecretary of economic of development in the Italian government), Igor Crnadak (foreign minister of Bosnia and Herzegovina), Stanislaw Tillich (president of the Federal Council of Germany), Marcelo Rebelo de Sousa (president of Portugal), Matthias Fekel (French minister of external trade), and Dimitri Rogozin (Russian vice president). There were also several visits by Federica Mogherini, the foreign policy minister of the European Union, who was finally able to broker a deal with Havana. During her most recent visit in January 2018, she announced EU development assistance in sustainable agriculture and renewable energy projects, promoted greater investment and trade by the European Union, and criticized the US embargo.

In 2016 several other wealthy industrialized nations strengthened ties with Cuba. Canada, which had a particularly cool relationship with Cuba under former prime minister Stephen Harper, made a major effort to show that—under Justin Trudeau—a new approach would be followed. Accordingly Trudeau visited Havana (as his father had done in 1976) and shortly thereafter issued an emotional communiqué on the death of Fidel Castro. In addition the Canadian government arranged for the frigate *Fredericton* to visit Havana—a first for the navy. Not to be outdone, the French navy frigate *Germinal* also visited the island.

Cuba also courted international connections with the Global South, especially through its program of medical internationalism—but also through other education, construction, culture, and sports cooperation initiatives. Throughout the years when Raúl Castro was president, foreign politicians traveled to Havana. Again, taking 2016 as a benchmark to analyze the depth of Cuba's international relations, many leaders and ministers from Latin America, Africa, and Asia traveled to Havana. In February former Colombian president Ernesto Semper, secretary-general of the Union of South American Nations, was received by Raúl Castro, as was former president of Uruguay José Mujica. Later in the month Uraguayan vice president Raúl Fernando Sendic was received by his Cuban counterpart, Miguel Díaz-Canel. Also in February Peru's president, Ollanta Humala, led a trade delegation to Cuba. Later that year Juan Orlando Hernández, president of Honduras, also visited Havana, while Ethiopia's foreign minister, Tedros Adhanom Ghebreyesus, came to Havana in June.

In March and April, respectively, Argentina featured prominently, with Foreign Minister Susana Malcorra and President Mauricio Macri visiting Havana. Between March and May Raúl Castro received several leaders from Latin America and the Caribbean, including Evo Morales (Bolivia), Jimmy Morales (Guatemala), Keith

Christopher Rowley (Trinidad and Tobago), David Arthur Granger (Guyana), Jocelerme Prévert (Haiti), Desiré Delano Bouterese (Suriname), and Andrew Michael Holness (Jamaica). At the June summit of the twenty-five-country Association of Caribbean States, hosted in Havana, Raúl Castro also met with the prime ministers of Saint Martin, Antigua and Barbuda, and Curaçao, as well as the governor of Puerto Rico, Alejandro García Padilla. It is worth noting that both Macri and Morales are extremely conservative presidents, sharing little in common with the ideology of revolutionary Cuba—yet their presence illustrates how ties to Cuba with even neoliberal governments in Latin America have continued to grow. Andrés Serbín provides a well-argued analysis of the evolution of Cuba's relations with Latin America, illustrating the pragmatism that is a common feature of Havana's relations with the area.

In late 2016 several African leaders visited Cuba at the invitation of the Cuban government. They included Peter Hitjitevi Katjavivi, president of the National Assembly of Namibia, who came to Cuba in January. Prime Minister Pakalitha Bethurel Mosisili of Lesotho (received by Vice President Díaz-Canel), former president Sam Nujoma of Namibia (received by Raúl Castro), President José Mario Vaz of Guinea-Bissau (who visited Fidel Castro at his home), and Algerian prime minister Abdelmalek Sellal (received by Raúl Castro) also visited Cuba. Asia was not omitted, with visits by key members of the Chinese Politburo, including Sun Zhengcai (April) and Kim Yong Chol (May), while Chinese premier Li Keqiang visited in September. All were received by Raúl Castro. In fact Havana was a particularly busy capital in September, with visits by the Chinese premier almost overlapping with that of Japanese premier Shinzo Abe (the first visit by a Japanese leader) and also with visits by President Tsakhiagiin Elbegdoy of Mongolia and Iranian president Hassan Rouhani.

Apart from this long list of distinguished foreign visitors to Cuba, there were several other significant events which took place there and testify to the government's careful attention to cultivating foreign relations with both developing and industrialized countries. Some are of important symbolic importance, such as the decision of the Czech Republic to appoint an ambassador to Cuba for the first time in twenty-seven years. The former socialist ally had been a particularly acerbic critic of Cuba after the dissolution of the Soviet Union and the socialist common market (Council for Mutual Economic Assistance). The same could be said about Poland. Significantly, in June 2017 Witold Waszczykowsi came to the island—the first visit by a Polish foreign minister in thirty years. In terms of international politics, more significant was the brief February meeting in Havana between Patriarch Kirill of the Russian Orthodox Church and Pope Francis. (The patriarch was on an official visit to Cuba, whereas the pope was en route to Mexico.) This meeting—the first between the leaders of these churches—came after a profound rift between the churches which had lasted over a thousand years.

The visit of President Obama to Havana in March 2016, shortly before a massive outdoor concert by the Rolling Stones, was enormously important and probably the most significant international visit of the decade. It was a bold and courageous step by Obama that was generally well received by the Cuban people, although it was criticized by many in the Communist Party of Cuba. Both before and after the Obama visit, there have been scores of high-profile visits from the United States—by members of Congress, leaders of business and agricultural associations, and tourism managers. But it was the president's visit which legitimized all subsequent visits and paved the way for a better bilateral understanding.

The January 2017 visit of Thomas Donohue, head of the U.S. Chamber of Commerce, during which he met with Raúl Castro and members of his economic cabinet, was also particularly important, coming days before the inauguration of Donald Trump. Long an opponent of the embargo, the Chamber of Commerce had consistently promoted the process of normalizing bilateral relations while urging the revolutionary government to be more supportive of U.S. investment. Concerned with potentially negative reactions to these goals by the incoming Trump administration, Donohue sought to remind Trump of the significant interest of American business in not turning back the advances of the Obama administration.

While the United States–Cuba axis has understandably dominated North American media, it is important not to lose sight of the significant relationships that Cuba has been developing around the globe. The meeting between Pope Francis and the patriarch of the Russian Orthodox Church in Havana is a potent symbol of the international significance of this relatively small Caribbean island of just 11 million people (roughly the size of Ohio or Georgia). Also important was the role of Cuba in supporting for almost four years the Colombian peace process, arguably the most significant development in Latin American politics for years. In 2016 this resulted in the signing of a peace accord between the guerrilla Revolutionary Armed Forces of Colombia–People's Army (Fuerzas Armadas Revolucionarias de Colombia—Ejército del Pueblo, or FARC-EP) and the Colombian government. The civil war there had lasted for fifty-two years, resulted in over two hundred thousand deaths, and displaced 5 million people.

Under the mediation of Norway and Cuba, both sides had been meeting in Havana since December 2012. In June 2016 an agreement was finally reached, and a famous photograph of the time shows Colombian president Juan Manuel Santos grasping the hand of Timoleón Jiménez, chief negotiator of the guerrilla group, with Raúl Castro between the two. Several key political figures attended the ceremony, including Norwegian foreign minister Borge Brende, UN Secretary-General Ban Ki-moon, and Presidents Michelle Bachelet (Chile), Nicolás Maduro (Venezuela), Danilo Medina (Dominican Republic), and Salvador Sánchez Cerén (El Salvador). Cuba's role in brokering the peace negotiations and hosting both sides for nearly four years was clearly an extraordinary piece of international diplomacy and needs to be recognized.[22]

Cuba's international standing has clearly risen substantially during the careful nurturing of bilateral and multilateral relations under Raúl Castro. In part this was because the countries of Latin America had developed a closer working relationship, assisted by the increase of socialist and social democratic countries since the first election of Hugo Chávez. There was, therefore, a sense of self-confidence in the area. But Havana had also made a deliberate attempt under Raúl Castro to build a broad network of international relations not based solely upon ideology. While no basic principles had been renounced, pragmatism had clearly made its presence felt.

CONCLUDING THOUGHTS

On one level there are serious challenges facing Cuban foreign policy as the presidency of Raúl Castro comes to an end. To a large extent this is due to the circumstances surrounding the weakening of the "pink tide" in Latin America and the decline in support for the Latin American Left. The case of Venezuela-Cuba ties has also been mentioned, and the major challenges faced by the Maduro government have made for an increasingly difficult time in Havana. Another major blow for Havana came from the scandalous impeachment of Dilma Rousseff in Brazil and the threat of legal proceedings against her predecessor, Lula da Silva. These acts have severely reduced the influence of the Workers' Party in Brazil, a former major ally of Havana, as Regiane Nitsch Bressan notes. While there is no doubt that this was the result of immoral and dishonest machinations and a hostile press, the end of thirteen years' rule by the Workers' Party has been a major blow to Cuba.

Likewise the determined opposition to Cristina Fernández de Kirchner and the Peronistas led to the defeat of her handpicked successor in the November 2015 elections. Again, the new government, led by Mauricio Macri, has pursued a relentless legal battle against the former president. In Bolivia Evo Morales lost a legislative battle to stand again as a candidate for the presidency, while in Ecuador Rafael Correa left the presidency in 2017, although he was replaced by a good friend of Cuba, Lenín Moreno. Given the symbolic importance of these severe dents to the unity of the Latin American Left and the significant impact of these events upon Cuba's international trade and investment prospects, these are challenging times indeed, as is indicated in the concluding chapter.

However daunting these may appear, they pale in comparison with the challenges faced in the past by the Cuban revolutionary process. From the defeat of Fulgencio Batista's vastly superior military forces in the late 1950s to the survival of the revolution during decades of U.S. attempts at regime change—and it must be remembered at all times that Cuba is a mere ninety miles from the superpower—the government has managed to blaze a trail and overcome these obstacles.

The end of the privileged relationship with the former Soviet Union and its socialist allies in Eastern Europe also affords a useful point of comparison with the challenges faced by Cuban foreign policy today. Mervyn Bain in his chapter analyzes how the relationship between Havana and Moscow has evolved, in political and economic terms, and shows that Russia is still a major trading partner of Cuba. The loss of erstwhile allies, the decimation of its decades-old commercial relationships, and a disastrous drop in GDP—seen most clearly in the 1989–1994 period—provoked enormous difficulties for Cuba during the ensuing Special Period. This complex and depressing reality lasted for over a decade, and its effects are still felt in Cuba. But it also provided an important learning moment, and since then Havana has moved to broaden its international ties in terms of both trade policy and international relations. In addition, in good times and bad, Cuba has continued its policy of international cooperation, providing medical care to dozens of developing countries, as outlined in the chapter by John M. Kirk.

But major challenges face Cuba as Raúl Castro leaves the presidency. The major difficulties of Cuba's main trading partner for over a decade, Venezuela, and the potential impact on Cuba, as well as the U.S. policy of the Trump administration, undoubtedly constitute the two single most important issues on the Cuban foreign policy agenda. Speaking in January 2017 at a conference of Caribbean and Latin American leaders, Raúl Castro welcomed incoming president Trump, while noting, "Cuba and the United States can cooperate and live side by side in a civilized manner, respecting our differences and promoting all that is of benefit for both countries and people. . . . But it should not hope that to achieve this Cuba will make concessions inherent in its independence and sovereignty."[23] Since that day bilateral tensions have increased substantially, with the Trump administration seeking to place obstacles in the path of improving ties between Washington and Havana.

Given Cuba's desire to spread its trade relationship over several countries and not remain dependent upon Venezuela, for several years Havana has been diversifying its trade relations. Indeed, as Mercy A. Kao has noted, Chinese trade with Cuba has been steadily increasing during this time, and China may well replace Venezuela as the second-largest exporter of goods to the island. Kao notes how China's exports have ranged from $1.17 billion to $1.53 billion for the past eight years but rose to $2.33 billion in 2015 (fully 52 percent above 2014 figures). At the same time, trade with Venezuela fell 46.14 percent in 2015, a situation which could otherwise have proved disastrous to the Cuban economy. However, with China clearly taking up the slack as a trading partner for the island, Cuba was able to offset the significant shortfall.[24] Adrian H. Hearn and Rafael Hernández analyze the evolution of this key relationship, increasingly important for Cuba as Venezuela faces mounting challenges.

Writing in June 2016, Reuters correspondent Marc Frank analyzed the different path being followed by Cuba under Raúl Castro, noting, "Cuba's long-term trading partners are using debt forgiveness, swaps and new financing to try to win investment opportunities on the island before U.S. companies turn up following its detente with Washington."[25] He commented upon how the Paris Club of wealthy nations had forgiven $8.5 billion of $11.1 billion in defaulted debt and had arranged a variety of financial deals with most members. By June some fourteen nations had signed bilateral debt arrangements with Cuba. In 2014 Russia had done something similar, forgiving $30 billion in Soviet debt, while investing the remaining $3.5 billion in Cuba. The Cuban government, which in earlier years had opposed the idea of any form of debt swap, is now keen to diversify trading ties, avoiding the earlier cycles of historical dependency on Spain, the United States, and the Soviet Union—and also preparing for the future without Venezuela. This topic is dealt with in detail in the chapter by H. Michael Erisman.

Throughout the decades of the revolutionary process, there is one major element which needs to be stressed—namely, the tenacity of the government in adhering to principles of the right of countries to establish their own path of political sovereignty. Self-determination has, since 1959, been a major position of Havana. The attempts of other governments to exercise undue influence on Cuba, from the Common Position of the European Union to the crude attempts at regime change practiced by Washington until the Obama administration, have always failed. Put simply, revolutionary Cuba has not given in to external pressure, even during the traumatic years of the Special Period. As the Trump administration develops its own Cuba policy and, in the words of the president, seeks to arrange a better "deal" with revolutionary Cuba, the famed pragmatism of Raúl Castro and the decades-long respect for these principles will not be sacrificed. At the same time, Cuba's resolve will be sorely tested by increased bilateral tensions, and the first post-Castro president will face serious challenges in seeking an improved relationship with the United States.

Raúl Castro's leadership has resulted in a well-drafted, balanced, and intelligent foreign policy. This can be seen in the deliberate strategy of broadening trade relationships in case the Maduro government falls (along with Havana's privileged access to subsidized oil and payment for Cuban medical services). It can also be seen in the web of international connections involving high-profile visits (both of foreign dignitaries to Cuba and of Cuban ministers to other countries). Writing at a time when the possibility of a Trump victory seemed remote and U.S. commercial interests were in the ascendancy, William LeoGrande emphasizes the remarkable success of Raúl Castro's government in diversifying its options: "Even as Cuban officials welcome dozens of U.S. trade missions, they are building a robust and diverse network of international ties to hedge. If normalization succeeds, Cuba will not be drawn back into a dependent relationship with the Colossus of the North; and if normalization fails, Cuba will have no shortage of alternative partners."[26] In light of this broad network of political, diplomatic, investment, and trade connections, the claim of Jorge Domínguez regarding the extent and reach of Cuban foreign policy referred to earlier, although logically different in view of changing world circumstances, remains as valid today as it did then—fully four decades ago.

Continuity in the form of many basic principles since the origins of the revolutionary process still constitutes the backbone of Cuban foreign policy, which is also well-equipped with a strong element of pragmatism. Solidarity and cooperation are still enormously important, albeit with some changes in Havana's goals. The fundamental principles of Cuban foreign policy were summarized clearly in late 2016: "non-intervention in internal matters, respect for national sovereignty, equality of rights and the self-determination of peoples; support for friendship and cooperation between nations; the practice of tolerance and peaceful coexistence, and complete respect for the inalienable right of every state to choose their own political, economic, social and cultural system."[27] They remain as pertinent in 2018 as they were almost sixty years ago.

NOTES

1. Julia Cooke, "Cuba's Imaginary Isolation," *New York Daily News*, March 23, 2016. In her article Cooke notes, "Those of us who've spent time there have watched with some combination of amusement and frustration as familiar lines are trawled out this week. The word 'isolated' peppers news reports. . . . What's more dangerous about the self-congratulatory language . . . is that it ignores the global community that already exists in Cuba. . . . The problem with the current media narrative is that the country is reduced to what it is to Americans, not within the larger context of the world."

2. To understand the extent of these changes, see Philip Brenner et al., eds., *A Contemporary Cuba Reader: Reinventing the Revolution* (Lanham, MD: Rowman & Littlefield, 2008); Philip Brenner et al., eds., *A Contemporary Cuba Reader: The Revolution under Raúl Castro* (Lanham, MD: Rowman & Littlefield, 2015).

3. "Bush Reaffirms Cuba Embargo," *CNN*, October 25, 2007, www.edition.cnn.com/2007/POLITICS/10/25/bush.cuba.

4. William LeoGrande, cited in H. Michael Erisman, "Raúlista Foreign Policy: A Macroperspective," in Brenner et al., *A Contemporary Cuba Reader: The Revolution under Raúl Castro*, 224–25.

5. Jorge Domínguez, "Cuban Foreign Policy," *Foreign Affairs*, no. 57 (fall 1978): 83.

6. "The Castro regime is failing to address even the most basic humanitarian needs of the Cuban people. Chronic malnutrition, polluted drinking water, and untreated chronic diseases continue to affect a significant percentage of the Cuban people." A detailed prescription to resolve all of Cuba's social, economic, and political needs is then provided. See Condoleezza Rice and Carlos Gutiérrez, "Commission for Assistance to a Free Cuba, Report to the President," CubaNet, July 2006, www.cubanet.org/htdocs/ref/dis/07170602.htm.

7. Wayne S. Smith, "Bush's Dysfunctional Cuba Policy," Foreign Policy in Focus, November 6, 2006, http://fpif.org/bushs_dysfunctional_cuba_policy.

8. Helen Yaffe and Jonathan Watts, "Top Diplomatic Negotiator in Cuba Warns Trump: 'Aggression Doesn't Work,'" *Guardian*, January 17, 2017.

9. See the EFE agency report "Cuba desaprovechó el deshielo para rescatar su economía, según un informe," *El Nuevo Herald*, December 20, 2016.

10. For an analysis of the Obama policy on Cuba, see "Charting a New Course on Cuba," White House, https://obamawhitehouse.archives.gov/node/352651 (accessed January 18, 2018).

11. "In the good times under Mr. Chávez, who cast himself as Fidel Castro's spiritual son, Venezuela restarted and expanded the oil refinery here in Cienfuegos, making it the city's largest employer. Venezuela built new houses and brought in new city buses. . . . Reselling subsidized oil from Venezuela on the open market earned Cuba billions of dollars." Anatoly Kurmanaev, "Cuba and Venezuela's Ties of Solidarity Fray," *Wall Street Journal*, December 13, 2016.

12. See "10 Achievements of the ALBA Alliance in 10 Years," *Telesur*, March 17, 2015, http://www.telesurtv.net/english/telesuragenda/10-Achievements-of-the-ALBA-Alliance-in-10-Years-20141213-0024.html.

13. Ibid.

14. See Marc Frank, "Cuban Trade with Venezuela Plunges over Two Years," *Reuters*, August 18, 2017.

15. "EU-Cuba: Council Opens New Chapter in Relations," Press Release 712/16, Council of the EU, December 6, 2016.

16. See "96/697/CFSP: Common Position of 2 December 1996 Defined by the Council on the Basis of Article 3.2 of the Treaty on European Union, on Cuba."

17. Jakub Klepal, "EU Common Position on Cuba: Alternatives and Recommendations" (paper prepared for the Association for International Affairs, People in Need and Pontis Foundation, Prague, April 2006).

18. Sarah Stephens, "The EU Has Recognized That Its Common Position Has Failed to Improve Human Rights in Cuba. It's Time for the U.S. to Do the Same with its Embargo," *Americas Quarterly*, summer 2014, http://www.americasquarterly.org/content/eu-has-recognized-its-common-position-has-failed-improve-human-rights-cuba-its-time-us-do.

19. "EU-Cuba."

20. One example of the Cuban government seeking to strengthen bilateral political relations around the globe can be seen in the number of parliamentary delegations that visited Cuba's own parliament, the Asamblea Nacional. Between December 2015 and May 2016, for example, forty-five delegations came to visit from abroad. Among the newcomers were groups of politicians from the Czech Republic, Finland, Indonesia, Turkey, Algeria, and Saint Vincent and the Grenadines. Other visitors were the president of the Uruguayan Senate, the president of the Legislative Assembly of El Salvador, and the president of the Foreign Relations Commission of the Mexican Senate. Delegations also came from the Chinese National Assembly, the socialist wing of the European Parliament, and a group of French parliamentarians. See "Fortalece parlamento cubano sus vínculos a novel internacional," *Juventud Rebelde*, July 4, 2016.

21. While this section provides an exhaustive list of international visitors to Cuba, it is also important to recognize that Cuban politicians were also busy traveling around the globe at the same time. In February 2016, for example, Raúl Castro visited France, repaying the May 2015 state visit of President François Hollande (the first French president to visit the island), and Colombia in September to attend the ceremonies around the final signing of the Peace Accord. At the September summit of the Non-Aligned Movement in Venezuela, he met with leading politicians from North Korea, India, and Palestine. Foreign Minister Bruno Rodríguez, for example, visited Germany in May, and at the UN General Assembly in September, he met with his counterparts from Romania, Ireland, Peru, Lithuania, and the Dominican Republic. He also traveled to Qatar and the United Arab Emirates. First vice president Miguel Díaz-Canel represented Cuba at the January 2016 CELAC meeting in Ecuador and in May also visited Belarus, Venezuela, and Russia (where Vladimir Putin received him). In June he represented Cuba at the opening of the Panama Canal extension and met with President Juan Carlos Varela. Similarly extensive trips were undertaken by Esteban Lazo (president of the National Assembly), Deputy Minister of Foreign Affairs Marcelino Medina, Vice President of the Council of Ministers Ricardo Cabrisas, and Vice President of the Council of State Salvador Valdés-Mesa. This extensive foreign policy continued throughout 2017.

22. Daniel García Peña, former high commissioner for peace in Colombia, summarized the role well: "The Cubans have, from the very beginning, offered a very significant support for the process. The FARC, as many guerrillas in Colombia and throughout Latin America, see the Cuban revolution and the Cuban government . . . with great respect. And the pressure that the Cuban government has put on the FARC and the guerrillas has been quite significant, but also the way that they have been very discreet in allowing the Colombians, both the government and the guerrillas, to really take the lead and to drive this process. . . . The presence of Raúl Castro in today's event will symbolize the role, the very crucial role, that the Cubans have played throughout this whole process." See "Colombia & FARC Agree to Ceasefire in Historic Peace Deal, Begin Long Process of Implementation," *Democracy Now*, June 23, 2016, https://www.democracynow.org/2016/6/23/colombia_farc_agree_to_ceasefire_in.

23. See Marc Frank, "Cuba's Castro Warns Trump to Respect Country's Sovereignty," *Reuters*, January 25, 2017.

24. Mercy A. Kao, "China-Cuba Relations: Assessing US Stakes," *Diplomat*, December 24, 2016, http://the diplomat.com/2016/12/china-cuba-relations-assessing-us-stakes.

25. Marc Frank, "Rich Nations Use Cuba Debt in Hopes of Prying Open Opportunities," *Reuters*, June 6, 2016.

26. William M. LeoGrande, "Cuba Reaches Out to Partners Far and Wide to Hedge against U.S. Engagement," *World Politics Review*, October 11, 2016, http://www.worldpoliticsreview.com/articles/20145/cuba-reaches-out-to=partners-far-and-wide-to-hedge-against-u-s-engagement.

27. Juana Carrasco Martín, "Cuba y su proyección internacional en 2017," *Juventud Rebelde*, December 29, 2016.

I

KEY ISSUE AREAS

2

The Defense Contribution to Foreign Policy

Crucial in the Past, Crucial Today

Hal Klepak

In the last years of the government of Fidel Castro, and now those of his brother Raúl, the armed forces' role as an arm of Cuba's foreign policy has grown after many years of reduced status following their dramatic role in that policy in the early years of the revolution. This chapter will attempt to show briefly how that evolution took place in order to address the question as to the nature and importance of that role at the present time.

THE PAST WEIGHS HEAVY

The Cuban Revolutionary Forces (Fuerzas Armadas Revolucionarias de Cuba, or FAR, with their ministry, termed MINFAR) were officially founded as such only in the autumn of 1959, when the old army, navy and air force of the Batista dictatorship were abolished in favor of the current structure and placed under the command, as minister, of twenty-nine-year old *comandante* Raúl Castro. In order to understand their ethos and behavior over the years since, it is nonetheless necessary to set them in the context of a revolutionary struggle for full independence going back to the first war for independence from Spain, the Ten Years' War of 1868–1878; the subsequent war for that goal from 1895 to 1898, truncated in its objective by U.S. intervention in that conflict; and the long battle to achieve real independence from the neocolonial status of the current revolutionary movement dating back to 1953.

The FAR see themselves not just as harking back to those earlier struggles but rather as the *direct* continuation of the heroic military efforts of the past and the guarantors that there will never be a return to a colonial or neocolonial status. This approach, anchored in their training, indoctrination, ceremonial celebrations, orders and awards, and public statements, is ever present.[1] This worldview is underscored by the absolute pride the institution takes in thus being "revolutionary" armed forces divorced, in their view, from so many of the traditions and practices of armed forces in most of Latin America. In particular, this is embodied in the central pillar of *el ejército no tira contra el pueblo* (the army does not fire on the people), a stance of vast importance with both theoretical and practical implications for the institution and the state.

Thus we are dealing with an unusual military institution which fits ill into the wider Latin American experience and often undertakes tasks that would be considered quite different from the traditional role of the armed forces in most of the developed world. Indeed, even in a Latin American context, where militaries often take on many jobs related to national development, the FAR are truly unique. In the Cuban revolutionary experience since 1959, they have been called upon to produce ideas and personnel to carry out a vast range of such nontraditional tasks as running the agrarian reform program in the early years, organizing the arrangements for the seizure of property abandoned by wealthy émigrés in the first wave of elite exodus from the country, founding an agricultural "army" to assist in feeding the population, leading the organization of the national effort to neutralize the worst effects of natural disasters, helping out in the literacy campaigns and the spread of national health services to the whole of the country, managing much of the economy today, and a long list of other responsibilities .

Even better known are the FAR's more traditional military efforts in what are termed "internationalist" assistance projects abroad, such as their defeat of the Bay of Pigs invasion of 1961, their victory in the struggle with "bandits"—that is, the counterrevolutionary movements which spread in many parts of the country later in the 1960s—their successful deterrent role in the stand-off with the United States, and their major effort in the export-of-revolution stage of Cuban foreign policy. All of these diverse efforts were in direct support of that policy and its main objective of ensuring the revolutionary government survived.

Raúl Castro

This institution, regarded by almost all specialists as exceptionally successful in both peace and war, had been headed directly by Raúl Castro for well over four and a half decades before he assumed the presidency in 2006, although he continued to fill the defense ministerial portfolio as well until 2008. It is also true that, with his enormous knowledge of the institution and Cuban defense problems, Raúl has maintained a strong interest in the FAR throughout his presidency. This author has argued elsewhere that if Fidel has been the undoubted key strategist of Cuba's defense over these long and beleaguered years, Raúl has been his direct architect of the central institution of the revolution, which is the FAR.[2]

Raúl's own past has been even more linked to the military than that of his brother. Having taken part in the ill-starred July 26, 1953, attack on the Moncada Barracks as a mere soldier of twenty-three, he then spent most of the next years in prison or in exile preparing the return to the island in late 1956 of the tiny exile force that was to grow into the Ejército Rebelde and defeat Batista's forces only a little over two years later.[3] Over that time Raúl had a major role in teaching his fellow prisoners and later in training the future insurgents in exile in Mexico, in getting them to Cuba in the celebrated yacht *Granma*, in supporting Fidel in the mountains in the first months of the fighting and commanding some of the most brilliant military activities there, and eventually in heading off on his own to found a new front in the north of Oriente Province, where his command and political skills would be tested and honed even further.

He was a great success at everything to which he turned his hand. As a result Fidel chose him to be his minister of the armed forces and thus the person also responsible for the president's own security in those days of attempted assassination, widespread sabotage, and eventual foreign invasion. Few in Cuba would doubt that he was the man for the job and not just selected because he was a trusted brother. The man who was to become acting leader of Cuba on July 31, 2006, and president de jure in February 2008 thus had vast military and defense administrative experience when he finally moved on from the minister's position to become head of state. He likewise had for long taken on a central role in foreign policy, negotiating many of the main arrangements with the Soviet Union, replacing Fidel at international meetings when his brother could not attend, and overseeing many internationalist ventures himself. And especially since 1989, he had taken on many of the tasks of wider government formerly done by Fidel in order to free the *comandante en jefe* for endeavors in which he took a special interest, such as medical internationalism and public health at home.

The FAR and Foreign Policy under Fidel

The institution that Raúl had forged under Fidel's inspiration had been the armed instrument of Cuban foreign policy ever since Raúl took over the FAR and arguably even earlier. From the Cuban perspective, as the revolution in those early years became ever more besieged internationally, the policy of threatening those governments which cooperated most with U.S. efforts to unseat Fidel, known as the "export of revolution," became a real if constantly denied pillar of foreign policy. As a result the FAR trained rebel groups in Cuba and many countries of Latin America and even further abroad. And as seen in the Dominican Republic that first year, Cuba was prepared to use its forces on occasion in direct support of such "progressive" forces abroad.

At the same time the FAR took part in several campaigns on the side of friendly political movements or governments, most markedly in Algeria and Syria in the 1960s and 1970s. FAR assistance was equally present in support of African liberation movements, especially those aiming at independence from Portugal. But nothing like the major interventions in southern Africa in the mid-1970s or in the Horn of Africa shortly afterward, involving over fifty thousand Cuban troops, had ever occurred or even been conceived of as possible by Western experts. As Nelson Mandela repeatedly made clear, the decisive defeat of the South African invasion of Angola and the Cuban role in Namibia were nothing less than key to the fall of the apartheid regime and the liberation of the region.[4] Cuba was "punching above its weight" in the international community and was doing so largely because of the FAR's exceptional size, training, professionalism, organization, and access to Soviet equipment at no or nominal cost. Cuba was able to take center stage in many international fora, and it was often Raúl's FAR which allowed it not only to be there but to be listened to as an actor of weight on the global scene.

The Cuban military and other assistance to Sandinista Nicaragua during the revolution against the Somoza regime and after the insurgents took power in the summer of 1979 was likewise very great indeed. And elsewhere in Central America, reduced but still important aid was given to rebel movements in both El Salvador and Guatemala. Fidel's brother had the most direct of roles in preparing and implementing this policy of support throughout these years, as well as in the difficult job of dealing with the often vexed Soviets, who wished Cuba's international behavior to take more account of both U.S.-Soviet relations and the damage that such Cuban "adventurism" could cause to the central concern in Soviet policy: good relations with Washington.[5]

The Year 2006 and Raúl in Government

By 2006, however, much of this context had changed massively. The end of the Soviet connection brought in its wake the "Special Period," declared in the summer of 1990 and resulting in the greatest belt-tightening Cubans had known since independence.[6] The economy went into free fall, and, uniquely for an authoritarian government, the FAR were to feel the crunch more than any other ministry. Instead of increasing their strength in these times of internal crisis, the FAR saw their budgets collapse, their postings abroad dry up, their training dwindle, and their international linkages atrophy. From probably the best military intelligence structure in Latin America, the FAR declined to a state where they deployed a tiny group of a mere nine defense attachés as their sole military eyes and ears abroad.

Raúl had to implement massive changes in a nearly shattered force. The budget fell by nearly half in five years, and even then that figure does not reflect the fact that the Cuban peso declined from one to the dollar to 150 times that, at least in the early years.[7] The country could no longer afford the size of defense establishment it had maintained for thirty years, and national service was reduced to two years instead of the long-established system of three years. In the vital area of fuel provision to units for training and operations, some less essential formations saw their allocation fall by up to 90 percent, while even forces vital to deterrence found themselves with 30 percent or even more of a reduction in this crucial area. Training dried up at home considerably and abroad entirely. Senior courses and those related to joint operations, usually taken in the Soviet Union, disappeared entirely, as did essentially all defense connection with that country. Within a couple of years, the last of those links with the USSR, the much discussed espionage center in Lourdes, closed and was replaced by a computer school.

In the United States hard-line views soon became dominant, and Washington closed in for what was generally considered an easy kill of yet another tottering communist state. The FAR was crucial in the blocking of this design as the institution, despite huge cuts in personnel (nearly three-quarters in these years) and budgets, moved into the economy with trained officers, personnel, and, most importantly, ideas. FAR officers, handpicked by Raúl in the mid-1980s in the context of an already faltering economy, were sent to study modern economics and business administration in Spain and some Latin American countries. Thus the FAR could already be considered reformist in the years before 1990. Now, in the context of the disaster of the "Special Period," these officers were brought to the fore and guided much of the national economic recuperation of the next half decade and beyond.[8]

THE FAR TODAY: WHAT DOES THIS FOREIGN POLICY INSTRUMENT ACTUALLY LOOK LIKE?

It is important to spend some time examining the FAR today in order to understand more fully any current or potential foreign policy support the institution gives, or might in the future give, to the current president or his successors. As can be imagined from what has been said above, the Cuban armed forces, for all their loyalty, flexibility, success in combat abroad and at home, prestige with the public, utility to the state, and professionalism, are still a deeply wounded military force.

Twenty-six years of a savaged defense and security budget, the cannibalization of equipment and weapon systems such as few countries' militaries have endured (even with the famous post–Cold War "peace dividend"), massively reduced training programs, essentially no replacement of key materiel or weapons for all that time when most of the world has been adjusting to what is termed the "revolution in military affairs," and the virtual end of courses and postings abroad have left a profoundly changed and vulnerable military on the island. Yet it is almost astounding to witness the continuing high level of morale in today's FAR and their continued ability to recruit loyal and good officers and other ranks, to engage large numbers of promising youth of both genders in the "Camilito" junior military school program, and most particularly to mobilize very large reserve forces indeed, even in such difficult times, for alerts or exercises.[9]

That high morale does not mean there are not serious problems for the forces, even beyond the obvious ones of old equipment and weaponry, less effective training, poor intelligence acquisition, promotion bottlenecks, lowered numerical strength, overtaxed personnel, and so much else. Yet, perhaps paradoxically, high morale may be linked to those challenges. Indeed, despite its reduced budgets, manpower, fuel, and other resources, since 1990 the FAR have been given more roles rather than fewer. And they have more than justified, once more in their history, the confidence their commanders put in them in even these most trying of times.

The FAR were asked to do essentially five things:

1. Continue to act to deter enemy attack through a high degree of combat readiness
2. Contribute to economic recovery and survival through retooling for agricultural production of food vitally needed for the population
3. Contribute to economic recovery through the posting of competent and loyal officers to the most needed sectors of the national economy in order to run key industries
4. Undertake, in cooperation with the Ministry of the Interior (MININT), increased activity in counternarcotics and illegal immigration operations in order to build confidence with the United States and especially that country's security forces
5. Continue and improve the FAR role in key popular activities such as disaster preparation and relief, weather prediction, and other civil defense roles

They were to do all this with less than a third of their former numerical strength, in the direst of financial circumstances, and with, in addition, all the very serious challenges already mentioned in training, fuel, equipment, and weaponry. Soon they were directly or indirectly running what is estimated as some 60 percent of the national economy, or at least its most dynamic, foreign-currency-earning sectors.[10] There is a caveat necessary to bring forward here. Most analysts have tended to use the terms "military industry" and "military control of the economy" as if these phenomena are straightforward and refer to the same kind of operations. Thus one sees reference to companies which have perhaps only one retired officer of the FAR heading them placed in the same category as firms which have serving military heads and active military staffs and produce military equipment for the armed forces. To date, alas, there has not been much effort to eliminate this lack of precision in the use of terms, and the result is a simplistic portrayal of the military in commercial enterprises.

Be that as it may, the FAR, especially with the Youth Labor Army (Ejército Juvenil de Trabajo, or EJT) of some one hundred thousand men who received less military training than other conscripts and worked essentially only in agricultural production, became a vital part of feeding the population as many Cubans faced real hunger for the first time in many years. Crucially, promotions to lieutenant colonel as of the early 1990s required that the officer in question had taken courses in management of agricultural and industrial enterprises. This was in addition to the fact that fewer officers had earlier been selected to attend modern economic management courses abroad. With this requirement it was hoped to build a significant pool of senior officers with credentials in these now vital fields.

The generally accepted figure for FAR strength, leaving out the only partially trained conscripted force of the EJT, is in the area of some fifty to sixty thousand, including all ranks. They are divided into the Eastern, Central, and Western Armies, with each "army" having attached naval and air force assets. The Eastern Army is based in the provinces of Guantánamo, Santiago de Cuba, Granma, Holguín, Las Tunas, and Camagüey. The Central Army is in the provinces of Ciego de Ávila, Sancti Spíritus, Santa Clara, Cienfuegos, and Matanzas. And the Western Army covers the rest of the island, as well as the city of Havana, the special district of the Island of Youth, Pinar del Río, and the new provinces of Mayabeque and Artemisa. After the disastrous years of the early to mid-1990s, there was a slow recovery in the percentage of the government budget for defense and internal order at the turn of the century, but this was soon reversed again. It was not until 2008–2009 that one saw the beginning of a more sustained, if still irregular, progression in an increase in the budget, although in 2015 and 2016, in line with Raúl's desire to improve conditions of service for military personnel, there was a significant increase in spending in this sphere.[11] However, the fact that all of this is stated in pesos (*moneda nacional*), worth one-twenty-fourth of the convertible pesos, which are in turn equivalent roughly to the U.S. dollar, means that one is still speaking here of a budget that is a fraction of what it was in 1990, when the Special Period was declared.

The Revolutionary Navy was deeply hurt by the Special Period from the beginning in the loss of courses, materiel, ships, smaller craft, and repair facilities provided before by the USSR. It soon found itself transformed into a coastal defense force, largely fighting illegal migrations and the narcotics trade instead of remaining the impressive oceangoing "blue water" force it had become in the years of the Soviet defense connection. While one or two larger ships of the tender, supply, and landing ship types are still kept in service, the navy is now no longer able to boast modern escort vessels, a submarine fleet of some size, or any of the other attributes of a major naval force. That said, this has not meant it no longer has jobs of immense importance to the nation and especially to its foreign policy objectives.

The air force, termed the Anti-Air Defense and Revolutionary Air Force, was hardest hit of the three services when the events of that fateful year struck. More dependent even than the navy on high technology, modern weaponry, and equipment, the Cuban air force was soon little more than a shadow of its former self, although a highly professional one still. From operating large numbers of the very latest types of fighter, light bomber, fighter ground attack, reconnaissance, and transport aircraft coming from the Soviet Union, it was soon cannibalizing most of those aircraft in order to keep at least a few flying.

It is the land force that came out best from the Special Period, although it also suffered greatly. A vast number of its vehicles were handed over to the civilian population for other uses in the years after the summer of 1990. Tank transporters, visible in large numbers as the famous, or infamous, *camello* (camel) buses on which Cuba was to become so dependent, were only some of these many thousands of light and heavy trucks and jeeps which took over so much of the economy and civil life on the island. However, less dependent on high technology, the army weathered the storm better than either of the other services.

The army's key asset, manpower, was of course still there, and indeed the prospect of three meals a day, reasonable accommodation, free uniforms, and the opportunity to learn a trade kept the regular force well manned and made it possible to take the difficult step of reducing the time of service from three years to two in the early to mid-1990s. With an army so much smaller than before, it proved quite easy to keep it up to its revised strength without calling on much of the young male population to come directly into the armed services. Many men could now choose to do national service of a nonmilitary kind, for instance, related to the Customs Service, Immigration, antidengue campaigns, the fire brigade, or any of a large number of other services generally, but not always, under the wing of MININT.

This, however, has led to the greatest change in Cuba's military posture imaginable. This is because the Cuban people had been for decades part of a nationwide system of preparation for defense aiming at a true "nation in arms," based on the French revolutionary model but modified in large part to follow the more relevant experience of modern-day Vietnam.[12] The aim was to produce a military force of essentially the whole nation, a "wasp's nest," in Raúl's celebrated phrase, that could deter any U.S. invasion through the obvious fact that while the United States would win any war between the two nations, the cost to the northern neighbor of such an adventure would be out of all proportion to any potential gains.

This has been the anchored strategy of Cuba over almost the whole period since the revolution "triumphed," to use the Cuban term. But it clearly depends on Cubans taking seriously their period of active military service, their compulsory time in the varied reserve forces in place, the required refresher and other training connected to it, their continuing devotion to the idea of *trabajo, estudio, fusil* (work, study, rifle), and much else. For good or for ill, this heightened state of readiness is no longer with us. Due to the reduced force and better retention, the need for a large intake of new soldiers from each year's male youth pool is so much less than in the past that only a small percentage of the nation's male youth actually serve in the regular force.

Moreover, those who do not serve in this capacity rarely receive any more than the short, five-week *previa* course of very basic training given to the EJT and some other temporary members of MININT doing national service. And perhaps even more troubling is that a very large percentage of young males do no training at all, never serve in the reserves, and do not consider themselves part of any wasp's nest except in the sense that many are still prepared to defend the country, even if they are entirely untrained in how to do so.

This is not to say, however, that this defense posture has been abandoned in its entirety. As repeated alerts and exercises involving the reserve forces have shown, perhaps especially that of 2006 when Fidel was taken ill, the FAR are still able to mobilize hundreds of thousands of people to man the country's defenses when needed or when the system needs to be tested. This is simply an unheard-of capacity in a region such as Latin America, where reserve forces elsewhere are either unimaginable or, at best, in their infancy. Cuba is thus not at all in the enviable position of a few years ago, where the nation-in-arms concept fitted well with the defense posture of the state. But it still leaves other regional countries far behind and has the resources of manpower on which it can still draw even in this new and dangerous era.

Training has of course been curtailed, as mentioned, but it still goes on. And constant calls for vigilance and hard work in national defense remain part and parcel of Cuban life.[13] Probably an equally troubling issue, however, remains new equipment and especially weaponry. As mentioned, the world is deeply into what is termed in military circles the "revolution in military affairs." The impact of new technologies across the board, new intelligence and information systems, new weapons, robotics, cyber defense, and a whole host of other novel elements on the defense scene has resulted in the FAR being well behind most other countries in many essential defense fields and of course entirely outstripped by the capabilities of their most likely adversary. If Cuba was never able to do more than give an initial "bloody nose" to any invading force coming from the United States, it is now unlikely to be able to do even that very effectively. Stealth aircraft, precision munitions, drones, and longer-range and faster-firing missiles and naval artillery, not to mention the more human factor that the United States now has the most battle-hardened armed forces in the world as a result of its constant military operations of recent decades, cannot have left the old possibilities open to the FAR as true planning options.

KEY CHALLENGES FOR TODAY AND THE FUTURE

Several factors have affected the efficiency of the FAR and thus their utility as an instrument for the furtherance of national policy and, perhaps especially, foreign policy. They have been through scarcities of all kinds for the past quarter century. In addition, after long decades of significant combat experience, they have now known none over the last two and a half. Moreover they are ill paid, poorly equipped, worse armed, and undertrained and are asked permanently to undertake nonmilitary tasks. Perhaps the most serious challenges are the dangers of corruption, of potential divisions in the officer corps, of the growing gap between the lifestyles of many personnel and their civilian counterparts (a factor complicated by related racial issues), and of the decline in the number of personnel with operational and especially combat experience. These, combined with the already mentioned and extremely important weakening of the nation-in-arms concept, are causes of considerable concern at the present time.

As can be imagined, armed forces with such a major role in the economy, and at the higher level dealing with businessmen from international corporations of great power and influence, can find themselves tempted by the contexts in which they find themselves and by the business practices of some such firms. To date there have been surprisingly few cases of high-level corruption, and in those that arise punishments can be swift and draconian, resulting in dismissal with disgrace, imprisonment, and cashiering. MININT and the FAR maintain a directorate to check on any such improper actions on the part of senior officers, and there is little doubt that it does its work of surveillance well.

More troubling for some is that this corruption is also present among the other ranks of the armed forces, having, as they often do, high levels of access to goods that are scarce in Cuban society as a whole and thus much sought after. While this is doubtless less of a problem than in wider society, where theft from state enterprises is often little less than a way of life, the impact on military discipline and the high prestige of the FAR in society makes senior officers nervous on this point. The current extensive programs of education on anticorruption are only a small response to this major problem.

Even beyond this difficulty is the fact that FAR officers posted to these rather prestigious positions must logically have cars, if not of their own then at least available constantly to them, and often must entertain at home as well as in the pleasant surroundings of bars, restaurants, clubs, and the like. They take priority when repairs are needed to their living spaces or their means of transport. Such perks are rarely available to officers in more traditional military jobs in training, headquarters administration, and operations, where they are often very far away indeed from big cities and such temptations but equally far from such emoluments. The intention to produce the large pool of trained business and agricultural managers in the FAR, to which reference has already been made, has not changed the reality that good managers are not easy to withdraw from these tasks, which are central to national recovery. Thus some key officers have spent several or even many years in such positions and have not seen normal military service during all that time.

If all this change has occurred in the armed forces, it has not been absent from foreign policy either, where things have of course changed almost entirely, at least when observed from outside. Cuba has abandoned the export of revolution, has in many senses become a much more conservative state, and, while still calling for a new economic (and political) order internationally, has been much more inclined to be patient in its calls for such reform. Cuba simply could not do any longer what it had attempted to do in the past, although its efforts regarding internationalism in medicine, sports, education, and the arts increased over this period.

The FAR might have been expected to have played a vastly reduced role in any new foreign policy which eschewed most support of insurgencies abroad, accepted a reduced role for the country internationally, and well understood that a much greater dose of realism was necessary for Cuba to survive in the new context. In many senses this was what happened, and Cuba's departure from Africa entirely by 1991, after it had already abandoned its major role in Sandinista Nicaragua the year before, was emblematic of the new context. With these moves, the heyday of Cuban military internationalism was left behind, and the FAR learned to live with its reduced means and in some sense its reduced status as well.

The United States in All This

In fact, however, a new role had already been present in embryo for many years, and far from finding their role in foreign policy reduced under Raúl as president, the

FAR and their dependent, highly interconnected Ministry of the Interior were to see just the opposite occur. In the crisis times of 1990 and after, the priority of Cuban foreign policy had to change to finding a modus vivendi with the United States. To a considerable extent, the priorities of U.S. security and defense were to become shared with Cuba, even if little was to be made publicly of the change for some time.

This needs further nuance. At no time in Cuba's history, revolutionary or otherwise, has the United States been anything but the primary concern of Cuban foreign policy. This is of course true for all of that superpower's neighbors and thus applies to Canada, Mexico, and the Bahamas as well. The United States also has an overwhelming presence in the foreign policies of all states in Central America and the Caribbean and indeed most in Latin America.

Napoleon's famous dictum that "Geography is nine-tenths of policy" is nowhere more clearly seen than in this region. But with the end of the Soviet connection, the socialist common market (Council for Mutual Economic Assistance), the Warsaw Pact, and the "socialist division of labor," there was no further possibility of finding a counterweight to U.S. hostility and power for Cuba. The country would therefore have to go into deep damage control via a much greater opening up to Latin America and a massive increase in its relations with western Europe and Canada. That said, the crisis remained, and remains, profound, despite the undoubted advances of more recent years. And even with greater relations with these others, the improvement of relations with the United States had to become an even greater priority.

To the surprise of many observers, the context for such a slow improvement was evolving in a favorable fashion, at least to some degree, and in ways in which the FAR could find a major role. In the late 1980s no one could fail to see that with the end of the Cold War, U.S. security concerns were shifting. The "war on drugs," already declared in the early 1970s, took on formal and permanent form, and the armed forces, for the first time, were given a role in its conduct overseas. And anyone who did not think that the consequences of failing to cooperate with Washington on the matter were likely to be serious found they had to think again, as U.S. policy in the region took up fighting the drug trade with a vengeance—even to the extent of overthrowing Panama's deeply corrupt and narcotics-linked Manuel Noriega government in 1989.

Cuba had similarly been accused in 1987 of cooperating with drug cartels in getting narcotics into the United States. The Cuban response was immediate and strong. Already known in most of the world for its exceptional record in dealing with the scourge both at home and in cooperative efforts internationally, Cuba issued a detailed statement of its approach to fighting the trade while at the same time both beefing up its own efforts in that regard and strengthening its links with like-minded nations. In this the FAR and MININT were to have the main roles, and their importance in the support of key foreign policy objectives was thus to return to nearly the levels of the early revolutionary years.[14]

While MININT no doubt officially has the lead role in fighting narcotics, such a view needs further examination. In fact, this ministry is subordinate to MINFAR in almost all senses and linked to it in almost all areas. Indeed, in Cuba members of both are termed *militares* (soldiers). And while MININT manpower and maritime assets are often emphasized more than the role of the FAR, in fact in logistics, training, doctrine, tactics, communications, command, and even personnel, the junior ministry's dependence on the FAR is clear. In addition, while at sea MININT craft work most closely, if to date indirectly, with the U.S. Coast Guard; it is the air force that does most aerial work and the army and reserve army which tackle highly manpower-intensive jobs such as searches for drugs left in *bombardeos* on Cuba's shores or in its territorial waters.[15]

During the government of Raúl Castro, bilateral military cooperation is much more direct, if more MININT-dominated, in the area of illegal immigration, where proper accords have maintained this very close and successful cooperation since the *balsero* (rafter) crisis of the mid-1990s. Even here, however, the FAR are never out of the picture. In this regard, it is important to understand the degree to which MININT is subordinate to MINFAR. This has always been the case but became especially so after 1989, when links between three MININT officials and key *narcotraficantes* ended with a purge of the ministry and the replacement of large numbers of officials with ones seconded from the FAR. Command of MININT has rested directly with a FAR officer ever since, as was seen in the naming of the most recent MININT minister during the winter of 2016–2017.

In fact, direct U.S.-Cuban military cooperation is much more wide-ranging even than discussed so far. The two defense forces cooperate very closely over the management of the Guantánamo naval base, on overflights especially for natural disaster relief in the region, and in weather-forecasting arrangements and have done so on a limited basis in military health efforts in Haiti. The exceptional professionalism of the FAR in these and other areas of mutual concern has repeatedly brought them the highest praise from U.S. senior officers who have had occasion to work with them.[16]

Thus we see in Raúl's absolutely key priority area of improving relations with the United States that the FAR play a major and much-appreciated supporting role.[17] And he has wished to increase that cooperation, especially, but not only, with an antinarcotics cooperation accord similar to the one already in operation for illegal migration. Recent talks on this and other collaborative military efforts with regard to weather warnings, health, counterterrorism, and some smaller areas have also taken place since the American and Cuban presidents reached agreement on reestablishing relations in December 2014. To the surprise of many, there have even been reciprocal visits between U.S. and Cuban officials in key centers of shared work in these fields, and Cuba is even attending U.S.-sponsored conferences on Caribbean security, although up to now this has been by MININT and not directly by MINFAR. All of this would of course have been unthinkable only a few years ago.

Allies . . . More or Less

The other main field in which one might expect to find FAR support for foreign policy is not surprisingly in working with other Bolivarian Alliance for the Peoples of Our America (Alianza Bolivariana para los Pueblos de Nuestra América, or ALBA) militaries in the variety of initiatives taken by that radical grouping in defense. As ALBA is styled an "alliance," it brings with that designation almost an assumption of at least some defense cooperation among the members of the group. Cuba, however, was from the beginning extremely reluctant to go very far in this regard, as it was well aware that if U.S. reactions were to harden even further regarding the group, the island would be at the forefront of any blow that might come from the superpower. It was felt that for Caracas it was easy to make anti-American comments and to speak of resisting by all means Washington's efforts to continue to control Latin America. But for Havana no such ease could be felt, and to have any such sign as the visible founding of an anti-U.S. alliance given internationally was not a welcome idea in Cuba. Although it did accept the need for the designation as a sort of show of unity in the face of events in the region and as the "pink tide" that put these movements in power gained steam in the early 2000s, Havana was clear that the military dimension of the grouping was limited and that any suggestion of a muscular anti-U.S. alliance to which Cuba would seek admittance was a nonstarter.

President Hugo Chávez's rhetoric on many issues of U.S. policy in the region, hemispheric defense and other cooperation, economic warfare, and propaganda soon surpassed that of Fidel and other Cuban leaders, who, especially in security and defense affairs, hoped for an improvement in relations with Washington and not for a continuation of the downward spiral of that connection. In this regard, Caracas could often be a liability for Cuba in its slow building of confidence, at least with key sectors of the U.S. defense community. This was of course classic confidence building in the sense of the creation in the adversary state of a body of opinion which does not share a sense of threat where one's own country is concerned.[18] It was a slow and difficult process and not one which Cuba wished to see derailed by too much activism on the defense front in ALBA.

The FAR do of course have a fairly close relationship with the Venezuelan armed forces and have had such since early after Chávez came to power in 1998. Cubans have been active in providing training to the Venezuelans at a number of levels, most prominently, at least in coverage by the press in the North, to intelligence and security bodies set up by the new government in Caracas as opposition to it hardened over the first years of its rule. At least as important, however, has been the FAR's training of the Venezuelan military in its exceptional natural disaster preparation and relief operational techniques.

The Venezuelans soon took on the Cuban approach of having "brigades" to handle such tasks as clearance of tree branches that could threaten electrical wires in case of storms, opening up of drains for water control under such circumstances, weather watching and especially information handling for the general public in the country as a whole and particularly in exposed areas, preparation of shelters, evacuation planning and execution, and the like. However, in other fields the differences between the two armed forces are much more obvious than the similarities. The FAR are serious military forces with great traditions in peace and war. Even the most generous observer of the Venezuelan armed forces could not suggest such a state of affairs for that country's military. While the Venezuelans have traditionally had the money, the equipment, and the weaponry that the FAR lack, the FAR are much the more competent and battle-tried force. And corruption, doubtless a problem for the FAR, is not in any way at the level of what is seen in Venezuela's military forces.

The links with other ALBA armed forces are even slimmer. While Cuban defense attachés are sent to those capitals, there is not much work for them to do. Cuba is not in a position to offer much; nor are these potential partners able to offer much to Havana. A joint staff school has been set up in Bolivia that is supposed to stimulate common approaches to defense among the countries of ALBA and even to help if the planned eventual joint staff were actually created and made to work in bringing to light a joint strategic concept and perhaps some sort of shared planning. In fact, however, all of this has rather remained in abeyance, in part because of Cuban realism on the matter. The occasional visit of an Ecuadorean cadet training ship or a Nicaraguan mission interested in how Cuba maintains its aged Soviet helicopters does take place, but these are simply not major missions for the Cuban armed forces. For the FAR, the alliance remains one in name only.

Other Links with NATO Countries

Connected with the U.S. dimension of the FAR's contribution to the achievement of Cuban foreign policy goals is the relationship with the United Kingdom, France, and the Netherlands, the three European nations still with territorial connections in the Caribbean Basin. This link is still largely under the formal control of MININT, but, as we have seen, that distinction is greatly blurred by the close integration of both ministries in key roles under discussion here.

The United Kingdom has territories particularly close to Cuba with the Cayman Islands, formerly administered from Jamaica but now a separate entity still in a dependent relationship with London off Cuba's south-central coast, and the Turks and Caicos Islands well to the northeast at the eastern tip of the Bahamas. Farther afield in the Caribbean are the other British territories of Anguilla, Montserrat, and, well to the north of Turks and Caicos, the Atlantic island of Bermuda. Little wonder then that the British have long had the largest cooperative arrangement with the Cuban security forces on the vital matter of the illegal drug trade so present in the Caribbean area.

This connection is most visible in the large and impressive UK-funded training program for MININT personnel in this field. Not only is such training conducted in Cuba, but Cuban officials have frequently gone to the United Kingdom to train in the most recent techniques, to learn how to operate the latest related equipment, and to liaise with their British counterparts. In addition, London has furnished a great deal of equipment to Cuba for use in the struggle.

Royal Navy ships and support vessels of the Royal Fleet Auxiliary visit Cuba frequently and are assured of a warm welcome. Cooperation is fluid and constant and includes the passage of information to U.S. authorities from their Cuban counterparts, when appropriate, on suspicious activities which may threaten U.S. drug-control efforts. Such cooperation has often received lavish if low-key praise from the U.S. Coast Guard and other agencies of the American government.

Of course there is also some British defense connection with the Bahamas to Cuba's north and with Jamaica to its south. The Royal Bahamas Defence Force had experienced real problems in its dealings with the FAR in the early years after Bahamian independence in 1973. Indeed, a serious incident in the late 1980s brought about actual exchanges of fire between the two forces, and relations reached a low ebb. Since then, however, cooperation to some degree in both illegal immigration and counternarcotics operations and the signing of defense and security agreements by Nassau and Havana have cemented a closer and much friendlier relationship between both countries, notably in defense and security but, as is usual in Cuba's connection with the anglophone countries of the Caribbean, across the board as well. The Jamaica Defence Force has much less often needed to work with its Cuban counterparts, but there are also defense and security agreements between these two countries, which enjoy an overall diplomatic relationship stretching back to Jamaican independence in 1962 and even beyond. Here again, the major elements of the linkages are in the counternarcotics field.

French and Netherlands territories in the Caribbean Sea are considerably farther afield and not so closely linked to Cuba, the largest island of the Antilles. The concerns of Paris for its defense and security responsibilities for the islands of Guadeloupe, Martinique, and Saint Martin or even for its continental territory of French Guiana are again largely in the counternarcotics field. And despite questions of greater distance reducing any likely Franco-Cuban defense and security relationship mirroring that between Havana and London, in fact Paris has long had a small training program for Cuban counternarcotics personnel and proffered other assistance to Cuba in that area of endeavor. French naval vessels visit Havana and other Cuban ports with some frequency in connection with joint efforts in this field. The French government is deeply aware that ships leaving French territories in the Caribbean do not normally face any further Customs requirements before entering metropolitan France, a clear indication of why France is keen on maintaining control of the scourge of the illegal narcotics trade as far afield as possible. Finally, France, for obvious historic and cultural reasons, is extremely pleased with the huge Cuban effort to assist Haiti, some of which has a distinct Cuban defense as well as humanitarian element to it as well.[19]

The Netherlands territories of the Netherlands Antilles, Aruba, and roughly half of Saint Martin (shared with France), as well as its historic connection with Suriname, now independent and formerly Netherlands Guiana, remain of defense and security concern to The Hague, and there is a very respectable military presence on the insular elements of this patchwork of lands. But here again distance makes a strong connection with Cuba less likely, although it should not be forgotten that this has not stopped Havana from cooperating with the Dutch in this field, and there is a security agreement between the two countries. As for French territories in the area, so with the Dutch, where there is usually no further Customs check to goods leaving these islands before they enter the Netherlands and thus the European Union.

Thus here is a wide-ranging series of arrangements, practices, training initiatives, and operations involving MININT directly and the FAR indirectly, which are useful for Cuban foreign policy goals with other nations but also have a direct impact on the central relationship with the United States. And that impact is seen by both Washington and Havana as profitable and important. All these major initiatives have been strengthened during the years that Raúl Castro has been president.

CONCLUSION

The FAR is in any case hardly in a position in its present reduced straits to play a major role in anything which is not the first priority of the nation's foreign policy, and that is without doubt the improvement of relations with its neighboring superpower. Efforts of a confidence-building type are not new between the armed forces of the two countries and have often received kudos for their role in softening approaches to détente on both sides of the Florida Strait.

Nothing else is so important to Cuba's foreign policy objectives as the relationship with the United States. Raúl made this clear in his first major foreign policy speech in 2006 and has insisted upon it throughout his leadership. And the creation of a body of officials within the defense and other security apparatus of the United States who see Cuba as a positive force useful for major goals of U.S. foreign and domestic policy, rather than as an enemy with whom one should not even deal, is a massive achievement of the FAR, MININT, and the Cuban state as a whole. The existence of that significant body of opinion, deep within the defense community of the superpower, can only stand Cuba in good stead as the challenges posed by a new government in Washington become clearer. Nobody knows this better than Cuba's president and his armed forces.

NOTES

1. See throughout the exceptional interviews of senior Cuban officers in Luis Báez, *Secretos de generales* (Barcelona: Losada, 1997); Mary Alice Waters, *Haciendo historia: Entrevistas con cuatro generales de las Fuerzas Armadas Revolucionarias de Cuba* (Havana: Editora Política), 2006.

2. Hal Klepak, *Raúl Castro and Cuba: A Military Story* (London: Palgrave/Macmillan, 2012).

3. The Moncada attack is taken in Cuba as the beginning of the armed struggle to topple the Batista regime, and its date of July 26 gave this movement its name.

4. See Piero Gleijeses, *Conflicting Ends: Washington and Havana in Africa* (Princeton, NJ: Princeton University Press, 2001), for the most complete study of this period.

5. For a good overview of the Soviet-Cuban relationship over those years, see Yuri Pavlov, *The Soviet-Cuban Alliance, 1959–1991* (New Brunswick, NJ: Transaction Publishers, 1993).

6. Homero Campo and Orlando Pérez, *Cuba: Los años duros* (Mexico City: Plaza y Janes, 1997).

7. Cuba, Oficina Nacional de Estadísticas, *Anuario estadístico de Cuba*, 1996.

8. Domingo Amuchástegui, "Las FAR: Del poder absoluto al control de las reformas," *Encuentro con la Cultura Cubana* 26/27 (autumn/winter 2002–2003): 133–47.

9. The highly visible Camilo Cienfuegos pre-officer-training scheme, present in every province, produces a large percentage of the future officer corps of the FAR. Cienfuegos was the almost mystical commander of the northern "invasion" force moving west from the Sierra Maestra in the effort to unseat the Batista government in late 1958. He died soon after the rebel victory in an aircraft incident for which there has so far been no full explanation. See "La luz de quien nace todos los días," *Juventud Rebelde* 62, no. 93 (February 5, 2017): 1.

10. This figure is accepted widely, but in fact the exact amount of the economy under military "control" is (not surprisingly) unknown. For context, see Omar Everleny Pérez Villanueva et al., *Cuba: Reflexiones sobre su economía* (Havana: CEEC, 2002), 19–40; Arnoldo Brenes and Kevin Casas, *Soldados como empresarios: Los negocios de los militares en Centroamérica* (San José: Arias, 1998).

11. Marcela Donadio, *A Comparative Atlas of Defence in Latin America and the Caribbean 2016* (Buenos Aires: RESDAL, 2016), 144–46.

12. See Hugo Rudea Jomarrón, *Tradiciones combativas del pueblo cubano: Las milicias cubanas* (Havana: Editora Política, 2009).

13. See, for example, the recent "En interés de la defensa del país," *Granma* 27, no. 2 (February 2017): 1.

14. For example, a large number of antinarcotics agreements were signed with Caribbean and other countries, beefing up cooperation in the field. For a wide-ranging study of this, see throughout Francisco Arias Fernández, *Cuba contra el narcotráfico: De victimas a centinelas* (Havana: Editora Política, 2001).

15. A *bombardeo* (bombardment) is the term used for the jettisoning of their cargos by threatened aircraft or boats bringing drugs north when intercepted by security forces. Cuba's coasts are very vulnerable to such actions.

16. See Marc Frank, "Former U.S. Drug Tsar Meets Castro in Cuba," *Reuters*, March 3, 2002. See also U.S. Department of State, *International Narcotics Control Strategy Report* (Washington, DC, 2005).

17. See the interview with the former commander of the brigade responsible for the border with Guantánamo, Brigadier General José Solar Fernández, in Báez, *Secretos de generales*, 277–78.

18. See, for classic treatments of these themes, James Macintosh, *Confidence-Building in the Arms Control Process: A Transformation View* (Ottawa: Department of Foreign Affairs, 1996); Andrew Richter, *Reconsidering Confidence and Security Building Measures: A Critical Analysis* (Toronto: York University, 1994).

19. For the wider story of Cuba's medical role in its neighboring country, see John Kirk, *Salud pública sin fronteras* (Santiago de Cuba: Editorial Oriente, 2016), 185–208.

3

Cuba's International Economic Relations

A Macroperspective on Performance and Challenges

H. Michael Erisman

> "No man is an island, entire of itself. Every man is a piece of the continent, a part of the main."
>
> —John Donne

Poet John Donne was referring above to membership on the part of individuals in what is today known as the "global village." But this characterization can likewise be easily applied to countries, with "interdependence" being the descriptive term often used here. Smaller island nations are particularly prone to this phenomenon, especially in an economic sense because they are almost always heavily dependent upon exporting and importing various resources, goods, and services in order to support and especially to improve their peoples' standard of living. As such, the dynamics and viability of their international economic relations represent a crucial dimension of their foreign affairs agendas.

Cuba, a nation whose 2015 population was listed at 11,248,783, readily fits this profile. Many of the inputs into its economy are imported, petroleum being a crucial example, and it relies heavily on its web of international ties to generate its ability to finance them. Accordingly, this chapter seeks to present a descriptive macroperspective on Cuba's international economic relations, focusing on various key elements thereof to see what their performance patterns have been during Raúl Castro's tenure as president and what new initiatives Havana has injected into the overall equation.

Most of the data upon which this overview is based comes from Cuban sources, especially various editions of the *Statistical Yearbook of Cuba* (*Anuario estadístico de Cuba*), published by the National Office of Statistics (Oficina Nacional de Estadísticas, or ONE). Some analytical conclusions pinpoint those sectors of Cuba's international economic network that have been functioning efficiently and those where significant challenges exist, which, if resolved, will very likely bode quite well for the island's future economic prospects.

But before delving into these more specific sectoral issues, let us look at some background information on Cuba's economy in general and the state of its international economic relations.

A PERFORMANCE MACROPERSPECTIVE

Table 3.1 uses the growth of Cuba's Gross Domestic Product (GDP) as a rough indicator of how its economy has performed during Raúl's tenure.[1] The overall trend since the initial halcyon years of 2006 and 2007 has been downward, as might be expected, given the high bar set during that period. Nevertheless, with the exception of a few years, the island has experienced modest but respectable GDP progress, with the growth rate hovering in the 2.5 to 4 percent range.

Counterbalancing these positive trends are the country's balance-of-trade figures. The island has, like many other nations, consistently imported more than it has exported (see table 3.2), thereby enhancing its international debt burden. However, contrary to many other cases (e.g., Greece being an extreme example), Cuba appears to have been somewhat successful in managing its obligations over the past few years, as indicated by the data in table 3.3, which shows that Havana's overall external debt during the 2011–2014 period has been reduced significantly, as has the debt as a percentage of various measures such as GDP. Another key development has been the recent willingness of some of Havana's major creditors to extend it debt relief. The breakthrough here came in 2014 when Moscow agreed to write off 90 percent of the debt that the island incurred to the USSR during the Cold War era.[2] Subsequently, spurred at least in part by the improvement in U.S.-Cuban relations, other nations followed suit, with Reuters reporting,

> Cuba's long-term trading partners are using debt forgiveness, swaps and new financing to try to win investment opportunities on the island before U.S. companies turn up following its detente with Washington. . . .

Table 3.1. Cuban GDP Growth Rates (percentage)

2006	*2007*	*2008*	*2009*	*2010*	*2011*	*2012*	*2013*	*2014*	*2015*	2016
12.5	7.5	4.1	1.4	2.4	2.8	3.0	2.7	1.3	4.0	–1.0

Table 3.2. Cuba's Balance of Trade (millions of pesos)

2006	*2007*	*2008*	*2009*	*2010*	*2011*	*2012*	*2013*	*2014*	*2015*	*2016*
–6,573	–6,393	–10,570	–6,043	–6,094	–8,082	–8,224	–9,424	–8,180	–8,353	–7,953

Table 3.3. Cuba: External Debt by Creditor (US$ billions)

	December 2011	*December 2014*	*December 2016 (Projected)*
BIS banks	1.7	1.0	1.2
Paris Club[a]	30.5	14.6	7.6
Other official debt[b]	2.0	2.5	2.6
Suppliers[c]	4.4	2.3	2.5
Defaulted bonds and loans[d]	4.3	4.3	4.3
Total	42.9	24.7	18.2
Debt ratios			
Debt as percentage of GDP	62.5	34.0	18.0
Debt as a percentage of exports plus tourism	504.0	275.0	
Debt as a percentage of convertible exports plus tourism	839.0	458.0	
Debt as a percentage of exports of goods and services	262.0	143.0	

Sources: Luis R. Luis, "Cuba Restructures Its Visible External Debt," *ASCE Cuba Blog*, January 10, 2016, http://www.ascecuba.org/cuba-restructures-visible-external-debt; Luis R. Luis, "Cuba's External Debt Problem: Daunting Yet Surmountable," *ASCE Cuba Blog*, December 12, 2013, http://www.ascecuba.org/cubas-external-debt-problem-daunting-yet-surmountable.

[a]Official debt to major creditors; excludes interest on past-due interest.

[b]Brazil, China, and other official debt not in Paris Club based on author's estimates.

[c]Estimate based on ONE debt statistics.

[d]Defaulted bonds and commercial loans carried at face value; includes $1.25 billion from the London Club.

> In December [2015], Cuba struck a general accord with the Paris Club of wealthy nations to forgive $8.5 billion of $11.1 billion in defaulted debt and it has since reached follow-up bilateral deals with most members.
>
> Spain and France have pledged more than $700 million in outstanding Cuban debt for development projects on the island and Italy and Japan are expected to follow suit this month, their companies in line for any new business.
>
> France, which is Cuba's largest creditor in the Paris Club, agreed in February [2016] to drop more than $225 million of outstanding debt in a swap arrangement.[3]

As noted previously, Cuba's international economic relations play a vital role within this larger scenario. To determine how, and how well, they have been making their contribution, it is necessary to explore the performance patterns in such key areas as Cuba's regional trade profile, its export product menu, its shifting list of primary trading partners, and the primary policy initiatives that have recently been implemented under Raúl Castro's leadership.

Cuba's Regional Trade Profile

History has taught Cuba that overconcentration, regional or otherwise, with respect to its international economic networks is a very risky proposition. This

Table 3.4. Cuba's Regional Trade Profile, 2016

Region	*Percentage*
Western Europe	24.21
Eastern Europe	3.71
Asia	25.50
Middle East	.18
Africa	2.71
Latin America/Caribbean	33.07
North America	6.91
Others	3.71
TOTAL	100

harsh reality was driven home when the Soviet Bloc began to disintegrate in the late 1980s, taking with it the preferential relations which had led Havana to conduct approximately 85 percent of its foreign trade with Eastern Europe and ushering in the agony of the island's "Special Period." Today, however, one finds a radically different profile, as Havana has been extremely successful in pursuing a significantly diversified network of regional trade (see table 3.4).

Admittedly things were more uneven prior to 2016, when Venezuela occupied a dominant position in Cuba's overall trade profile. For example, in 2014 Caracas accounted for 40.6 percent of the island's total trade, thereby driving Latin America's share to 53.6 percent of the total. In 2016, however, the bottom had fallen out of Cuban-Venezuelan trade (see figure 3.1 in the section on Havana's primary trading partners); the overall total dropped by 5,033,474 million pesos from 2014, which represented a decline of 69.35 percent. Indeed, the contraction in Cuba's total trade from 2014 to 2016 (down 5,307,475 million pesos) was overwhelmingly driven by the precipitous drop in its relations with Caracas.

Cuba's Export Profile

Diversification has been achieved not only in terms of Havana's regional trade but also with respect to its export menu. Throughout most of its history, Cuba was renowned as one of the world's great sugar islands. It maintained this status until the end of the twentieth century, with sugar constituting its only export of any great significance (see table 3.5). But like many other things, as the island transitioned into the post-Soviet era, this tradition was abandoned in favor of diversification (see table 3.5). Medical services did not produce any significant export income during the Cold War because Havana normally did not demand any compensation (aside from some local logistical support) from the developing countries that were the primary recipients of its aid programs.[4] Raúl Castro, however, adopted a somewhat different approach after he assumed leadership of the country in 2006. Certainly he remained committed to the principle of medical internationalism and indeed dramatically expanded the scope of participation therein (see table 3.6). However, while some

Table 3.5. Cuba's Export Profile (percentage)

1990	*2008*	*2014*
Sugar: 76.0	Services: 49.1 (mostly health)	Health services: 52.6
Nickel: 7.0	Tourism: 18.9	Tourism: 16.3
Merchandise: 4.8	Nickel: 11.9	Minerals: 4.8
Tourism: 4.0	Merchandise: 6.4	Pharmaceuticals: 4.7
Citrus: 2.5	Pharmaceuticals: 2.4	Sugar (and products): 2.7
Pharmaceuticals: 0.02	Alcoholic beverages = 2.0	Tobacco products = 1.5

Sources: Carmelo Mesa-Lago, "Convirtiendo el desempleo oculto en visible en Cuba," *Espacio Laical* (Havana Cuba, 2000): 366; Comisión Económica para América Latina y el Caribe (CEPAL), *La economía cubana: Reformas estructurales y desempeño en los noventa*, 2nd ed. (México DF: Fondo de Cultura Económica, 2000), table A38.

Table 3.6. Cuban Medical Aid Personnel

1999	*2001*	*2003*	*2005*	*2006*	*2007*	*2008*
3,600	3,800	15,000	24,950	28,664	29,809	36,770
2009	*2010*	*2011*	*2012*	*2013*	*2014*	*2015*
38,000	37,000	40,000	38,000	50,715	52,000	55,000

Source: Created by the author using data gleaned from various IGO and media sources. An especially useful source of data and information about Cuba's medical aid activities is the *MEDICC Review*, available on the Internet at http://www.medicc.org/index.php.

especially needy countries still got complete subsidization, others were now asked to make payments for such assistance. This shift from pure cost-free humanitarianism to a more conventional trade model has produced significant dividends for Havana. Specifically, such programs generated an inflow of approximately CUC$5 billion in 2013, with CUC$8.2 billion estimated for 2014, thereby becoming, by a large margin, the island's leading source of export income. This has since declined following the reduction of medical personnel from both Venezuela and Brazil but probably still generates some $6 billion for the Cuban government.

Tourism, which at one time was touted as the island's greatest potential source of hard currency, represents Havana's other major generator of service-based export income. Table 3.7 summarizes the sector's performance over the past few years. There is, however, a major problem that typically plagues the industry in the Caribbean and other developing areas, which is the considerable "leakage" of the revenue generated from the host country (e.g., to pay for external goods and services associated with tourism). An average discount rate in the 60 percent range is estimated for the Cuban tourism industry (which is in line with the average figure for Caribbean tourism in general). This phenomenon is illustrated in table 3.8, using 2016 tourism and revenue data provided by the Cuban government. The line in table 3.7 referring to the international travel income accruing to Havana is indicative of this quandary. International transportation is, along with hotels and food, one of the major expense

Table 3.7. Tourism Revenues (millions of convertible pesos)

	2007	*2008*	*2009*	*2010*	*2011*	*2012*	*2013*	*2014*	*2015*	*2016*
Total	2,236	2,347	2,082	2,218	2,503	2,613	2,608	2,546	2,819	3,069
From international tourism	1,982	2,090	1,899	2,025	2,283	2,326	2,325	2,367	2,601	2,907
From international travel	254	257	183	193	220	288	283	179	218	162

Table 3.8. Tourism Revenue Leakage, 2016

	Total Tourists	*Total Cuban Revenue*	*Total Tourist Expenditures*	*Cuban Percentage of Total Expenditures*	*Percentage Leakage*
At $2,500 per tourist	4,002,317	$3,068,600,000	$10,005,792,500	30.7	69.3
At $3,000 per tourist	4,002,317	$3,068,600,000	$12,006,951,000	25.6	74.4

categories for people visiting the island. But most tourists do not travel on Cuban carriers. For example, Canadians (who represent the largest contingent of visitors) are likely to fly on Air Canada rather than Cubana, the result being that Havana loses this highly lucrative source of hard tourist currency. This pool of lost revenue could expand significantly when relations with the United States are fully normalized and the predicted flood of American visitors materializes.

Cuba's Primary Trading Partners

The recent evolution in the pattern of Cuba's primary trading partners is summarized in table 3.9. During the Cold War, of course, Havana's network of international trade relations was heavily dominated by the USSR and its Eastern European allies, which normally constituted 80 to 85 percent of the total. Today that profile has changed considerably as Cuba has developed a much more variegated menu of partners to replace its disintegrated Soviet Bloc connection. Indeed, aside from Brazil's rise to the top five, the composition in 2016 was not radically different from that in 2006, when Raúl's tenure began.

There was, however, a period of reconcentration, which began with the emergence of Hugo Chávez's government in Caracas (1999) and continued under the Nicolás Maduro administration. As indicated previously, Cuba was making progress, even before Raúl's administration, in terms of diversifying its regional trade and its export product profiles. A different dynamic emerged, however, when one looked at the percentage of total trade held by key trading partners. Here what had been a fairly respectable distribution in 2006 became much more concentrated, the zenith coming in 2012 when Venezuela's share reached 44.2 percent of the island's total trade. The core of this close relationship essentially revolved around two elements: medical services on Cuba's part and vital oil exports to the island by Venezuela (see figures 3.1 and 3.2 regarding the overall growth of this trade relationship, which peaked in 2012). Admittedly Havana's Venezuelan connection was not nearly as extensive as was the case with the Soviet Bloc, but the gap between Caracas and Cuba's other main trading partners had grown considerably over the years.

Table 3.9. Cuba's Primary Trading Partners (percentage of total trade)

2006	*Percent*	*2016*	*Percent*
Venezuela	21.26	China	20.5*
China	14.61	Venezuela	17.7**
Spain	8.18	Spain	10.4
Canada	7.22	Canada	4.8
Netherlands	6.89	Brazil	4.0

* Up from 7.6 percent in 2014
** Down from 40.6 percent in 2014

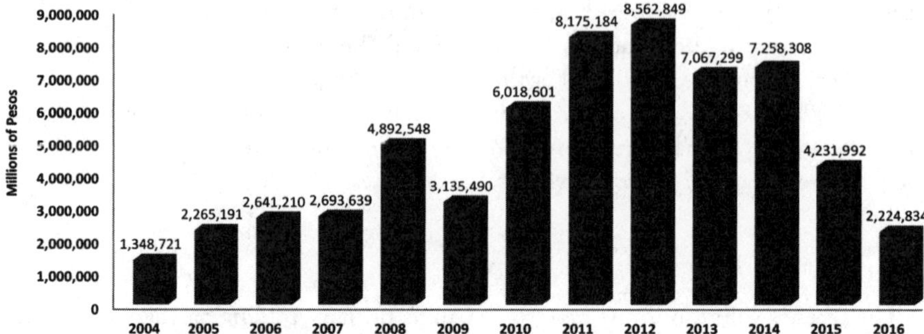

Figure 3.1. Cuban-Venezuelan total trade (millions of pesos). The 2016 figure is down 74.02 percent from the high in 2012.

There was, however, an important characteristic involving this relationship that favorably distinguished Havana's dealings with Venezuela from those with its other primary trading partners. Cuba's exports to these other countries, which generally exhibit rather high levels of economic/social development, have tended to be rather negligible. On the other hand, as shown in figure 3.2, beginning in 2010 Havana had developed and until 2016 had maintained a comparatively robust and certainly more balanced two-way trade relationship with Venezuela.[5]

Havana's trade relationship with its other main partner, China, has been somewhat uneven. From 2007 to 2014, the trend was generally downward, with Beijing's share of total Cuban trade bottoming in 2014 at 7.6 percent. This was somewhat surprising since China has in recent years launched a major economic campaign in Latin America, and therefore one might reasonably have expected to see an expanding Chinese presence in Cuba's foreign trade profile. Instead Beijing, like Havana's

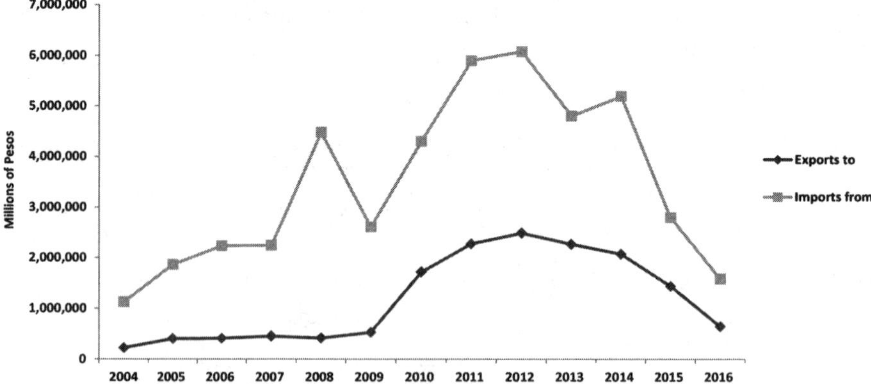

Figure 3.2. Cuban exports/imports with Venezuela (millions of pesos).

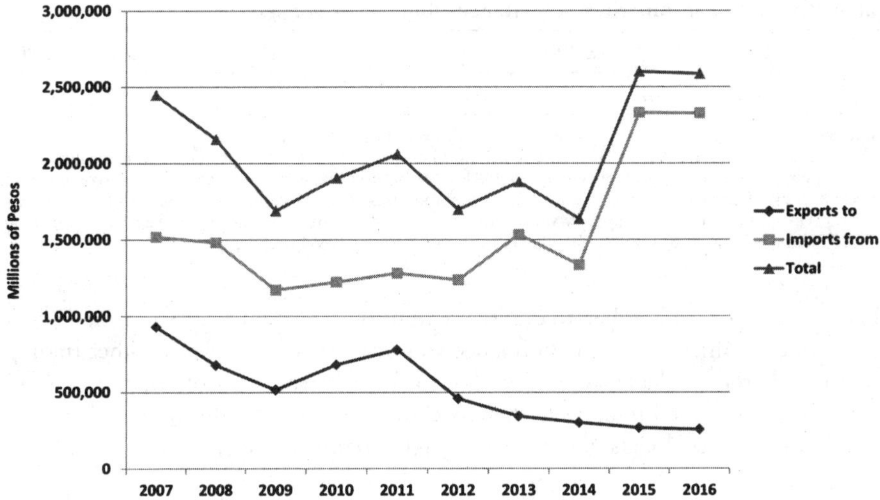

Figure 3.3. Cuban trade with China (millions of pesos).

other main trading partners, was increasingly overshadowed by Venezuela. It has been suggested in the *Economist* that this negative pattern may have been due to the fact that "wages in China have increased and high energy prices have raised the cost of shipping goods from China to America."[6] In any case, there was a dramatic turnaround in 2015–2016 that saw the figures on China's total trade with and its exports to Cuba rocketing above its 2007 marks, culminating in 2016 with Beijing displacing Caracas as Havana's premier trading partner. The one exception to this rising trend is the low and declining level of Cuban exports to China in recent years, which, as was mentioned previously, is characteristic of Havana's trade profile with most of its major partners.

Cuban American Remittances

Cuban commercial trade with the United States has been negligible due to the draconian sanctions to which Washington has remained committed for over fifty years. The few transactions that have occurred have displayed the following characteristics: they have not been reciprocal, consisting almost solely of U.S. sales to Cuba; most of the trade has involved agricultural sales approved by Washington; and the annual amounts have usually fallen in the $300 million to $400 million range, although in 2008 there was a spike to $711.5 million.

There has been, however, one glaring gap in Washington's effort to restrict U.S.-Cuban economic relations, which are the remittances in both cash and goods that Cuban Americans send to relatives on the island. The recent transfer of cash remittances is summarized in table 3.10. A significant amount of this hard currency is

Table 3.10. Cuban-American Remittances (billions of dollars)

2006	*2007*	*2008*	*2009*	*2010*	*2011*	*2012*	*2013*	*2014*	*2015*
1.251	1.363	1.447	1.653	1.92	1.295	2.605	2.8	3.5	3.3

Sources: Chart created from data contained in Emilio Morales and Joseph L. Scarpaci, *Remittances Drive the Cuban Economy* (Miami: Havana Consulting Group, 2013), http://thehavanaconsultinggroups.com/index.php?option=com_content&view=article&id=345%3Aremittances-drive-the-cuban-economy&catid=48%3Aremittances&lang=en; Luis R. Luis, "Economic Impact of the New Cuba Measures," *ASCE Cuba Blog*, December 24, 2014, http://www.ascecuba.org/ economic-impact-new-cuba-measures; Jack Evans, "Remittances Support Budding Cuban Economy," *Cuba Today*, July 11, 2016.

likely, in one way or another, to eventually find its way into the coffers of the Cuban government, which can use it to finance vital imports from Havana's other trading partners. If the blockade were lifted due to full normalization of relations and all restrictions on capital flows were thereby eliminated, the already considerable wave of U.S. remittance dollars would almost surely become a tsunami.

RECENT CUBAN INITIATIVES

During most of Raúl Castro's presidency, Havana's economic relations with Brazil expanded rapidly. Trade volume, for example, increased 55.7 percent from 2007 to 2014 (see figure 3.4), thereby propelling Brazil up to Cuba's number five trading partner. Certainly one negative factor in this relationship from Havana's perspective has been, as noted on the chart, the low level of Cuban exports to Brazil. It was anticipated, however, that this situation would improve somewhat due to plans to dispatch large numbers of Cuban medical personnel to Brazil who would be paid for their services, thus generating export income for Havana. Operating within the context of Brazil's Mais Médicos (More Doctors) program, Havana initially (late summer 2013) contracted to send 4,000 doctors to Brazil on three-year contracts; by February 2014 that number had increased to 7,400, and by January 2015, to 11,429. As is noted in table 4.1 of John Kirk's chapter, as of May 31, 2016, there were 10,994 medical personnel in Brazil. The influx of hard-currency income from the Mais Médicos program was estimated to reach at least $528 million a year at 2014–2015 levels.

Another key dimension in this strengthened relationship during the Rousseff era was the leading role that Brazil has played in the $900 million upgrade of the port of Mariel. It is here that a giant free trade zone (FTZ) and container port have been constructed. According to Dr. Carmelo Mesa-Lago, a prominent observer/analyst of the Cuban economy, the port and FTZ are by far the most important current development projects on the island.[7] Among the incentives that Havana has instituted to encourage foreign companies to locate in the FTZ are a zero tax rate on profits for eight years and full expatriation of profits.

The Mariel project is part of a larger effort to expand Cuba's international economic relations by attracting foreign investors to the island. Havana's prior track

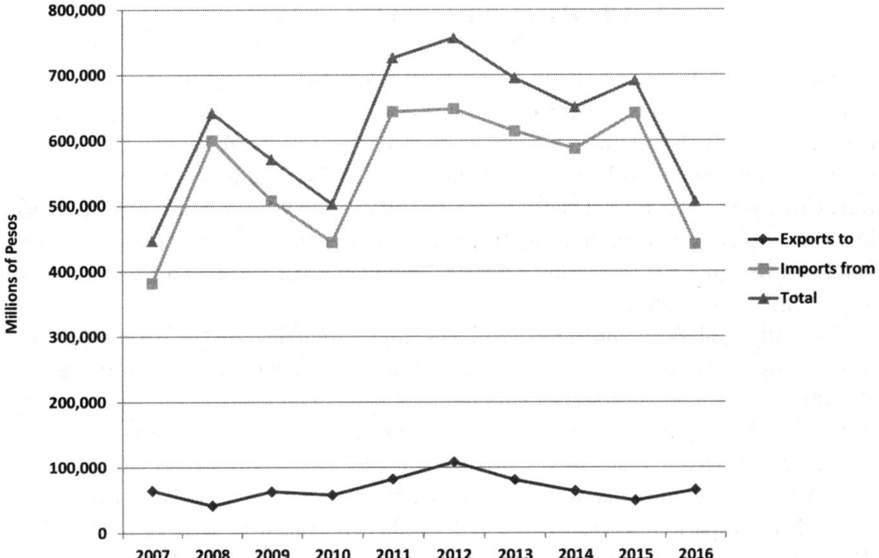

Figure 3.4. Cuban trade with Brazil (millions of pesos).

record in this regard had been rather lackluster. Indeed the number of foreign firms with direct investments in the country's economy dropped from more than 400 in 2002 to 190 in 2013. To rectify this situation, a new foreign investment law was passed in March 2014. According to William LeoGrande, President Raúl Castro "deemed the law so important that he called the [Cuban National Assembly] into special session to pass it rather than wait for the regularly scheduled session in July."[8] Among the law's investment incentives, which represent a significant improvement over its 1995 predecessor, are that it cuts the tax on profits from 30 to 15 percent for most industries, allows 100 percent foreign ownership, provides an eight-year exemption from all taxes on profits for joint ventures, and removes the 25 percent tax on labor costs.

This momentum in Cuban-Brazilian collaboration has, however, been disrupted by political turmoil in Brazil. In 2016 pro-Cuban leftist president Dilma Rousseff was impeached and then removed from office on allegations of corruption by conservative elements in the country's legislature. Speculating on the potential foreign relations fallout, a Brazilian diplomat who had served in Cuba said, "There will be a short-term review of our Cuba policy, because the money has run out and because there are some serious governance questions regarding the [Mariel-related] loans. Everything will be put on hold."[9] This pessimism proved to be prescient as total trade between the two countries plummeted 26.7 percent in 2016 (see figure 3.4). As such, the future prospects for close, cooperative relations do not appear to be promising.

A LONG-TERM CHALLENGE

In 2008 reports began to circulate about the potential for significant oil deposits north of Cuba in the island's offshore exclusive economic zone. The estimates ranged from approximately 5 billion barrels (U.S. Geological Survey) to 20 billion barrels (Cuban government). If the mid- to higher range of these estimates proves to be correct, Cuba will enter an exclusive club as one of the top twenty nations of the world in terms of oil reserves. Even using the lowest (U.S.) estimate, Canada and Venezuela would be the only nations in the Western Hemisphere to surpass Cuba on the basis of per capita oil reserves.

Currently Cuba's oil industry produces approximately 50,000 barrels per day, while daily consumption is around 130,000 to 140,000 barrels, meaning that 80,000 to 90,000 barrels (i.e., approximately 62 to 64 percent of total consumption) must be imported every day to meet the domestic demand.[10] But, as Robert Sandels has observed, "finding reserves even at the lower end of the estimates would make Cuba energy independent, and eventually a net exporter. This would have an incalculable impact on its economy, and would send the U.S. sanctions policy into the dustbin of imperial miscalculations."[11] As a major exporter, Havana would be able to use the hard-currency revenues to finance its imports as well to underwrite various development projects. In short, oil could be the catalyst which allows Cuba to address some of its current economic problems and perhaps even usher in a new era of prosperity for the revolution.

This potential bonanza has, however, remained elusive. So far several test wells have been drilled by various international partners, but none have proven to be commercially viable due to geological problems (e.g., hard rock, which makes it extremely difficult to extract whatever oil may be present). Basically, then, while oil production remains an option to be pursued, Cuba will have to employ more conventional strategies in the near future to enhance the dynamics of its international economic relations.

CONCLUSION

Based on the preceding survey, what conclusions might be drawn regarding the contemporary structure and dynamics of Cuba's international economic relations under Raúl Castro's leadership? Not surprisingly, what emerges is a somewhat mixed performance picture.

Considerable success can be seen in five dimensions of the island's international economic agenda: regional trade diversification, modernization of the export product menu, the Mariel project, the new foreign investment law, and remittance flows. There are, of course, some matters within these areas which merit additional attention. For example, while the export products menu has been modernized and diversified, a pattern of increasing reliance on the exportation of health services has developed. Certainly advances in the public health sector have been one of the crown jewels (along with education) of the revolution. Cuba has achieved results in areas such as its infant mortality rates and its life spans, which are similar to and in some comparative cases (e.g., with the United States) better than those of the world's developed nations. It therefore makes perfect sense to take advantage of the international marketability of this expertise. However, as Cuba experienced from its prior overreliance on sugar, diversification is a highly desirable trading attribute which can serve as a buffer against setbacks in some area(s) of the overall trade equation. Therefore discretion suggests that Cuba be cautious with respect to the share allocated to medical services in its export activities.

With respect to the new foreign investment law, there are still some provisions that have been carried over from the old version which might create problems. Specifically, says LeoGrande, "Two important elements of Cuba's FDI landscape have not changed. . . . Major projects will still require approval by the Council of State or Council of Ministers, which has led to lengthy delays in the past. And investors will still have to hire workers through the state's labor exchange rather than hiring them directly, limiting firms' control over the skills and incentives of their labor force. These conditions have been major deterrents to FDI in the past and will undoubtedly be a drag on new investment unless the Cuban government finds ways to mitigate their negative effects."[12]

There likewise are uncertainties about the prospects for U.S. enterprises to make nontourism investments should the blockade be lifted. If the experiences of other Caribbean nations are any indication, the prospects and potential benefits with regard to U.S. investments might be minimal. As in Cuba, domestic demand in Caribbean countries usually is not large enough to attract a great influx of outside capital. Hence there must be some other compelling reason for U.S. companies to locate subsidiaries in the islands, with one inducement that at one time gained popularity being the possibility of using the Caribbean as a low-cost manufacturing/export platform to service the U.S. market. Subsequently, however, the tendency for North American companies has been to shift the focus of such operations to Mexico and Central America due to the advantages afforded by the North American Free Trade Agreement.

Moving to the problematical side of the ledger, the primary challenges confronting Havana encompass the leakage of tourism revenues and finding replacement sources for its lost trade with Venezuela, especially with respect to crucial oil imports. Regarding tourism, it probably would be very difficult for Havana to restructure dramatically its financial arrangements with well-established, major providers of tourists such as Canada in order to capture more of the revenue flow. However, a very lucrative opportunity appeared to be developing across the Florida Strait when in 2015 President Barack Obama initiated steps to move beyond Washington's outdated, ineffective adversarial policies toward Havana, including the controversial travel restrictions that prevented most U.S. citizens from visiting the island (see LeoGrande's chapter for details).[13] If these restrictions were completely eliminated, "tourism experts estimate Cuba could receive up to five million U.S. visitors within two years."[14] In all probability, this scenario would require an extensive number of agreements/contracts, which, if negotiated shrewdly on Havana's part, should allow Cuba to recoup a larger share of the (U.S.) tourist dollar. Such speculation (and optimism) came to a screeching halt, however, with Donald Trump's election. Having indicated during the presidential campaign that he might adopt a hard line toward Cuba, he proceeded to do so in June 2017 by rolling back some of Obama's reforms. He could do this easily since they were based on executive orders (not legislation), which could likewise be rescinded by such actions on Trump's part. There were two main provisions affecting travel: (1) people who previously were allowed to make their own low-cost arrangements to go to Cuba under the general license provision permitting individual "people to people" visits now had to do so via group excursions operated by U.S. companies certified by Washington to provide such services, thereby limiting travel opportunities and raising the probability of significantly increased costs; and (2) U.S. companies and citizens were prohibited from doing business with any enterprise (e.g., a hotel or restaurant) linked to the Cuban military. The latter proviso, which admittedly might be hard to enforce, was potentially quite sweeping and restrictive, given the wide participation by members of the Cuban armed forces in the island's economy (see Hal Klepak's chapter for details).

The trading relationship that Havana has developed with Venezuela is both complicated and delicate. On one hand, there can be no doubt that it has been highly beneficial to Cuba, especially with regard to meeting the island's energy needs. The emergence of Hugo Chávez's radical government in Caracas (1999) ushered in an era of especially close ties between the two countries (see the section on Cuba's primary trading partners), which has continued under Nicolás Maduro, who assumed the Venezuelan presidency after Chávez died in 2013. Under Maduro, however, the country has experienced increased economic problems and political unrest, which have begun to affect Cuba adversely. Indeed, according to William LeoGrande,

> Shock waves from Venezuela's precipitous economic collapse have finally reached Cuba. They are forcing drastic cuts in energy consumption, slashing economic growth from 4 percent last year to just 1 percent in 2016. . . . Cuba's predicament was foreshadowed by the plunging price of oil on the world market and Venezuela's declining production, down 12 percent in the past year alone. Nevertheless, for several years Venezuela continued to meet its obligation to ship some 80,000 to 90,000 barrels of oil daily to Cuba at subsidized prices in exchange for the services of some 40,000 Cuban medical and educational professionals. Cuba resold some of the Venezuelan oil on the world market for a tidy hard currency profit. . . . Now, however, the inevitable has come to pass: Venezuelan oil shipments to Cuba are declining, down 20 percent this year, impacting both Cuba's domestic energy supply and its hard currency reserves.[15]

If Maduro's opponents are successful, as many expect them to be, in their attempts to have him removed from office, the result will almost certainly be a new government in Caracas that is much less friendly toward and willing to cooperate with

Cuba. While the recent interest in closer ties with Havana expressed by both Russia, which at one time supplied all of Cuba's oil requirements, and the European Union could serve to soften somewhat the blows of a disruption of the Cuban-Venezuelan relationship, the more pessimistic observers foresee a scenario rivaling the disastrous "Special Period" that the island experienced in the early 1990s after the collapse of the Soviet Bloc.

What can be said with certainty, however, is that Cuba has, despite Washington's arrogant and ultimately ill-fated attempts to prevent it, embraced John Donne's dictum and worked hard to become a part of the international economic main. There still are, of course, challenges which need to be confronted and overcome, but in the final analysis this macroperspective suggests that Havana has in in many respects succeeded under often very difficult circumstances to become a vibrant member of the global economic village.

NOTES

1. Unless otherwise noted, the charts and tables were created by the author using data from Oficina Nacional de Estadísticas, *Anuario estadístico de Cuba* (Havana, 2015).

2. For details, see "Russia Writes Off $32bn Cuban Debt in Show of Brotherly Love," *Guardian*, July 10, 2014.

3. "Rich Nations Use Cuba Debt in Hopes of Prying Open Opportunities," *Reuters*, June 6, 2016, http://www.reuters.com/article/cuba-debt-idUSL4N18V01G.

4. For comprehensive overviews of Cuba's medical aid programs, see Julie Feinsilver, *Healing the Masses: Cuban Health Politics at Home and Abroad* (Berkeley: University of California Press, 1997); John Kirk and Michael Erisman, *Cuban Medical Internationalism: Origins, Evolution, and Goals* (New York: Palgrave Macmillan, 2009); John Kirk, *Healthcare without Borders: Understanding Cuban Medical Internationalism* (Gainesville: University Press of Florida, 2015).

5. This growth in Cuban export income was almost certainly a reflection of the large number of medical personnel that Havana has dispatched to Venezuela. Indeed, Caracas has been by far the leading recipient of such Cuban health services.

6. "Why Has China Snubbed Cuba and Venezuela?," *Economist*, July 6, 2013.

7. Reported in Eoghan Macguire, "Cuba Libre: Could Port Herald New Economic Age for Communist Island?," *CNN*, November 20, 2013, http://edition.cnn.com/2013/11/20/business/cuba-libre-could-new-port-communist.

8. William LeoGrande, "Cuba's New Foreign Investment Law Is a Bet on the Future," *World Politics Review*, April 2, 2014. LeoGrande's article provides an excellent summary of the new investment law, upon which this overview draws heavily.

9. "Rousseff's Fall in Brazil Casts Cloud on Cuba," *Reuters*, May 12, 2016, http://www.reuters.com/article/idUSKCN0Y32T7.

10. Mimi Whitefield, "Economists Debate How Hard Venezuelan Economic Storm Will Hit Cuba," *Miami Herald*, July 28, 2016, http://www.miamiherald.com/news/nation-world/world/americas/cuba/article92430592.html.

11. Robert Sandels, "An Oil-Rich Cuba?," *Monthly Review*, July 3, 2012, http://monthlyreview.org/2011/09/01/an-oil-rich-cuba.

12. LeoGrande, “Cuba’s New Foreign Investment Law.”

13. While not able to eliminate totally the travel ban, Obama did relax the restrictions, resulting in approximately 614,500 U.S. citizens visiting the island in 2016, which was an increase of 35.8 percent over 2014 (the year before the restrictions were relaxed).

14. “Delta to Resume Cuba Charters from Atlanta,” TravelMole, June 30, 2015, http://www.travelmole.com/news_feature.php?news_id=2017371.

15. William LeoGrande, “Venezuelan Contagion Hits Cuba’s Economy, Putting Reforms in Jeopardy,” *World Politics Review*, August 1, 2016, http://www.worldpoliticsreview.com/articles/19522/venezuelan-contagion-hits-cuba-s-economy-putting-reforms-in-jeopardy.

4

The Evolution of Cuban Medical Internationalism

John M. Kirk

In July 2016 there were fifty-five thousand Cuban medical professionals working in sixty-seven countries—including more than twenty-five thousand doctors.[1] To put this in context, that is almost a quarter of all Cuban physicians and would be the same as having two hundred thousand American physicians working in developing countries. Indeed, since 1960 (when the first medical mission left to tend to victims of an earthquake in Chile), some 325,000 Cuban health personnel have provided medical services in 158 countries. And this, it must be remembered, has occurred in a developing country of just over 11 million people. Moreover, currently Cuba has more medical personnel working abroad than all of the industrialized countries combined. (Given the reduction in numbers of Cuban medical personnel in Venezuela and Brazil, it can be assumed that there are currently about 10,000 fewer, although probably working in the same countries.)

There is no doubt that the medical internationalism program was a major initiative of Fidel Castro, and for nearly five decades he was the driving force behind its key components. Among these was the founding of the Latin American Medical School (Escuela Latinoamericana de Medicina, or ELAM) in 1999, from which some twenty-eight thousand doctors from over ninety countries have graduated to date. This includes some 170 from the United States. Significantly, most have graduated without any charge for the six-year program, which has been praised by Dr. Margaret Chan, director general of the World Health Organization (WHO).[2] Also important is Operación Milagro, a program of ophthalmology services offered at no charge in many Latin American and Caribbean countries, which has provided over 23 million consultations to people of modest means. Some 3.9 million people in thirty-four countries have received free eye surgery through this program.[3] This was an initiative of Fidel Castro, assisted by Hugo Chávez, with Cuba providing the medical personnel and Venezuela the financial support. Of particular importance for Fidel Castro was the Henry Reeve Brigade, established in September 2005 and designed to send large teams of Cuban medical staff specializing in natural disasters to assist those living in affected areas around the globe. The brigade's first mission was to the Kashmir region of Pakistan, following a massive earthquake. In all, Cuba sent 2,564 medics, set up thirty-four large field hospitals (subsequently donated to Pakistan), and provided one thousand six-year medical scholarships to Pakistani students. Since then there have been dozens of missions—from tsunamis to earthquakes, volcanoes to flooding—that the Henry Reeve Brigade has dealt with. Of these one of the most significant was the 2014 Ebola outbreak in West Africa. The most recent was in late November 2017, when Cuban specialists in emergency medicine helped survivors of an earthquake in Oaxaca, Mexico. Worth noting is that, in the wake of Hurricane Irma in late 2017, and despite major damage to Cuba, Havana sent 750 health workers to assist the populations of several devastated Caribbean islands.

In sum, largely because of the personal interest of Fidel Castro, for decades medical internationalism has been a major commitment of Cuba. At first these initiatives were provided at little or no cost to poor developing countries—and initially began with generous subsidies from the Soviet Union. But after the implosion of the USSR and the onset of the "Special Period" (with its devastating social and economic impact beginning in 1990, including a 35 percent drop in GDP and the disappearance of over 80 percent of its external trade), it was clear that the empathy and revolutionary solidarity of the past would have to be curtailed, or at least severely reduced.

This was not immediately apparent under Fidel Castro's leadership, however, as Cuba continued to send medical brigades abroad—in 1999 alone to Colombia (earthquake), Honduras (dengue epidemic), and Venezuela (floods). Moreover, in 2005 Cuba offered to send fifteen hundred medical personnel to the United States after Hurricane Katrina devastated Louisiana, an invitation rejected by the administration of George W. Bush. Largely assisted by financial support from the recently elected government (in 1999) of Hugo Chávez in Venezuela, Cuba's medical missions continued apace. But the health problems faced by Fidel Castro (who temporarily ceded power to Raúl in July 2006 following intestinal surgery and then resigned as president in February 2008) and the death of Chávez in March 2013 had a major impact on Cuba. What should the government of Raúl Castro do in terms of medical internationalism? Given its own economic difficulties (without taking into account the massive difficulties of its largest trading partner, Venezuela), could Cuba afford to maintain the program? Unlike his more ideologically inclined brother, Raúl Castro has usually been considered extremely pragmatic. Given the challenging circumstances, many thought that medical cooperation programs would soon vanish, or at least be severely curtailed. In fact there has been a strategy of both continuity and change. This chapter analyzes some of the more significant changes that have taken place in Cuba's medical internationalism program under Raúl Castro.

MEDICAL INTERNATIONALISM UNDER RAÚL CASTRO: SOME GENERAL REFLECTIONS

Since 2006 there has clearly been a refocusing of medical cooperation (a term preferred by Cuba over the rather paternalistic "aid"), and some programs have been scaled back—while new initiatives, largely designed to generate funding for the underperforming economy, have been introduced. The essence of this new policy can be seen in the April 2011 "Resolution on the Guidelines of the Economic and Social Policy of the Party and the Revolution," passed at the Sixth Congress of the Communist Party of Cuba.[4] The objective of the *Lineamientos* (as the document is referred to in Spanish) was to update the socialist nature of the economy. In the section on trade, Articles 80 and 81 are pertinent to this discussion. Article 80 is a general statement, noting, "A comprehensive strategy must be designed for the export of services, in particular, professional services," while Article 81 emphasizes the need to maximize income from the exportation of medical goods and services: "A strategy must be designed and implemented to secure new markets for the export of both health-care services and Cuban medical and pharmaceutical products." To illustrate the pragmatic and rather hard-nosed way in which medical services are viewed by the government, the very next article (82) notes, "The export markets for seafood (lobster and shrimp) must be recovered and maximized." For the government headed by Raúl Castro, any export—be it goods or services—that supported the ailing economy was welcome. Lobster and shrimp, medical services, and pharmaceutical products all fell under the same rubric.

The section on international "cooperation" adopts a similar tone in its analysis. Article 110 emphasizes the need for a proper analysis of all solidarity projects, with the need to keep accurate financial and statistical records "for assessment purposes: in particular, cost analyses." Articles 111 and 112 are complementary. The former is a distinct departure from the traditionally generous approach to Cuban medical internationalism, wherein the cost of humanitarian missions was not considered particularly important. Instead the official policy now seeks to make all projects at least cost-neutral: "Where practical, consider a payment requirement to cover at least the costs incurred by Cuba in its solidarity cooperation projects" was the advice given. Article 112 is more pointed, encouraging government planners to "promote multilateral cooperation, particularly with UN agencies, as a way to obtain financial resources and technologies in keeping with Cuba's national development priorities." In other words, medical internationalism was to be continued, but instead of rushing to assist poor nations in need of Cuban support, wherever possible funding should first be sought in order to subsidize the initiative. As can be seen, the traditional approach to international solidarity continues—but is now accompanied by a set of guidelines designed to make it more cost-effective, a useful means of assisting Cuban economic development.

Clearly, it is hard to ignore several decades of humanitarian support around the globe, involving tens of thousands of Cuban medical staff. At the same time, given the pragmatic nature of the Cuban president and also the need for Cuba to develop a sustainable economy, it is clear that a different path was being taken. While in the 1990s tourism had been the immediate source of badly needed hard currency in the most difficult years of the Special Period, by 2008 a broader, more diverse approach was needed to modernize the socialist economy. Since Cuba had a surplus of doctors (over eighty-five thousand—more than the number found in Canada, a wealthy industrialized nation with more than three times the population), an emphasis was now increasingly placed on exploiting the potential resulting from that wealth of human capital.

GENERAL THOUGHTS ON MEDICAL INTERNATIONALISM AFTER THE *LINEAMIENTOS*

Since 2010 some aspects of the medical internationalism program have remained constant, while others have changed fairly dramatically. The preamble to the Cuban constitution emphasizes the need for revolutionary Cuba to commit to internationalist duties, particularly to the people of Latin America and the Caribbean, and this is viewed as a time-honored commitment in which Cubans feel extensive pride. Moreover, for many Cuban medical personnel the opportunity to work abroad is extremely useful. There are several reasons for this. First, and most important, it provides them with the opportunity to earn far better salaries than they could at home. This also helps the Cuban government deal with the inverted social pyramid dilemma that exists as a result of the Special Period, since workers in the tourism industry and the self-employed currently earn significantly more than those in the state sector, including doctors. Moreover, in many ways working abroad has become a rite of passage, with approximately a quarter of Cuba's eighty-five thousand physicians on internationalist duty. There is also an educational value of being exposed to conditions that they have only read about in textbooks. Meanwhile there are advantages for the revolutionary government since the exportation of their professional services brings in over $8 billion annually, the largest single source of hard currency for the Cuban economy.

While the largest program of Cuban medical support is that found in Venezuela (where there are approximately twenty-eight thousand Cuban doctors, nurses, and technicians), the major program introduced under the leadership of Raúl Castro is that found in Brazil, which started in 2013. Despite the need for thousands of doctors in underserved areas (mainly in the impoverished northeast), and despite a government campaign inviting local physicians to serve in the Mais Médicos program, few Brazilians volunteered to work there. The Pan American Health Organization then organized a major recruiting campaign, and some 11,430 Cuban physicians applied—making up 79 percent of all physicians in the Brazilian program. The health of the underserved population understandably improved significantly, and despite complaints from the conservative medical federations, the program was renewed—

even after the government of Dilma Rousseff was impeached and removed from office in 2016. Her successor, Michel Temer, encountered widespread opposition to any plans to terminate the program, and as a result it was renewed until 2018.

The Mais Médicos program in Brazil illustrates the value of Cuban medical internationalism in several ways. The most obvious, and the most important, is the delivery of medical services to people who traditionally have been excluded or underserved. But it also provides significant financial incentive to both the Cuban government and the physicians themselves. The Brazilian government pays approximately $4,200 per doctor for contracted medical services each month. Of that amount, the physician receives approximately $1,200, with the balance going to Havana. The monthly amount paid by the Brazilian government represents a welcome contribution to the state coffers but also is fifteen to twenty times what the doctors would have received in Cuba.

An analysis of the dozens of countries where Cuban medical staff are currently employed is telling (see table 4.1 for the complete list). In Latin America and the Caribbean, there are large numbers in Venezuela (28,351), Brazil (10,994), Bolivia (721), Ecuador (710), Haiti (567), Guatemala (415), and Guyana (181). In Africa the largest Cuban medical presence is found in Angola (1,712), South Africa (9,344), Mozambique (303), Guinea (221), Namibia (125), and Gambia (113). There is also a sizeable Cuban medical presence in Timor-Leste (151), as well as in the Arab countries of Bahrain (11), Saudi Arabia (148), and Qatar (462). The last three examples are an indication of Cuba's ongoing search for fresh, lucrative markets to which medical expertise can be exported.

An analysis of the form of payment received by Cuba for medical services illustrates the unusual and somewhat complex income schedule and the basic pragmatism at play. In essence, if a country can afford to pay for medical services, then it is required to do so, and there is a sliding schedule, based on ability to pay. As a result, and to give examples of this sliding scale of payment, Cuba charges high medical rates to the government in Qatar (where Cuban personnel run a large, technologically sophisticated hospital) but very little to the governments of Bolivia and Gambia, which have a greatly reduced ability to pay. Somewhere in the middle are Angola and South Africa, both of which have valuable mineral resources. To complicate matters (and following on from Article 112 of the *Lineamientos*), Cuba also receives payment for its medical services from several countries, including Norway and Brazil (to support Cuban medical services in Haiti) and South Africa (for medical support in Lesotho). Venezuela offers another distinct approach to payment. For while the value has decreased in recent years, during the Chávez years Cuba received approximately one hundred thousand barrels of oil daily at significantly reduced rates in exchange for medical services. It is worth noting that, while Cuban medical services are well remunerated in richer countries, the amount received is significantly less than would be paid for European- or North American–trained staff.

This sliding scale approach employed by the government of Raúl Castro is also found in medical education provided by Cuba. Again, those who can pay, do so—

Table 4.1. Cuban Health Collaborators around the World (as of May 31, 2016)

Country	*Total*	*Doctors*
Latin America and the Caribbean		
Antigua and Barbuda*	46	9
Argentina	2	1
Bahamas*	39	5
Belize	90	44
Bolivia	721	366
Brazil	10,994	10,987
Colombia	1	1
Curaçao*	2	2
Dominica*	30	14
Ecuador	710	639
El Salvador	16	8
Grenada*	24	20
Guatemala	415	223
Guyana*	181	79
Haiti	567	125
Honduras	90	56
Jamaica	148	34
Nicaragua*	55	35
Saint Kitts and Nevis*	14	8
Saint Lucia*	21	11
Saint Vincent and the Grenadines*	2	2
Suriname	7	2
Trinidad and Tobago*	157	34
Uruguay	24	9
Venezuela*	28,351	8,764
On Other Continents		
Algeria	931	347
Angola*	1,712	815
Bahrain*	11	3
Botswana	100	50
Burkina Faso	25	19
Cape Verde*	52	41
Chad	22	7
China	7	2
Congo	46	28
Djibouti	26	26
Eritrea	2	1
Ethiopia	25	16
Gabon	44	30
Gambia*	113	64
Ghana	1	1
Guinea*	221	135
Guinea Bissau*	33	26
Guinea Conakry	15	11

Country	*Total*	*Doctors*
Kiribati*	6	5
Lesotho	3	3
Mozambique	303	221
Namibia	125	55
Niger	6	4
Qatar	462	95
Portugal	52	50
Russia	1	1
Sahrawi Arab Democratic Republic	4	3
São Tomé and Principe*	9	9
Saudi Arabia	148	144
Seychelles*	46	45
South Africa	9,344	337
Swaziland	20	18
Timor-Leste*	151	108
Tanzania*	29	26
Uganda	6	4
Vanuatu	2	2
Zimbabwe	45	25

*Countries in which Cuban personnel also offer medical training
Source: Nuria Barbosa León, "Cuba's International Health Cooperation," *Granma*, November 7, 2016, http://en.granma.cu/mundo/2016-07-15/cubas-international-health-coo (accessed November 7, 2016).

albeit at a significantly reduced rate compared to the international market. As a result, many foreigners studying medicine at specialized hospitals in Cuba will pay tuition to the government—depending on their ability to do so. Conversely, those who are from poor countries will receive their training at no cost. This is seen clearly at ELAM in Havana, where South African students are paid for by their government, while others—such as those from Haiti—receive six years of medical training without their government having to pay. During Fidel Castro's leadership there was no charge for any students, whereas now the ability to pay is a key component of the Cuban approach under his brother.

THE CHILDREN OF CHERNOBYL PROGRAM: 1990–2013

A useful yardstick for measuring Cuba's medical support for the marginalized is the treatment given to the victims of the Chernobyl nuclear meltdown in the Ukraine following the implosion of a reactor there in 1986. Fidel Castro invited those affected by the accident to come to Cuba for medical treatment. The first patients arrived on March 29, 1990, and until 2011 Cuba continued to receive patients—in all some twenty-six thousand, mainly children.[5] For years, the town of Tarará, east of Havana, had housed a large camp for Cuban youth. It was quickly converted into a 350-bed hospital, with housing for four thousand people. At its peak, some fifty doctors and nurses, with some three hundred support staff, worked there. The children who came were housed and fed by Cuba and usually accompanied by a relative (who also stayed for free in Tarará). The only cost borne by the Ukrainian government was transportation.

While most children who participated in the program usually stayed for only forty-five days, there were many others with life-threatening conditions who remained for months and indeed years while their conditions were treated. During this period, over seven thousand operations were carried out by Cuban surgeons at Havana pediatric hospitals on those worst affected. It is important to bear in mind the historical context. This was at a time when the Soviet Union had ceased to exist and Cuba's trade had been decimated. The resulting Special Period in Cuba led to massive economic difficulties as factories were closed down, trade was decimated, and Cubans faced severe shortages of food. At that time the average Cuban male lost twenty pounds and the average female fifteen pounds. Pharmaceutical products—like everything else—were in short supply. Yet, while this was happening to the Cuban populace for over a decade, the government continued to receive children from Chernobyl—to house and feed them and provide them with medical care, all at no cost to the patients. There was a resultant frustration shared by many: How could Cuba continue to treat these children, when local children were suffering due to the fall of the Soviet Union?

Despite the temptation to close the Tarará program—particularly when there were clearly no economic benefits that could accrue to Cuba at this desperate economic juncture—the government of Fidel Castro maintained it. The medical treatment of twenty-six thousand patients over two decades, as well as their housing and feeding, must have cost billions of dollars—and this at a time when Cuba was facing a disastrous economic situation. Yet Havana continued this program until 2013, supported by Fidel Castro, who noted, "They are going to have the best doctors, the best medical care, the best hospitals, the best medicines that exist in the world. This cooperation of ours is a very basic duty."[6]

In October 2011 Ukrainian president Viktor Yanukovych visited the Tarará hospital and stated that his government would start to pay for the medical care of children. Former Ukrainian president Leonid Kuchma had visited Cuba a year earlier, making the same commitment for the Kiev government. To date, however, no financial contribution has been delivered, and so in early 2013 the last of the Ukrainian patients returned home. Cuba under Raúl Castro had decided that the Ukraine had received sufficient Cuban humanitarian support and compassion. So, if they were not prepared to pay for the health care of their own children after more than two decades of Cuban generosity, the Tarará facilities could be more effectively employed. As a result, a scaled-down version of the medical facilities is now being used to support the health-care needs of foreign students living nearby, as well as the local population.

BIOTECHNOLOGY UNDER RAÚL CASTRO

As noted earlier, following extensive public consultation, the government issued the *Lineamientos*, a series of guidelines designed to revive the ailing economy. One of these recommendations (Article 81) specifically encouraged the exportation of Cuban pharmaceutical products, an area of great economic potential. To a large extent this process has been greatly developed under Raúl Castro. The fundamental biotechnology initiative was initiated in the 1980s by Fidel Castro, who understood the potential of Cuba's not only producing its own pharmaceutical products but also exporting them to other developing countries. As a result plans were drawn up for a series of high-tech science research centers grouped in what is referred to as Havana's Polo Científico. This is an area where over twenty thousand qualified scientists, engineers, and technicians are working in some thirty large modern complexes to carry out highly advanced scientific research. The significance of Cuba's contribution to biotechnology was recognized in a 2009 editorial in the prestigious journal *Nature*, terming it "the developing world's most established biotechnology industry which has grown rapidly even though it eschewed the venture-capital funding model that rich countries consider a requisite."[7] The fame and prestige have only increased since then.

Cuba produces approximately 65 percent of its own medications, and the price for the public is extremely low. In recent years it has also developed its export potential, and the sale of biotech products brings in approximately $800 million, although potentially this could increase significantly. In recent years there has been increasing talk about Cuba selling a variety of its biotechnology products to its logical market: the United States, just ninety miles away. The diplomatic initiatives undertaken by Presidents Barack Obama and Raúl Castro have proven successful in many ways, not the least of which has been identifying potential joint ventures in this area. In October 2016 scientific collaboration in medical research was approved by Washington, and Cuban researchers were given permission to seek approval from the U.S. Food and Drug Administration for clinical trials of several drugs. American companies involved in biotechnology and pharmaceutical products have not been slow in seeking to collaborate with Cuban scientists—although it remains to be seen how the election of Donald Trump will affect U.S.-Cuban relations, even in humanitarian projects such as these.

"The country has a whole arsenal of unique drugs locked behind the U.S. embargo," according to a recent article in the *Atlantic*.[8] The author focuses on CIMAvax, a lung cancer vaccine that Cuba developed several years ago at the Center for Molecular Immunology (Centro de Inmunología Molecular, or CIM) and now of interest to Roswell Park Cancer Institute in Buffalo, New York. In fact the drug is now undergoing clinical trials in the United States. Since the 1980s, when Cuban scientists were encouraged to focus on the significance of interferon, the country has made significant progress in a number of biotechnology products. Rob Wright provides some relevant data on Cuba's successful (but hitherto largely unknown) biotechnology industry, noting that Cuba holds some twelve hundred international patents, sells pharmaceutical products in more than fifty countries, and has over three hundred biotechnological centers.[9]

Another product of interest to multinational drug companies is Heberprot-P, a treatment for diabetes which has been registered in twenty-five countries. The drug is injected into ulcers of diabetic patients and has been extremely successful—reducing the need for amputation for a large number of patients. There are many other products exported, such as the world's first synthetic vaccine against *Haemophilus influenzae* type b (Hib), the bacteria responsible for almost 50 percent of flu infections, as well as Nimotuzumab and Racotumomab, two other anticancer products.

Under Raúl Castro there has been a reinvigorated interest in biotechnology and specifically products with export potential. As Cuba is a revolutionary, socialist country, however, the profit margin is not the only concern, since Raúl Castro sees biotechnology as an avenue to both assist other developing nations (and, lately, industrialized ones) and to generate badly needed capital for Cuba. That said, there is an essential difference between the Cuban approach and that used in capitalist countries. Cuba focuses its research attention on products that will be of the greatest health benefit to the Cuban people and by extension people in other nations who need the medical treatment. Supporting human health is the primary goal of the Cuban approach, with making profits a secondary one. While this is gradually changing over time, it still remains the essence of Havana's strategy. As an example, rather than producing drugs that will support hair growth or provide a cosmetic benefit, Cuban biotechnology focuses its research on diseases that affect global health, such as malaria or dengue.

The spirit of the *Lineamientos* thus causes a dilemma for Cuban biotechnology. For decades it has focused on producing high-quality medicines designed to improve the health of the Cuban people, while at the same time starting to provide at modest prices goods and services for export to other developing countries. Now, however, while continuing to follow these goals, it is also working to generate hard currency for the state. In November 2012 BioCubaFarma was formally established, bringing under one umbrella organization the many research institutes and biotechnology centers working on these products. Some twenty-one thousand researchers are now working together for one large scientific enterprise, pursuing these twin goals. This centralization of technology would have been unthinkable in earlier years but has now become feasible, and indeed necessary, under Raúl Castro.

Another important element of the Cuban approach to biotechnology under Raúl Castro is the increased interest in cooperating with other developing countries, both in joint research projects and in selling Cuban technology. This harkens back to the *fidelista* humanitarian goals, where profit was not as important as saving lives. In recent years joint ventures have been established with companies in many countries, including India, Algeria, Malaysia, Iran, and, in particular, China and Brazil. Of key importance in these ventures is the need to transfer technology so that other developing nations can learn to produce the needed products and not depend on a single source. This process has increased under Raúl Castro, and by 2008 Cuba had signed agreements in technology research with thirty-two developing countries. As a sign of the importance of Sino-Cuban collaboration in medical research, in 2009 President Hu Jintao presented Dr. Agustín Lage, director of CIM, with an international award for collaboration in the treatment of Chinese cancer patients. Four years later the large Sino-Cuban Center of Molecular Immunology was established in Beijing.

Another significant research center is LABIOFAM, originally focused on the domestic farming market. It is now a major part of the strategy to export a number of biotechnology products. One of its most successful products is a rodenticide, used in dozens of developing countries, from Peru to Mongolia, Benin to Nicaragua. In addition to selling Cuban products, it follows up to ensure that the host nation is capable of maintaining a sustainable program. Bioplagicides and insecticides have also been developed to control vectors, and biolarvicides (used as a means of reducing malaria) have been applied in sixty countries. The appropriate technology is introduced in these programs in order to eradicate malaria, and factories have been built in several African countries.

Clearly under Raúl Castro biotechnology is becoming an increasingly lucrative facet of Cuba's economic development strategy. It is estimated that Cuba is now the largest single medicine exporter in Latin America and, as indicated by the *Lineamientos*, will continue to focus its strategy on exports. The election of Donald Trump in November 2016 remains a major unknown, since his conservative stated policies toward Cuba could badly undermine both joint research programs with U.S. institutes and pharmaceutical producers and the potential of exporting medications to the United States. At the same time, Cuba's exports to the developing world continue to grow, and regardless of the Trump administration's approach to Cuba, biotechnology—closely allied with the exportation of medical professional services—will remain enormously important.

THE HENRY REEVE BRIGADE AND CUBA'S RESPONSE TO NATURAL DISASTERS

Perhaps no other facet of Cuba's medical internationalism has captured the imagination as much as the efforts of this group, now several thousand strong, of professionals trained in dealing with a variety of natural disasters. Its activities since 2005 also provide a good example of how its use under the government of Raúl Castro has evolved. The brigade, named after an American citizen who fought in Cuba's first war of independence (1868–1878), was established in 2005, in the wake of Hurricane Katrina. As noted earlier, Cuba had offered the support of some fifteen hundred Cuban medical staff to assist the affected area. After the administration of George W. Bush refused to even acknowledge the Cuban offer, Havana found an outlet for its newly formed medical army following a massive earthquake in Pakistan on October 5, 2005. Prior to the formation of this particular brigade, Cuba had sent medical missions to many countries in the wake of natural disasters. One of the largest had been sent to Central America in 1998, following Hurricane Mitch, and it is generally estimated that there were over thirty thousand fatalities across Honduras, Guatemala, and Nicaragua. Significantly, Cuba did not have diplomatic relations with these countries, yet did not hesitate when international support was requested—and some two thousand Cuban medical personnel were sent. Later they stayed, developing a Comprehensive Medical Program in these countries, as hundreds of medical personnel were sent by Cuba to work and live (usually on two-year contracts) in largely underserved rural areas. Perhaps more important was the establishment of ELAM in 1999: for the initial years of the medical school's functioning, the largest group of medical students came from the countries affected by Hurricane Mitch. All these students from Central America were given a six-year medical scholarship. In sum, while the tradition of responding to natural disasters was thus deeply rooted prior to 2005 and the founding of the Henry Reeve Brigade, it was after 2005 that it became formalized, with a nationwide training schedule and structure put in place.

In 2015 the Henry Reeve Brigade was nominated for the Nobel Peace Prize, largely because of its work in three countries of West Africa (Guinea, Liberia, and Sierra Leone), where a massive Ebola outbreak occurred in late 2014. Over eight thousand people died, and panic spread throughout the industrialized world, as a handful of cases developed there. When the United Nations and WHO appealed for medical personnel, the first country to reply was Cuba. In all, 256 specialists were selected from the 10,000 who volunteered. They were sent to the areas in West Africa that were most affected. This was the largest Cuban medical contingent responding to a natural emergency in recent years, although Cubans had responded to calls for various earthquakes, tsunamis, and floods, sending smaller brigades around the globe. As suggested in the *Lineamientos*, financial support for the Cubans came from the WHO, which paid for their work during the six months that they were there.

Although much smaller, in many ways the Cuban support for Haiti following Hurricane Matthew in October 2016 was more significant. Cuba itself was already reeling from the impact of Matthew—which caused massive damage in Guantánamo Province—yet did not hesitate in sending the Henry Reeve Brigade to Haiti. In all, some thirty-eight specialists in emergency medicine flew to Haiti, joining over six hundred Cuban medical staff already working in what is the poorest country in the Western Hemisphere. In passing it is worth noting that Cuba has had medical staff working in Haiti since 1998, when Hurricane Georges wreaked havoc there. At that time over 230 Haitians were killed, 80 percent of crops were destroyed, and 167,000 people were left homeless. Cuba responded immediately to requests for assistance, and since 1998 over six thousand Cuban medical personnel have served in Haiti. Perhaps even more important is the fact that Cuba has trained—at no cost to that impoverished country—over one thousand Haitian physicians, who have been steadily replacing the Cubans stationed there.

In the 2010 earthquake, when over two hundred thousand Haitians were killed, Cubans again played a major role. This was largely because there were already some six hundred medical personnel working in the country, and they were soon joined by others from the Henry Reeve Brigade, who arrived within twenty-four hours of the earthquake. They remained for three months, also dealing successfully with a major cholera outbreak that erupted shortly after the earthquake. Their contribution to the health of the Haitian population at this critical time was significant. Indeed, between January 12, 2010, and March 31, according to official figures, Cuban medical staff gave 260,000 consultations, took part in seven thousand surgeries, attended fourteen hundred births, and vaccinated one hundred thousand people. All of this was delivered by 783 Cuban medical personnel, assisted by 481 Haitian doctors trained in Cuba and 278 other medical staff all trained in Cuba.[10]

The Henry Reeve Brigade remains as active as ever under Raúl Castro, responding to calls for assistance from all over the globe. In general, however, its missions are much smaller than the large delegations sent to Haiti in 1998, Pakistan in 2015, or even West Africa in 2014–2015. More typical now are those sent to Nepal after an earthquake in 2015 or to Ecuador after the August 2016 earthquake there. International funding—as was the case in dealing with the Ebola crisis in West Africa—is also appreciated, as noted in the *Lineamientos*. The mission to Oaxaca in late 2017 was the twenty-seventh mission of the Henry Reeve Brigade, an extraordinary record. Given this wealth of training, talent, and experience, it is surprising that the WHO has not requested that Cuba form an international body, funded by the WHO and the United Nations and based upon the Henry Reeve Brigade, to be on call for international disasters across the globe. This would provide a high-quality response to natural disasters (which continue to increase as a result of climate change) while providing Cuba with badly needed income. Certainly Cuba has the experience of several decades, the numbers of well-trained medical personnel who are specialists in dealing with natural emergencies, and the political will to assist.

THE POTENTIAL OF MEDICAL TOURISM

One area which is increasingly being developed as a revenue stream for Cuba is the potential offered by medical tourism. Data are extremely hard to find, largely because this is such a recent facet of medical internationalism, but it is steadily emerging as an area that brings in significant funding. The focal point for this initiative is the company specifically established by the Cuban government, Servicios Médicos Cubanos S.A. A visit to its website (www.smcsalud.cu/smc) shows the wide variety of services offered. Clients are made aware of the Facebook account of the company, which also has a Twitter feed. All these treatment programs are intended for foreigners, who pay in convertible pesos (roughly the equivalent of the U.S. dollar). The last aspect—second opinion consultation—is intended for people who have been given a diagnosis of their medical condition and yet want to have another specialist examine the evidence and either confirm or reject it. Also included are recommendations for further, or alternative, treatment in Cuba.

The section on health-care programs has an extremely long list of medical conditions which can be treated at a number of local hospitals. As can be imagined, they cover everything from herniated disks to lung cancer, Hodgkin's disease to diabetes. For each one there are details provided on the procedure, the time the patient would stay in Cuba, the tests that would be given, daily medication provided, and so forth. Transportation in Cuba, airport reception and departure, and accommodation details are also provided. One of the longest programs (lasting twenty-one days), "Quality of Life for Senior Citizens," starts with a thorough checkup and is followed by a battery of tests, including eye and dental examinations. An exercise program, podalogy, electrotherapy, alternative medicine, ozonotherapy, and saltwater therapy are among the many aspects of the treatment provided. Significantly, prices are not provided for any of the treatments, and instead potential clients are asked to fill in appropriate application forms, after which prices are given.

This multifaceted revenue potential run by Servicios Médicos Cubanos has been developed in recent years, and while it is still too early to appreciate its value to the Cuban economy, it will undoubtedly grow significantly—as has been the case with medical tourism around the globe. In the case of Cuba, the widespread international reputation, developed over decades, will help this initiative—particularly in the Americas.

A NEW APPROACH TO MEDICAL INTERNATIONALISM UNDER RAÚL CASTRO?

In terms of medical cooperation, on one level Cuba gives the appearance of maintaining its traditional approach. After all, in Havana ELAM continues to graduate thousands of doctors from around the globe (most of whom still pay no tuition). On an official visit in January 2014, UN Secretary-General Ban Ki-moon termed ELAM "the most advanced medical school in the world" and praised "the ingenious contributions of the school, for being leaders in South-South cooperation and in the forefront of international health."[11] In addition, the ophthalmology program, Operación Milagro, continues its work throughout Latin America and the Caribbean, seeing an estimated fifteen thousand patients (who pay nothing for their medical care) daily. Throughout the developing world, Cuban physicians and nurses continue to deliver basic primary health care through their Comprehensive Health Program in underserved, usually rural settings—from Guatemala to Burkina Faso, Guyana to Chad. Finally, Cuban medical professors working abroad are still teaching in a number of medical faculties, the largest being in Venezuela, where over twenty thousand physicians have already been trained.

But there have been changes, largely as a result of Cuba's economic challenges and the underlying pragmatism of Raúl Castro. On one important level the humanitarian approach of Cuba now is very much the same as it was when it was a passion of Fidel Castro.[12] What has changed, however, is—in the case of the Henry Reeve missions, to take one example—the process of deciding where to send medical cooperation, how large an operation to establish, and how to fund it. Another example might perhaps illustrate this new direction in medical internationalism. In November 2016 Bolivia's President Evo Morales praised the Operación Milagro ophthalmology program there. In his country, he noted, there were over seven hundred Cuban medical personnel, while the eye hospitals operated by Cuban personnel had benefited some 676,000 people. In Bolivia cataract surgery costs almost $1,000 in private clinics, and he estimated the cost of eye care provided by the Cubans in Bolivia to date as being $338 million—yet this had always been provided at no cost to patients by the Cubans. He was therefore giving $719,000 to Cuba as a symbolic contribution and act of solidarity. If this happens with a poor, developing country, one can imagine how Cuba can lobby with wealthier countries such as Qatar and Saudi Arabia for financial support.

Moreover, new ways of generating funding through the experience of decades of medical training and experience in Cuba have been discovered and are being increasingly developed. The whole concept of medical tourism is slowly evolving in Cuba. While still in its infancy, this program has tremendous potential under the Servicios Médicos Cubanos company. Likewise the area of biotechnology is increasingly becoming professionalized and continues to look abroad for joint venture partners. To date this has been occurring in developing countries, reflecting both the difficulties of competing with the large transnational drug companies and its ideological origins. But it is clear that, depending upon the U.S. government, its logical partner for many research initiatives is to be found to the north. In any event, the internationalization of the biotechnology industry will continue apace.

In essence, the spontaneous humanitarianism of Fidel Castro has been replaced by his brother's more cautious pragmatism and fiscal prudence. Like Fidel, Raúl takes an interest in humanitarianism, in support for developing countries, and in channeling the natural wealth of medical talent that Cuba possesses. Yet there are significant differences. In 2013, in an interview with José Miyar Barruecos, a physician and longtime confidant of Fidel Castro, I asked why medical internationalism was such an obsession for the former president. "It's because of his medical condition, the 'síndrome del sí' [yes syndrome]," he replied. I asked for some clarification, and he explained that Fidel Castro found it impossible to turn down valid requests for medical assistance from any developing country and therefore agreed to provide it when it was needed. Under Raúl Castro, while this commitment remains, it has shifted considerably. Indeed, while no valid request is turned down, greater consideration is given to the cost—and he is influenced by the *síndrome del quizás*, the "perhaps" syndrome. Now, many other elements are considered carefully before a commitment of medical cooperation is given—yet another sign of an evolving foreign policy under Raúl Castro.

NOTES

1. Nuria Barbosa León, "Cuba's International Health Cooperation," *Granma*, July 15, 2016, http://en.granma.cu/mundo/2016-07-15/cubas-international-health-cooperation (accessed November 7, 2016).

2. "I know of no other medical school that offers students so much, at no charge. . . . For once, if you are poor, female, or from an indigenous population, you have a distinct advantage. This is an institutional ethic that makes this medical school unique." Quoted in John M. Kirk, *Healthcare without Borders: Understanding Cuban Medical Internationalism* (Gainesville: University Press of Florida, 2015), 42.

3. See "Misión Milagro: 12 años al servicio de los más necesitados," *Telesur*, July 8, 2016, http://www.telesurtv.net/telesuragenda/Mision-Milagro-11-anos-20150708–0020.html (accessed November 7, 2016).

4. Quotations in this section are from "Sixth Congress of the Communist Party of Cuba, Resolution on the Guidelines of the Economic and Social Policy of the Party and the Revolution, Adopted on April 18th, 2011, 'Year 53rd of the Revolution,'" available at https://www.google.com/url?sa=t&rct=j&q=&esrc=s&source=web&cd=1&cad=rja&uact=8&ved=0ahUKEwjGvO-B_PHYAhVW7GMKHdO2AJsQFggnMAA&url=http%3A%2F%2Fanterior.cubaminrex.cu%2FEnglish%2FActualidad%2F2011%2Fjulio%2FLineamientos%2520en%2520INGLES%2520(version%2520final).doc&usg=AOvVaw3qDn5F0PhT4yGBi9JZXUO9.

5. A report issued by the staff at Tarará in early 2012 noted that 26,114 patients were treated there, of whom 21,874 were children, most under the age of fourteen. In all, 86 percent were from the Ukraine, with almost 3,000 from Russia and 730 from Belarus. See Kirk, *Healthcare without Borders*, 247.

6. Ibid., 252.

7. Ibid., 140.

8. Sarah Zhang, "Cuba's Innovative Cancer Vaccine Is Finally Coming to America," *Atlantic*, November 7, 2016, http://www.theatlantic.com/health/archive/2016/11/cubas-lung-cancer-vaccine/505778/?utm_cource=eb (accessed November 9, 2016).

9. Rob Wright, "Will Cuba Be the World's Next Leading Biotech Hub?," *Life Science Leader*, October 17, 2016, http://www.lifescienceleader.com/doc/will-cuba-be-the-world-s-next- (accessed November 9, 2016).

10. Kirk, *Healthcare without Borders*, 208.

11. Ibid., 43.

12. The approach employed by Cuba under Fidel Castro was summed up eloquently by Nelson Mandela in 1991: "What other country can point to a record of greater selflessness than Cuba has displayed in its relations with Africa? Where is the country that has sought Cuban help and had it refused." Cited in ibid., 1.

II

CUBA'S REGIONAL RELATIONS

5

Cuba and Latin America and the Caribbean

Andrés Serbin

This chapter focuses upon the basic question of whether, since Raúl Castro's succession as the head of the Cuban government in 2008, Latin America was—or is—relevant for Cuba, and vice versa. Particularly important in this regard is the question of Cuba's links with the new wave of regionalism in Latin America that started at the beginning of the century and the influence of this regionalism on recent Cuban political and economic evolution. Our main argument here is that the development of the so-called postliberal or posthegemonic regionalism within a propitious context of an economic international environment was closely intertwined with a simultaneous significant shift in Latin American and Caribbean (LAC) politics (with the electoral accession to power of center-left, left-wing, and populist movements and parties). Thus the conditions were created for the establishment of a new pattern of relationships between Latin American countries and Cuba, moving from Havana's initial strong involvement in "exporting revolution" to a more cooperative role for the Cuban government—eventually as a facilitator and an "honest broker" in conflict situations in the region[1] and a provider of professional services. This new pattern not only helped to reinstate Cuba as a full member of the LAC and hemispheric community but also succeeded in developing a new relationship with the United States.

Within this framework, however, some of the questions that remain unanswered are related to the role that Cuba played in the building of this new regionalism, as well as the influence of this development on changes in Cuba. To answer these questions, this chapter is structured in three parts. The first part analyzes the development of LAC's new regionalism and its importance in terms of its increasing autonomy from the United States within the changing international landscape. The second part focuses on the current evolution of the relations of several key Latin American nations with Cuba and their role in the regionalization process. This section concentrates upon the economically powerful and politically most influential actors of LAC. Finally, the third part analyzes Cuba's contribution to this development as a key political and symbolic reference and as an important player in the hemisphere and discusses the future evolution of this process in the framework of a new international environment. The main argument underlying this analysis is that since the 1990s, the new regionalism in LAC and Cuban foreign policy developed in intertwined processes strongly influenced by Cuba's renewed political links with the region, which at the same time brought political and economic support and cooperation to the failing Cuban economic system.

In order to contextualize the changes in Cuban foreign policy after Raúl Castro took full control of the government and the Cuban Communist Party (CCP) in 2008, it is necessary to briefly underline some important precedents that contributed to shape current Cuban foreign policy.

After the collapse of the Soviet Union, it became gradually evident to the Cuban military and political elite that Cuba was in need of both new international political allies to counterbalance the U.S. embargo and economic partners to keep the political system alive. The Cuban economic model clearly showed structural problems that urgently needed to be addressed and solved if the existing political system was to survive. The hardships that followed were characterized by the government as the *Período Especial para Tiempos de Paz* (Special Period in Times of Peace), but the difficulties confronted at this new stage also marked a gradual change in the pattern of Cuba's involvement in Latin America and the Caribbean. The references to proletarian internationalism and support for national liberation processes were now nuanced, and new emphasis was directed toward the search for regional peace. The objective was to emphasize Cuba's intention of becoming part of the process of integration and collaboration with Latin America and the Caribbean, and this was later reflected in the modifications of the 1976 constitution by the National Assembly of Popular Power.[2]

After the 1990s, Cuba was in need of a diversified and broader foreign policy to support the goals of the revolution. In a geostrategically unipolar post–Cold War world, it was difficult to find political allies, and it was more difficult to find economic partners who were able to help replace the support previously provided by the USSR. Fortunately Cuba was able to count on the political capital acquired in previous years when the export of the revolutionary model and the country's role as a global player and champion of the Third World were important assets that could be used as the basis for a renewed foreign policy.

Cuba used its nationalist and revolutionary credentials to call for the political unification of Latin America and the Caribbean around the anti-imperialist struggle and the cultural revitalization of the basic concept of a distinctive Latin American identity.[3] Consequently, Cuba was seen as a symbol of a staunch anti-imperialism and a reference point for a Latin American socialist model, which, in the 1970s and 1980s, was supposed to be achieved through armed struggle with the assistance of revolutionary Cuba. But support to different left-wing movements and to armed groups struggling in Latin America against both military dictatorships and weak democratic governments alienated most of Cuba's potential Latin American allies. In 1962 Cuba was suspended from the Organization of American States (OAS) and strongly condemned by a majority of LAC governments in the organization. At the beginning of the 1970s, the exceptions to these condemnations were four independent English-speaking Caribbean countries (Jamaica, Trinidad and Tobago, Guyana, and Barbados),[4] but the existing diplomatic relations between those countries and Cuba did not lead to its incorporation into the fifteen-nation Caribbean Community (CARICOM),[5] even if in the 1980s some of these countries were trying to establish socialist regimes. Moreover, the U.S. invasion of Grenada in 1983 was a strong warning to the Caribbean countries not to follow the Cuban revolutionary path.

In the 1990s, the regional environment began to change, and particularly significant was the rapprochement of Cuba with Mexico (the only country in the Western Hemisphere, along with Canada, that did not sever its diplomatic relations with Havana in the previous period). The unity of Mexico along with Venezuela and even Colombia (the Group of Three, or G-3), as well as improved ties with the Caribbean and several Central American countries (particularly Nicaragua after the arrival of the Sandinistas to power), opened the possibility for a first attempt by Cuba to become a legitimized player in the region following the creation of the Association of Caribbean States (ACS) in 1994. This was followed, in a more economic dimension, by Cuba's incorporation into the Latin American Integration Association (Asociación Latinoamericana de Integración, or ALADI) between 1994 and1998. Also, beginning in the early 1990s, Cuba was invited by Mexico and Spain to attend the Ibero-American Summits, a step which represented a significant breakthrough regarding Cuba's regional isolation.

However, the changes in Cuba's relations with LAC were still strongly defined by political, ideological, and diplomatic ties and not by trade and economic relations, due largely to the difficult economic situation imposed by the U.S. embargo. Within this context, initially Canada and some EU members (Spain and the Netherlands) became Havana's most active economic partners. The continuation of relations with Mexico also facilitated Mexican investments and trade. Later, at the beginning of the twenty-first century, as a result of China's growing Latin American presence and the consolidation of Hugo Chávez's government in Venezuela, both countries became Cuba's main trading partners. Later they were joined by Brazil, particularly after the election of Lula da Silva as president.[6]

The ideological and political atmosphere at the end of the century and during the first decade of the twenty-first century was propitious for the predominantly political nature of Cuba's relations with LAC. The "pink tide" and the leftward turn of some of the elected governments in the region were coincidental with previous strong ties with the Cuban Revolution, forged during the guerrilla years and at the São Paulo Forum and other venues. Cuba was perceived as an important symbol of LAC resistance to U.S. hegemony and a stalwart of political autonomy in both the hemisphere and the world. The accession of left-wing governments to power through elections in several Latin American countries was associated with and propelled by a favorable international economic environment. In addition the demand for commodities generated a boom for most of the regional economies and allowed for the implementation of social and development policies aimed at both increasing social inclusion and reducing poverty and inequality.

This was the propitious regional juncture when Raúl Castro became head of state and leader of the CCP in 2008, replacing the ailing Fidel. Within this context, the new regional organizations emerging at the beginning of the century as part of the new wave of postliberal or posthegemonic regionalism excluded the United States and Canada and included Cuba as a full member or, in some cases, as an observer country. This postliberal or posthegemonic regionalism crystallized with the creation of both the Bolivarian Alliance for the Peoples of Our America (Alianza Bolivariana para los Pueblos de Nuestra América, or ALBA) and the Community of Latin American and Caribbean States (Comunidad de Estados Latinoamericanos y Caribeños, or CELAC). Moreover, beginning in the 1990s, the Cuban government—starting with Fidel Castro (who was invited to attend several presidential inaugurations) and continuing with Raúl and other high officials—participated in various regional summits and even in meetings of the Common Market of South America (Mercosur). While Cuba never joined either Mercosur or CARICOM as a full member, it was accepted as an observer.

At that point, Cuba became omnipresent in LAC, helped by the close alliance with Hugo Chávez and by the sustained support of the Brazilian government of Lula da Silva. Such support was instrumental in strengthening the Cuban presence in LAC in its new role as "honest broker" (particularly in Colombia with the beginning of the peace process, but also in the relationship between Colombia and Venezuela during the escalation of tensions). Cuba's growing regional role also contributed to significant pressure being placed on the Barack Obama administration to both accept this presence at the hemispheric level and eventually to start to "normalize" U.S.-Cuban relations in December 2014. In this latter regard, LAC countries were widely perceived as political allies of Havana in the confrontation with the United States. Cuban participation in the new regional mechanisms was mostly of a political (and eventually symbolic) nature. Based on its experience with the CARICOM-Cuba Joint Commission, as well as with the creation of the ACS, ALBA, and CELAC, Cuba, following its statist model and its antineoliberal stand, did not sign full free trade agreements with other LAC countries. Instead it assumed other types of commitments for trade and cooperation based on fair exchange and solidarity or on bilateral economic complementarity, but at all times rejecting anything that would imply an acknowledgment of a market economy. In fact, Cuba inspired and supported the struggle by social movements, trade unions, and several LAC governments to oppose the Free Trade Area of the Americas (FTAA) promoted by the United States, the so-called Washington Consensus and accompanying neoliberal reforms, and the globalization process, condemning them as expressions of capitalism and market economies. This position was in line with the new narrative—postliberal or posthegemonic[7]—developed by the new regionalism emerging in LAC at the time. Therefore, Cuba's ties with Latin America were mostly ideological and political, aimed at strengthening LAC's support to end the U.S. embargo and, more recently, to access economic cooperation and foreign investments, particularly with Venezuela and Brazil, in several sectors of the Cuban economy after the process of *actualización económica y social* (updating of the social and economic model) started.

Cuba and the New Latin American Regionalism

Since the 1950s, the evolution of Latin American regionalism has been characterized by three distinct stages. The first phase, encompassing the 1960s through the 1980s (during which the United States still exercised strong hemispheric hegemony), was built around the aspiration for greater regional autonomy through the creation of regional markets and regional strategies of industrialization and import substitution. A second phase took shape at the end of the 1980s and the beginning of the 1990s as a neoliberal approach was introduced into the regional processes, now focused on trade liberalization, an economic opening, and the elimination of trade barriers, a process which was strongly influenced by the Washington Consensus and by the concept of open regionalism held by the Economic Commission of Latin America and the Caribbean. Trade, investment, and economic issues became dominant in the new regional agenda. However, after the collapse of negotiations over the FTAA at the Summit of the Americas in Mar del Plata in 2005, new modalities of regional political cooperation, as well as social and economic integration, began to emerge which were "postliberal" or "posthegemonic" in nature, as evidenced by newly created organizations such as the Union of South American Nations (Unión de Naciones Suramericanas, or UNASUR), ALBA, and CELAC.

The profound changes that the international system has undergone since the beginning of the century have been reflected in the region. After the end of the Cold War and especially after September 11, 2001, the United States reoriented its strategic priorities and generally paid less attention to Latin America (apart from its closest neighbors, Mexico, Central America, and the Caribbean). This fundamentally weakened the U.S. relationship with the region as well as the inter-American system. The euro crisis further accentuated the decline of the European presence in the area. Links among Latin American states grew, but not through a single and coherent process of regional integration. China, India, Korea, and other Asian countries increased their presence in the region as Japan had done earlier, but—with the exception of China—they limited their ties mostly to economic matters. Other actors such as Russia and Iran also began to establish closer ties with the region, benefiting from the "geopolitical vacuum" created by the partial withdrawal of the United States in the region.

Slowly things began to change in the international economy. After the 2008 financial crisis, the U.S. economy has mostly recovered. Also, notwithstanding "Brexit," the eurozone is not in any immediate danger of collapse, and despite an economic slowdown, China has avoided a hard landing of its economy and has increased its presence in LAC. Nonetheless, although the international system may appear more stable, it also shows greater signs of multipolarity and polycentrism. Thus Latin American countries, particularly in South America, have exhibited a greater autonomy from the United States, a process in which closer economic ties with China have played a significant role.

Within this framework, in the last decade different regional organizations have been created in Latin America, based on varying political, economic, and ideological approaches that characterize this greater autonomy from the United States and the resurgence of the Bolivarian vision of a community of Latin American and Caribbean Nations.[8]

In 2004, Cuba and Venezuela formed the Bolivarian Alternative for the Peoples of Our America, later renamed the Bolivarian Alliance for the Peoples of Our America, as an organization of South-South cooperation and assistance with a strong anti-U.S. rhetorical bent. In May 2008, UNASUR was founded in Brasília, encompassing twelve South American states, including Guyana and Suriname. In February 2010 in Cancún, CELAC was formed with the participation of all Latin American and Caribbean governments, creating an inter-American organization that excluded the United States and Canada, as ALBA and UNASUR had also done. CELAC now took on the role of the Rio Group, which had served as a forum for political coordination and consultation since the 1980s. The Rio Group had a significant impact in preventing and resolving several conflicts within the region, while CELAC assumed a more extraregional role and has developed a series of extraregional initiatives with actors such as the European Union, China, India, and Russia. The creation of both the Latin American Economic System (Sistema Económico Latinoamericano, SELA) in the mid-1970s and of the Association of Caribbean States (Asociación de Estados del Caribe, AEC) in the mid-1990s, which again excluded the United States, paved the way for this process. SELA was envisioned as becoming the economic body of CELAC, a scenario which, due to several factors, never in fact occurred. Finally, it is worth mentioning the creation of the Pacific Alliance—founded in 2012 by Colombia, Chile, Peru, and Mexico—which had started out fundamentally as a revitalized free trade agreement between these four countries. The Pacific Alliance members stand to gain from a reduced form of the Trans-Pacific Partnership, signed in October 2015, despite threats from the Donald Trump administration to reject it.

Nevertheless, the dominant trend of a combination of regional political coordination and increasing autonomy from the United States has prevailed in the region for the last two decades, notwithstanding the persistent fragmentation and the lack of consolidated institutions, particularly regarding the roles of ALBA, UNASUR, Mercosur, and CELAC. Within this context, Cuba was increasingly invited to attend regional summits and high-level meetings and became a frequent, active participant at the meetings of these organizations. Treaties and cooperation agreements of different kinds were signed between Cuba and various Latin American countries during this period, and Cuba was one of the founders of CELAC. The culmination of this process was the second summit of CELAC held under the Cuban pro tempore presidency in Havana in January 2013, with the participation of LAC presidents and heads of state and the attendance of the secretary-general of the OAS. This gradual inclusion of Cuba into the LAC community went very smoothly, punctuated by declarations of support for the Cuban government and denunciation of the U.S. embargo at different international fora.[9]

This increasing Cuban involvement in the LAC region in recent years has several relevant precedents,[10] but one of the most important steps was taken when Presidents Fidel Castro and Hugo Chávez of Venezuela decided to create the ALBA-TCP in 2004. This was the main organization for regional integration and cooperation in which Cuba participated at the beginning of the twenty-first century, representing an important alternative political mechanism to promote both economic relations and political and ideological identity and also to strengthen coordination among its members. There is abundant literature on the role played by Cuba in fostering this organization and on the close relationship established with the Bolivarian Republic of Venezuela, but it is also important to note that this process was simultaneously associated with and contributed to an increasing Cuban involvement in other regional summits and conferences. Starting with its participation in the Ibero-American Summits in the 1990s, Cuba attended the meetings in Brazil and Mexico of the Summits of Latin America and the Caribbean on Integration and Development (CALC), which paved the way for the creation of CELAC. The emergence and development of all of these organizations, particularly ALBA, UNASUR, and CELAC, is primarily due to the leadership of a few LAC countries.[11] With the exception of the Pacific Alliance members, most of them have emphasized the role of the state in economic matters, politics, and development and have promoted an intergovernmental approach (often on a strongly interpresidential basis). They have also introduced an innovative regional agenda that prioritizes new issues through the framework of primarily or exclusively intergovernmental initiatives, with relevant importance given to the summits of heads of state and a lesser role for other political actors. This "presidentialist" approach—and the emphasis on the role of the state and on governmental agreements—was quite compatible with Cuba's political system. Another relevant topic on the regional agenda was the issue of South-South cooperation, which also was in line with Havana's international orientation.

Despite the convergence on a general thematic agenda, which included not only political agreements and social issues but also issues of energy, finance, infrastructure, and security, there were varied perspectives in the region associated with the distinct interests, priorities, and visions of different countries.[12] Thus a single unified vision did not take shape with regard to global transformations and challenges and the role of the region in the international economic system. As a result, regional fragmentation and diversified foreign policy objectives persisted through this phase of the new regionalism. Cuba was not an exception in simultaneously pursuing its own national interests while participating at several newborn regional organizations. What was particularly noteworthy was that there was no questioning of the Cuban political system and the official government program of *actualización del modelo* (updating of the system) to preserve the predominance of a centralized economy.

The predominant regional trend at the time toward increasing autonomy (to a variety of degrees and employing different modalities of contestation) from the United States and the diversification of international relations in a multipolar international system clearly reflected similar trends expressed by Cuban foreign policy, particularly since the 1990s. Similarly, the anti-U.S., antineoliberalism, and antiglobalization approach promoted by social movements during their struggle against the FTAA, goals shared by the Cuban government, permeated—to different degrees and with varying nuances—most of these initiatives. There is no way of establishing precise relations between the two processes, but it is clear that the increasing Cuban presence in the Latin American and Caribbean community contributed to the inclusion of some of these topics in both the agendas and the spirits of the regional organizations. This process lasted until the regional political map started to change and the international environment became more hostile.[13]

The Role of the Key Latin American and Caribbean Countries

Since the mid-1990s and particularly at the beginning of the twenty-first century, three primary leading actors have emerged in the region—Venezuela, Brazil, and Mexico[14]—with different capacities and regional influence and with distinct patterns of relations with Cuba. One might also add to these three players the weight of Argentina's strategic association with Brazil (which was not without its own tensions and rivalries) and the close ties between the Cuban government and the administrations of Néstor Kirchner and Cristina Fernández de Kirchner in Argentina. Colombia also played an emerging role as the third most significant economy in the region, while simultaneously going through peace negotiations between the government and the guerrillas. (As noted in the introduction to this book, the role of Cuba in supporting and hosting the peace negotiations between 2012 and 2016 was extremely important and made a significant contribution to ending decades of civil war there.) However, the weight of these two latter actors as leaders of regional processes during the last twenty years was much less than that of the three nations (Venezuela, Brazil, and Mexico) mentioned initially. The following section analyzes the role of their relations with Cuba.

The rise of Brazil in the international system at the beginning of the twenty-first century has been notable and is part of the increasing role of emerging countries in a world economy fueled by a commodities boom. The magnitude of this process and the regional implications for South America, Latin America, and the inter-American system remain unclear, particularly due to the ambiguous global and regional roles that Brazil seeks to play, a process that changed significantly after the impeachment of Brazilian president Dilma Rousseff in 2016.[15] However, the impact of the economic and political weight of Brazil in the region and in the global scene is significant. The "strategic void" initially left by the United States in Latin America in the

1990s, with its repercussions and its impact on the current evolution of the Organization of American States, was partially filled by Brazil's growing leadership and its promotion of a South American space with greater autonomy. This promotion was linked both to the creation of Mercosur in the early 1990s and to the establishment of UNASUR in 2008 as a follow-up to the efforts to counterbalance the FTAA promoted by the United States.

As the world's seventh-largest economy, Brazil—notwithstanding its current crisis—is the most important power in South America and has become an increasingly important actor at the global level, particularly with the creation of the BRICS (Brazil, Russia, India, China and South Africa) bloc. Within this framework, during the last two decades, Brazil developed a cautious but sustained diplomacy oriented toward strengthening its regional and global leadership,[16] progressively consolidating its influence in South America despite the reluctance of some countries in the region to accept it. At the time, its objectives were oriented toward regional stability and development, as well as the creation of international coalitions, combining "benign leadership" with a strategy of incremental concentric circles, intergovernmental relations, weak regional institutionalization, and restricted commitments to supply the resources and pay the costs of regional integration, all of which supported a projection of Brazilian power into Latin America and Africa.[17] In contrast to Venezuela, and despite challenging some of Washington's policies, the Brazilian governments of Lula and Dilma Rousseff did not take an openly antagonistic position toward the United States, even in circumstances as complex as the case of electronic espionage against President Dilma Rousseff's government in 2012. At the same time, since 2007, Brazil had developed a strategic association with the European Union which was advancing EU-Mercosur negotiations on a free trade agreement (a process still being negotiated).

For Brazil, two trends reached a tipping point in 2010: China surpassed the United States as Brazil's primary trading partner,[18] and Brazil exported more commodities than manufactured goods for the first time since 1978. However, the decrease of international commodities prices, the new direction of the economy, and slower economic growth affected Brazil's international visibility and influence in the coming years, a situation aggravated by the crisis that led to the impeachment of President Rousseff and the appointment of President Michel Temer. As a result, Brazil's role as a regional leader was severely reduced.

Within this context, the close ties between Brazil and the Cuban government constituted one important piece in building Brazil's projection on the regional level and indeed beyond South America, as the Brazilian governments not only supported the Cuban position regarding the condemnation of the U.S. embargo but also invested in Cuban economic reforms through the building of the port of Mariel as well as through an initial attempt by the national Brazilian petroleum company, Petrobras, to join Cuban Petroleum (CUPET) and foreign oil companies in the exploration of deep-water resources in the Gulf of Mexico.

On the diplomatic level, bilateral visits of high officials (including the respective heads of state) increased during the Workers' Party (Partido dos Trabalhadores, or

PT) governments. While president, Lula visited Cuba four times and Dilma Rousseff two, last in 2014 to inaugurate the port of Mariel and to attend the Second CELAC Summit in Havana. For his part, Raúl Castro has visited Brazil three times since 2008, and both ex-presidents from Brazil (Lula and Rousseff) flew to Havana to attend Fidel Castro's funeral in December 2016. After leaving office Lula visited Cuba again, apparently to support Odebrecht, the Brazilian construction company with significant investments in Cuba. With funding from the Brazilian National Bank for Economic and Social Development, Odebrecht was the main company responsible for the building of Mariel, now equipped to handle "post-Panamax" vessels that will benefit from the expansion of the Panama Canal. The subtle and cautious support and leadership of the PT Brazilian governments and of Lula da Silva in particular[19] was a key factor in this process. Brazil was able to manage both support for Cuba and condemnation of the U.S. embargo while maintaining cordial diplomatic relations with Washington.

However, as Regiane Nitsch Bressan explains in her chapter, Brazil's policies toward Cuba were more influenced by economic interests than political concerns.[20] Since 2003, when Lula launched the Brazilian-Cuban alliance, Brazil had become an important trading partner for Cuba. Between 2003 and 2013, Brazil's bilateral trade with Cuba grew 580 percent, and Brazil became the third-largest Cuban trading partner after Venezuela and China.[21] Nevertheless, the current recession and political crisis have reduced Brazil's capacity to increase its cooperation and trade with Cuba. The recent Petrobras and Odebrecht corruption scandals, involving Brazilian officials, are also significant factors in the decrease in Brazilian investment interest. Under conservative president Michel Temer, the Mais Médicos program in which Cuban doctors play such a key role has also been reduced. In sum, within a difficult international economic environment and with the transformation of the political map in Latin America, the recession and the political changes in Brazil have affected relations with Cuba in both economic and political matters. Brazil's recent support of the suspension of Venezuela—a close ally of Cuba—from Mercosur is not helping to improve the current relations.

Since January 1959, the approach taken by Mexico toward the Cuban Revolution has been inconsistent, strongly conditioned by the priorities imposed by its relations with the United States. Mexico, without taking on an explicit role of regional leadership, finds itself among the ten largest economies in the world, with a government that seeks to reposition the country on the regional and global levels. However, Mexico has historically not demonstrated consistent or sustained leadership in the region, primarily exercising its influence on economic issues and in global fora. At the regional level, it has been limited in taking on a leadership role, principally because of its close relationship with the United States and its membership in the North American Free Trade Agreement (NAFTA). It is perennially torn between its ties with North America and its ability to be part of and have some influence on the Latin American community. Mexico aspires to overcome its biregional identity by promoting a foreign policy based on multiple goals. These include strengthening its

Latin American credentials, boosting its declining regional influence (especially in South America because of its exclusion from organizations like UNASUR), diversifying its international presence, and assuming its external role as a middle power, but without the aspirations of a clear regional power.[22] Despite its limited presence in Latin America, Mexico is beginning to resume its traditional hemispheric position in addition to its ties with North America, as illustrated by its more proactive foreign policy and the part it has played in reactivating the Rio Group as an alternative regional political forum to the OAS. Also significant are its efforts in the creation of CELAC (with the exclusion of its NAFTA partners), its rebuilding of ties with Cuba, and its role as a founding member of the Pacific Alliance. Mexico, which for many decades has served as a diplomatic bridge between Washington and Havana, also faces a troubled domestic front due to the escalation of organized-crime-related violence and political instability.[23]

Cuba's relations with the Mexican government headed by Enrique Peña Nieto have evolved noticeably. Initially his 2012 electoral victory concerned Havana, which saw him as a man determined to bring back the Washington Consensus as the dominant ideology in the region. Indeed, from Cuba's perspective, Mexico was still too closely aligned with Washington to serve as a diplomatic partner. Peña Nieto acknowledged this and therefore opted to put aside discussions on democracy and human rights (preferring them to be discussed at the United Nations) and instead to concentrate on Mexican trade and investment opportunities in Cuba.[24]

The first meeting between Raúl Castro and Peña Nieto happened in Chile during the first CELAC summit in 2013, followed by the new Institutional Revolutionary Party government's condoning of the Cuban debt to Mexico of US$487 million. In January 2014 Peña Nieto made an official visit to Havana (where he met with Fidel Castro), which was reciprocated by Raúl Castro in November 2015. Mexican trade and investment have continued to grow. In 2013 bilateral trade reached US$386 million, while Mexican investments in the island in 2015 reached US$730 million. According to the World Trade Organization, Mexico became at the time the seventh destiny for Cuban exports, while the island increased its imports from Mexico by 28.6 percent.[25]

The reestablishment of diplomatic relations between Cuba and the United States in December 2014 acted as an "accelerator" for Cuban-Mexican relations.[26] The relaunching of Cuban-Mexican relations was related to the official Mexican position of interest in the economic reforms on the island.[27] However, on the economic level, those relations are still relatively limited, despite trade and investment involving Mexican companies such as CEMEX, Industria Molinera de La Habana, Aeromexico, and Interjet. In 2016 there were thirty-one Mexican investment projects planned. After Venezuela and Brazil, Mexico is Cuba's third-largest trading partner in Latin America.[28] Currently two Mexican companies, Devos Caribe (a paint manufacturer) and Richmeat of Cuba (beef products), are operating in the Mariel free trade zone,[29] but the tourist and energy sectors also offer future investment opportunities.

In terms of key bilateral issues, migration and drug trafficking are extremely important for both countries. The election of Donald Trump poses interesting questions since the reformulation of U.S.-Mexican relations and the post-Obama approach to Cuba can also influence the future possibilities for the improvement of Cuban-Mexican economic relations. The review of the NAFTA agreement, a key platform issue for Trump, can affect both this relationship and indeed Mexico's relations with the rest of the Caribbean. It is highly possible that the historical triangle of U.S.-Mexican-Cuban relations will prevail and condition the evolution of Cuban-American links. Meanwhile, economic reforms in Cuba open the opportunity for increased Mexican economic interests on the island, as shown by the active presence of several Mexican companies.

In recent years no country has been more important for Cuba's economic development than Venezuela, as Carlos Romero illustrates in his chapter. At the beginning of the century, under the presidency of Hugo Chávez, it momentarily emerged as a strong contender for regional leadership, moving beyond its traditional influence in Central America and the Caribbean to the rest of the continent.[30] Although Venezuela was never before one of the major players in South America, over the last eighteen years it has promoted strategies using its oil wealth to build international alliances. Chávez cultivated and bought the loyalty of countries that were within Brazil's sphere of influence, such as Bolivia and Ecuador, in addition to several Central American and Caribbean countries. A foreign policy based on oil wealth is subject to the whims of the international price of a barrel of oil, and Venezuelan foreign policy has been overextended, subsidized by the high price of oil and characterized by a highly charged ideology.

Venezuela also resorted to the creation of regional organizations in order to increase its influence. Since the 2004 creation of ALBA in close association with Cuba, the Bolivarian government has sustained the organization's large outreach program through oil assistance. It has also extended its influence by incorporating into ALBA countries with similar antihegemonic and anti-U.S. attitudes in the Caribbean, Central America, and South America. However, in recent years under President Nicolás Maduro, Venezuela has lost its influence as a regional leader due to the drop in international oil prices that has led to severe economic problems in Venezuela. Also significant are the inherent difficulties involved in replacing a charismatic leader such as Chávez. Venezuela maintains a two-pronged foreign policy based on both a soft-balancing strategy designed to weaken the U.S. hegemonic presence and a growing militarization of its bureaucracy in its domestic social and political affairs.[31] Similarly, while Cuba continues to be a close ally of Venezuela, the economic reforms on the island are going in a slightly different direction compared with the growing statist policy of the Bolivarian government.[32]

Venezuela played an important role in the crusade for Cuba's inclusion in the LAC community, particularly after the establishment of ALBA, an organization generally associated with an inflammatory anti-U.S. rhetoric. With the election of Chávez to the presidency of Venezuela in 1998, the South American country gave unconditional support to the Castro government, support that has continued in the post-Chávez era. Economically, Cuba depended on Venezuela as its main trading partner. Venezuela provided cheap oil supplies to Cuba in return for teachers, doctors, and intelligence advisers. Politically, Caracas relied on Havana as its intimate political adviser and bulwark of anti-imperialist socialism, but the political and economic crises that followed the election of Nicolás Maduro after the death of Chávez have clearly hindered Venezuela's capacity to maintain economic support for Cuba. According to several sources, in 2016 Venezuela reduced its shipments of oil to Cuba by 40 percent. From an estimate of more than 105,000 barrels a day, they dropped in 2016 to 77,000, and supplies of crude oil to the Cienfuegos refinery (managed by a joint Cuban-Venezuelan company) were drastically reduced, stopping production.[33]

In 2014, the main recipients of Cuban exports were Venezuela, the Netherlands, Canada, China, and Spain, and the main exporters to Cuba were Venezuela, China, Spain, Brazil, and the United States,[34] a trading relationship which shows a high level of concentration of Cuban trade with a reduced group of countries. In general, however, economic relations with Latin America have improved during this century, as Michael Erisman explains in detail in his chapter. For example, in 2003 the trade with LAC countries represented 33.4 percent of the total exchange but in 2012 reached 61.2 percent. According to a 2014 report, Cuban exports to the region grew from 21.7 to 28.6 percent, while imports from the region went from 31.3 to 48.8 percent. In 2012 the main recipients of Cuban products in the region were Venezuela and Brazil (46.4 percent of exports to the region, which, with the exports to Argentina and Mexico, reached 53.1 percent).The export of professional services, particularly health services, is one of the main components of the exports, particularly in the case of Venezuela and Brazil.[35]

As noted earlier, Latin American nations have been deepening diplomatic relations with Cuba since the mid-1990s, both on a bilateral level and within existing and emerging multilateral and intergovernmental organizations such as SELA, the Rio Group, ALBA, UNASUR, and CELAC. One of the most significant developments to illustrate this was the decision taken by the Panamanian government to invite Cuba to the Seventh Summit of the Americas in 2015, a decision which illustrated the regional process of including Cuba in the hemispheric community as a full actor—and this despite several voices that echoed their distrust regarding Cuban democracy and human rights performance, as well as the limited reach and slow pace of the economic reforms on the island.

The growing role of Cuba within Latin America can also be seen in the support provided for the renewal of Cuban-U.S. relations. Two factors contributed to this process: the changing landscape of regional governance after the end of the Cold War and, as a result of the gradual strategic disengagement of the United States from the region, the role of some key Latin American and Caribbean countries in influencing U.S. positions toward Cuba. The two factors are intertwined, as the emerging new Latin American regionalism was closely linked to the leading roles played by Brazil, Venezuela, and Mexico in this process. A third additional factor is also pertinent:

from the 1970s, beginning with the closer ties established by Havana with the CARICOM countries, to the 1990s, when, after the collapse of the Soviet Union, the country was admitted to ALADI, Cuba developed a consistent strategy of broadening and deepening its relations with Latin America within its "concentric circles" foreign policy strategy. This grew dramatically after the gradual accession to power by left-wing or populist parties and movements, most of which were sympathetic to Cuba's revolution. Seasoned and skilled Cuban diplomacy was a crucial factor both in the process of developing closer ties with Latin American and Caribbean countries and in preparing the ground for the U.S.-Cuban bilateral talks.[36]

Within this context, Cuba's direct or implicit participation in the evolution and expansion of the so-called postliberal or posthegemonic regionalism since the 1990s is crucial to understanding the closer ties forged with LAC after the end of the Cold War and the end of the policy of exporting the Cuban Revolution to the region (never officially announced). Cuba continued as the main symbolic reference point in the highly anti-U.S. and antihegemonic rhetoric of this new regionalism. In addition, Havana continued developing closer links on a bilateral level with most of the relevant players in the region, who, at the same time, were some of the leading promoters of this new wave of regionalism.

Cuba and Latin America and the Caribbean: The Current and Future Situations

On December 17, 2014, Presidents Barack Obama and Raúl Castro announced the reestablishment of diplomatic relations. Even if, beginning with the Fifth Summit of the Americas held in Port of Spain in 2009, most LAC governments continued to denounce the U.S. embargo on Cuba, expectations had been increasing regarding Cuba's return to the inter-American system. The Sixth Summit of the Americas, held in Cartagena in 2012, confirmed this trend, with LAC states increasingly calling for Cuba's participation. The June 2009 OAS General Assembly decision to withdraw the 1962 suspension of Cuba reinforced this trend and showed that most of the Latin American and Caribbean governments (not just those aligned with ALBA) were keen on a rapid reincorporation of Cuba into the hemispheric community.

Given this context, in 2016 Cuba remained active in hemispheric matters. It was a signatory of the ALADI agreements, a full member of SELA and ACS, and an active founding member of ALBA and CELAC.[37] It persisted, however, in its reluctance to sign free trade agreements with its neighbors, even if it continued as an observer at CARICOM and Mercosur. In the case of UNASUR, Cuba repeatedly received support for its demand for an end to the U.S. embargo and in addition was consistently praised for the positive role that Havana played in the Colombian peace process.

At present Cuba is at a crossroads. Raúl Castro is to stand down as president this year (2018), and thus for the first time in sixty years there will be no Castro leading the country. There is also the challenge of dealing with the Trump administration and a multitude of potential complications on this front. The national economy is also faring poorly. On December 27, 2016, President Raúl Castro stated that, because of the reduction in the supply of fuel and financial tensions, Cuba experienced a reduction in the annual growth of its gross domestic product of 0.9 percent.[38]

Within this context, the current reconfiguration of the regional political landscape poses some new and serious challenges to the Cuban government. Havana's main Latin American trading and political partners are in retreat. Venezuela has substantially reduced its oil assistance, forcing the Cuban government to establish severe adjustments in the consumption of energy on the island and to acquire elsewhere additional oil supplies at international oil prices. The Cuban-Venezuelan Cienfuegos refinery was temporarily closed. The Brazilian government reduced the participation of Cuban doctors in the Mais Médicos program, with a significant impact on the $US500 million that it provided for services to the Cuban government. In addition, Brazil has reduced Cuban imports while the Odebrecht scandal expanded—limiting Brazilian investment in Cuba. Mexico continues struggling with a new relationship with the United States after the arrival of the Trump administration, a process that will probably hinder its interest in and support for Cuba. For Argentina and Colombia, Cuba still represents a symbolic reference point but will not become an important target for trade or investment. After the Panama Summit, the more radical postliberal organizations and governments are weakening or are prioritizing issues other than Cuba on their agendas. The regional political environment has changed, and the new wave of postliberal/posthegemonic regionalism has been progressively vanishing, together with the power and influence of the organizations that it created and nurtured.

The window of opportunity offered by the reestablishment of Cuban-U.S. relations during the Obama administration, with the sustained support of Latin American and Caribbean countries, to open the economy and attract foreign investment now seems to have closed. The contradictory statements by the new U.S. president, torn between the advice of conservative Cuban Americans to reverse the normalization process and the pressures of U.S. business sectors to develop it further, do not help us anticipate how (and in what directions) relations with Cuba will change.

The election of Trump as U.S. president arrived as a shock, both for Cuba and for the rest of LAC, while at the same time the death of Fidel closed an important chapter of Cuban influence in LAC and opened serious questions about the continuity of the special relationship between Cuba and LAC. Nevertheless, these two events should be contextualized not only in terms of the birth of a new stage of regional and inter-American relations but also with regard to the emerging new international environment. A new global situation, with the eventual realignment of relevant global players such as China, the United States, and Russia, and the Trump administration's foreign policy understandably raise questions about both the survival of the "normalization process" between Cuba and the United States and the future of a Latin American regionalism which was sympathetic with Cuba.

As suggested by Richard Feinberg in a recent volume, there could be several very different scenarios for the process of internal reforms in Cuba. The first one—

"inertia and exit"—can show that "the forces of inertia and authoritarian resilience—the one-party monopoly and bureaucratic control—[can] prove too powerful for those Cubans pushing for profound change." The second one—"botched transition and decay"—suggests a scenario in which Cuba "comes to look more like other Caribbean countries, manifesting many of their less desirable traits," including systemic corruption and organized crime. Finally, the third scenario—"soft landing-sunny 2030"—implies that "by 2030 Cuba will be well on the road toward becoming firmly integrated into the global economy," with a stable hybrid economy and a vibrant political life.[39] Within the current regional and international environment, and bearing in mind the internal constraints presented by the three scenarios, on the regional level it is difficult to envision a new distinctive role for LAC in any of them. After achieving the full reincorporation of Cuba within the hemispheric community, and after helping to reestablish Cuban-U.S. relations, in the new stage LAC as a region will not be able to perform the same role as in the past, both on the political front and in terms of investment and trade. Moreover it is difficult to foresee Cuba playing a similar role in the region as in previous years. Cuba is part of Latin America and the Caribbean, and as such it probably will be forced to confront similar challenges and constraints in the foreseeable future, while trying, at the same time, to make its national interests and priorities prevail on a drastically different regional and world stage.

NOTES

1. See Carlos Alzugaray, "Cuba's External Projection," in *Routledge Handbook of Latin America in the World*, ed. Jorge Dominguez and Ana Covarrubias (New York: Routledge, 2015), 193.

2. See Ricardo Domínguez Guadarrama, *Revolución cubana. Política exterior hacia América Latina y el Caribe* (Mexico City: UNAM, 2013), 182.

3. Carlos Alzugaray, "La Revolución Cubana y su influencia sobre la Izquierda latinoamericana y caribeña," in *Pensamiento Propio* (Buenos Aires: CRIES), no. 32 (July–December 2010): 161–85.

4. And, for a brief period, Chile, while the Salvador Allende government lasted, and Argentina during the short presidency of Héctor José Cámpora in 1973. Mexico, however, maintained its special links with Cuba.

5. In 1992 Cuba requested observer status at CARICOM. The next year a Cuban-CARICOM Joint Commission was established, which paved the way for the Trade and Economic Cooperation Agreement. CARICOM-Cuba was signed in 2000 and opened the possibility for a limited free trade agreement between CARICOM and Cuba with the aim of fostering the development of the Association of Caribbean States, which was created in 1994.

6. In 1990, through a joint initiative by Fidel Castro and Luiz Inacio Lula da Silva, a first meeting of left-wing parties and organizations was convened. The meeting became known later as the São Paulo Forum, in which the process of restructuring and programmatic redefinition of the Latin American and Caribbean Left started.

7. For a discussion of the extent of those concepts, see the introduction and first four chapters of Andrés Serbin, Laneydi Martinez, and Haroldo Ramanzini Jr., eds., *El regionalismo post-liberal en América Latina y el Caribe* (Buenos Aires: CRIES, 2012).

8. See Andrés Serbin, *Chávez, Venezuela y la reconfiguración política de América Latina y el Caribe* (Buenos Aires: Editorial Siglo XXI, 2010).

9. See Antonio Romero, "Cuba, su política exterior y la nueva arquitectura de la gobernanza regional en América Latina y el Caribe," in *Pensamiento Propio* (Buenos Aires: CRIES), no. 42 (July–December 2015): 107–33.

10. This was analyzed in Andrés Serbin, "Círculos concéntricos. La política exterior de Cuba en un mundo multipolar y el procesos de 'actualización,'" in *Cuba, Estados Unidos y América Latina frente a los desafíos hemisféricos,* ed. Luis Fernando Ayerbe (Buenos Aires: CRIES-Icaria Editorial, 2011), 229–67.

11. See José Briceño León, "¿Gobernanza regional o soft balancing de Estado revolucionario? El discurso y la práctica del ALBA," in *Pensamiento Propio* (Buenos Aires: CRIES), no. 42 (July–December 2015): 189–90.

12. A clear example of this is the lack of coordination among the three Latin American members of the G20 (Argentina, Brazil, and Mexico). Within that group, the existing rift between Mercosur and the Pacific Alliance, which the current governments of Chile and Argentina are trying to overcome, have complicated attempts to unify a common agenda at CELAC to engage global actors such as the European Union, Russia, India, and China.

13. For a further discussion of the current situation of most of these organizations, see Wolf Grabendorff, ed., "La arquitectura de gobernanza regional en América Latina. Condicionamientos y limitaciones," special issue, *Pensamiento Propio* (Buenos Aires: CRIES), no. 42 (July–December 2015).

14. Andrés Serbin, "Tres liderazgos y un vacío: América Latina y la nueva encrucijada regional," *Anuario CEIPAZ, 2008–2009* (Madrid: CEIPAZ, 2009).

15. For a more detailed description, see chapters on Brazil by Vigevani and Aragusuku and by Miriam Gomes Saraiva in Grabendorff, "La arquitectura de gobernanza regional en América Latina," and in Andrés Serbin, ed., *¿Fin de ciclo y reconfiguración regional? América Latina y las relaciones entre Cuba y los Estados Unidos* (Buenos Aires: CRIES, 2016).

16. Matías Spektor argues that the Brazilian policy toward South America is built on two main pillars. First, it protects against threats and preserves Brazil's freedom of action against regional instability, U.S. interference, and the negative effects of globalization. Second, regional activism is a tool to increase its power and support Brazil's broader interests in the world. See Matías Spektor, "Idéias de ativismo regional: A transformação das leituras brasileiras da região," *Revista Brasileira de Política Internacional* 53 (January–July 2010): 25–44.

17. See Alcides Costa Vaz, "Coaliciones internacionales en la política exterior brasileña: Seguridad y reforma de la gobernanza," *Revista CIDOB d'Afers Internacionals*, no. 97–98 (April 2012): 176; Elsa Llenderozas, "Política exterior latinoamericana y la comunidad de estados latinoamericanos y caribeños," in *Desafíos estratégicos del regionalismo contemporáneo: CELAC e Iberoamérica,* ed. Adrián Bonilla and Isabel Álvarez (San José, Costa Rica: FLACSO-AECID, 2014), 129–49.

18. After Argentina as its most important partner.

19. The links with Fidel started when the Sandinistas took power in Nicaragua in the 1980s and have continued until today. Lula was also instrumental in the inclusion of Cuba in the Río Group in 2009.

20. See Federico Merke, "The New Cuban Moment: Can Latin American States Help Spark Reform," Carnegie Endowment for International Peace, Washington, DC, September 2015, 3.

21. See Regiane Nitsch Bressan, "O espaco de America Latina na política exterior brasilera," in Serbin, *¿Fin de ciclo y reconfiguración regional?*, 322.

22. Llenderozas, "Política exterior latinoamericana," 133–34.

23. Merke, "The New Cuban Moment, 3.

24. Ibid.

25. See Raúl Benitez Manaut, "México y la nueva dinámica de las relaciones Cuba–Estados Unidos," in Serbin, *¿Fin de ciclo y reconfiguración regional?*, 191–207.

26. Ibid., 202.

27. "10 datos sobre las relaciones Mexico-Cuba," gob.mx, https://www.gob.mx/presidencia/articulos/10-datos-sobre-la-relacion-mexico-cuba (accessed November 6, 2015).

28. Benitez Manaut, "México y la nueva dinámica."

29. "Mariel, el naciente polo de inversión extranjera en Cuba," *El Nuevo Herald*, November 4, 2016, http://www.elnuevoherald.com/noticias/mundo/america-latina/cuba-es/article112534382.html (accessed November 4, 2016).

30. Serbin, *Chávez, Venezuela y la reconfiguración política.*

31. See Andrés Serbin and Andrei Serbin Pont, "Quince años de política exterior bolivariana: Entre el soft balancing y la militarización," in *Pensamiento Propio* (Buenos Aires: CRIES), no. 39 (January–June 2014): 287–325.

32. See Andrei Serbin Pont, "¿Aliados incómodos? Venezuela y el impacto de la normalización de las relaciones Cuba-EEUU," in Serbin, *¿Fin de ciclo y reconfiguración regional?*, 167–90.

33. Carmelo Mesa-Lago, "El porvenir de Cuba con Trump," *Política Exterior*, December 20, 2016.

34. See José Luis Rodríguez, "La economía cubana y América Latina: Oportunidades y desafíos," *CubaDebate*, March 10, 2014, http://www.cubadebate.cu/especiales/2014/03/10/la-economia-cubana-y-america-latina-oportunidades-y-desafios-iii/#.WmTqgTdOk2w

35. Ibid.

36. Particularly significant was Cuba's role in supporting the peace accords in Colombia between the government and the FARC guerrilla movement. The civil war in Colombia had lasted for more than five decades, resulting in 220,000 dead, 80,000 missing, and 7 million displaced. Under Fidel Castro and later his brother Raúl, Havana convinced the guerrillas to accept a binding peace agreement with the Juan Manuel Santos government. From 2012 to 2016 Cuba hosted the peace negotiations, and a final agreement was signed in November 2016.

37. SELA, *Análisis y recomendaciones para fomentar el comercio entre la república de Cuba y los países de América Latina y el Caribe* (Caracas, August 2013), http://www.sela.org/media/265315/t023600005452-0-di_12_-_analisis_y_recomendaciones_para_fomentar_el_comercio_entre_cuba_y_alc__rev_3_sep18.pdf.

38. AFP, "Cuban Economy in Recession for 2016: Castro," *Independent*, December 29, 2016, http://www.theindependentbd.com/arcprint/details/74383/2016-12-29.

39. Richard Feinberg, *Open for Business: Building the New Cuban Economy* (Washington, DC: Brookings Institution Press, 2016), 202–21.

6

Cuba and Africa

Recasting Old Relations in New but Familiar Ways

Isaac Saney

"Humanity has a debt to African people. We cannot let them down."

—Abelardo Moreno, UN Permanent Representative of Cuba[1]

Abelardo Moreno's statement at the September 16, 2014, meeting of the United Nations Security Council to discuss the Ebola epidemic in West Africa illustrates the privileged position that Africa occupies in the Cuban Revolution's foreign policy, under the leadership of both Fidel Castro and Raúl Castro. This special relationship is the product of a unique interaction between two sides of what has been termed the "Black Atlantic," a space created by the histories of the transatlantic slave system, colonialism, and anticolonial struggles. The intersection of all three connects Cuba to Africa, undergirded by Cuba's deep historical and cultural ties with the continent that predate the Cuban Revolution.[2] From 1763 to 1862, 750,000 enslaved Africans were brought to Cuba to work primarily in the sugar plantation system.[3] The island's history of African slavery laid the basis for the enduring link to Africa. Today Cuba has diplomatic links with every country in Africa, with the exception of Morocco (explained by Havana's ongoing support for the independence of Western Sahara, which Morocco occupies). Cuba was among the first non-African member states or organizations (actually the fourth) to be accredited to the African Union (AU).[4]

Havana's privileging of Africa in its foreign policy is mirrored in the deep respect accorded the island nation within the African continent. For six consecutive years, the African Union, representing fifty-four-countries, has unanimously adopted a resolution condemning U.S. economic sanctions against Cuba.[5] On May 23, 2013, the fifty-four foreign ministers of the African Union unanimously adopted "a motion of support and gratitude to Cuba, for its contribution to the emancipation of Africa[,] . . . categorically in favor of lifting the U.S. economic blockade against the Caribbean island."[6] Fidel Castro's death underscored this special relationship as African leaders and civil society organizations responded with outpourings of messages extolling his and Cuba's various contributions to Africa. Nigerian president Muhammadu Buhari described Fidel Castro as "a great friend to Africa."[7] In Angola, where the ties to Cuba are particularly poignant, a new highway in Luanda Province was named "Comandante em Chefe da Revolução Cubana Fidel de Castro Ruz Motorway."[8] Erastus Mwencha, deputy chair of the African Union, declared,

> You cannot write the history of Africa or Cuba, without Castro. . . . Cuba, through Castro, gave resources, gave soldiers, trained combatants, and did everything it could to assist Africa gain independence. As you know, Cuba provided support in the form of medical doctors and has also trained a number of doctors from Africa in Cuba. And most recently when we had the problem of Ebola, Cuba was one of those countries, challenged as it is under sanctions, that sent doctors and did everything that they could to assist the countries that were affected by Ebola. And so Cuba has been standing with Africa and working with Africa throughout whether it was through independence but also during development time.[9]

Mwencha speaks directly to the unique status of Cuba in African discourse and imagination. While Cuba is situated in the Caribbean, the African Union considers the island nation part of Africa due to its location within the African Diaspora.[10] The African Union has designated the African Diaspora as its sixth region or department, in short, incorporating all communities of African descent into the formal structure of the African Union. The AU defines the African Diaspora as "[consisting] of people of African origin living outside the continent, irrespective of their citizenship and nationality, and who are willing to contribute to the development of the continent and the building of the African Union."[11] However, as Mwencha noted, Cuba is bound to Africa in ways that transcend simply the existence of a large population of African descendants.

At the Havana memorial to Fidel Castro, South African president Jacob Zuma emphasized the singularity of Cuba's engagement with Africa, stating that "the deep and undying special relationship between Cuba and Africa was cemented by the blood of heroic Cuban soldiers who paid the supreme sacrifice for their belief in anti-imperialism, freedom and justice."[12] Using South Africa as an example of Cuba's ongoing assistance to Africa, Zuma emphasized, "South Africa has gained many Cuban doctors in our hospitals and clinics, often in the most remote areas of our country. In addition, many of our youth have qualified as medical practitioners in Cuba and many are continuing to study in this country."[13]

This active historical memory of Cuba's contributions to African anticolonial and national liberation struggles and the present concrete benefits of the medical and educational assistance have been a potent force in shaping and determining Havana's relationship with Africa. Therefore, while the assumption of the Cuban presidency by Raúl Castro in 2006 introduced a new dynamic in general within Cuban politics and policy creation, it is has not changed the fundamental contours of the relationship with Africa established when Fidel Castro was at the head of the Cuban revolutionary leadership. This relationship continues to be defined and shaped by the deep historical ties that were forged in the 1960s and 1970s, driven by an ideological and moral commitment to assist Africa without regard to significant resource acquisition or financial remuneration. Indeed, to paraphrase Karl Marx, history weighs profoundly on Cuban policymakers with regard to Africa.[14] While there is a growing emphasis on ensuring that Cuba's internationalist missions are economically sustainable and less of a drain on the island's resources, it has had a minimal impact on the various Cuban missions in Africa. The focus on creating a more efficient and productive economy—a more sustainable and prosperous socialism—has not diminished the commitment to assisting and cooperating with Africa. Cuban internationalist missions, especially those with Africa, continue to be "driven by proletarian internationalism, as well as other philosophical/idealistic principles."[15] In short, under Raúl Castro continuity has been the dominant feature.

"THE PAST IS NEVER DEAD. IT'S NOT EVEN PAST":[16] A LATIN AFRICAN PEOPLE

Africa has been central to Cuba's revolutionary internationalist foreign policy. Cuba's distinctive relationship with Africa is sui generis: no country has made such a sustained contribution and commitment to African anticolonial and national liberation struggles and social development. Since the triumph of the Cuban Revolution on January 1, 1959, Cuba has engaged in ongoing solidarity with the peoples and the continent of Africa. Diplomatic support, training, military aid, and other forms of concrete material assistance were provided to, for example, the National Liberation Front of Algeria in its struggle for independence from France and in the Congo, where Che Guevara led a guerrilla group. Training material, aid, and medical personnel were given to Guinea-Bissau's liberation struggle against Portugal. In 1977, the Cuban armed forces were critical in expelling a Somalian invasion of Ethiopia. Amilcar Cabral, leader of the liberation movement in Guinea-Bissau, poignantly captured that essence of Cuba's engagement with Africa: "I don't believe in life after death, but if there is, we can be sure that the souls of our forefathers who were taken away to America to be slaves are rejoicing today to see their children reunited and working together to help us be independent and free."[17]

The most dramatic internationalist mission was Cuban military assistance to help the Angolan government repulse South African aggression. From 1975 to 1990, more than 330,000 Cuban volunteers participated in repelling several South African invasions, with more than 2,000 Cubans losing their lives. Cuban military involvement in southern Africa has been repeatedly dismissed as surrogate activity for the Soviet Union. This position has been unequivocally refuted. In his acclaimed book *Conflicting Missions: Havana, Washington and Africa, 1959–1976*, Piero Gleijeses demonstrates that the Cuban government—as it had repeatedly asserted—decided to dispatch combat troops to Angola only after the Angolan government requested Cuba's military assistance to repel the South Africans, refuting Washington's assertion that South African forces intervened in Angola only after the arrival of the Cuban forces; the Soviet Union had no role in Cuba's decision and was not even informed prior to deployment. In short, Cuba was not the puppet of the USSR.[18]

As the survival of the racist South African state depended on establishing its domination of all of southern Africa, the region was transformed into a vast arena in which, for more than a decade, the forces for and against apartheid clashed. This was underscored by the South African Truth and Reconciliation Commission, which concluded, "It would appear that conflicts in southern African states, particularly in Mozambique, Namibia and Angola, were often inextricably linked to the struggle for control of the South African state."[19]

From 1975 to 1988, the South African armed forces embarked on a campaign of massive destabilization of the region. The war of destabilization wrought a terrible toll. Between 1981 and 1988, an estimated 1.5 million people were (directly or indirectly) killed, including 825,000 children.[20] This was the result of Pretoria-sponsored insurgencies (namely, UNITA in Angola and Renamo in Mozambique) and direct military actions by the South African armed forces. South Africa launched numerous bombing raids, armed incursions, and assassinations in surrounding countries.

The decisive military confrontation with South Africa occurred around the southeastern Angolan town of Cuito Cuanavale. Cuito Cuanavale was a critical turning point in the struggle against apartheid. From November 1987 to March 1988, the South African armed forces repeatedly tried and failed to capture Cuito Cuanavale. The Cuban commitment was immense, providing the essential reinforcements, materiel, and planning. Fidel Castro stated that the Cuban Revolution had "put its own existence at stake, it risked a huge battle against one of the strongest powers located in the area of the Third World, against one of the richest powers, with significant industrial and technological development, armed to the teeth, at such a great distance from our small country and with our own resources, our own arms. . . . We used our ships and ours alone, and we used our equipment to change the relationship of forces, which made success possible in that battle. We put everything at stake in that action."[21]

This military effort culminated in the decisive defeat of the South African armed forces at the town of Cuito Cuanavale. The defeat of the South African Defense Forces at Cuito Cuanavale in 1987 and 1988 drove the apartheid army out of Angola and altered the balance of power in southern Africa. South Africa was forced to the negotiating table, which directly resulted in Namibian independence and accelerated the dismantling of apartheid in South Africa.[22]

A poignant example of Cuba's dedication to the antiapartheid struggle was the generosity extended to the children who survived the notorious Kassinga massacre at a Namibian refugee camp in Angola that was perpetuated by the South African armed forces on May 4, 1978, in which hundreds were killed and hundreds were taken prisoner.[23] In response, the Cuban government offered to educate all the survivors on the Isla de la Juventud. Former Namibian ambassador to Cuba Grace Uushona was one of those children: "There were 600 of us who came. I went to high school and prep school there." She described Cuba as "my second country."[24] The resolve to educate the survivors of the Kassinga massacre was part of a general and continuing Cuban goal to provide education to all of Africa.[25]

The Cuban leadership justified the military intervention in southern Africa as both defending an independent country from foreign invasion and repaying a historical debt owed by Cuba to Africa. Fidel Castro frequently invoked Cuba's historical links to Africa. On the fifteenth anniversary of the Cuban victory at Playa Girón (Bay of Pigs), he famously declared, "Those who once enslaved man and sent him to America perhaps never imagined that one of those peoples who received slaves would one day send their fighters to struggle for freedom in Africa. . . . We are a Latin-African people."[26]

This sentiment did not solely belong to Fidel Castro; it prevailed within the revolutionary leadership. Jorge Risquet, Havana's principal diplomat in Africa from the 1970s to 1990s, was also unambiguous in explaining Cuba's military intervention in terms of Cuba's historic and moral obligations as a consequence of slavery and the slave trade. Most significantly, Raúl Castro was an avid supporter and shaper of this policy. In a 1976 report to the Cuban Communist Party's Politburo about his two-month visit to Angola, the Republic of the Congo, and Guinea, he emphasized that coming to the aid of African national liberation movements was "an internationalist duty."[27] In other official documents shared within the revolutionary leadership, he consistently articulated the necessity to "continue to help Africa" in the anti-imperialist struggle.[28] For example, in a 1985 meeting with Mikhail Gorbachev, he declared, "Africa is literally dying, while the United States exploits it."[29] Beyond these statements of support for Africa, it was Raúl Castro who created and then developed the Fuerzas Armadas Revolucionarias into the formidable force that was able to wage successful campaigns in Africa.[30] His commitment to the anti-imperialist struggle and the politics it requires was concretized in the instrument that the Cuban Revolution, under Fidel Castro's leadership, would deploy so decisively in Africa.

In 1991, Nelson Mandela, as a very public recognition of Cuba's role in the antiapartheid struggle, deliberately chose Cuba as one of the first countries outside Africa and the first in Latin America to visit after his release from twenty-seven years of imprisonment. Mandela declared, "The Cuban people hold a special place in the hearts of the people of Africa. The Cuban internationalists have made a contribution to African independence, freedom and justice unparalleled for its principled and selfless character."[31] He continually reiterated these sentiments during his 1994–1999 presidency of South Africa, and his successors have continued in this vein, with Thabo Mbeki and Jacob Zuma on several occasions echoing those sentiments.[32] Physical monuments in South Africa to the antiapartheid struggle also pay homage to Cuba. On the Wall of Names in Pretoria's Freedom Park, the names of 2,106 Cubans who died in Angola during the 1975–1991 Cuban military missions are inscribed.[33]

Inside Cuba, Raúl Castro has continued to valorize Cuba's role in southern Africa. Hector Fraginals de la Torre (coordinator for North and Central America, Department of International Relations, Communist Party of Cuba) underscored that the Cuban leadership places a premium on the preservation and projection of the historical memory of Cuba's role in Africa's anticolonial struggles, especially in southern Africa.[34] In 2007, Cuban television broadcast a twenty-two-episode series, *La epopeya de Angola*, on the internationalist mission. Numerous memoirs have also been published, coupled with regular commemorative events. On March 24, 2008, Raúl Castro presided over a major ceremony, which reiterated the internationalist mission in Angola (as embodied in the victory at Cuito Cuanavale) as a defining period in the trajectory of the Cuban Revolution.[35] In 2012, as Cuba's official representative at a conference honoring Kwame Nkrumah's pan-Africanism, Jorge Risquet pointed out, "Cuban fighters came to ancestral Africa to fight side by side with the people against colonialism and the oppressive apartheid regime. For 26 years, 381,000 Cuban soldiers and officers fought alongside African populations—between April 24, 1965, when Ernesto Che Guevara and his men crossed Lake Tanganyika, and May 25, 1991, when the remaining 500 Cuban fighters returned home triumphant. . . . Twenty-four hundred Cuban internationalist fighters lost their lives on African soil. Today we no longer send soldiers. Now, we send doctors, teachers, builders, specialists in various fields."[36]

Cuban society is suffused with the retelling of the internationalist mission in southern Africa. It has become central to Cuba's national narrative. Raúl Castro has reinforced this process of preserving the integrity of this historical memory. This exercise in national memory not only serves to keep alive among Cubans the story of Cuba's sacrifices in southern Africa but also ensures that Africa and Africans do not forget.

ONGOING MEDICAL INTERNATIONALISM

While the military mission in southern Africa was the most dramatic manifestation of Cuba's commitment to Africa, the medical missions are no less important in illustrating the privileged position of the continent in Havana's foreign policy. Cuba's first medical mission was to Algeria. This set the stage for the deep medical engagement with Africa. By 1988 there were Cuban medical missions in twenty-two African countries. Africa was the principal area for Cuban medical personnel. For example, in 1981 40.8 percent of Cuban medical personnel serving overseas were stationed in Africa, and by 1988 it was 47.3 percent. By 2015, it was estimated that seventy-six thousand Cuban medical personnel had served in Africa.[37] The extent of Cuba's involvement goes beyond simply the number of countries. Cuban doctors did not simply augment the existing health-care system; in many cases they were the health-care system. By 1977 Cuba was the crucial, if not central, provider of health care in six African countries. Cuba's medical internationalism also extended to training Africans as doctors and in other health-care capacities. By 1990–1991, 2,524 doctors from Africa had been trained in Cuba, 1,507 of them from sub-Saharan Africa.[38]

This commitment to Africa and Africans has not only continued but also been expanded under Raúl Castro. A 2016 *Granma* article stated that Cuba's missions in Africa were designed "to contribute to the development of the receiving nation . . . an act of unconditional solidarity."[39] The focus on creating a more efficient and productive economy encompasses Cuba's various internationalist missions but has not had a significant impact on the programs in Africa. Havana's aim to reduce the cost of the medical programs to Cuba was based on a sliding scale. As noted in the chapter by John Kirk on Cuba's medical internationalism, the objective was to have those countries that could afford to pay without compromising their own development goals contribute to covering a portion, if not all, of the costs of the medical missions. This would help offset the expense of maintaining Cuban doctors in the field and in the hospitals. However, the poorest countries would—and do—continue to receive the medical assistance "at no cost or at a heavily subsidized rate."[40] Thus, Africa, particularly sub-Saharan Africa, continues to receive the service of Cuban health-care workers at very low cost. The only exceptions are Angola and South Africa. This policy was reaffirmed in the two strategic documents adopted at the April 2016 Seventh Congress of the Communist Party of Cuba, which reiterated the commitment to internationalism as an important part of the Cuban model of socialist development. Article 326 of the "Conceptualization of Cuban Socialism" emphasized building relations "with sister nations of the South based on solidarity."[41] Article 200 of the "2030 National Economic and Social Development Plan" identifies internationalism as of the fundamental "values, practices and attitudes that distinguishes our society."[42]

Cuban medical assistance to Africa is unprecedented, under the tenure of both Fidel Castro and Raúl Castro. Indeed, the thrust established by Fidel has not only continued but been expanded and enhanced. At the time of Fidel Castro's formal resignation from the presidency in 2008, Cuba had medical missions in twenty-two African countries, involving 1,184 medical personnel (including 832 doctors).[43] By 2012, Havana's medical missions in Africa had expanded to encompass thirty-five countries on the continent, with more than four thousand health-care workers.[44] By 2013, the contingent had grown to more than fifty-five hundred.[45] Thus, under Raúl Cuba's medical missions in Africa have grown from encompassing 41 percent of countries in Africa to 65 percent, with the actual size of the overall African mission growing by more than 4.5 percent. Specific examples illustrate Havana's ongoing commitment to assist the poorest African countries. In Mozambique another 30 doctors were sent, increasing the total to 160. Rwanda was added to Cuba's African medical map in 2010, when thirty-one doctors were dispatched. In Botswana an eye clinic was established.[46] Indeed, from 2007 to 2013, 32,314 Africans have received specialized eye treatment as part of Operación Milagro, the program launched jointly by Cuba and Venezuela to provide access to ophthalmological care for basic ailments such as cataracts. Initially aimed at Latin America, the program grew to include Africa.[47]

Havana has also expanded its medical educational projects in Africa. As Kirk points out, "There is no evidence that, since Raúl Castro came to power in 2006, Cuba has in any way reduced its interest in training doctors for the Third World."[48] The evidence is to the contrary. By 2016 it was estimated that thirty thousand students from Africa had graduated from Cuban universities.[49] The Latin American School of Medicine continues to waive the tuition for students from the poorest African countries.

During the tenure of Fidel Castro, Cuba participated in setting up six medical schools across Africa, with Cuban professors as the principal instructors. The goal is to build indigenous health-care capacity by directly training doctors in their native countries. Medical schools were established in Ethiopia (1984), Uganda (1986), Ghana (1991), Gambia (2000), Equatorial Guinea (2000), and Guinea-Bissau (2004).[50] Cuba has continued to support the goal of achieving African health-care independence. For example, an additional eleven doctors were sent to teach at Tamale University in Ghana.[51] In 2008, the medical program in Gambia was expanded to provide training for community doctors. In the new program twenty-nine Cuban professors taught thirty-five students.[52] This quite incredible instructor-to-student ratio illustrates the importance placed by Cuba on the necessity to create within African countries the medical expertise vital to improving social and human development.

Havana is also committed to providing low-cost medicines to countries of the South, especially sub-Saharan Africa. One objective is to ensure that medicines are much more affordable, so that expense is no longer a barrier to effective treatment; another is to foster independence from the West's monopoly on drug creation and production. This has meant directly challenging the grip of the pharmaceutical giants on the international markets. A successful instance of this approach was the creation and distribution of a low-cost vaccine for meningococcal meningitis, a bacterial infection that attacks the outer membranes of the brain and spinal cord. The result can be severe brain damage, with a 50 percent mortality rate if not properly treated. In 2006–2007, due to unusually dry weather, sub-Saharan Africa faced the possibility of a deadly outbreak across "what is known as Africa's *meningitis belt*, a band that stretches across 23 countries, from Senegal in the west to Ethiopia in the east, home to 430 million people."[53]

However, at the time the only producer of a vaccine against the disease, Sanofi Pasteur, a U.S.-based corporation, was discontinuing production. In response, the World Health Organization (WHO) issued an urgent call for the production of a vaccine. Cuba's Finlay Institute and Brazil's Bio-Manguinhos immunobiological institute responded and cooperated in producing a very low-cost vaccine. Their cost was $0.95 per dose as opposed to $15 to $20.[54] Cuba and Brazil had produced a vaccine that was fifteen to twenty-one times cheaper than the vaccine of Sanofi Pasteur. The vaccine was distributed across the "meningitis belt," with the main targets being Mali, Ethiopia, Burkina Faso, Nigeria, Niger, and Chad, which had been deemed to be facing the greatest threat. In the end, more than 19 million doses were distributed.[55] WHO specialist Alejandro Costa noted that Cuba and Brazil "were able to produce a vaccine at the lowest cost, which contributed to reducing the cases of meningitis."[56] Ramón Barberá, Finlay Institute vice president for production, described the vaccine's creation, production, and distribution as "a victory of unity."[57]

Perhaps the most convincing demonstration of the continuity with Fidel of Raúl's commitment to Africa was the 2014 Ebola epidemic that ravaged West Africa. Raúl Castro immediately recognized the gravity of the situation and jointly with the WHO and the Pan American Health Organization convened an international conference in Havana on the epidemic.[58] Cuba also went further. As Ebola ravaged Guinea, Liberia, and Sierra Leone, the island nation offered "to send to Sierra Leone 103 nurses, and 62 doctors."[59] In total 256 medical personnel were deployed in those three countries, with 53 sent to Liberia and 35 to Guinea. In Sierra Leone, Cuban doctors treated one thousand patients and were able to halve the Ebola mortality rate. Cuban doctors are estimated to have saved 260 lives; in Guinea they saved 150 lives.[60] Cuba also trained 13,286 people in Africa in the protocols and techniques necessary to deal with and prevent the spread of Ebola.[61]

The Cuban medical mission was by far the largest sent by any country. As Jorge Lefebre Nicolás, Cuba's ambassador to Liberia, declared, "We cannot see our brothers from Africa in difficult times and remain there with our arms folded."[62] Such was the magnitude of Cuba's solidarity with Africa that even the corporate media, usually unduly harsh in their views concerning Cuba, had to give the Caribbean nation plaudits for its actions. On October 9, 2014, the *Wall Street Journal* noted, "Few have heeded the call, but one country has responded in strength: Cuba."[63]

A TRULY SPECIAL RELATIONSHIP: CUBA AND SOUTHERN AFRICA

Within Africa, it is with southern Africa, particularly South Africa, that Cuba has developed the most extensive and multifaceted relationship. This relationship revolves around the decisive role of Cuba in the long fight for southern African national liberation. This is consistently reflected in the valorization of Cuba; indeed, Cuba has become integral to the regional metanarrative. The shared history of the antiapartheid struggle serves as the base upon which Cuba and southern African nations have developed and maintained strong political and diplomatic relations. While this weight of history finds expression in frequent rhetorical flourishes and symbolic gestures, it is often, however, invoked as the rationale for the implementation of policies to forge a closer relationship in the postapartheid and post–Cold War eras. Mozambican foreign minister Tomaz Salomao declared, "We believe that to reciprocate that attitude toward Cuba and its people for Africa is very important."[64]

For example, former Namibian president Sam Nujoma in his autobiography highlights Cuba's crucial role in the realization of Namibia's independence.[65] The twentieth anniversary commemorations of the battle of Cuito Cuanavale poignantly illustrate this valorization. A number of events were organized across the region. In Brazzaville, the Angolan and Cuban embassies jointly hosted celebrations.[66] In 2008, then Namibian president Hifikepunye Pohamba awarded Namibia's highest honor, the Order of the Most Ancient Welwitschia Mirabilis, to Fidel Castro, declaring, "We are indebted to the Cuban Government and the heroic Cuban people for this support and we shall never forget this unparalleled example of selfless internationalism."[67]

Cuba maintains the strongest relationship with South Africa. Full diplomatic relations were established on May 11, 1994. President Mandela stated that "in accordance with South Africa's policy towards countries with which it has normal diplomatic relations, it would endeavor to foster trade and economic, cultural and sporting links with Cuba that would be mutually beneficial." Medical internationalism is an important element of this relationship. The medical program with South Africa was initiated in 1996 when the first Cuban doctor arrived. On August 2, 2012, Malebona Matsoso, director general of South Africa's Ministry of Health, emphasized that South Africa "needs health care workers, especially in rural areas, and we want to train more doctors. We therefore want to sustain this relationship with Cuba."[68] Trade and Industry Minister Robert Davies also noted, "Cuba continues to provide training for SA doctors and provide vaccines that are used in the public health sector in SA and contribute to eradicating very serious diseases."[69]

The medical mission has steadily grown to meet the needs in rural areas. In 2016, an additional 29 Cuban medical personnel were sent to the province of Gauteng, increasing the size of the Cuban medical contingent in South Africa to 424.[70] Several cooperative agreements have been reached, including one deal to provide primary health-care education in Cuba to South Africans.[71] In November 2016 Havana and Pretoria signed "a cooperation agreement in Basic Education, joining to the existing ones in health, water resources, human settlements and professional training on the island."[72]

Havana's relationship with Pretoria is indicative of the approach that has emerged from the deeply entwined Cuban relationship in the thirty-year southern African anticolonial and national liberation struggles. The widening of this relationship goes beyond the sphere of Cuban internationalist missions. In 2010, South Africa also made a series of loans to the island, amounting to $137 million. However, on December 9, 2010, during a visit to Cuba, South African President Zuma, invoking Cuba's contribution to the struggle against apartheid, announced the cancellation of Cuba's $137 million debt to South Africa, taking the opportunity to hail the "Cubans' depth of internationalist feeling."[73] This action was praised by South Africa's National Union of Mineworkers, which stated, "This gesture should serve as a basis for renewing our fraternal relations with Cuba, which were born out of a concrete struggle for freedom and liberation of the oppressed people of our country and the southern African region."[74] The sentiment of a debt owed to Cuba by South Africans cannot be overstated as a dominant principle shaping Pretoria's relations with Cuba. During a November 2012 visit to Cuba, Trade and Industry Minister Davies stated, "If it had not been for the contributions and sacrifices that Cuba made . . . I think we might well find ourselves battling with the demon of apartheid for several more years, and possibly a decade longer than we did."[75]

Nevertheless, the relationship between Cuba and South African has not been, as Minister Davies observed, "underpinned by robust economic relations."[76] Cuba's economic relationship with South Africa has been conditioned by the relatively small size of the Cuban market and the island's foreign exchange difficulties.[77] In 2011, Cuba ranked 83rd out the 216 countries as a recipient of South African exports and 120th for imports.[78] In 2012, Davies noted that efforts had been made since the emergence of a democratic South Africa to strengthen economic links between the two countries: "We have tried a number of things on various occasions but some of these things have not delivered the results."[79] While there are a number of projects in mining, tourism, construction, and manufacturing, in 2014 trade between the two countries only amounted to $8.6 million.[80]

Nevertheless, the South African government launched an initiative to redress this situation through a February 2012 agreement that was ratified in May 2012. Pretoria provided an economic assistance package of R350 million (US$50 million). Crafted as a means to assist Cuba in dealing with the significant damage caused by the 2008 hurricanes, the agreement was divided into three phases. Through the African Renaissance Fund, Cuba was initially granted R100 million, comprised of a nonrepayable R40 million grant to purchase seeds in South Africa and abroad (R5 million in South Africa, the rest in other countries). The second phase provided a R100 million nonrepayable solidarity grant. The third phase extended a R210 million credit line to be repaid by 2019. Pretoria also opened the South African construction sector to Cuban state firms.[81] On July 19, 2016, Cuban and South African representatives met to discuss "economic relations."[82] The gathering included the ten largest South African companies. Celia Labora Rodriguez, international relations director of the Cuban Chamber of Commerce, pointed out the opportunities that now existed in Cuba. She emphasized that "economic collaboration will be bolstered by the economic changes in her country and the new investment law that seeks to attract foreign capital."[83]

While South Africa, due to its strategic regional role, has developed the most significant economic relations with Cuba, other countries in the region are strengthening those ties. Angola has long extolled Cuba's role in defending Angolan independence. Angolan minister of defense Candido Pereira Van-Dunen emphasized in Havana, Cuba, "Our people have written with blood and sweat, glorious moments that resulted in the consolidation of freedom, national independence and sovereignty of Angola after a heroic battle against the enemies."[84] Cuba continues to engage in several educational programs with Angola. In 2016, 2,386 Angolans were studying in Cuba in a variety of disciplines, with 1,186 enrolled in medicine.[85]

The Angolan-Cuban cooperation in the health and education sectors is accompanied by a growing role in other areas. For example, the Angolan consortium Sonangol is participating with the Cuban oil company CUPET in oil exploration off the Cuban coast. Cuban companies are also involved in oil exploration in Angola. Through Sonangol, CubaPetróleo was able to obtain a 5 percent share in an offshore block in Cabinda. Havana also has a presence in Angolan construction, being involved in road repair and bridge construction. Cuba participated in the building of ten bridges. During a May 2013 economic mission to Angola, Cuban vice president Ricardo Cabrisas stated, "Concerning the construction sector, Cuba is ready to continue to participate with its human capital in the drafting and implementation of large projects."[86]

In the case of Namibia, a 2015 agreement stipulated that 750 Namibian students would attend medical school in Cuba from 2015 to 2018.[87] However, despite this agreement and biennial Cuban and Namibian discussions, as well as economic, commercial, and technical cooperation, relations remain relatively undeveloped in comparison to Angola and South Africa. Hage Geingob, then Cuban-Namibian trade and industry minister, recognized this as he observed that the "Namibian-Cuba friendship started way back during the country's liberation struggle. Now we must do more in strengthening economic cooperation. . . . As you sacrificed your lives during Africa's bitter struggle, let us find ways on how to cooperate economically as partners."[88] Namibian foreign minister Utoni Nujoma discussed extensively the possibility of a much-expanded Cuban economic presence, particularly in mining and infrastructural development.[89] In 2016 the Namibia-Cuba Joint Working Group was established to expand trade and commercial relations. The group's central focus is on developing three stalled projects in the manufacturing sector, particularly the delayed construction of a pharmaceutical plant in Namibia.[90]

Whether a more substantial—quantitatively and qualitatively—economic relationship between Cuba and southern Africa will emerge remains to be seen. At present, the economic and commercial relations lag behind the scale of Cuba's internationalist missions. In 2016, of the more than 5,000 Cubans serving in various missions in Africa, the overwhelming majority—3,718—were serving in six southern African nations, all of which were frontline states in the struggle against apartheid: Angola (2,742), Mozambique (389), South Africa (424), Namibia (113), Botswana (99), and Zimbabwe (46).[91] These six countries have more Cubans serving in them than the other twenty-nine African countries combined. Even when it is factored in that both Angola and South Africa pay significantly above the subsidized rates for Cuban doctors ($1,100 per month per doctor in the case of Angola), these Cuban mission figures underscore the significance that Cuba attaches to the region.

However, there is considerable political will—particularly in South Africa—to forge deeper economic ties. These economic initiatives have emerged during the presidential tenure of Raúl Castro. They are in line with the focus on Cuban economic development. Greater efficiency and productivity in the domestic sphere are mirrored by a more efficacious and materially beneficial foreign policy. However, one can overstate the impact of placing greater emphasis on the creation of concrete economic relations. The emergence of this new dimension in Cuba's relationship with southern Africa also appears to represent continuity with past practice and a policy of deepening engagement based on the very recent shared history of the region's anticolonial struggle.

CONCLUSION

During his tenure at the helm of the Cuban government, Raúl Castro has put the emphasis on the economic sustainability and prosperity of the Cuban socialist project. Nevertheless, while relations with Africa have been attenuated due to Cuba's economic, commercial, and national development imperatives, there has been no rupture or significant departure from principles that governed the entwined relationship that has bound Cuba and Africa together. Ideological and moral grounds continue to predominate. Despite the accentuation of the economic links, the cooperative relationship not only continues but also has been expanded and enhanced.

Cuba is ineluctably bound to Africa and is an integral part of the African Diaspora. As Fidel Castro declared, Cuba is a Latin African nation. With the United Nations' declaration of the International Decade for People of African Descent for 2015 through 2024, Cuba's solidarity with Africa assumes greater poignancy.[92] In reiterating its support for the decade at the 71st United Nations General Assembly, Havana stated, "We share the view that the International Decade for People of African Descent provides an opportunity that should be seized by all States to focus on the challenges to be faced in combating racial discrimination; to draw policies that allow us to solve identified problems and to strengthen international cooperation in order to achieve a world where equality, mutual respect and social justice prevail."[93]

Aside from supporting the International Decade for People of African Descent, Havana also champions the lawsuit of fourteen countries of CARICOM, the English-speaking Caribbean Community, against the United Kingdom, France, and the Netherlands for reparations for the legacy of the transatlantic slave trade. At the April 2016 summit of the Community of Latin American and Caribbean States, Raúl Castro declared his support for the lawsuit: "We support the just demand for compensation launched by the member states of the Caribbean Community. People from the Third World are still feeling the effects of the inhuman exploitation."[94] His statement echoed Fidel's September 1, 2001, address to the World Conference against Racism, Racial Discrimination, Xenophobia, and Related Intolerance, where he stated, "Cuba speaks of reparations, and supports this idea as an unavoidable moral duty to the victims of racism. . . . The irrefutable truth is that tens of millions of Africans were captured, sold like a commodity and sent beyond the Atlantic to work in slavery while 70 million indigenous people in that hemisphere perished as a result of the European conquest and colonization."[95]

The Cuban Revolution has been—and is—united with Africa by the Black Atlantic and the shared burden of overcoming the legacy of imperial domination and underdevelopment. The centrality of Africa to Cuba is reflected in the size and scope of the various internationalist missions that the island nation has deployed on the African continent: from the nearly half million who served as soldiers during the era of the anticolonial and national liberation struggles to the thousands of medical personnel and educators who ply their trade in the second decade of the twenty-first century. The ideological and political parameters—at least for the unpredictable life expectancy of historical memory—is shaped by the shared experience of the transatlantic slave system, colonialism, and underdevelopment.

The island's internationalist missions in Africa are a profound challenge to those who argue that relations among the world's nations and peoples are—and can only be—determined by self-interest and the pursuit of power and wealth. Cuba is often described as the only foreign country to have gone to Africa and gone away with nothing but the coffins of its sons and daughters who died in the struggles to liberate Africa. Under the leadership of both Fidel and then Raúl, Cuba provides the example that it is possible to build relations based on genuine solidarity and social love, thereby demonstrating the alternatives to neoliberalism and that another more equitable world is possible.

NOTES

1. "Cuba Confirms Support in Fight against Ebola at Security Council Debate," *Telesur*, September 19, 2014.

2. Paul Gilroy, *The Black Atlantic: Modernity and Double-Consciousness* (Cambridge, MA: Harvard Press, 1995).

3. Louis A. Pérez Jr., *Cuba: Between Reform and Revolution* (Oxford: Oxford University Press, 2015), 66.

4. *African Union Handbook 2016* (African Union, 2016), 167.

5. "Cuba Thanked African Support in Fighting US Blockade," *Prensa Latina*, May 24, 2016.

6. "Foreign Ministers Back Cuba," *Prensa Latina*, May 23, 2013.

7. "Fidel Castro: Africa Leaders Praise a Fallen Comrade," *Deutsche Welle*, November 27, 2016.

8. "Angola Has Named Its Newest Highway after the Late Fidel Castro," *Quartz Africa*, December 6, 2016.

9. James Butty, "African Union Official Remembers Fidel Castro," *VOA News*, November 28, 2016.

10. Marylín Luis Grillo, "Cuba es también parte de África," *Juventud Rebelde*, May 25, 2016.

11. Hakima Abba, "From Roots to Branches: The African Diaspora in a Union Government for Africa," in *Towards a Union Government for Africa: Challenges and Opportunities*, ed. Timothy Murithi (Pretoria: Institute for Security Studies, 2008), 1.

12. "Qhawe Lamaqhawe! President Zuma's Moving Tribute to Fidel Castro," *Mail-Guardian*, November 30, 2016.

13. Ibid.

14. This is an allusion with much more positive connotations to Marx's famous statement from *The Eighteenth Brumaire of Louis Bonaparte*: "The tradition of all the dead generations weighs like a nightmare on the brain of the living." Karl Marx, *Karl Marx: A Reader* (Cambridge: Cambridge University Press, 1999), 277.

15. John M. Kirk and Michael Erisman, *Cuban Medical Internationalism: Origins, Evolution and Goals* (Basingstoke, UK: Palgrave Macmillan, 2009), 87.

16. William Faulkner, *Requiem for a Nun* (New York: Vintage, 1994), 73.

17. Piero Gleijeses, *Conflicting Missions: Havana, Washington, and Africa, 1959–1976* (Chapel Hill: University of North Carolina Press, 2001), 198.

18. For a detailed discussion, see Gleijeses, *Conflicting Missions*; Isaac Saney, "African Stalingrad: The Cuban Revolution, Internationalism and the End of Apartheid," *Latin American Perspectives* 35, no. 5 (September 2006): 81–117.

19. Truth and Reconciliation Commission of South Africa, *Truth and Reconciliation Commission of South Africa Report*, vol. 2: *Repression and Resistance* (New York: Macmillan Reference Limited, 1999), 3–4.

20. Africa Watch, *Accountability in Namibia* (New York: Africa Watch, 1992); International Defence and Aid Fund, *Remember Kassinga* (London: International Defence and Aid Fund, 1981); Truth and Reconciliation Commission of South Africa, *Report*, 46–55.

21. Fidel Castro, "We Will Never Return to the Slave Barracks," in Nelson Mandela and Fidel Castro, *How Far We Slaves Have Come!* (New York: Pathfinder Press, 1991), 34–35.

22. For a detailed discussion, see Piero Gleijeses, *Visions of Freedom: Havana, Washington, Pretoria, and the Struggle for Southern Africa, 1976–1991* (Chapel Hill: University of North Carolina Press, 2013); Saney, "African Stalingrad."

23. Africa Watch, *Accountability in Namibia*; International Defence and Aid Fund, *Remember Kassinga*; Truth and Reconciliation Commission of South Africa, *Report*, 46–55.

24. Patricia Grogg, "Cuba-Africa: Decades of Assistance and Cooperation," *Inter-Press Service*, July 2, 2004.

25. Laura Prada, "Cuba-Africa Collaboration: A Bridge between Sister Nations," *Granma*, May 20, 2016.

26. Fidel Castro, *Cuba's Internationalist Foreign Policy, 1975–1980* (New York: Pathfinder Press, 1981), 110, 129; Fidel Castro, *2nd Congress of the Communist Party of Cuba: Documents and Speeches* (Havana: Editora Política, 1981), 55.

27. Raúl Castro, "Informe al Político Buró del Segundo Secretario del Comité Central del Partido Comunista de Cuba acera de su visita a África (19 de abril a 7 de junio de 1976)," June 14, 1977, 5.

28. Raúl Castro, "Memorandum of Conversation between Raúl Castro and Samora Machel," December 17, 1977.

29. Raúl Castro, "Memorandum of Conversation between Raúl Castro and Mikhail Gorbachev," March 20, 1985.

30. Hal Klepak, *Raúl Castro and Cuba: A Military Story* (Basingstoke, UK: Palgrave Macmillan, 2012), 45.

31. Nelson Mandela, *Nelson Mandela Speaks: Forging a Democratic Non-racist South Africa* (New York: Pathfinder, 1993), 119. See also the video excerpt "Fidel Castro in South Africa

with Nelson Mandela," video posted to YouTube by Moodesty Inthemood, August 21, 2009, https://www.youtube.com/watch?v=NWzqBisf624.

32. Thabo Mbeki, "Letter from President Thabo Mbeki: Cuba's Selfless Contribution to African Liberation Driven by a Genuine and Passionate Humanism," *ANC Today*, March 30–April 5, 2001, http://www.anc.org.za/ancdocs/anctoday/2001/at10.htm; Thabo Mbeki, "Address at the University of Havana," March 28, 2001, http://www.dfa.gov.za/docs/speeches/2001/mbek0328.htm. See also "Zuma Leads ANC Delegation to Cuito," *Mail and Guardian*, March 22, 2008; "Zuma Salutes Combatants of Cuito Cuanavale," *Mail and Guardian*, March 25, 2008.

33. "Media Release: Che Guevara's Daughter Pays Homage at Freedom Park to Fallen Cuban Freedom Fighters," *Freedom Park*, October 22, 2009, http://www.freedompark.co.za/cms/index.php?searchword=cuba&ordering= newest&searchphrase=all&Itemid=42&option=com_search.

34. Meeting with Hector Fraginals de la Torre, Coordinator for the North and Central America, Department of International Relations, Communist Party of Cuba, May 3, 2016.

35. Alberto Núñez Betancourt, "Preside Raúl acto de conmemoración por la victoria en Cuito Cuanavale," *Granma*, March 25, 2008.

36. Abayomi Azikiwe and Jorge Risquet, "Cuban Revolutionary Leader in African Affairs, Dies 40 Years after Angolan Campaign," *Global Research*, October 6, 2015.

37. John M. Kirk and Chris Walker, "Cuban Medical Internationalism: The Ebola Campaign of 2014–15," *International Journal of Cuban Studies* 8, no. 1 (spring 2016): 16.

38. John M. Kirk, *Healthcare without Borders: Understanding Cuban Medical Internationalism* (Gainesville: University Press of Florida, 2015), 23–26.

39. Prada, "Cuba-Africa Collaboration."

40. Kirk, *Healthcare without Borders*, 26.

41. *Conceptualización del modelo económico y social cubano de desarrollo socialista* (Havana: Partido Comunista de Cuba, 2016), 15.

42. *Plan nacional de desarrollo económico y social hasta 2030* (Havana: Partido Comunista de Cuba, 2016), 24.

43. Robert Huish and John Kirk, "Cuban Medical Internationalism in Africa: The Threat of a Dangerous Example," *Latin Americanist* 53, no. 3 (September 2009): 135; John Kirk, "Cuban Medical Internationalism and Its Role in Cuban Foreign Policy," *Diplomacy and Statecraft*, no. 20 (2009): 281.

44. Kirk, *Healthcare without Borders*, 40

45. Kirk, *Healthcare without Borders*, 40; Luis Grillo, "Cuba es también parte de África."

46. John M. Kirk, "Cuban Medical Internationalism under Raúl Castro," *Bulletin of Latin American Research* 31, no. 1 (February 2012): 87.

47. Kirk, *Healthcare without Borders*, 116.

48. Kirk, "Cuban Medical Internationalism under Raúl Castro," 80.

49. Prada, "Cuba-Africa Collaboration."

50. Kirk, "Cuban Medical Internationalism and Its Role in Cuban Foreign Policy," 281.

51. Kirk, "Cuban Medical Internationalism under Raúl Castro," 87.

52. Kirk, *Healthcare without Borders*, 27–28.

53. Patricia Grogg, "Cuba, Brazil Unite for Africa's Health," *Inter-Press Service*, October 25, 2010.

54. Grogg, "Cuba, Brazil Unite"; Kirk, *Healthcare without Borders*, 155.

55. Kirk, *Healthcare without Borders*, 155.

56. Grogg, "Cuba, Brazil Unite."
57. Ibid.
58. Kirk and Walker, "Cuban Medical Internationalism," 20.
59. Kirk, *Healthcare without Borders*, ix.
60. Kirk and Walker, "Cuban Medical Internationalism," 18.
61. Ibid.," 17; Gail Reed, "Meet Cuban Ebola Fighters: Interview with Félix Baez and Jorge Pérez: A MEDICC Review Exclusive," *MEDICC Review* 17, no. 1 (January 2015): 10.
62. "Ebola West Africa: Cuba Leads Way on Medical Effort," *BBC News*, October 22, 2014.
63. Drew Hinshaw and Betsy Mckay, "Cuban Doctors at the Forefront of Ebola Battle in Africa," *Wall Street Journal*, October 9, 2014.
64. Ibid.
65. Sam Nujoma, *When Others Wavered: The Autobiography of Sam Nujoma* (London: Panaf Books, 2001), 362–63.
66. "Local, Cuban Embassies in Brazzaville Celebrate Cuito Cuanavale Battle," *AllAfrica-GlobalMedia*, March 21, 2008, http://www.allafrica.com/stories/printable/200803210378.html.
67. Kuvee Kangueehi Windhoek, "Castro Gets Highest Honour," *AllAfricaGlobalMedia*, March 25, 2008, http://www.allafrica.com/stories/printable/200803250368.html.
68. SA News (November 6, 2012).
69. "South Africa Looks to Grow Trade Relations with Cuba," *Economy News*, November 7, 2012.
70. "Cuban Medical Collaboration Expanding in South Africa," *Granma*, August 3, 2016; "Cuba and South Africa Sign Cooperation Agreement in Basic Education Pretoria," *Prensa Latina*, November 23, 2016.
71. See, for example, "New Group of 80 South Africa Students to Study Medicine in Cuba," *Cuban Business and Economic News*, September 10, 2012.
72. "Cuba and South Africa Sign Cooperation Agreement in Basic Education Pretoria," *Prensa Latina*, November 23, 2016.
73. "Zuma Writes Off Cuba's £86m Debt," *Morning Star*, December 9, 2010; "South Africa's Zuma Wraps Up Cuba Visit," *Latin American Herald Tribune*, December 9, 2010. See also Jacob Zuma, "Lessons from Cuba for Our Youth," politicsweb, December 12, 2010, http://www.politicsweb.co.za/politicsweb/view/politicsweb/en/page71654?oid=215044&sn=Detail&pid=71616.
74. Ibid.
75. SA News (November 6, 2012).
76. Press Release, South African Department of Trade and Industry, November 5, 2012.
77. Xavier Carim, *Agreement between South Africa and Cuba on Economic Assistance* (Pretoria: International Trade and Economic Development Division, 2012), 3.
78. Press Release, South African Department of Trade and Industry, November 5, 2012.
79. "South Africa Looks to Grow Trade Relations with Cuba," *Economy News*, November 7, 2012.
80. "Cuba, South Africa to Enhance Economic Ties," *Xinhua*, July 20, 2016.
81. Carim, *Agreement between South Africa and Cuba*, 3–8; "South African Minister in Havana to Promote Deals," *Cuban Business and Economic News*, November 2, 2012.
82. "Cuba, South Africa to Enhance Economic Ties."
83. "Cuba, South Africa to Enhance Economic Ties."

84. “Defence Minister Highlights Relations between Angola and Cuba,” *Angop*, August 6, 2011.

85. “Cuban Medical Collaboration Expanding in South Africa,” *Granma*, August 3, 2016.

86. “Cuba Seeking More Construction Projects in Angola,” *Angop*, May 21, 2013.

87. “Namibia and Cuba Strengthen Economic Ties,” *Southern Times*, November 2, 2015.

88. “Minister Encourages Namibian and Cuban Governments to Find Ways to Cooperate on Economic Level,” *Africa News Wire*, October 4, 2012.

89. Larry Moonze, “Cuba, Namibia Eternal Allies—Utoni Nujoma,” *Post Newspapers Zambia*, October 7, 2010.

90. Namibia and Cuba Strengthen Economic Ties,”

91. Prada, “Cuba-Africa Collaboration.

92. 2015–2024 International Decade for People of African Descent (http://www.un.org/en/events/africandescentdecade).

93. “71 UNGA: Cuba at the Third Committee on ‘Elimination of Racism, Racial Discrimination, Xenophobia and Related Intolerance’ and ‘Rights of Peoples to Self-Determination,’” *Representaciones Diplomáticas de Cuba en el Exterior*, November 1, 2016.

94. “Cuba Backs Caribbean Nations in Slavery Compensation Bid,” *Telesur*, April 1, 2016.

95. “Key Address by Dr. Fidel Castro Ruz, President of the Republic of Cuba at the World Conference against Racism, Racial Discrimination, Xenophobia and Related Intolerance, Durban, South Africa,” United Nations, September 1, 2001, http://www.un.org/WCAR/statements/0109cubaE.htm.

7

Cuba and Asia and Oceania

Pedro Monzón and Eduardo Regalado Florido

Cuba's foreign policy toward the Asia-Pacific is based upon general principles that are seen in the government's approach to all areas and which have been in place since the early days of the Cuban Revolution. The essence of this approach has not varied, despite the evolution of historical circumstances in the Asian countries studied here as well as domestic dynamics. There is a profound ethical basis for this policy, based on the traditional revolutionary philosophy of Cuba. This has evolved since the wars for independence in the late nineteenth century and the development of a national identity, influenced by many factors, especially the important impact of the complex relationship with the United States. Cuba accepts the fundamentals of the UN Charter and the basic principles of international law, including respect for nations' sovereignty, independence, and territorial integrity. Cuba accepts that a peaceful resolution to diplomatic challenges is to be sought, based upon the firm conviction that peace is absolutely necessary for the development of humanity. This is only attainable on the basis of equality between states and peoples, as well as respect for self-determination and rejection of any form of external interference in the internal affairs of any country.

There are several key aspects of Cuban foreign policy, recognized internationally, including its independent nature and the creativity employed in its development. Also significant is the question of internationalism, a particularly distinctive aspect of Cuba's foreign policy, which has been particularly focused on Latin America and Africa but has also been applied in Asia. Another important component is its basic anti-imperialism, its solidarity (which includes international cooperation in a variety of spheres), and its support for unity in Third World countries. Cuba has condemned colonialism and all forms of external interference as well as the use of threats or force in interstate relations, the adoption of unilateral coercive measures, aggression, and any form of terrorism, including state terrorism. Cuba has consistently defended respect for fundamental human rights and the creation of a just economic, financial, and international monetary order. These precepts are included in the country's constitution, which also condemns any kind of discrimination on the basis of race, political belief, or opinion.

While Cuba respects diverse ideas and political systems, in the last analysis there are essential priorities among its objectives. One essential and strategic component has been the support shown to develop socialism and communism. Goals that are also important are the national liberation of exploited peoples, the defeat of imperialism, and the elimination of colonialism, neocolonialism, and all forms of exploitation and discrimination.

These have been common themes in all speeches by Raúl Castro since he assumed the presidency in 2006. During the Sixth Congress of the Communist Party of Cuba in April 2016, and in the context of the reestablishment of diplomatic relations with the United States,[1] he stated that Cuban foreign policy would continue to support these long-established principles. He declared that Cuba would never renounce them or make any concessions concerning national independence or sovereignty. In addition, he stated that Cuba would not renounce its traditional ideals in terms of foreign policy, which remained committed to just causes, self-determination of nations, and support for allies.

Since the "Special Period" after the end of the Soviet Union and during the current international situation, Cuban foreign policy has faced several difficulties that have required significant adjustments in Cuba's foreign relations. There have been other complicating factors, including the ongoing deficit in the external financial balance of trade, a basic inefficiency and lack of productivity in the domestic economy, a disappointing overall economic growth, limitations for consumers, unequal distribution of income, obstacles resulting from an excessively bureaucratic approach, and demographic challenges. The process of reforming and updating the national economy and the need for a new socialist model have resulted in prioritizing economic aspects in Cuba's diplomatic initiatives as well as a greater rationalization of domestic economic resources and foreign policy.

In addition to these internal challenges facing Cuba, there is also another major influence on the country's foreign relations. The key factor in this scenario was the reestablishment of diplomatic relations with the United States in December 2014. Despite this important development, the embargo against Cuba has continued, with only minor amendments, with little impact on trade restrictions, and it is clear that the process of normalizing bilateral relations is still a long way off. That said, this development has resulted in an explosion of interest in Cuba from other countries. High-level visits by diplomats and businesspeople have increased notably. These developments will have a major influence on the island's economy, providing that the embargo's sanctions can be reduced and that better conditions for investment and trade result. These changes in the internal and international context have also been an important influence for Cuba's traditional relations with the Asia-Pacific region.

Asia is the largest continent, both in terms of size and population. It covers an area of about 45 million square kilometers (roughly 8.65 percent of the Earth's surface) and includes some 60 percent of the world's population, making it the area with the greatest concentration of inhabitants in the world. It has an impressive economic dynamism—with almost 40 percent of the world's gross domestic product (GDP) and 27 percent of global commerce. It also contributes the most to the growth of the world's GDP. In terms of gross national product, and on a global scale, the People's Republic of China and Japan are the second and third largest (after the United States). Together with India they represent three of the largest economies on earth. As a result, many studies have shown how this region is rapidly becoming the epicenter of the world economy, displacing the traditional role of the industrialized West.

There is clearly an increasing interest in Latin America and the Caribbean being shown by Asia—especially in terms of mutual benefits in commerce, finance, and investment. As a result, we can witness the creation of alternative trading and investment opportunities and a new type of Asian involvement with the region. For example, the role of Asian finance is becoming increasingly significant, given the accumulation of international reserves, the strength of the currency and national financial markets in some countries, a greater capacity to finance investments, and the creation and consolidation of new multilateral institutions.

Asia-Oceania is also advancing rapidly in terms of regional economic integration, as seen most clearly in the Association of Southeast Asian Nations, with particular interest being taken in China, Japan, and India. This has led to financial support for different poles of economic power, which go beyond their regional limits. Numerous free trade treaties, of both intra- and extraregional natures, have been established. These strengthen the process of liberalization as well as the promotion of trade and investment relations within regional and global networks. The consolidation of their spaces of integration and regional support have acquired a notable geostrategic value, while at the same time consolidating multilateral institutions that offer an alternative and/or complement to the institutional global framework.

From the political perspective, there are four socialist countries in the region, some of which are immersed in developing a program of active economic reform, a process which in turn has strengthened their economic and political sustainability as well as their international connections. Besides the countries with communist parties in power, progressive political parties in opposition to other established governments also play an important role—as is the case in India and Japan. The same can be said about the growth in environmental groups, as the effect of negative changes in the environment is noted.

The consolidation of the strategic association of China and Russia has been particularly important, especially in coordinating actions surrounding international topics, as an expression of interest shared by both countries in promoting multipolar goals in order to meet national objectives. This bilateral relationship plays an important role in dealing with and containing Washington's ambitions to maintain its strong influence in the region. It also assists in supporting its goal of promoting a new economic and financial global order, as well as strengthening international political relations.

In addition the growing cooperation between these two powers strengthens new, alternative approaches to multilateralism, as seen in the Shanghai Cooperation Organization and the BRICS association, a useful counterweight to U.S. hegemony. The combined approach of the two countries is strengthened with India's participation in certain shared interests, such as the promotion of triangular commercial and financial interests and, in bilateral terms, cooperation on military and security matters. In sum, the role of actors such as China, Russia, and India on bilateral and multilateral levels is contributing to promote a multipolar international system, based upon an axis of asymmetrical interdependence with other actors from outside the region. In addition, twenty-three countries of the region are members of the Non-Aligned Movement, a process which represents a source of significant political capital for developing countries.

This is the international background for Cuba's insertion into the region. During the last decade, Cuba's relationship with the Asia-Oceania region has been based upon the general established principles of the government, contingent upon the new national and international context. The basic objectives of Cuban foreign policy in the region since 2006, taking into account the overall currents of continuity and change, are

To continue developing support in the region in order to overturn the U.S. embargo, which continues to affect seriously the international economic relations of Cuba, especially in the financial sphere, since there are still serious and persistent sanctions against companies from third countries that maintain relations with Cuba. This objective and the accompanying policy of international collaboration has resulted in Cuba's maintaining excellent diplomatic relations with thirty-eight of the thirty-nine countries in the region. Cuba has eighteen diplomatic missions here covering all of the countries, as well as three consulates general. In 2016 Cuba also opened a diplomatic mission in Singapore but closed the one in the Philippines following the closure of that country's mission in Havana—although this has not affected diplomatic relations between the two. In addition, the countries of the region have fourteen diplomatic missions in Cuba.

To continue to develop friendly relations at the political and economic level with the countries and political movements in the region, regardless of the governing system or ideology. This is done as a means of developing relations in those sectors in which Cuba possesses clearly established experience and prestige, such as public health and education. Related to this is the goal of obtaining financial and technological support for the development of infrastructure and industry in Cuba, as well as stimulating commercial exchange. From a commercial perspective, Cuba's foreign trade with the region represents approximately 16 percent of the island's total foreign trade. Of particular trade importance are several key food products, especially rice. In addition, the region has been the source of relevant financial support for Havana, while Cuba also has several significant investments there.

To study pertinent characteristics in certain capitalist countries with notable economic growth in order to determine useful information that could be of assistance to the current process of updating the Cuban economy.

To maintain a spirit of internationalism and solidarity based upon pertinent principles and political criteria.

These characteristics also characterize the multifaceted relations with the four socialist countries in the region, although in these cases political connections play an important role in the relationship and provide a special interest in learning about their experiences in reforms that have been undertaken there.

Relations with the People's Republic of China have a strategic, multifaceted character. Over the past decade there has been a significant growth in bilateral connections, and the political dialogue between both countries has been strengthened, based upon an exchange of high-level visits and similarities in political philosophy. Among these visits one should note that of President Xi Jinping to Cuba in July 2014, which resulted in twenty-nine multisectoral agreements being signed. Also important were the visits of the vice premier and minister of the Politburo of the Communist Party of China and of Vice President of the Central Military Commission Fan Changlong. As an illustration of this reciprocal interest, many functionaries, business representatives, and political leaders from Cuba have visited China, including Salvador Valdés Mesa, vice president of the Council of State, and First Vice President Miguel Díaz-Canel, who participated in Chinese commemorative ceremonies of the victory against fascism. In 2016 Chinese prime minister Li Keqiang visited Cuba for the first time, while Cuba also participated in the First Ministerial Meeting of the China–Community of Latin American and Caribbean States Forum.

Between Cuba and China there is also a degree of mutual support in the multilateral sphere, with an emphasis on issues of national interest for both countries, including the questions of human rights, the U.S. embargo, and the policy of recognizing a "single China." Cuba has not changed its position, and will not do so, on the question of Taiwan being an inalienable part of China. This explains the lack of relations with Taiwan, since this would imply recognition of it as an independent country. In terms of commercial relations, China is the second trading partner of Cuba and one of the major sources of financing.

The special session of the intergovernmental commission that exists between both countries has resulted in effective participation in the development of key sectors of the Cuban economy for the 2016–2020 period. One key aspect is the development of tourism interests, with Chinese tourists now flying to the island following the opening of an Air China flight from Beijing to Havana via Montreal. A number of strategic agreements have contributed to the development (at both short and medium terms) of cooperation with China and have resulted in economic plans being drawn up from the present until 2030. Among these projects are plans in biotechnology, telecommunications and information technology, infrastructure development, construction (among others, the port terminals in Santiago de Cuba and Moa), petroleum, and renewable energy. As part of this close relationship, in recent years there have been exchanges examining both countries' respective processes of socialist construction, reflecting an important component of this political dialogue.

Relations with Vietnam are extremely important for Cuba, and for many years there has been a respectful political dialogue, which continues. There have been some significant visits, including that of the Vietnamese prime minister to Cuba in 2014 and that of General Tran Dai Qang, minister of national security, in 2015. That same year several Cuban government representatives visited Vietnam, including Darío Delgado Cura, attorney general of Cuba; Ana María Machado, vice president of the National Assembly; Ulises Guillarte de Nacimiento, secretary-general of the Confederation of Cuban Workers; Salvador Valdés Mesa, vice president of the Council of State; and José Ramón Balaguer, head of the Department of International Relations of the Communist Party of Cuba.

Vietnam is Cuba's second-largest trading partner in Asia, with bilateral trade continuing to grow and reaching $270.3 million in 2014 (11 percent of all of Cuba's trade with the Asia-Pacific region). Cuba also has a completely owned business in Vietnam (Labiofam Vietnam), which produces and distributes pharmaceutical, biological, and chemical products. There are also discussions underway with Vietnamese investors in sectors dealing with the exploration and development of petroleum deposits, food production, tourism, and construction, among others. The trade balance remains unfavorable to Cuba, and rice constitutes 62 percent of Vietnamese exports to the island. In 2015 the thirty-third session of the intergovernmental commission took place in Hanoi, where it was decided to continue implementation of the five-year Bilateral Economic Agenda, signed during the March 2014 visit of the Vietnamese prime minister. The objective is to base improved economic-commercial ties upon the excellent existing political-diplomatic relations.

Relations with Japan have been steadily improving in recent years. In 2013 the official short-term debt of Cuba was restructured, and 80 percent of it was cancelled. The announcement of the reestablishment of diplomatic relations with the United States caused a significant commercial and economic impact for both countries. It led to a renegotiation of Cuba's debt to Japan, as well as an increase in bilateral visits and business proposals. First Vice President Díaz-Canel and Vice President Ricardo Cabrisas visited Tokyo, while Foreign Minister Fumio Kishida visited Cuba, followed by Prime Minister Shinzo Abe, all truly unprecedented events.

Relations between Cuba and other countries in the region are positive. Despite the closure of embassies in both countries, Cuba's relations with the Philippines remain positive. Likewise, there have been discussions with Malaysia in terms of the international agenda, and important exchanges have taken place during the first decade of the twenty-first century. The legacy left by the former prime minister of Malaysia, Mahathir Mohamad, has been substantial since his nationalist, anti-imperialist policies resulted in great potential for strengthening bilateral relations and developing strong personal ties between the leaders and governing parties of the two countries. Relations between Cuba and Indonesia, which were strengthened through the Non-Aligned Movement, have also remained strong over the years.

Cuba has historical diplomatic relations with the People's Republic of Korea (PRK), which are based on political/philosophical agreement and solidarity resulting from both countries' commitment to socialism as well as both also being subjected to international pressure. Based upon a position of principles, Cuba has maintained a policy of support for the PRK, a country that has not been able to develop normal international relations since the end of World War II and has faced systematic threats from the United States, a country that plays the role of the aggressor in its relations with Pyongyang. On the contrary, the isolated and besieged PRK has been defending its sovereignty and national integrity in the face of increasing threats from the Donald Trump administration. The diplomatic relations with the PRK explain the fact that Cuba does not have diplomatic relations with the Republic of Korea. However, this has not been an obstacle to the maintenance and promotion of growing links in the fields of the economy, trade, and culture with Seoul. Cuba's position on the question of poor bilateral relations is that the current tensions should be negotiated peacefully by both sides, with the ultimate goal of seeking a policy of disarmament, avoidance of any conflicts, and the reunification of the Korean Peninsula without any foreign interference. In addition, Cuba is against the development and possession of nuclear arms by any country, since their accidental use could trigger a devastating war against all of humanity. In terms of multilateral relations, there is strict agreement on priority issues, especially in terms of human rights. The visit to Cuba of Foreign Minister Ri Su Yong on the fifty-fifth anniversary of the establishment of diplomatic relations and the recent visit of Vice President Salvador Mesa to Pyongyang have contributed to strengthen bilateral relations.

Cuba has maintained a policy of developing greater ties with the islands of the Pacific (these include Nauru, the Solomon Islands, Vanuatu, Kiribati, Tonga, and increasingly Papua New Guinea), as well as with Timor-Leste and Australia. Havana has diplomatic relations with fourteen of these countries, and one of them—the Solomon Islands—opened an embassy in 2012 with the goal of having it serve as a bridge with other islands in the area, particularly in terms of Cuban medical collaboration there. Most of these islands have resisted pressure and historically have voted to support Cuba's resolution against the U.S. embargo at the United Nations. At the Seventieth General Assembly of the United Nations, all countries in the region voted to support Cuba's position on this question, including Micronesia, Palau, and the Marshall Islands, which also established diplomatic relations with Cuba in 2015. (Please see Tim Anderson's chapter for a thorough discussion of the growth of Cuba's ties with the islands of the South Pacific.)

Since 2006, cooperation has developed between Cuba and these countries on issues of health care and education (especially literacy) as well as on climate change. Hundreds of Cuban doctors have been sent to the islands with the objective of improving health care, and hundreds of scholarships to study medicine have been granted to youth there. Indeed, hundreds of people from the islands have studied at the Latin American School of Medicine (Escuela Latinoamericana de Medicina, or ELAM) in Havana, and at the time of this writing there were two hundred students (mainly from the Solomon Islands) studying to be doctors.

In recent years this foreign policy has also led to negotiations which have resulted in the partial or complete payment of health-care and education services, depending on the ability to pay of these countries—as is analyzed by John M. Kirk in his discussion of the evolving role of medical cooperation. This has taken place on a case-by-case basis and has resulted in a more rational policy of solidarity. Those countries which, because of their limited level of development, cannot pay for the medical services provided continue to receive the traditional level of support from Cuba. In addition, some of the countries in the region pay Cuban medical personnel reduced stipends, while there are other countries where salaries are slightly higher. Finally, there are others with the ability to pay salaries which are substantially higher—although always less than the international market rates for qualified medical personnel. This explains why Cuba, in addition to providing medical scholarships to students without the means to pay for their studies, has also begun to charge those who can afford to pay for their education. Based upon this policy, Cuba has encouraged a form of triangular cooperation in these projects, with the financial support of Australia and New Zealand. Several joint scoping missions have been undertaken to some of the Pacific islands, resulting in various projects in health cooperation with Cuban medical personnel.

As part of this development of Cuba's foreign policy, and within the framework of a multilateral strategic focus, Cuba has promoted its relations with the Pacific Islands Forum, to which it has belonged as an observer nation since 2013. It has organized meetings with these countries through United Nations initiatives and has promoted ties with Latin America and the Caribbean through several organizations such as the Community of Latin American and Caribbean States, the BRICS association of countries, and the Forum for East Asia–Latin America Cooperation. There are also plans to strengthen ties through collaboration in sports, education, and biotechnology and to continue exchanges on methods of combating climate change.

Cuba has particularly good bilateral relations with Timor-Leste, which can be traced back to the historical ties and support for its independence. There have been several high-level visits in recent years. Former prime minister Ramos Orta has visited the island, both when he was the country's leader and after leaving his post. Prime Minister Ruy María de Araujo also visited Cuba in October 2015. There has been a current of mutual support on topics which are priorities for both countries, including the U.S. embargo of Cuba. It is possible that in the future Cuba might be able to support several sectors of the economic base, such as in the enclave of Oecusse in the western part of Timor, with the export there of professional services.

Cuban collaboration with Timor-Leste in the medical sector has been particularly successful, and Timor-Leste is the country in this region which has received the greatest level of support. Hundreds of Cuban doctors have worked there, seeking to improve the health-care system. Approximately a thousand Timorese doctors have trained in Cuba, resulting in Timor having the best ratio of doctors to patients in the region. Most have become doctors because of scholarships given by Cuba to study at ELAM as well as at the Faculty of Medicine established in the Timorese capital, Dili, by Cuban professors of medicine. An important literacy program, "Yo, Sí Puedo" (Yes, I Can), has also been established there.

Despite the election of a new government in Australia in 2013, bilateral ties have continued to develop favorably, and there is keen interest in Cuba's cooperation within the Pacific area. Although Australia is a developed country, its regional collaboration programs have gone beyond a strictly external triangular approach. Over three years ago Cuba began a literacy program with several Aboriginal communities. This has proved to be particularly important since this population, traditionally marginalized, has encountered many problems obtaining proper education in Australia. As a result, the high level of illiteracy represents an important social and political challenge for this developed country. There have been other examples of this closer bilateral relationship, as seen in the visits of high-ranking Australian politicians. Particularly important was that of Australian minister for trade and investment Andrew Robb in 2016. Several possibilities in the areas of cooperation, investment, and trade were discussed, with particular interest in the agriculture and energy sectors.

In recent years closer ties have also resulted with New Zealand. Pertinent factors in this discussion are the campaign of New Zealand to seek a seat on the United Nations Security Council and the impact of Cuban cooperation in the Pacific region. In addition, Cuba has been studying, among other models, the New Zealand approach to development, with the objective of obtaining information that could be useful for its own development process.

Relations with India remain very positive, with a sound level of political coordination based upon traditional ties and agreement on multilateral topics. The exchange of visits at the highest levels has strengthened these ties and given fresh impetus to commercial and economic relations, which are the least developed. In 2013 Foreign Minister Bruno Rodríguez Parrilla visited India, followed in 2015 by First Vice President Miguel Díaz-Canel. Diplomatic ties with Sri Lanka are stable, and it is hoped that these will remain firm under the new government. Since the sending of the Henry Reeve Brigade in 2005 to Pakistan, bilateral relations have been strengthened. Following the withdrawal of the approximately twenty-five hundred Cuban medical personnel, Havana provided one thousand scholarships to Pakistani students to train as doctors in Cuba. The last of these doctors graduated in 2015.

Some Observations on the Future

Based upon all the information available and looking toward the future, the following tendencies can be expected:

At the commercial level, trade between Cuba and the countries in the region will continue to grow steadily, but with an expected increase in the commercial deficit for Havana. The principal Cuban exports will be nickel, sugar, and biotechnological products.

In terms of investments, a gradual, discrete increase of Asian investment in Cuba is expected, especially in the sectors dealing with tourism, manufacturing, renewable energy, and biotechnology.

With regard to financial arrangements, an increase in financial support is expected, especially in the areas of renewable energy, information technology, transportation, agriculture, and hydraulic resources.

In the areas of science and technology, the region will increase its role as a source of access for new technologies to Cuba, especially in relation to information and communication technologies and manufacturing.

Cooperation and collaboration will remain an important aspect of Cuba's relationship with Asia and will gradually increase, especially in areas of agriculture, health care, generation of renewable energy, and hydraulic resources.

An increase in the field of tourism is expected, following investment in tourist facilities in Cuba as well as an increase in Asian tourists to the island.

In terms of political relations, dialogue and exchanges concerning topics of mutual interest will continue to grow in both bilateral and multilateral agendas.

FINAL OBSERVATIONS

Cuba maintains the same principles in its foreign policy, based upon both international norms and the profound ethical roots of the revolution, as it has done for decades. That said, the application of these principles is nuanced by the evolution of Cuba's specific interests in the region and by the international context.

Cuba's relations with Asia and Oceania are extremely important due to the dynamic of regional economic development, political potential, and the significance of socialist governments in the region. These relations have taken on added importance in the last decade, a process which has also been influenced by the reestablishment of diplomatic relations with the United States and, as a result, by the new stage of dialogue with the European Union, as well as the development of a multipolar reality in international relations. In addition, this has influenced the search for a solution to Cuba's external debt to the Paris Club nations, which in turn has facilitated relations with the area.

During the presidency of Raúl Castro, Cuban foreign policy has been characterized by the continuity of solid foreign relations developed by the government. The nuances shown by this policy in no way alter the fundamental policies and have been determined essentially by the updating of the Cuban economic model and regional contexts. In almost all cases, Cuba has encouraged the exchange of visits at different levels, the objective of which is to consolidate friendly relations, sign agreements, and stimulate commercial-economic exchange. In Cuba's policy toward Asia, the priority given to China and Vietnam is significant in the visits carried out there by President Raúl Castro. These relations are expected to continue to develop.

NOTE

1. See the "Informe Central al 7mo. Congreso del Partido Comunista de Cuba, presentado por el Primer Secretario del Comité Central, General de Ejército Raúl Castro Ruz, La Habana, 16 de abril de 2016, Año 58 de la Revolución."

8

Cuba and the European Union

Susanne Gratius

> "Fidel Castro was a man of determination and an historical figure. He passes away in times of great challenges and uncertainties."
>
> —Federica Mogherini, November 26, 2016

Fidel Castro's death on November 25, 2016, ten years after his brother Raúl Castro assumed the presidency, will change the course of the Cuban Revolution that has been closely tied to its supreme leader. Absent Fidel Castro, the ideational element of the regime and the symbolic figurehead that tied the Cuban elite and the society together has disappeared. The consequences are unpredictable, but without Fidel, who retired from power but stayed behind the scenes as the guardian of the revolution, the Cuban government will introduce major changes into the economy and the political structure of the country and accelerate the reform process (one which Fidel tended to oppose).

The postrevolutionary generation that might assume the presidency in 2018, when Raúl Castro has promised to retire, will be measured by results and reforms and no longer by history and emotions. The armed forces will have a key role both in Cuba's immediate political future and after the end of Castroism. Whether Raúl's successors can preserve the positive legacies of the revolution—among others a strong state and excellent public health-care and education systems—is as uncertain as the outcome of a new political game that started with the disappearance of Fidel Castro. The Comandante has been a global symbol of social justice, independence, and resistance to U.S. hegemony, but also of intolerance, arbitrary leadership, fear, and authoritarianism. Cuba's new political chapter has yet to be written.

In September 2018, after Raúl Castro's mandate as president has ended, the European Union and Cuba will celebrate thirty years of uninterrupted diplomatic relations, developmental assistance, and economic relations. Since the 1990s, the

EU (that is, the countries that make up the European Union) has been Cuba's major investor, donor, and trade partner. Its economic weight in Cuba contrasts with a rather distant political relationship that has been conditioned for two decades by the Common Position of the EU on Cuba, approved on December 2, 1996, to increase diplomatic pressure for reform on the Castro government. The signing of the Political Dialogue and Cooperation Agreement between Cuba and Brussels twenty years later will open a new chapter in relations after endless debates on the additional conditionality in the Common Position imposed by the former Spanish government of José María Aznar in order to strengthen the Atlantic axis of foreign policy.[1]

This chapter will make a case for a pragmatic, interest-driven change in Cuban-EU relations as a consequence of three major factors: economic and foreign policy shifts under Raúl Castro, a less value-oriented foreign and security policy of the EU, and the rapprochement in Cuban-U.S. relations under Barack Obama (2009–2017). These three factors will be discussed in the first part. The second section concentrates on the nature, progress, and challenges in Cuban-European political, social, and economic relations. The last section identifies major trends and prospects in Cuban-EU cooperation connected to the three factors analyzed in the first part of the chapter and analyzes potential developments in the 2017–2018 period after Donald Trump's assumption of the U.S. presidency, following elections in Germany and France, and under a new Cuban government.

CYCLICAL RELATIONS DRIVEN BY PRAGMATISM AND EXTERNAL FACTORS

Within a broad framework of cooperation, relations between Cuba and the EU have been cyclical. Constant shifts in relations from rapprochement to distance can be explained by both the behavior of different actors and structural change at the regional and international levels. In general, the ups and downs in bilateral cooperation had been more dependent on external than on internal factors. Cuba's traditionally tense relations with Washington and the EU's close transatlantic partnership strongly conditioned bilateral patterns of cooperation and together make up by far the most important variable of change in relations.[2]

On the domestic front, ideological factors had a strong influence on the temperature and degree of relations between Havana and Brussels. This happened particularly during the 1996–2011 period when Cuba was an issue of domestic struggles between the Spanish Socialist Workers' Party (Partido Socialista Obrero Español, or PSOE) and the conservative Popular Party (Partido Popular, or PP) or when Cuba reminded eastern and central European countries like the Czech Republic and Poland of their own socialist pasts—which they perceived as a negative historic experience. Over time, both sources of controversy were replaced by a broad European consensus in favor of constructive engagement with the island. That said,

Cuban socialism and resistance against U.S. hegemony are still controversial issues between the European liberal, left- and right-wing political parties represented in the European Parliament.

Pragmatism has been at the intersection between Cuban and EU foreign policies since 2014, when Havana and Washington announced the resumption of diplomatic relations and Brussels began to negotiate the Political Dialogue and Cooperation Agreement. The mutual shifts from ideological controversy to pragmatic engagement have different explanations. Changes in Cuba's foreign policy responded to economic reforms as the main source of Raúl's political legitimacy and survival.[3] The decision of the EU to replace its traditional policy of conditioned engagement with an approach of constructive engagement in its relations with the island occurred in the context of its most severe identity crisis and the gradual abandoning of its image as a normative, value-driven actor.[4]

These changes in Europe responded to a global trend toward the weakening of liberalism in international relations as a result of the return of antiliberal Western policies such as nationalism, protectionism, patriotism, realist self-interest, and the end of military interventions to protect human rights. Compared to the 1990s, when the missionary promotion of individual human rights and democracy dominated the foreign policies of many Western countries, these policies had clearly declined. This was due to several causes, including the economic crisis of 2008, the failure of the Arab Spring, and the gradual retrenchment of the EU and particularly the United States.[5] Donald Trump in the United States and right-wing political parties in Europe represented the return of national sovereignty, noninterference in domestic affairs, and a lower commitment to the idea of democratic peace.

The decline of democracy promotion and political conditionality in the West had been developing over a number of years. This was seen first in the policy of Canada (a country that has held uninterrupted diplomatic relations with Havana since 1945) and then in 1988 by the EU, in the 1990s by Latin America, and in 2014 by the United States. The worldwide recognition of Castroism has also been the result of a huge diplomatic effort and an active role of Cuba in international organizations to promote the legitimacy of the revolutionary regime and to denounce U.S. sanctions. The abstention of the United States at the annual UN ritual to condemn the embargo in 2016 (under Obama) was another diplomatic victory for Raúl Castro.

EU political pragmatism and Cuba's economic reform agenda under Raúl facilitated a dramatic change in relations. As a consequence of a European and global shift toward a new pragmatism, under the government of Raúl Castro ties between Cuba and the European Union moved from "conditioned" to "constructive" engagement. Consequently, the Common Position of the EU that had dominated relations with Cuba for the last two decades demanding democratic progress was replaced in December 2016 by the Political Dialogue and Cooperation Agreement.

For decades, the Common Position of the EU and its special democracy clause had been perceived as a major obstacle to a full normalization of political relations with Havana. The December 2016 decision to terminate the bilateral Political Dialogue and Cooperation Agreement without any type of democratic concession or regime transformation in Havana can be interpreted as an implicit recognition that the strategy of conditioned engagement of the Common Position had failed. It not only missed the goal to promote political change on the island but was even counterproductive since it justified a united regime facing the external threat (in this case the EU). Moreover, political distance between Cuba and the European Commission was contradicted by full and normal bilateral relations held by nearly all EU member states with Cuba.

The restoration of diplomatic relations with Washington has been both an obstacle and an incentive in EU-Cuban relations. On the one hand, during the Obama presidency it meant the end of the special place that the EU had occupied, rather by accident, in Cuba's foreign policy since 1996—parallel to the approval of the U.S. Helms-Burton law. On the other, Obama's radical policy shift paved the way for a transatlantic and hemispheric consensus on engagement with Cuba that facilitated the successful conclusion of the Cuba-EU agreement.

PRAGMATIC SHIFTS IN CUBAN FOREIGN POLICY AS A GUARANTEE FOR REGIME CONTINUITY

Foreign policy shifts under Fidel and Raúl Castro have been instrumental to the political continuity of Castroism, and often these shifts have been forced by external factors. Both presidents displayed an extraordinary capacity to adapt to international changes through constant shifts in foreign policy. As a small island without strategic resources and facing sanctions from the United States, Cuba needed strong allies. Consequently, the maintenance of the revolutionary regime depended on the assistance of powerful external partners that offered both economic subsidies and ideological support.

In the first years of the Cuban Revolution, U.S. hostility and the embargo forced the regime to join the Socialist Bloc to guarantee its economic and political survival during the Cold War. During these thirty years, the Third World "revolutionarism" of the Cuban regime created tensions with orthodox Soviet socialism, for Cuba was never a satellite state; rather, it was an independent actor that used its external allies for economic survival.[6]

The second radical change in Cuban foreign policy under Fidel was the opening to capitalist countries at the beginning of the 1990s. This included the EU, which for ten years became its main economic partner and donor. In 2000, when negotiations with the EU on Cuba's integration into the Cotonou Agreement of the African, Caribbean, and Pacific group of states failed, Fidel Castro began to develop a strategic alliance with Venezuela that offered high economic benefits based on cheap oil supplies in exchange for Cuban human resources to deepen the Bolivarian Revolution. Hugo Chávez's death in 2013—during Raúl's presidency—illustrated both Cuban political leadership and a strong bilateral interdependence between the two countries.

Like Fidel, President Raúl Castro valued political control and the maintenance of power over economic gains, modernization, and social progress. This overarching system-stabilizing goal and the presence of Fidel until 2016 explained the rather limited economic opening to the private sector and the continuity of a highly centralized and authoritarian single-party system under Raúl. Yet, while continuity characterized his economic and social policy, major shifts have been introduced in foreign policy in order to guarantee the survival of the regime and to prepare the ground for the post-Castro period.

In the ten years since 2008, when he formally assumed the presidency, Raúl Castro introduced changes in Cuban foreign policy[7] and de-ideologized it. As opposed to his brother's arbitrary and emotional leadership, rational choice, cautious pragmatism, and economic interests characterized Cuban foreign policy under Raúl Castro. Highly beneficial strategic alliances with strong economic partners—the Soviet Union during the Cold War, China and Venezuela in the post–Cold War era, and the United States during Obama's second term—served as both oxygen for Castroism and as a vaccine against the economic costs of the U.S. embargo.

Within this broad political framework, compared to Fidel's charismatic personal leadership, Raúl readapted Cuban foreign policy to focus on economic goals and reforms as a major source of his personal legitimacy. Unlike Fidel, Raúl did most of what he promised and is seen by Cubans as a more reliable and predictable political leader, but also as a less charismatic figure. He introduced four major changes in Cuba's external relations: (1) increased efforts for international recognition, (2) rapprochement with Washington, (3) the signing of an agreement with the EU, and (4) a shift toward a pragmatic, economic-interests-guided process of de-ideologizing external relations, including those with the Bolivarian Alliance for the Peoples of Our America (Alianza Bolivariana para los Pueblos de Nuestra América, or ALBA) and Venezuela.

International Recognition

In the 2008–2018 period Cuban foreign policy concentrated a huge amount of effort and resources upon the need for external recognition and support, accompanied by some political changes (among others, the release of hundreds of political prisoners since 2010 and the end of waves of repression against dissidents). This strategy has been very successful. Cuba is no longer isolated but holds diplomatic relations with nearly every country in the world, including the United States and the Vatican. More than a hundred nations have opened embassies in Havana, and Cuba is fully integrated with Latin America and the Caribbean.[8] Despite the democracy clause, the island is a full member of the Community of Latin American and Caribbean States, belongs to the Caribbean Community (CARICOM) and the Association of Caribbean States, and is a founding state of the ALBA initiative.

Dialogue with Washington

When Raúl assumed the presidency, he promised to restore relations with Cuba's historic enemy. Full recognition by all the countries of Latin America and the Caribbean increased the pressure on the United States to recognize the regime and reduce the "iron curtain" as the last symbol of the Cold War. Gradually, Obama began to adopt the European, Canadian, and Latin American strategy of engagement. The first step was the elimination, in 2009, of the veto clause that prohibited Cuban membership in the Organization of American States. The next was the restoration of diplomatic relations with the United States, and the third was the participation of the island in the Summit of the Americas in 2015. Neither the EU nor Spain played any role in this rapprochement, although Canada and the pope monitored the bilateral negotiation process. President Barack Obama's historic visit to Cuba as the first U.S. president to travel to Havana in eighty-eight years consolidated the reestablishment of diplomatic relations and dialogue after more than five decades of mutual distance and mistrust. Bilateral reconciliation and the elimination of restrictions generated a climate of confidence and economic optimism in Cuba, although the embargo (introduced in 1960) remained in place.[9] These initiatives also had the potential in the medium and long term to restore economic relations with the United States that could serve to replace Havana's risky alliance with the Venezuelan government, which was coming under increasing pressure due to the disastrous economic and political situation in that country.

Agreement with the EU

Raúl also envisaged a gradual normalization of relations with the EU. As a consequence of regional recognition, the EU admitted Cuba to its interregional summits with Latin America and the Caribbean, following the path of the Ibero-American Community, which included Cuba as a full member from its very beginning in 1991. In 2008, the EU lifted the restrictions imposed in 2003 as a response to a new wave of repression against dissidents under Fidel Castro. The lifting of the "four measures"—fewer cultural exchanges, reduced developmental cooperation, more limited diplomatic contacts, and inviting dissidents to official celebrations—was the first step in a gradual process of political rapprochement between Havana and Brussels. Unlike Fidel in his attempts to formalize relations, Raúl did not demand the abolition of the Common Position as a precondition for negotiations concerning the pending cooperation agreement envisaged since the 1990s as the last step for full bilateral relations. This pragmatic stance concerning the lack of preconditions facilitated the internal decision-making process in the EU in favor of a dialogue with Cuba. In 2014 the European Commission received the mandate to negotiate the Political Dialogue and Cooperation Agreement, which was announced in March 2016 and signed in a record time of only nine months.

Pragmatism and De-ideologization

Under Raúl, a mix of economic realism and liberalism has replaced ideological neo-Marxist discourse as the dominant pattern in Cuba's foreign policy. Instead, preserving national interests such as economic stability and political control have gone hand in hand with full international insertion without major changes in the regime. Along these lines, Raúl abandoned Fidel's ideological projects such as the "battle of ideas" at home and the Economic Forum on Globalization, intended to demonstrate Havana's rejection of capitalism and U.S. hegemony that was celebrated at the annual meetings of the Cuban Economic and Social Forum. Raúl also adopted a low profile in other left-wing alliances against capitalist globalization and U.S. domination such as the G-77 and ALBA. In short, Havana no longer projects itself to the world as a proactive defender of neo-Marxist structural change and as a symbol of resistance against capitalism and imperialism, preferring instead to lower its international profile and visibility under Raúl.

Cuban foreign policy frequently has been as lucrative in economic terms as it has been risky in political terms. In the past, the initial strategic alliance with the Soviet Union and the Socialist Bloc guaranteed economic survival and a Caribbean welfare state, while their unexpected disappearance provoked the severest economic crisis in Cuban history. History could repeat itself with the new ally of the post–Cold War period: Venezuela. The possible political, social, and economic collapse of Venezuela and the end of the Bolivarian Revolution represent a serious risk for the continuity of the strong interdependence between both countries. Oil supplies from Venezuela to Cuba have already begin to decline. According to Carmelo Mesa-Lago,[10] approximately 21 percent of Cuban gross domestic product depends upon trade with Caracas. But Venezuela's record inflation rate of over 300 percent in 2016, a deep recession of around –8 percent, and a serious debt crisis, all combined with relatively low oil prices, present a somber picture for future cooperation with Cuba.[11] A similar risk exists in the uncertain evolution of relations with the United States. The prospect of gradually lifting restrictions and sanctions imposed since the 1960s by the United States was threatened by the presidential election on November 8, 2016.

Thus, although the scenarios are still uncertain, in the worst short- or medium-term case, Cuba could lose both its strategic partner Venezuela after a change of government or an economic collapse and the United States as a political and potential economic partner. This situation would again make dealing with Europe a significant priority on Cuba's foreign policy agenda.

THE EU'S METAMORPHOSIS FROM A NORMATIVE TO A PRAGMATIC ACTOR

Cuban foreign policy under Raúl coincided with a new EU pragmatism. If Raúl Castro adopted a less ideological, Marxist, and anti-imperialist foreign policy, for its part the EU abandoned part of its external image in Latin America as a soft-power, value-oriented normative actor that projected its own visions, including human rights and democracy, to the world.[12] A second coincidence between Cuba and the EU was the return to introspection and the high priority of economic issues on their respective agendas. From different angles, both partners de-ideologized their foreign policies and adopted a more pragmatic stance.

Cuba's centralized external relations contrast with the EU's multiactor and multilevel foreign and security policy. The supranational European Parliament and the European Commission, on the one hand, and still-powerful EU member states with national interests, on the other, are the main players in Europe's foreign and security policy. In addition there are nonstate actors such as human rights activists, nongovernmental organizations, and private companies representing influential lobbies that further complicate decision-making processes within the EU and particularly regarding Cuba.

Although the EU is still a multilayer actor, the gradual upgrading of the common diplomatic European External Action Service resulting from the Lisbon Treaty strengthened the external image of the EU as a coordinated actor. This happened in the midst of a multifactor crisis involving the Brexit, the rise of nationalist right-wing political parties, a debt crisis, and the arrival of millions of refugees from a conflict-prone North Africa.

EU High Representative for Foreign Affairs and Security Policy Federica Mogherini recognized the EU's "existential crisis."[13] Unlike the former idealistic and optimistic European Security Strategy, approved in 2003 by the first EU high representative, Javier Solana, the EU Global Strategy reflects a more realistic stance on foreign and security policy, closer to the realistic position of Cuba's external projection under Raúl. "Principled pragmatism" is the new external branding of the EU.

This label, literally introduced by the EU Global Strategy, changes the traditional soft- and civilian-power approach of the EU as a normative global power strongly committed to regional and global governance based on shared rules and principles. As opposed to the European Security Strategy in 2003, when security was seen "as a pre-condition of development" and anchored in an "irreplaceable Transatlantic Relationship," "strategic autonomy" is the new goal of the EU Global Strategy and is aimed at "serving national interests" and "the protection of citizens."

Following Robert Putnam's "two-level game," internal threats such as the terrorist attacks in France, Belgium, Spain, and the United Kingdom, as well as the Brexit, the refugee crisis, and the increasing power of anti-EU nationalist parties, all had a major impact on Europe's image and role in the world. The EU projects itself no longer only as a normative soft power exporting regional governance and values to the world but also as a collective security actor with military capabilities and "national" European interests that have to be protected against external threats. The gradual shift from "liberal constructivism" to "liberal realism" or "realpolitik" in EU foreign and security policy[14] changes the nature of its external relations, now less focused on development and shared global values and principles than on "pragmatic security interests." Although the EU is still committed to a rule-based global governance in a UN framework, altruism and solidarity tend to be replaced by a self-interested discourse on protection and interests.

In line with the announcement of President Trump to reduce the U.S. engagement in and financial contribution to the North Atlantic Treaty Organization and transatlantic relations, the EU has assumed a more independent, self-reliant role in its defense and foreign policy. The increasing weight of military hard power and collective security has begun to change the nature of the EU as a supranational normative actor in international relations. This shift from normative actorness to "principled pragmatism" facilitated the conclusion of negotiations with Cuba as part of the Western alliance and as an important partner in triangle relations between Latin America, the United States, and Europe.

The EU Global Strategy as the guiding foreign and security policy instrument consolidated the EU's gradual change from a normative, value-oriented policy toward a pragmatic, more interest-driven policy. In Latin America this shift, together with homegrown problems caused by right-wing governments undermining the EU's own principles, contributed to a decline of democratic conditionality in external relations, including with Cuba. Additionally, the weak political status of Spain for some 350 days without a functioning government (from December 2015 to November 2016) after two electoral processes facilitated the agreement with Cuba, a country that traditionally has been the source of ideological conflicts between the two main political parties PSOE and PP in the Spanish past. These internal problems generated a metamorphosis of the EU from an idealist collective actor into another "nationalist" player. The spill back of the EU's integration process by the Brexit and the threat of renationalization by the electoral preference of right-wing parties in key member states has significantly changed its external image.

Another element of change is the high priority of other issues—the Transatlantic Trade and Investment Partnership (TTIP), refugees, the Brexit, the debt crisis—that replaced Cuba on the European agenda and de-ideologized the debate. Especially during the presidency of Fidel Castro, for ideological reasons, Cuba had been a controversial issue of dissent between more pragmatic or "constructive" EU member states and their counterparts, the liberal democracy promoters and/or Atlanticists, such as Spain, Germany, and the ex-socialist eastern European countries, and the Nordic human rights activists (Sweden, Denmark, and the Netherlands). These debates and controversies over whether to exercise greater pressure or instead to promote more engagement dominated the EU Council debates on Cuba for years.[15]

These differences vanished following the "Europeanization" of foreign policy under High Representatives Catherine Ashton and Federica Mogherini and the diplomatic service. Other factors were important, including a lower profile of Spain in the EU's Cuba policy, a shift in U.S. policy under Obama, and other external priorities. The combination of all these factors allowed the EU to abandon its Common Position on Cuba that had for more than twenty years introduced a negative conditionality into relations without provoking any political concessions on Havana's part as initially envisioned by the former Spanish government of the conservative José María Aznar.

THE UNITED STATES CONDITIONS CUBAN-EU RELATIONS

In 2018, the position of the EU in Cuba's foreign policy again depends on external factors, in this case Havana's relations with the United States and Venezuela. The more distant Cuba's relations with its two key partners are, the more intense its cooperation with the EU will be. The opposite scenario is also true: the closer its relationship with the United States and Venezuela, the lower the priority of the EU in Cuba's foreign policy.

The behavior of the United States has conditioned relations between Cuba and the European Union. Major shifts in Cuban-European cooperation can be mainly explained by shifts in Cuban-U.S. or EU-U.S. relations. Since the end of the Cold War, the EU has compensated for part of the U.S. absence in Cuba's foreign relations in terms of trade, investment, and developmental cooperation flows. Cuba is still the only market in the world without the direct competition of U.S. firms. Spain in particular is Cuba's main European partner, with large investments in the tourist and other sectors, as the chapter by Joaquín Roy illustrates. The EU has always opposed the U.S. embargo, as seen at the annual voting celebration at the United Nations, when most countries have condemned U.S. sanctions. While the EU is an important economic partner for Cuba, for Europe the Caribbean island offers the opportunity to challenge or present an alternative to U.S. power by adopting a policy of engagement.

Nonetheless, the EU's relations with Cuba were subordinated to the much more important transatlantic relations, while Cuba used its relations with the EU to seek international legitimacy and recognition. Meanwhile tensions in Cuban-U.S. relations generated changes in EU policy and an alignment with the United States. A clear example was the crisis in 1996, when Fidel Castro's government shot down two airplanes from the United States and Bill Clinton approved the Helms-Burton law. The EU response, designed by Spain—which at that time was pursuing an Atlanticist foreign policy—was the Common Position of the EU on Cuba to increase pressure for political change on the regime and a later deal with Washington to minimize the effects of extraterritorial sanctions for Europe.

Another moment of mutual hostility and increasing mistrust came during the eight years under President George W. Bush, when Cuba was considered comparable to countries included in the "axis of evil" and new restrictions on relations with the island were adopted—involving, among other things, remittances and people-to-people contacts. In addition the Cuba transition coordinator tried to impose a U.S. blueprint for transition in Cuba. Caleb McCarry traveled regularly to the EU to convince Brussels to be "hard on Castro" and avoid a formal EU-Cuban agreement. The EU, again pushed by the conservative government of Spain, approved in 2003 the four restrictive measures as a response to Washington's pressure and the crackdown on dissidents by Fidel Castro during the so-called black spring of 2003. Repression in Cuba and Washington's hard-line policy thus limited a further advance in relations between Havana and the EU.

Obama's radical shift from the traditional U.S. policy of regime change to constructive engagement and Raúl's pragmatic foreign policy facilitated the EU-Cuban agreement. The United States was no longer seen as an obstacle in bilateral relations, and, for different reasons, Cuba and the EU concentrated their foreign policies on Washington. The reconstruction of dialogue and confidence building with its historic enemy dominated Cuba's diplomatic efforts, and the EU dedicated a large amount of its resources and time to the negotiation of the Transatlantic Trade and Investment Partnership with the United States. The restoration of relations between Cuba and the EU preceded the signature of the Political Dialogue and Cooperation Agreement, but both processes occurred in separate channels.

Nearing the end of Obama's presidency, transatlantic relations, once a core issue for Cuba and the EU, had already begun to decline as a priority in both actors' foreign policies. For Havana and Brussels, relations with the Republican government of Donald Trump are unpredictable and, without any doubt, much different than they were under President Obama. From the EU perspective, the TTIP project has reached a dead end as a consequence of harsh rejection and opposition in large parts of Europe and the United States. If the TTIP fails and Donald Trump's announcement to withdraw from Europe comes true, the transatlantic axis in EU's foreign policy will further decline. The consequences of Trump's presidency for U.S.-Cuban relations are even more difficult to foresee.

A distant relationship with the United States by both Cuba and the EU could have either positive or negative effects on the bilateral agenda. As a positive consequence, the return to tensions between Washington and Havana could bring the EU back as a key economic and political partner for Cuba. On the negative side, the end of the transatlantic consensus toward engagement under the Republican president could again provoke an EU-U.S. controversy on Cuba with two possible results: a closer stance for Brussels with Washington, including more pressure on the Cuban regime, or a cooling of relations, with a clear commitment of the EU to constructive engagement and full relations with Havana.

GRADUAL PROGRESS TOWARD FULL NORMALIZATION IN CUBAN-EU RELATIONS

Relations between Cuba and the EU have shifted between periods of rapprochement and distance. Traditionally, Cuba perceived Europe as the eastern axis of the Western alliance and the transatlantic partnership with the United States. Particularly at the end of the Cold War, and closely related to the Helsinki peace process with Eastern European countries, Europe offered a platform or bridge between the United States and the Socialist Bloc.

Since the reestablishment of diplomatic relations in 1988, the EU has been, apart from Canada, Cuba's most constant and liable partner. When Raúl Castro is scheduled to leave power in 2018, Cuba and Europe will celebrate thirty years of uninterrupted diplomatic contacts, regular economic exchanges, and developmental cooperation. Significantly, close economic relations have been unaltered by changes in political relations between Havana, Brussels, and Madrid.

In a sense, the EU saved Cuba from economic collapse at the beginning of the 1990s. Trade and developmental cooperation from Europe contributed to avoiding the end of the regime that since 1960 has been the main target of the U.S. embargo. The EU's clear rejection of U.S. sanctions, illustrated by, among other things, the annual votes at the United Nations General Assembly and declarations of the Ibero-American Summits against the embargo, offered Cuban leaders a certain recognition of the regime and of the legitimacy of its revolution. Until today, together with Canada and Latin America, the EU is part of the international alliance to support Cuba's defense against U.S. sanctions.

As noted earlier, relations have shifted between conditioned and constructive engagement according to the internal situation in Cuba, the power constellation within the EU, and relations with the United States. Since the 1990s, both sides have reestablished developmental cooperation. EU flows have been rather modest: between 2008 and 2014 Cuba received €90 million for technical cooperation, including social modernization and management capacities. Another €55 million has been committed in the 2014–2020 period for food security, the environment, and social projects.

Under Raúl Castro, relations were gradually upgraded without major incidents. In 2008, the EU lifted its restrictive measures and transformed the EU representation in Havana, established five years before, into a full delegation. The restoration of full developmental cooperation with EU member states and close relations with Spain under the governments of José Luis Rodríguez Zapatero (2004–2011) and Mariano Rajoy since then have contributed to the transition from conditioned to constructive engagement.

The release of political prisoners in 2010—following a hunger strike by Guillermo Fariñas—and economic reforms under Raúl were seen in Brussels and Madrid as a signal for goodwill and a clear political opening. In 2014, following previous consultations with Havana, the Council of the EU approved a negotiation mandate with Cuba, a process that concluded after seven rounds in March 2016 in Havana. Like other treaties, the agreement includes human rights and nonproliferation clauses accepted by the Cuban government and insisted on by EU institutions.

"Mutual respect, reciprocity and respect for their sovereignty" (rather a concession to Cuba than a reference to the EU as a semi-supranational entity) are the guiding principles of the first legal framework between both partners. Like any other agreement, it is founded on the three pillars of political dialogue, cooperation, and trade relations and is monitored by a joint council and a joint committee. The signing on December 12, 2016, marked the end of the EU's Common Position on Cuba and guaranteed full normalization of relations at all levels.

The EU is Cuba's main foreign investor, donor, and trade partner and accounts for a third of its tourists. Economic relations are highly asymmetric: Cuba's share of Europe's total trade in 2015 was approximately 0.1 percent, while the EU represented 26.6 percent of the island's total trade. The EU's leading position in Cuba's trade relations, ahead of China (19.7 percent) and Venezuela (16.9 percent), indicates the return to the situation that pertained before the strategic alliance between Havana and Caracas. Much like what happened in 1990 after the dramatic decline of Cuba's economic relations with the Soviet Union, the EU could, for the second time, replace the loss of another strategic partner, Venezuela, which in 2012 accounted for 44 percent of Cuba's exports.

The weight of the EU for Cuba depends on the evolution of two highly uncertain factors: relations with the United States under Donald Trump and the result of the domestic conflict in Venezuela, Cuba's main economic and political ally. If Havana manages to maintain beneficial relations with these two key partners, the EU will not be of utmost importance for Cuba. A return to an ice age in Cuban-U.S. relations and the breakdown of the strategic alliance with Venezuela (depending on the maintenance of the Bolivarian regime and oil prices) would bring the EU back to the top of Cuba's foreign policy agenda. Relations with the EU might be tedious and complicated but ultimately less risky than other partnerships.

Bilateral pragmatism on the Cuban and European side paved the way toward the Political Dialogue and Cooperation Agreement signed in March 2016, twenty years after the approval of the EU's Common Position on Cuba. The hemispheric context helped to redirect the traditional EU policy of conditioned engagement to the constructive engagement that other partners like Latin America and Canada pursue. Apart from the hemispheric context, the abolition of sanctions and democratic conditionality by the EU and the signing of the agreement have also been the result of the "principled pragmatism"—guided by national sovereignty on the Cuban side and by values in the case of the EU—of both partners that allowed mutual interests to overshadow ideological differences that are still there but don't condition relations any more.

CONCLUSION

> "With agreeing on the Political Dialogue and Cooperation Agreement last spring, the European Union opened a new chapter in relations that have always been strong through decades with the Cuban people."
>
> —Statement of EU High Representative Federica Mogherini on the passing away of Fidel Castro, Brussels, November 26, 2016

During Raúl Castro's presidency, relations with the EU were normalized, and Cuba no longer has an exceptional role as in the immediate past when the island was the only Latin American partner without a legal framework and a regular political dialogue with Brussels. The agreement also symbolizes the minor influence of Spain and the Europeanization of the EU's Cuba policy compared to former years when member states were divided into Atlanticists (Germany, the United Kingdom, and eastern Europe), human rights defenders (the Nordic countries), and the engagement bloc (France and others).

As opposed to the United States, the EU has always had strong ties with and a large presence in Cuba due to such factors as the Spanish heritage, the alliance with Eastern European countries and the German Democratic Republic, and, more recently, relations with the European Commission. Political change in Cuba after the end of governments headed by Fidel and Raúl Castro should not have dramatic consequences for bilateral relations. The foreseeable end of the Common Position or its irrelevance when the agreement is finally in place erases the major obstacle in relations. At the same time, it means that the EU will no longer envisage political and economic reforms through democratic conditionality

As long as regime change—the declared goal of U.S. policy—does not happen, the U.S. embargo will be maintained, and the EU, Canada, and/or Latin American countries will fill the gap left by Cuba's "natural partner" as a consequence of the ideological dispute between the revolutionary regime in Cuba and the liberal opposition of Cuban Americans living in the United States. The death of Fidel Castro was the first step toward the postrevolutionary period in Cuba. Any successor to his brother Raúl will lack the historic legitimacy of the guardians of the revolution and will need to legitimize him- or herself by economic, social, and political results and by gaining the support of a broad range of actors, including the powerful armed forces.

The Cuban Revolution has promised much, lasted long, and delivered less than expected, particularly for the generation that was born after 1959 and identifies the revolution with privations and hardship. That group will change the course of Cuban history and the island's relations with the outside world. In this process, Europe will be more an observer than an actor, but it has the advantage, compared to the United States, of a large presence, knowledge, and a relationship of trust with Cuban authorities and society. If Donald Trump returns to the Cold War narratives of the past, he will again open a gap in relations with Cuba and end the gradual convergence with the EU toward a mutual political "engagement" with the island.

The role of the EU, in the medium and long term, depends on the evolution of relations between Havana and Washington (along with Miami) on the one hand and with Venezuela on the other. In this broad framework, Europe has probably been the most reliable and constant partner of the Cuban regime and, by accident, has been in some periods of the cyclic relations its most important source of developmental cooperation, investment, and trade.

The EU could compensate for a decline of Cuba's strategic partnership with Venezuela and the likely backlash of the timid reconstruction of relations with the United States. In case of a regime change after Raúl Castro, the EU would be reduced to its natural weight as a secondary partner of Cuba, compared to the strong role the United States will without any doubt play in the country's postrevolutionary period.

In the meantime, the EU might again serve to compensate for economic hardship as it did in the 1990s. Given the difficult situation of Cuban relations with Venezuela and the United States, the EU (and Spain) could recover, at least temporarily, its former high position in Cuba's external relations. Thus, the importance of the EU and Spain in Raúl Castro's last years of government depends on the evolution of Venezuela's crisis and on Washington's Cuba policy under a Republican administration.

Donald Trump's remarks on the death of Fidel Castro, characterizing him as "a brutal dictator who oppressed his own people for nearly six decades," contrasted with the official statement of the White House still occupied by Obama: "In the days ahead, they will recall the past and also look to the future. As they do, the Cuban people must know that they have a friend and partner in the United States of America." Time will tell if Obama's radical shift toward rapprochement with Cuba will persist or be replaced by the old Cold War formula of aggressive democracy promotion that proved to be counterproductive by legitimizing Cuba's political unity as a defense against an external enemy.

Donald Trump, who assumed office on January 20, 2017, might push for a dramatic change in U.S. Cuba policy. The Republican electoral program perceived Obama's "opening to Cuba as a shameful accommodation to the demands of its tyrants. It will only strengthen their military dictatorship." A return to the old-style Cold War policies of antiregime propaganda, the open support of the opposition, and the setback of people-to-people contacts would provide the EU and Spain a broader space in Cuba's foreign policy.

Even if the United States under Trump maintains formal diplomatic relations with its historic enemy, which is supported by a clear majority of U.S. citizens and Cuban exiles, the short period of the transatlantic consensus toward engagement with the island will be over. Republican and Cuban American hard-liners will dominate their traditionally most important domestic or intermestic issue of power and influence: relations with Cuba. Trump won the state of Florida, the last bastion of anti-Castroism in the United States, and Republicans hold the majority in both chambers of the U.S. Congress.

For Cuba under Raúl Castro or his successor, a new ice age in relations with its biggest neighbor will be more difficult to manage than before because economic relations with Venezuela have declined and the agreement with the EU doesn't include any substantial increase of developmental or economic cooperation. But ultimately the biggest headache for the Cuban authorities entails not relations with the United States or the EU but rather the replacement of its highly beneficial strategic partnership with Caracas in the midst of a gloomy global economic outlook.

NOTES

1. Joaquín Roy, *Cuba, the United States and the Helms-Burton Doctrine: International Reactions* (Gainesville: University Press of Florida, 2000).

2. Susanne Gratius, "European Union Policy in the Cuba-U.S.-Spain Triangle," in *Debating U.S. Cuban Relations: Shall We Play Ball*, ed. Jorge Domínguez, Rafael Hernández, and Lorena Barberia (New York: Routledge, 2017).

3. Claes Brundenius and Ricardo Torres Pérez, eds., *No More Free Lunch: Reflections on the Cuban Economic Reform Process and Challenges for Transformation* (New York: Springer International Publishing, 2013); Marcia Solorza, "Reformas económico financieras en Cuba: Reinserción al capitalismo en una etapa de crisis," *Revista Problemas del Desarrollo* 185, no. 47 (April–June 2016).

4. Anna Ayuso and Susanne Gratius, "América Latina y Europa: ¿Repitiendo o reinventando un ciclo?," *Revista de CRIES* (Buenos Aires, 2016): 249–92.

5. Thomas Carothers, *Democracy Policy under Obama: Revitalization or Retreat?* (Washington, DC: Carnegie Endowment for International Peace, 2012).

6. H. Michael Erisman and John M. Kirk, eds., *Redefining Cuban Foreign Policy: The Impact of the "Special Period"* (Gainesville: University Press of Florida, 2006).

7. Carlos Alzugaray, "La actualización de la política exterior cubana," *Política Exterior* (Madrid) 161 (2014).

8. Andrés Serbín, coord., "Fin de ciclo y reconfiguración regional? América Latina y las relaciones entre Cuba y los Estados Unidos," *Anuario de la Integración Latinoamericana* (Buenos Aires: CRIES 2015).

9. Hiram Marquetti Nodarse, "El deshielo de las relaciones Cuba–Estados Unidos: Implicaciones económicas" (Bonn: Friedrich-Ebert-Stiftung, 2016).

10. Carmelo Mesa-Lago, "Normalización de relaciones entre EEUU y Cuba: Causas, prioridades, progresos, obstáculos, efectos y peligros," *Taller (Segunda Época). Revista de Sociedad, Cultura y Política en América Latina* 4, no. 6 (2015): 54.

11. José Manuel Puente, "Venezuela en colapso macroeconómico. ¿Qué se puede esperar?," *ARI* 63 (Madrid: Real Instituto Elcano, 2016).

12. Ayuso and Gratius, "América Latina y Europa."

13. European Union, *Shared Vision, Common Action: A Stronger Europe: A Global Strategy for the EU's Foreign and Security Strategy* (Brussels: European Union, June 2016).

14. Richard Youngs, *EU Global Strategy: How to Balance Interests and Values* (Brussels: Carnegie Europe, 2016).

15. Gratius, "European Union Policy."

9

Cuba, Oceania, and a "Canberra Spring"

Tim Anderson

Cuban engagement with Timor-Leste and the Pacific islands, particularly through powerful health cooperation programs, has helped reshape regional geopolitics. Most of the key initiatives came from the period when Fidel Castro was head of government, with strong continuity under Raúl Castro. The Caribbean island's medical cooperation with Timor-Leste, from 2003 onward, was the most powerful and successful move, transforming the health system of that new nation. Soon after that a series of health cooperation agreements with most of the Pacific islands catalyzed a new relationship between Cuba and Australia. At the same time, a mass literacy campaign in Timor had modest success in remote Australian indigenous communities. Cuba's influence in the region, though often understated, has been steadily changing ideas on public health and indigenous education.

This chapter reviews the Cuban presence in Oceania, concluding that there has been more continuity than change under the leadership of Raúl Castro. The updating and greater commercial emphases driven by Raúl—extending compensation regimes but falling well short of the commodification of health services—have mostly built on and made more sustainable Cuba's working relationship with the region. The chapter begins with an examination of the implications of Cuba's change of leadership before moving to a review of its health and education programs in Timor-Leste and the Pacific. It concludes with an interpretation of how Cuba catalyzed a new relationship with Australia, a "Canberra Spring." Washington's loyal ally in the Pacific decided well before its patron that it would be better to join with the Cubans than try to compete with them.

CONTINUITY AND CHANGE

Under Raúl Castro's leadership some new emphases in Cuban policy appeared. Most of these were aimed at consolidating and improving domestic livelihoods, but they had implications for the country's famous health cooperation programs. These economic reforms, which were consolidated into a 2010 Cuban Communist Party strategy paper, included a public-sector efficiency drive, greater management autonomy for the cooperative sector, a large opening for small business, and even a resurgence of (regulated) labor hire.[1]

It is important to observe, however, that these reforms were preceded by the even more wide-ranging reforms of the 1990s in response to the collapse of trade relations with the Soviet Bloc. These "Special Period" measures included the introduction of a dual currency system, a foreign investment law (1995) that set up mostly fifty-fifty joint ventures, and the introduction of mass tourism.[2] As the Cuban economy recovered from the late 1990s onward under the leadership of Fidel Castro, an expanded Latin American School of Medicine (Escuela Latinoamericana de Medicina) was established in 1999, the Bolivarian Alternative (later Alliance) for the Peoples of Our America (Alternativa [Alianza] Bolivariana para los Pueblos de Nuestra América, or ALBA) agreement with Venezuela was initiated in December 2004, and, with the economic benefits of that agreement, an "Energy Revolution" in 2005 renovated virtually all the country's power infrastructure.[3] Under Fidel there was also from the 1990s onward a renewed emphasis on the development of small-scale agriculture to limit the country's rising import food bill.[4] Linked to this were steps toward reform of the cooperative sector and in particular the agricultural UBPC cooperatives.[5] The government under Raúl built on this through the important new decree in mid-2008 on individual usufruct leases for unused land.[6]

Most of the large-scale foreign medical cooperation programs had been funded by Cuba itself, with a notion of contingent compensation from those countries with a capacity to pay. Often this simply meant the local government paying the salaries of resident Cuban doctors. However the ALBA agreement, pioneered by the late Hugo Chávez and Fidel Castro, showed that this idea of compensation could in some circumstances be of substantial benefit to Cuba.[7] The "oil for doctors" swap (in practice, a more detailed barter exchange which included exchange of scholarships and several integration agreements) involved Cuba committing "30,000 medical professionals, 600 comprehensive health clinics, 600 rehabilitation and physical therapy centers, 35 high technology diagnostic centers, and 100,000 ophthalmologic surgeries" as well as large training agreements in exchange for fixed-price (i.e., subsidized) oil sales and other assistance and training in energy and infrastructure.[8] That arrangement with Venezuela was the precedent for Raúl Castro's similar large-scale health-service deals with other wealthy countries like Brazil (with almost 11,000 Cuban doctors employed), Qatar (462 Cuban doctors), and Saudi Arabia (148 Cuban doctors).[9]

Cuban national accounts allow us to see continuity in the growth of services income between 2006 and 2014. Table 9.1 shows services as the main contributor

Table 9.1. Cuban Services, 2006–2014 (billions of pesos*)

	2006	*2007*	*2008*	*2009*	*2010*	*2011*	*2012*	*2013*	*2014*
Trade balance (G+S)	970	2,299	2,898	4,527	3,566	4,196	4,467	4,123	3,870
Export of services	6,554	7,865	8,761	9,189	9,358	10,597	10,744	10,962	10,659

* In constant 1997 prices.

Sources: Oficina Nacional de Estadísticas e Información (ONE), *Anuario estadístico de Cuba 2011*, 2012, http://www.one.cu/aec2011/datos/05%20Cuentas%20Nacionales.pdf; ONE, *Anuario Estadístico de Cuba 2014*, 2015, http://www.one.cu/aec2014/05%20Cuentas%20Nacionales.pdf.

to Cuba's positive external balance in goods and services. Of the positive service figures in recent times, tourism accounted for about $3 billion, with health services at almost $8 billion.[10] A U.S. government agency says that Cuba's "services exports are primarily concentrated in the health and travel services sectors. . . . Health services are estimated to account for 65 percent of Cuba's total services exports. . . . Travel services account for an additional 21 percent of Cuban services exports, primarily provided to tourists . . . [and the] remainder consists primarily of other services such as professional services and education."[11] Most of the latter is likely in health education.

Health services have become the leading edge in Cuba's external economy, drawing on the historical investment in human capital.[12] That is an emphasis that dates back to the Moncada Platform of the 1950s.[13] So it was well recognized, before Fidel's retirement, that reforms in higher education, as well as aiming to meet the human development needs of the Cuban people, would also serve to "convert education into the new locomotive which would drive the economy."[14]

I have stressed continuity in Cuba's reform processes, but it is clear that Fidel Castro in retirement, while supporting the new economic moves, maintained a powerful moral focus on international issues. A key emphasis under Raúl has shifted to economic sustainability, efficiency drives, and improved domestic livelihoods. The 2010 economic reform aimed to achieve greater productivity, meet expectations, break "self-deception,"[15] and elevate participation in management.[16] It was to be "completely Cuban, designed by ourselves" and was seen as an "updating" of the Cuban economic model.[17] Clearly this round of economic reform began well before and quite independently of the reopening of diplomatic relations with the United States in December 2014. That move was driven by Cuba's enhanced hemispheric prestige, as demonstrated by Cuba's assuming the presidency of the thirty-three-country, 600-million-person Community of Latin American and Caribbean States in 2013.

The Cuban Communist Party's 2010 reform proposal had the following as major themes for updating its socialist system: a more efficient economy with savings, increased productivity, and a combination of export orientation and import substitution; an expanded nonstate sector, particularly in small business and cooperatives; a new taxation system; a more commercially focused state enterprise sector; and the elimination of loss-making operations and reductions in state subsidies.[18] The new round of reforms was said to add "clarity" to a reform which addressed both global challenges and longer-standing internal problems, such as "excessive paternalism," while protecting "socialism and the achievements of the past 50 years."[19] The regulated price system would be revised to allow "a correct measure of economic costs, stimulus for the economy, an improvement of the trade balance and elimination of subsidies and unnecessary gratuities."[20] Senior official Ricardo Alarcón said that while Cuba was adapting to "the reality of the world . . . we are not going to privatize education, nor public health, nor are we going to dismantle the system of social security and assistance which all Cubans, without exception, enjoy."[21]

Cuban journalist Randy Alonso argues that the Cuban economy had become far stronger in a number of respects in 2016, compared to the 1990s. Trade partners and credit sources were far more diverse; foreign investment was wider and secured by law; tourism was ten times greater, attracting nearly $3 billion every year; the export of services had become the greatest source of foreign exchange, with health services drawing $8 billion per year; electricity generation and the national grid had been totally reconstructed; Cuba imported 59 percent of its fuel (compared to 98 percent in the 1990s); and 29 percent of workers were now in the nonstate (small business and cooperative) sector.[22] Cuba's top three trade partners in the 2006–2016 decade were Venezuela, the EU, and China. After that came Brazil, Canada, and Mexico.[23] This is a transformation that dates from the 1990s.

HELPING BUILD HEALTH SYSTEMS IN TIMOR-LESTE AND THE PACIFIC

Cuba's health assistance programs had traditionally focused on Latin America and Africa, barely touching the Pacific or Southeast Asia. Nevertheless, Cuban health cooperation in Timor-Leste, massive and systematic, was driven quite personally by Fidel Castro from 2003 onward. In the Pacific islands, a few years later, the programs were more modest but still substantial, reaching most of the islands and quietly shifting regional geopolitics. Within a few years there were around three hundred Cuban health professionals working in Timor and the Pacific. At the same time, Cuba was providing free medical training for more than twelve hundred medical students; a few years later nine hundred had graduated (see table 9.2). Within a short time, Cuba became the largest doctor trainer in Oceania.

There seems to be no immediate diplomatic goal for Cuba's offers of assistance to the Pacific islands. The countries were already linked through the United Nations' small island agencies and through the Non-Aligned Movement. Further, all except two U.S. island protectorates already voted at the UN against the U.S. economic blockade of Cuba. Although Cuba has a good relationship with China, there is nothing to suggest that the Caribbean country was linked to the rising U.S.-China power play in the region.

In any case, Cuban doctors and their training programs moved rapidly into their traditional role: that of helping build human capacity for public health systems. The doctors were contracted to local health departments, and the students were trained to be salaried public-sector professionals, with an emphasis on preventive care and health education as well as clinical practice. Dr. Margaret Chan, director general of the World Health Organization, said that Cuba's medical colleges were "a commitment and a contribution to a better training of the health professionals that the world needs today."[24] Yet, as in many other countries whose health systems are dominated by private doctors, this push to strengthen the public health sector raised local jealousies.

The aims of Cuban medical internationalism have not changed much in more than half a century. It is a principled humanitarian project which may have diplomatic, trade, or political benefits but is not formulated to that end.[25] Successive waves of health programs have been linked to Cuba's "battle of ideas,"[26] a broad program of revolutionary morality designed to build support for decent, humanistic social programs. Those characteristics are evident in the Oceania programs.

The finance and logistics of these training programs vary. In the case of countries without strong medical colleges, local governments transport their students to Cuba's colleges and then brings them home for holidays, if they can afford to. In the case of the Solomon Islands' students, in a friendly South-South gesture, the government of the Islamic Republic of Iran paid for their transport to Cuba, both in 2008 and in 2009.[27] In 2005 the Cubans helped build a Faculty of Medicine in Timor-Leste, and after that students were trained in the Spanish language but in Timor.[28] This university at first operated in the health centers where Cuban doctors practiced and were followed by small groups of students,[29] but the faculty soon acquired classrooms within Timor-Leste's national university.[30] All medical students in Cuba were on full scholarships, which include tuition, board, food, other services, and a small allowance of US$4 or US$5 a month. Some governments (e.g. Timor-Leste) paid their students an additional allowance, while others (e.g. Kiribati) did not. Non-Spanish-speaking students, like those from the Pacific, studied Spanish and science in their first year, in a premedical course.

For Timor-Leste the program grew from a meeting between Fidel Castro and Timor's then president Xanana Gusmao at the 2003 Non-Aligned Movement summit in Kuala Lumpur. At that time Timor-Leste was a new nation with a serious deficit in almost every area, including health professionals. Fidel's initial offer of scholarships was twenty, a decent program by international standards. The students were selected and sent to Cuba at the end of that year, and a small group of Cuban doctors arrived in Timor in April 2004.[31] However, in 2005 Cuba's offer was increased to three hundred, then one thousand places. Timor's then health minister Dr. Rui Araujo explained that in a six-hour meeting in Havana in December 2005, the Cuban leader asked Timor's then prime minister Mari Alkatiri and Dr. Araujo about the growing population of their country. The figure of one thousand scholarships was arrived at on the basis that one doctor per thousand people seemed a good start for the new country.[32] Essentially Cuba's program envisaged training an entire national workforce of doctors. This revised program gave Timor-Leste the largest health aid program in the world, outside Latin America. At that time the small country had perhaps sixty or seventy doctors, most of them in private practice.

Perhaps Fidel Castro was influenced by the news that the Timorese students were conscientious and dedicated, but there was another factor. Cuba's leader told Timorese leaders, "Perhaps we did not help you, in the past, as much as we should."[33] Cuba had indeed provided substantial assistance to all of Portugal's former African colonies, but when in 1975 Timor-Leste was effectively dominated by Indonesia, Cuba sat back. The role of Indonesia in the Non-Aligned Movement must have been a factor. In any case, a little over a decade later, Cuban health professionals had delivered on Fidel's promise; almost a thousand young Timorese had been trained as doctors, at no expense to the new nation.

During that time, however, Cuba's compensation system made some changes. In 2011, as oil and gas revenue came into Timor-Leste's state coffers, the new nation agreed to pay the salaries of Cuban doctors working in Timor. Prior to that, Cuba had paid its own doctors in Timor around US$300 per month, plus some other benefits. With improved Timorese capacity, those doctors moved onto a Timorese salary of between US$600 and US$1,000, with the higher ranks receiving more according to specialist qualifications. Cuban doctors on local salaries avoided the inflation introduced by other foreign professionals, and of course this was part of a program designed to replace the Cubans with Timorese. Unlike in the Venezuelan "oil for doctors" agreement, there was no payment to the Cuban health department. But in 2012, when postgraduate medical training places were offered to Timor, a fee was attached. The state was to pay, not the students, but it was considered that by this stage Timor had developed the capacity to compensate Cuba for its services.

The Cuban Medical Brigade in Timor differed from health aid programs from other countries. It moved rapidly into the rural areas. Initially a group of Cuban doctors was attached to the national hospital, but the majority were sent to rural areas, including to small clinics at the subdistrict level. Thus began the core of a rural doctor-centered health service, including the practice of house visits.[34] Cuban doctors provided most of the personnel for immunizations, tuberculosis treatment, general medical care, and skilled assistance at childbirth. Between April 2003 and mid-2008, the Cuban Medical Brigade carried out more than 2.7 million consultations. It is estimated that, over this period, it saved more than 11,400 lives.[35]

On September 3, 2010, the first group of eighteen East Timorese doctors graduated, amid proud celebrations at the national university. They had already carried out one-year internships at home after their six years of studies in Cuba.[36] These eighteen were immediately signed up as "general basic doctors" and sent to begin practice in rural areas. Graduations then occurred annually, the largest being for more than four hundred in late 2012. By early 2014 there were six hundred new doctors in the field, some with several years' experience.[37] None of them, by that time, had left the country or moved into private practice.

The development of Cuban health programs in the Pacific islands was somewhat different, though not in the values of training and practice. Separate agreements were made with each of the Pacific governments, and this most often required specialist Cuban doctors attached to the major hospitals. All the training was done in Cuba. Twenty students from Kiribati were studying in Cuba alongside Timorese when I visited them in 2007 and 2008; they were joined by another eleven in 2009.[38] In 2008 fifty Solomon Islands students began their studies;[39] they were joined by another twenty-five in 2009. By 2012 the Solomon Islands had ninety students in training. Several other island states were taking advantage of the program. There had been a Cuban program in Nauru in 2004, but that collapsed,[40] only to resume in 2009.

While there were far fewer Cuban doctors in the Pacific islands than in Timor-Leste, the thirty-three Cuban health personnel in the Solomon Islands, Kiribati, Tuvalu, and Vanuatu were said to account for a quarter of all the combined medical workers in those countries.[41]

The largest of all Pacific islands, Papua New Guinea (PNG), received an offer for a health cooperation program in September 2006.[42] However ten years later a PNG program had not yet begun. From conversations during my several visits to that country, it seemed that the large group of private doctors had managed to block the program.

In Vanuatu two groups of doctors worked at the hospitals in the capital, Port Vila, and at Luganville on the island of Espiritu Santo. In the Solomon Islands the doctors were attached to the national hospital in the capital, Honiara.[43] Graduates from the Solomon Islands have been returning from Cuba, and the challenge of an internship that adjusts them back to local systems is under discussion.[44] Return graduates from the little islands of Nauru and Tuvalu are taking advantage of an internship system set up in Kiribati.[45] The Cuban approach in the Pacific islands has been to assist in building public sectors, though not on such a massive scale as undertaken in Timor-

Table 9.2. East Timorese and Pacific Students in Cuban Medical Training, 2016

Country	*In Training*	*Began*	*Graduated*
Timor-Leste	200	2003	800+
Solomon Islands	65	2008	27
Kiribati	0	2005	30
Vanuatu	12	2008	18
Nauru	0	2009	9
Tuvalu	14	2008	8
Tonga	6	2012	0
Palau	3	2012	0
Fiji	8	2012	0

Sources: "Cuban Medical Collaboration: Democratic Republic of Timor Leste," Cuban Medical Brigade "Dr Ernesto Guevara de la Serna Che," Dili, July 2008; Jim Tulloch, Jorge Delgado, and Adrian Hearn, "Cuba-Australia Collaboration in the Pacific," Preliminary Findings, Joint Scoping Mission for Discussion with Sponsoring Agencies and Pacific Island Authorities, report, April 18, 2012; Carol-Anne Galo, "Private Medical Practitioners Disapprove Cuba Agreement," *Island Sun*, September 22, 2016, http://theislandsun.com/private-medical-practitioners-disapprove-cuba-agreement; Elliot Dawea, "Trainee Doctors Fail Exam," *Solomon Star*, August 29, 2016, http://www.solomonstarnews.com/news/national/11442-trainee-doctors-fail-exam; Kalyan Kumar, "New Zealand and Cuba Sign Agreement for Medical Cooperation in Pacific Islands," *International Business Times*, February 17, 2015, http://www.ibtimes.com.au/new-zealand-cuba-sign-agreement-medical-cooperation-pacific-islands-1421974; "18 New Ni-Vanuatu Doctors Begin Work in Vanuatu," *Vanuatu Daily Post*, January 16, 2016, http://dailypost.vu/news/new-ni-vanuatu-doctors-begin-work-in-vanuatu/article_0dee94dc-27ae-5d12-b11f-23e7465a24e1.html; Rita Narayan, "Nauru Medical Students Graduated from Cuba in Kiribati for Internship," *Loop*, August 1, 2016, http://www.loopnauru.com/content/nauru-medical-students-graduated-cuba-kiribati-internship; other personal communications, to November 2016.

Leste. Cuban doctor Huber Beltrán put it this way: "In Vanuatu the Cuban mission is very small . . . but compared to the doctors here it is significant, from 20 [local doctors] we have five more [Cuban doctors] lending a hand. We are helping these dear people, helping them resolve their problems."[46]

The rapid growth of public health systems almost always sparks a reaction from private doctors' associations, whose constituents remain concerned about the undermining of their own positions. This has been seen in Cuban health programs from South Africa to Honduras to Venezuela to Bolivia. Cuba doctor training does not contain Cuban political teachings, but it does carry many of the values of Cuban humanistic or social medicine. That often contributes to a clash of cultures and sometimes a difficult transition period. In the Solomon Islands there were private-doctor reactions to the arrival of the new graduates,[47] and many of the Cuban-trained graduates failed their initial local exams.[48] Similarly, graduates from Tuvalu were found to need improved internship training.[49] This has little do with the standard of Cuban training, which is widely recognized as world-class, but reflects two other things: first there is indeed a need for internships that adjust foreign-trained graduates to their own system and conditions; second, there seems always to be local resistance through the clash of medical cultures.

In Timor-Leste there were similar tensions, probably based on jealousy, as the first graduates entered the country's health system.[50] A large group of doctors trained with a public servant ethos challenges an older elite culture, where doctors are rare and enjoy a special status. From my observations there was a type of passive resistance from within the health department to the graduation and employment of the new doctors. There was also some jealousy of the Cuban role among sections of the Catholic Church. However that soon evaporated as Timorese culture—strongly rooted in community solidarity, inclusive Christian ethics, and an independent spirit—recognized and adopted many elements of the Cuban approach, such as free services, house visits, popular adult health education programs, and student training in the hospitals.[51] There was also support for the new approach from local clinics and professionals. Former health minister Dr. Araujo tried to prevent politicization of the health training, seeking the support of all sectors, including the church. Nevertheless, at the graduation ceremony in 2010, that history did not go unremarked. In her speech on behalf of all the new doctors, Dr. Ercia da Conceição said, "We know that during our study in Cuba the previous government received much criticism from many institutions, including the Catholic Church. . . . [However] we dedicated ourselves as Timorese looking for experience and intelligence in Cuba, but to return and live as Timorese."[52]

This new approach to health care also faced a type of cultural resistance from a people who did not have much contact with doctors or hospitals, or if they did, the experience was bad. The health system in Timor-Leste had been nurse based, with limited services. Pregnant women in rural areas were not used to traveling to a doctor or health center to give birth. Nevertheless, Cuban doctors had gradually encouraged them to do so.[53] Even in the capital, some women who had come to clinics for pregnancy checkups would give birth at home, sometimes resulting in the death of the baby.[54] Many mothers were reluctant to take sick babies to a district hospital because they associated the hospital with death: it was more traditionally seen as a place where people went to die.[55] If a hospital is associated with the terminally ill and regarded as "the end of the line," it is quite logical that mothers will fear taking their children there. Timorese graduate doctors were able to extend that confidence-building process, being native in language and culture.

Timor's first group of Cuban-trained doctors expressed strong ethical values, which can be traced back to traditions of social medicine rather than commercial private practice. Dr. Ildefonso da Costa, for example, spoke of the need to build the public health sector: "There has to be a balance between the private clinics and the public health system. . . . [W]e eighteen, we're going to do a project . . . which is social, which is human for this country."[56] Dr. da Conceição, in her keynote address at the September 2010 graduation ceremony, expressed ideas of solidarity, independence, and popular education: "Many people still cannot read and write. . . . [T]o escape from this path requires building high quality education, because if all Timorese are intelligent nobody can manipulate us, no one can defeat us and this nation will be strong and will never fall into the hands of others."[57] Dr. Colombianus da Silva spoke of the role of a humanist doctor: "In Cuba they taught us to work, but to work with love—as a doctor, a scientific doctor but a doctor with a heart. More than the work to cure illnesses, we have the responsibility to prevent it, to teach people so they can participate actively in the prevention of illness."[58]

After their return to Timor in August 2009, that first group treated infectious diseases that mostly do not exist in Cuba (malaria, cerebral malaria, tuberculosis, dermatitis, parasites, leprosy), delivered babies, attended emergency hospital receptions, sutured wounds (including caesarean wounds), participated in minor procedures, held regular consultations, vaccinated pregnant women and babies, developed educational materials on natural and traditional medicines, organized educative health discussion groups, including old peoples' discussion groups, and tried to assist in cases of malnutrition.[59] That helped to build their experience in their own country's unique health situation and system. With a total of 732 doctor graduations by 2013, Timor-Leste had risen from a country with one of the lowest rates of doctors to a nation with one of the higher rates.[60]

A "CANBERRA SPRING"

While the Timorese program was much bigger, it was Cuba's rapid development of health training in the Pacific that forced a rethink in Canberra. Australia had never dominated Timor-Leste in the way that it had dominated the Pacific. Yet within two or three years Cuba was training more Pacific island health professionals than Australia. Worse, most of the health professionals trained by Australia and New Zealand fairly quickly emigrated to—or were captured by—those same countries.[61]

This brain drain was powerful, facilitated by the small-scale and individualistic ethos of medical training. Canberra had begun a series of short "leadership scholarships"—now called Australia Awards[62]—and showed little inclination to enter into mass training. So it could not compete with Cuba but was concerned to maintain its influence in the region. In 2008 a newly elected Labor government decided to try a new approach.

The previous conservative government, led by John Howard, had tried to discourage Papua New Guinea's relationship with Cuba.[63] But after an internal review of regional aid policy, the Labor government led by Kevin Rudd decided to engage with Cuba in some kind of new regional partnership. Foreign Minister Stephen Smith visited Cuba in November 2009, the first such visit by an Australian foreign minister since 1995. He said the visit was "a fresh start to our relationship, to enhance the good working and productive relationship between Australia and Cuba."[64] Seven months later Smith welcomed Cuban foreign minister Bruno Rodríguez Parrilla to Australia, announcing that the two countries had already signed agreements on "general political and bilateral cooperation" as well as on "sporting matters" and were looking at further agreements on cultural contacts and development assistance.[65] However, the major focus was cooperation in health assistance. Smith observed, "Cuba is internationally renowned for the medical assistance work that it does. . . . [W]e're looking at what we can do together, in the Pacific, and also potentially in the Caribbean, in terms of collaboration on development assistance in the medical area." Rodríguez was also positive: "We could have [an] excellent exchange in our programs of international medical cooperation in this region."[66]

There was a natural logic to all this, given Australia's wealth and technical capacity and Cuba's proven skill in health training. However, the politics of such relationships are often not so straightforward. Australia has a hybrid health system based mostly on private doctors, underwritten by a public health finance system (Medicare) and a supplementary private insurance system. That is quite different from Cuba. Furthermore, Australia and Cuba maintain distinct mind-sets about how their foreign aid programs are developed. Australia embraces a regional hegemonic role, linked to Washington, which in turn seeks to contain the influence of independent powers, in particular China. On the other hand, Cuba has no particular regional ambitions but promotes a global public service ethos, maintaining focus on mass training and public institution building, themes which are neither prioritized nor negated in the Australian system. Australia, for its part, seeks influence in peak bodies and often operates in a unilateral way. For example, former prime minister Kevin Rudd's "Port Moresby Declaration" on regional cooperation, while announced in the PNG capital, was not subscribed to by any PNG leader.[67] Australian ministers speak of bilateral agreements with Cuba. Cuba, however, has stressed unique tripartite agreements, including each of the island states. Cuban foreign minister Bruno Rodríguez Parrilla welcomed the opportunity for "enhancing triangular cooperation" with the Pacific islands and "triangular cooperation in the Caribbean with the Haitian Government."[68] The Australian mind-set seems to have difficulties with this more contingent approach.

Cooperation in training faces not just a language barrier but also curricular differences. Australian medical training is typically more clinically focused, while Cuban pedagogy combines clinical, epidemiological, and social medicine with a strong emphasis on prevention and promotion through doctor practice, including "educational chats."[69] The Cuban doctors have fewer language problems than Australian doctors in Timor-Leste, where Portuguese is stronger than English and where there is now a large number of Spanish-speaking students and doctors who can assist. However, in the Pacific many Cubans doctors do need extra English-language training. English training and internship supervision are apparently areas in which Australia has expressed a willingness to assist.[70] However, that leaves the major question of how to develop the existing island medical colleges: in Fiji and Port Moresby (using English and with a Western curriculum, largely financed by Australia) and in Dili (using Spanish, created by the Cubans). A joint scoping mission[71] reported in 2012 on options, but many questions remain. Cuban-Australian health cooperation has been slow to develop, but cooperation in other fields has been wider, with agreements on sports, artistic exchange, and commerce in recent years. There has been some cofinancing of health and relief cooperation in Haiti. With the return of a conservative government to Australia in 2013, Canberra maintained its good relationship with Havana,[72] and neighboring New Zealand joined in soon after with an agreement for medical cooperation with Cuba.[73]

As Canberra developed its new relations, Cuba's adult literacy program "Yes, I Can" ("Yo, Sí Puedo") came to Australia. Academic Bob Boughton had studied the program in Timor-Leste and discussed with an indigenous health network the idea of bringing it to remote Aboriginal communities. Between 40 and 65 percent of Australian Aboriginal adults are functionally illiterate in English, and indigenous communities have often felt alienated from conventional Australian education programs. Using the Cuban method, with community participation at its center, a group of experienced community educators and Cuban advisers set to work. The program began as a pilot study through the University of New England in the remote rural town of Wilcannia with Australian government financing. In 2013–2014 a second pilot extended that program to the neighboring towns of Enngonia and Bourke.[74] The relative success of the first two stages of the program can be seen in table 9.3.

Table 9.3. "Yes, I Can" Australian Aboriginal Literacy Statistics, 2012–2014

	Wilcannia	*Bourke/Enngonia*	*Total*
Adult population	279	486	765
Estimated target population (40%)	112	194	306
Starters	40	78	118
Graduates	23	58	81
Completion rate	57.5%	74.4%	68.6%

Source: Bob Boughton and Deborah Durnan, "Cuba's 'Yes I Can' in Australia: Three Years On," ACAL National Conference, October 2014, http://acal.edu.au/14conf/docs/Cuba-Yes-I-Can-in-Australia.pdf.

The near 70 percent graduation rate compared very well with previous government-funded programs.

Both state and federal governments demanded a public-private partnership, and in May 2013 the Literacy for Life Foundation was created, which is a partnership between the National Health Research Institute, the Lowitja Institute, indigenous campaigner Jack Beetson, and the large construction company Multiplex. It remains centered on the Cuban method. This foundation has taken over what is now called the Literacy for Life Campaign, aiming to progressively reach as many communities as possible.[75] In 2015 and 2016 the program was extended to Brewarrina, and plans are afoot to move it into Walgett and Weilmoringle.

CONCLUSION: CUBAN INFLUENCE IN THE REGION

The Cuban role in health and education in Oceania remains a type of guilty secret. The island states are often shy about promoting the Cuban presence, for fear of alienating the big powers. This remains the case even in Timor-Leste, where every family has had direct contact with Cuban doctors and the Cuban-trained Timorese doctors. In Australia both major parties acknowledge that advances in indigenous literacy were only possible through the Cuban method, but the Cuban role is often downplayed. At the same time, across the region, private-doctor groups mobilize to protect their own interests.

Despite this, the Cuban presence has had a powerful impact on health systems in Oceania over the past decade. From the Cuban side this has come more from continuity than change. The chief instigator and driving force of these missions was Fidel Castro. Nevertheless, Cuban assistance in health and education in the region these days increasingly looks for partner financing or cofinancing. There is no single model or price for such cooperation, so we cannot speak of commodification of health services. Rather, Cuba appears to still apply the principle of appropriate compensation, depending on the capacity of the partner.

The health program in Timor-Leste has been the most systematic and successful, underwriting what is probably the fastest growth of any health system in the world. In eight Pacific islands (Papua New Guinea being the major exception) scholarships for more than two hundred medical students have provided valuable assistance to the islands' public health sectors, at the same time introducing Cuba's social medicine ideas to the region.[76]

The Pacific programs helped transform Cuba's relations with Canberra, opening some new possibilities. Australian-Cuban cooperation in health has been slow to develop, but the two countries now have agreements across a range of areas including sports, commerce, and the arts. Further, Cuba has made an important breakthrough in helping build indigenous literacy. As Julie Feinsilver wrote in 2006, Cuba's programs "have forced the re-examination of societal values and the structure and functioning of [local] health systems."[77]

NOTES

1. Tim Anderson, "The 'Cuban Model' and Its Microeconomy," *Latin American Perspectives* 41, no. 4 (July 2014): 89–110, http://lap.sagepub.com/content/41/4/91.

2. Tim Anderson, "Island Socialism: Cuban Crisis and Structural Adjustment," *Journal of Australian Political Economy*, no. 49 (June 2002): 56–86.

3. José Antonio Suárez et al., "Energy, Environment and Development in Cuba," *Renewable and Sustainable Energy Reviews* 16, no. 5 (June 2012): 2724–31.

4. "Cuba," World Food Program, 2016, https://www.wfp.org/countries/cuba

5. Alberto Matías González, "Agricultura campesina y ambiente en Cuba," *Eco-Portal*, August 31, 2004, http://www.ecoportal.net/Temas-Especiales/Suelos/Agricultura_Campesina_y_Ambiente_en_Cuba; "Agricultura sostenible en Cuba," *EcuRed*, 2006, https://www.ecured.cu/Agricultura_sostenible_en_Cuba.

6. "Decreto-Ley No. 259 sobre la entrega de tierras ociosas en usufructo," *Juventud Rebelde*, July 18, 2008, http://www.juventudrebelde.cu/cuba/2008-07-18/decreto-ley-no-259-sobre-la-entrega-de-tierras-ociosas-en-usufructo.

7. Rosa Miriam Elizalde and Luis Báez, *El Encuentro* (Havana: Oficina de Publicaciones del Consejo de Estad, 2004).

8. J. M. Feinsilver, "Oil-for-Doctors: Cuban Medical Diplomacy Gets a Little Help from a Venezuelan Friend," *Nueva Sociedad*, no. 216 (July–August 2008), http://www.ghd-net.org/sites/default/files/Nuevo%20Sociedad%20Cuba.pdf.

9. Nuria Barbosa León, "Cuba's International Health Cooperation," *Granma*, July 15 2016, http://en.granma.cu/mundo/2016–07–15/cubas-international-health-cooperation.

10. Randy Alonso Falcón, "Cuba y los interesados presagios: ¿Por qué la situación de hoy no es de los 90?" *CubaDebate*, July 22, 2009, http://www.cubadebate.cu/opinion/2016/07/22/cuba-y-los-interesados-presagios-por-que-la-situacion-de-hoy-no-es-la-de-los-90/#.V_4L_-B95hE.

11. United States International Trade Commission (USITC), "Overview of Cuban Imports of Goods and Services and Effects of U.S. Restrictions," USITC, March 2016, https://www.usitc.gov/publications/332/pub4597.pdf.

12. Carlos Fernández de Bulnes García, "Factores determinantes en la evolución de la productividad en años recientes," *Cuba: Investigación Económica* 14, no.1 (January–June 2008): 176–77; CEPAL, "Crisis internacional y oportunidades para la cooperación regional," Comisión Económica para América Latina y el Caribe, LC/R.2150 (diciembre 2008), Santiago de Chile: Naciones Unidas, 27.

13. Teresa Valenzuela García, "La educación en el programa del Moncada," *Radio Rebelde*, July 25, 2012, http://www.radiorebelde.cu/noticia/la-educacion-programa-moncada-20120725.

14. Victoria Pérez Izquierdo, "El nuevo papel de la educación en el funcionamiento de las políticas sociales en Cuba," *Cuba: Investigación Económica* 14, no.1 (January–June 2008): 152.

15. Raúl Castro, "The Solution Is to Raise Productivity," *Granma*, November 30, 2010, 1.

16. Camila Piñeiro Harnecker, "Cuba Needs Changes, to Take Us Forward Rather Than Backwards," *Espacio Laical*, no. 4 (October 20, 2010), 15–18, http://links.org.au/node/2106.

17. Yaima Puig Meneses and Leticia Martínez Hernández, "En este proceso quien decide es el pueblo," *Granma*, November 15, 2010, 4–5.

18. Partido Comunista de Cuba (PCC), "Proyecto de lineamientos de la política económica y social," VI Congreso del Partido Comunista de Cuba (1ro e noviembre, 2010) (Havana: Partido Comunista de Cuba, 2010), 6, 7, 10, 11, 14.

19. Luis Jesús González, "Los debates confirman la confianza de los cubanos en su Revolución" and "El socialismo se construye a voluntad," *El Economista*, December 19, 2010, http://www.eleconomista.cubaweb.cu/2010/nro390/lineamientos2.html and http://www.eleconomista.cubaweb.cu/2010/nro390/lineamientos1.html.

20. PCC, "Proyecto de lineamientos," 13.

21. "Cuba profundiza Revolución con actualización del modelo económico," [Telesur interview with Ricardo Alarcón in Caracas], *Prensa Latina*, January 2, 2011, https://laradiodelsur.com.ve/2011/01/cuba-profundiza-revolucion-con-actualizacion-del-modelo-economico.

22. Falcón, "Cuba y los interesados presagios."

23. USITC, "Overview of Cuban Imports," 7.

24. "Cuba Promotes South-South Health Cooperation," *Escambray* [Cuban digital newspaper of Sancti Spiritus Province], November 19, 2009, http://www.escambray.cu/Eng/cuba/cooperation091119752.

25. John M. Kirk and Michael Erisman, *Cuban Medical Internationalism: Origins, Evolution and Goals* (New York: Palgrave MacMillan, 2009), 170–83.

26. Antoni Kapcia, "Educational Revolution and Revolutionary Morality in Cuba: The 'New Man,' Youth and the New Battle of Ideas," *Journal of Moral Education* 34, no. 4 (December 2005): 399–412.

27. "Iran Pays for SI Students to Fly to Cuba," *Solomon Star*, November 30, 2009, http://solomonstarnews.com/index.php?option=com_content&task=view&id=13655&change=71&changeown=78&Itemid=26.

28. Cuban Medical Brigade, "Cuban Medical Collaboration: Democratic Republic of Timor Leste," Dili, July 2008.

29. Alberto Rigñak, interview with this writer, Dili, August 30, 2007; Alberto Rigñak, interview with this writer, Dili, July 16, 2008. Dr. Alberto Rigñak was head of the Cuban Medical Brigade in Timor-Leste from 2006 to 2009.

30. Rui Araujo, "A Snapshot of the Medical School, Faculty of Health Sciences, National University of Timor Lorosae, Democratic Republic of Timor Leste" (paper presented at the Expert Meeting on Finalization of Regional Guidelines on Institutional Quality Assurance Mechanisms for Undergraduate Medical Education, WHO/SEARO, New Delhi, India, October 8–9, 2009).

31. Francisco Medina, talk at Cuban Pavilion, World Social Forum, Caracas, January 28, 2006. Dr. Medina was head of the Cuban Medical Brigade in Timor-Leste between 2004 and 2006.

32. Rui Araujo, interview with this writer, Dili, September 1, 2007; Rui Araujo, interview with this writer, Dili, July 16, 2008. Dr. Rui Araujo was Timor-Leste's health minister between 2002 and 2007.

33. Araujo, interview, 2008.

34. Rigñak, interview, 2007.

35. Cuban Medical Brigade 2008; Tim Anderson, "Solidarity Aid: The Cuba–Timor Leste Health Program," *International Journal of Cuban Studies* 2 (December 2008), http://www.cubastudiesjournal.org/issue-2/international-relations/solidarity-aid-the-cuba-timor-leste-health-programme.cfm.

36. Tim Anderson, "Los Primeros/The First Group," YouTube, 2010, https://www.you tube.com/watch?v=wZx6_mZyd54.

37. Tim Anderson, "Timor's New Doctors," YouTube, 2014, https://www.youtube.com/ watch?v=Nzz0v2gtJ38.

38. "En Cuba nuevos estudiantes de las Islas del Pacifico," *Granma*, October 7, 2009, http://granma.co.cu/2009/10/07/nacional/artic15.html.

39. Moffat Mamu, "Cuban Doctors Bring Ease to Our Hospital," *Solomon Star*, September 20, 2008.

40. A. Asante et al., "Analysis of Policy Implications and Challenges of the Cuban Health Assistance Program Related to Human Resources for Health in the Pacific," *Human Resources for Health* 10, no. 1 (2012): 1–9, http://devstudies.unsw.edu.au/resources/publications/ analysis-policy-implications-and-challenges-cuban-health-assistance-program.

41. Ibid., 6.

42. José Ramón Balaguer, comments in discussion with Papua New Guinea prime minister Michael Somare, Havana, Cuba, September 13, 2006 (this writer was present); Yiliam Jiménez, comments in discussion with Papua New Guinea national planning minister John Hickey, Havana, September 11, 2006 (this writer was present).

43. Tim Anderson, "Not Really Europeans: Cuban Doctors in the Pacific," YouTube, 2013, https://www.youtube.com/watch?v=u3BqKrrkbVo.

44. Carol-Anne Galo, "Private Medical Practitioners Disapprove Cuba Agreement," *Island Sun*, September 22, 2016, http://theislandsun.com/private-medical-practitioners-disapprove -cuba-agreement.

45. Rita Narayan, "Nauru Medical Students Graduated from Cuba in Kiribati for Internship," *Loop*, August 1, 2016, http://www.loopnauru.com/content/nauru-medical-students -graduated-cuba-kiribati-internship; "Tuvalu Finds Cuban-Trained Doctors Need Skills Gap Filled," Radio Australia, February 9, 2015, http://www.radioaustralia.net.au/international/ radio/program/pacific-beat/tuvalu-finds-cubantrained-doctors-need-skills-gap-filled/1413571.

46. Anderson, "Not Really Europeans."

47. Galo, "Private Medical Practitioners Disapprove Cuba Agreement."

48. Elliot Dawea, "Trainee Doctors Fail Exam," *Solomon Star*, August 29, 2016, http:// www.solomonstarnews.com/news/national/11442-trainee-doctors-fail-exam.

49. Narayan, "Nauru Medical Students Graduated"; "Tuvalu Finds Cuban-Trained Doctors."

50. Tim Anderson, "Social Medicine in Timor Leste," *Social Medicine* 5, no. 4 (2010): 182–91, http://www.socialmedicine.info/index.php/socialmedicine /article/view/480/1028.

51. Ibid.

52. Ercia da Conceição, speech at graduation ceremony, National University of Timor Lorosae (UNTIL), Dili, September 3, 2010. Dr. Ercia da Conceição is one of the first group of Timor-Leste's doctors.

53. Geidi Martín Díaz, interview with this writer, Los Palos, Timor-Leste, August 28, 2007. Dr. Geidi Martín Díaz is a Cuban doctor who was posted in Los Palos, between 2006 and 2008.

54. Maité Llero, interview with this writer, Dili, July 2010. Dr. Maité Llero is a Cuban doctor who was posted in rural Viqueque and later in Becora, Dili, in 2010.

55. Irene Calderón Reynoso, interview with this writer, Dili, April 1, 2010. Dr. Irene Calderón Reynoso, a Cuban pediatrician, was posted to Maliana District Hospital in Timor-Leste between 2008 and 2010.

56. Ildefonso da Costa Nunes, interview with this writer, Dili, July 15, 2010. Dr. Ildefonso da Costa Nunes is one of the first group of Timor-Leste's doctors.

57. Da Conceição, speech, 2010.

58. Colombianus da Silva, interview with this writer, Dili, July 17, 2010. Dr. Colombianus da Silva is one of the first group of Timor-Leste's doctors.

59. Carlos Royuela Reyes, ed., "Vivencias de los estudiantes internos, sobre el desarrollo del internado," República Democrática de Timor-Leste, Brigada Médica Cubana, Facultad de Medicina, October 29, 2009.

60. "Health Workforce: Aggregated Data: Density per 1000," World Health Organization, 2013, http://apps.who.int/gho/data/node.main.A1444.

61. Joel Negin, "Australia and New Zealand's Contribution to Pacific Island Health Worker Brain Drain," *Australian and New Zealand Journal of Public Health* 32, no, 6 (2008): 507–11.

62. "About the Australia Awards," Australia Awards, 2015, http://australiaawards.gov.au/Pages/about.aspx.

63. "PNG Minister Attacks Downer over Doctors," *Sydney Morning Herald*, July 10, 2007, http://www.smh.com.au/news/World/PNG-Minister-attacks-Downer-over-doctors/2007/07/10/1183833470186.html.

64. Australian Minister for Foreign Affairs and Trade (AMFAT), "Joint Press Conference with Mr. Bruno Rodríguez, Cuban Foreign Minister," Minister for Foreign Affairs, June 8, 2010, http://foreignminister.gov.au/transcripts/2010/100608_press_conference.html.

65. AMFAT 2009.

66. AMFAT 2009.

67. Kevin Rudd, "Port Moresby Declaration," PM Transcripts, Australian Government, Department of Prime Minister and Cabinet, March 8, 2008, https://pmtranscripts.pmc.gov.au/release/transcript-15802.

68. AMFAT 2009.

69. Emilia Botello, interview with this writer, Dili, July 16, 2010. Dr. Emilia Botello was the Cuban dean of the Faculty of Medicine of the National University of Timor Lorosae at this time.

70. Pedro Monzón, personal communication with this writer, September 20, 2013. Pedro Monzón was the Cuban ambassador to Australia at this time.

71. Jim Tulloch, Jorge Delgado, and Adrian Hearn, "Cuba-Australia Collaboration in the Pacific," Preliminary Findings, Joint Scoping Mission for Discussion with Sponsoring Agencies and Pacific Island Authorities, report, April 18, 2012.

72. Monzón, personal communication, 2013.

73. Kalyan Kumar, "New Zealand and Cuba Sign Agreement for Medical Cooperation in Pacific Islands," *International Business Times*, February 17, 2015, http://www.ibtimes.com.au/new-zealand-cuba-sign-agreement-medical-cooperation-pacific-islands-1421974.

74. Bob Boughton and Deborah Durnan, "Cuba's 'Yes I Can' in Australia: Three Years On," ACAL National Conference, October 2014, http://acal.edu.au/14conf/docs/Cuba-Yes-I-Can-in-Australia.pdf.

75. "A Different Model for Literacy," Literacy for Life Foundation, 2016, http://www.lflf.org.au/about-csgz.

76. Anderson, "Social Medicine in Timor Leste."

77. J. M. Feinsilver, "Cuban Medical Diplomacy: When the Left Has Got It Right," Council on Hemispheric Affairs, October 30, 2006, http://www.coha.org/cuban-medical-diplomacy-when-the-left-has-got-it-right.

III

CUBA'S KEY BILATERAL RELATIONS

10

The United States and Cuba

William M. LeoGrande

In his first public statement after Fidel Castro fell ill, Raúl Castro offered an olive branch to the United States. Quoting Fidel's 1986 report to the Third Congress of the Cuban Communist Party, he said, "Cuba is not remiss to discussing its prolonged differences with the United States and to go out in search of peace and better relations between our people. But that would have to be on the basis of the most unrestricted respect for our condition as a country that does not tolerate shadows on its independence." Such a dialogue, Raúl continued, "would be possible only when the United States decides to negotiate with seriousness and is willing to treat us with a spirit of equality, reciprocity and the fullest mutual respect."[1] This position formed the cornerstone of Raúl Castro's policy toward the United States, and he would repeat it whenever the topic arose.

Raúl Castro underscored the continuity between his offer and Cuba's past stance toward its neighbor to the north by quoting Fidel's speech from two decades before.[2] But in practice, Raúl proved to be more willing than his older brother to pursue pragmatic engagement with the United States. Even as Washington continued policies aimed at casting "shadows" on Cuba's independence by weakening its government and promoting opposition, Raúl Castro was ready to accept the political challenges posed by engagement in order to reap its economic benefits.

U.S. RECALCITRANCE UNDER PRESIDENT GEORGE W. BUSH

But it takes two to tango—or salsa—so Cuba's offer to open a new chapter in relations with the United States required a willing partner in the White House. George W. Bush was not that partner. Beholden to conservative Cuban Americans in

Florida, Bush tightened U.S. economic sanctions, increased funding for "democracy promotion" programs supporting Cuban dissidents, and organized a presidential commission to plan for the overthrow of the Cuban government and the reconstruction of Cuba in the image of the United States.[3]

The Bush administration was convinced that the Cuban government was fragile, remaining in power only by virtue of the charismatic authority of its founder. Once Fidel Castro passed from the scene, U.S. officials believed, the regime would be short-lived. "Authoritarian regimes are like helicopters," mused Bush's assistant secretary of state for Western Hemisphere affairs, Thomas Shannon. "There are single fail point mechanisms. When a rotor comes off a helicopter, it crashes. When a supreme leader disappears from an authoritarian regime, the authoritarian regime flounders."[4]

Not surprisingly, when Fidel Castro's sudden illness removed him from the scene, U.S. officials anticipated that they were about to finally realize the dream of regime change harbored by most presidents ever since Dwight D. Eisenhower authorized the Central Intelligence Agency to begin plotting against Cuba's revolutionary government in 1960. They rejected Raúl Castro's offer of dialogue with contempt, denigrating Cuba's acting president as "Fidel's baby brother" and "Fidel Lite." The Department of State reaffirmed that the United States remained committed to regime change and the administration would "do everything we can to hasten that day."[5]

Nevertheless, for the next twelve months Raúl Castro continued to signal Cuba's interest in opening a dialogue. In December 2006, he repeated the offer more explicitly: "We take this opportunity to once again state that we are willing to resolve at the negotiating table the long-standing dispute between the United States and Cuba," he said, adding the same conditions he spelled out in August: "provided they accept . . . our condition as a country that will not tolerate any blemishes on its independence, and as long as said resolution is based on the principles of equality, reciprocity, noninterference and mutual respect."[6]

On July 26, 2007, Castro warned the Bush administration, "Our people will never give an inch of ground under the attempt of any country or group of countries to pressure us, nor will it make the slightest unilateral concession to send any kind of signal to anybody." But looking ahead to the next U.S. president, he reaffirmed Cuba's willingness "to discuss on equal footing the prolonged dispute with the government of the United States. . . . If the new United States authorities were to finally desist from their arrogance and decide to talk in a civilized manner, it would be a welcome change. Otherwise, we are ready to continue confronting their policy of hostility, even for another 50 years, if need be."[7]

PRESIDENT BARACK OBAMA PROMISES A NEW CHAPTER

When Barack Obama won election in 2008, it did not look like it would take another fifty years to finally normalize U.S.-Cuban relations. During the campaign, Obama pledged to follow a policy of engagement with Cuba. In April 2009, a few months after Obama's inauguration and on the eve of the Fifth Summit of the Americas in Trinidad and Tobago (to which Cuba was not invited), Raúl Castro traveled to Venezuela for a summit meeting of the Alianza Bolivariana para los Pueblos de Nuestra América (ALBA) countries. "We have let the American government know both in private and in public," he told the other heads of state, that Cuba would be happy to talk with the United States about human rights—"freedom of the press, political prisoners, everything, everything, everything they would like to talk about, but on an equal footing, with absolute respect for our sovereignty and for the right of the Cuban people to their self-determination."[8]

Obama appeared receptive. Addressing the Summit of the Americas, he reiterated his desire to engage. "The United States seeks a new beginning with Cuba," he said, to the applause of the assembled heads of state. "I'm prepared to have my administration engage with the Cuban government on a wide range of issues—from drugs, migration, and economic issues, to human rights, free speech, and democratic reform."[9] In June 2009, the United States voted (albeit with some reluctance) along with the rest of the Organization of American States membership, to repeal the 1962 resolution that suspended Cuba's membership.[10] In truth, the U.S. vote was aimed more at mollifying Latin America than engaging Cuba, but it was symbolic nonetheless of changing hemispheric politics and evolving U.S. policy. Cuba, as expected, declined to ask for its membership to be reactivated.

Semiannual migration consultations suspended by President Bush were resumed in July 2009, and progress seemed possible on a range of issues of mutual interest. In September, Deputy Assistant Secretary of State (DAS) Bisa Williams traveled to Cuba for talks on restoring direct mail service, suspended since 1968. She was given "unprecedented access to its state institutions," U.S. Interests Section Chief Jonathan Farrar reported. Vice Minister of Foreign Relations Dagoberto Rodríguez told Williams that by giving her a positive reception, "we meant to show our readiness to move forward in our relationship." To be sure, progress would require "confidence building," but "even within the existing diplomatic constraints, we see a way forward."

"It is hard to overstate just how markedly improved were our dealings with the Cuban Government and GOC institutions during . . . DAS Williams' visit," Farrar concluded his report. "As we did during the visit, we will continue to press the point that the GOC engagement with the Cuban people will do more to influence the bilateral relationship than its government-to-government engagement. Nonetheless, there are a number of action items from the various meetings that provide opportunity for us to test the GOC's willingness to continue to make progress on issues of interest."[11]

The road forward, however, was not smooth. While President Obama expressed his desire to open a new chapter in U.S. policy toward Cuba, Secretary of State Hillary Clinton was insisting on conditionality. Shortly after Obama lifted the limits on Cuban American family travel and remittances in April 2009, Secretary Clinton said that Washington could do little more to advance relations unless Cuba took reciprocal actions. "We would like to see Cuba open up its society, release political prisoners, open up to outside opinions and media, have the kind of society that we all know would improve the opportunities for the Cuban people and for their nation."[12]

By July, Secretary Clinton's list of conditions for further improvement in U.S.-Cuban relations sounded little different from George W. Bush's: "We have made it very clear that we could not do much more in dealing with Cuba unless Cuba changes," she declared. "The political prisoners need to be released. Free and fair elections need to be held. . . . So we are opening up dialogue with Cuba, but we are very clear that we want to see some fundamental changes within the Cuban regime."[13]

Speaking before Cuba's National Assembly a few weeks later, Raúl Castro replied directly. "Secretary of State Hillary Clinton said that they are open to a dialogue with Cuba but that they clearly want to see fundamental changes in the Cuban regime," he noted. "It is my obligation to respond to Mrs. Clinton, with all due respect, and also to those in the European Union who are asking for unilateral gestures in the sense of dismantling our social and political regime. I was not elected President to return capitalism to Cuba or to surrender the Revolution. I was elected to defend, preserve and continue to perfect socialism, not to destroy it." He went on to repeat the same message he had been sending Washington ever since he assumed the presidency in July 2006: Cuba was willing to hold a "respectful dialogue with the United States, on equal footing, without the slightest shadow to our independence, sovereignty and self-determination." He added, in case there was any doubt, "We will not negotiate our political or social system."[14]

Even the dialogue on issues of mutual interest came to a screeching halt in December 2009 after Cuba arrested U.S. Agency for International Development (USAID) subcontractor Alan Gross for building secure, independent digital networks in Cuba that linked to the Internet via encrypted satellite communications—part of USAID's "democracy promotion" programs. Cuba charged Gross with "acts against the Independence or Territorial Integrity of the Cuban State" and sentenced him to fifteen years in prison. Washington insisted Gross had done nothing wrong and that no further improvement in relations would be possible until Cuba released Gross unconditionally. The State Department cut off the recently resumed migration dialogue, and relations sank back into a deep freeze reminiscent of the previous administration.

Despite various attempts to restart discussions between the two sides, including efforts by Spanish prime minister José Luis Rodríguez Zapatero, Senator John Kerry, Governor Bill Richardson, and former president Jimmy Carter, Washington and Havana remained deadlocked over the issue of Alan Gross and the analogous plight of the Cuban Five (Cuban intelligence agents arrested in Miami in 1998 on a multiplicity of charges and sentenced to long prison terms).[15]

Yet, despite the impasse over the prisoners, Havana tried to restore momentum on issues of mutual interest by submitting to Washington a series of draft agreements on migration, counternarcotics cooperation, counterterrorism cooperation, environmental protection, natural disaster response, and trademark and patent protection.

Washington's constant refrain was unchanged: there could be no progress until Alan Gross was released, and the United States would not exchange him for the Cuban Five because there was no "equivalence." Gross was an innocent aid worker, and the Cubans were spies, Washington insisted.

In his report to the Sixth Congress of the Communist Party held in 2011, Raúl Castro excoriated the United States for "waging wars of conquest in Iraq and Afghanistan," supporting "corrupt and oppressive Arab governments," and attempting to destabilize progressive governments. The Obama administration was not only continuing the embargo, he said, but tightening it, disrupting Cuban financial transactions worldwide. Nevertheless, he reiterated Cuba's willingness to dialogue in order "to take on the challenge of having normal relations with the United States as well as to coexist in a civilized manner, our differences notwithstanding, on the basis of mutual respect and non-interference in the internal affairs."[16]

With U.S.-Cuban relations stalled, Cuba focused on strengthening its relations with other countries, especially in Latin America, as a counterweight to U.S. influence. Along with Venezuela, Cuba played a leading role in 2004 in the creation of the ALBA group of Latin American leftist governments. In 2010, Cuba supported the creation of the Community of Latin American and Caribbean States (Comunidad de Estados Latinoamericanos y Caribeños, or CELAC), a region-wide group excluding Canada and the United States, and in 2013 Raúl Castro was selected as president pro tempore. In its own immediate neighborhood, Cuba strengthened its ties with the Caribbean Community (CARICOM) by providing educational and medical assistance and disaster relief. In December 2014, Havana hosted the Fifth Cuba-CARICOM Summit.[17]

Beyond Latin America, Cuba continued to cultivate good relations throughout the Third World, having once again been elected to chair the Movement of Nonaligned Nations in 2006 (Cuba first chaired the movement in 1979). Havana sought to repair its relations with Russia and China as a means of diversifying its international economic ties.[18] In 2008, Russian president Dmitry Medvedev visited Cuba, followed in 2009 by Raúl Castro's visit to Russia. The result was deeper economic cooperation, culminating in a 2014 visit to Cuba by President Vladimir Putin, during which he announced that Russia would forgive 90 percent of Cuba's Soviet-era debt and restructure the remainder.[19]

Chinese president Xi Jinping also visited Cuba in 2014, signing more than two dozen cooperation agreements.[20] By then China had become Cuba's second-largest trading partner (behind Venezuela), and Chinese firms were investing in joint enterprises in key sectors such as nickel and petroleum.[21] In April 2014, Cuba began discussions with the European Union on replacing the Common Position (which was adopted by the EU in 2003 and conditioned relations on Cuban domestic political reforms) with a new agreement on political and economic cooperation that would mean an increase in trade, aid, and direct foreign investment.[22]

One measure of Cuba's success in cultivating good relations around the world was the annual vote in the United Nations General Assembly on Cuba's resolution demanding an end to the U.S. embargo. When first introduced in 1992, it won 59 votes in favor, 3 against, and 71 abstentions; in 2014, before Obama and Raúl Castro announced their intention to normalize relations, the vote was 188 in favor, 2 against (the United States and Israel), and 3 abstentions (the small island states—the Marshall Islands, Federated States of Micronesia, and Palau).[23]

THE BREAKTHROUGH

Building international solidarity proved to be a good strategy for Cuba. At the Sixth Summit of the Americas in Cartagena, Colombia, in 2012, President Obama faced a solid phalanx of Latin American presidents demanding that Cuba be included in the summit process if it was to continue at all. In the three years after the summit in Trinidad and Tobago, where Obama had promised a new beginning in relations with Cuba, U.S.-Cuban relations were essentially unchanged. The Cuba issue dominated the 2012 summit and had become, as Deputy National Security Advisor Ben Rhodes put it, "an albatross" crippling U.S. relations with the rest of the hemisphere.[24] Less than a year later, after winning reelection, Obama opened the secret negotiations that led to the announcements of December 17, 2014.

In April 2013, the White House sent a message to Raúl Castro outside normal diplomatic channels asking if Cuba was open to a highly confidential dialogue. Castro accepted, and the two presidents dispatched small teams of trusted aides to negotiate on their behalf. Obama sent Rhodes and Ricardo Zúñiga, a career Foreign Service officer on detail to the National Security Council staff. Castro sent a slightly larger team, including his son, Alejandro Castro, an Interior Ministry officer detailed to the president's personal staff. Neither the U.S. Department of State nor the Cuban Ministry of Foreign Relations was informed of the negotiations until they were well advanced.[25]

Cuba's principal objective in the talks was to win freedom for the Cuban Five. Despite U.S. promises that releasing Alan Gross could open the door to better relations across the board, the Cuban negotiators were unwilling to back away from their core demand. "They really weren't willing to put things on the table like diplomatic relations and normalization," recalled Ben Rhodes.[26] The U.S. negotiators repeated the familiar refrain that Alan Gross was not a spy and therefore could not be exchanged for spies. The impasse was only broken in 2014 when the United States proposed, and Cuba finally agreed to, trading the Cuban Five for Rolando Sarraff Trujillo, a Cuban intelligence officer imprisoned in Cuba for nearly twenty years for spying for the CIA. Cuba then released Alan Gross (along with fifty-three political prisoners) as a humanitarian gesture.

On December 17, 2014, in a televised address to the nation, President Obama announced his historic decision to normalize relations with Cuba. "In the most significant changes in our policy in more than fifty years, we will end an outdated approach that, for decades, has failed to advance our interests," Obama began. Instead of pursuing regime change, the United States would reestablish diplomatic relations and pursue a policy of engagement.[27]

Raúl Castro was more circumspect. The lead in his speech was the announcement that the Cuban Five had finally returned home, as Fidel had promised at the time of their arrest. The headline the next morning in *Granma*, the Communist Party daily newspaper, read, "Volvieron!" ("They have returned!"). Raúl devoted just a single sentence to the decision to normalize U.S.-Cuban relations. "We have also agreed to renew diplomatic relations," he declared, but quickly followed up by reminding people, "This in no way means that the heart of the matter has been solved. The economic, commercial, and financial blockade, which causes enormous human and economic damages to our country, must cease." Nevertheless, he was mildly optimistic, concluding, "The progress made in our exchanges proves that it is possible to find solutions to many problems. As we have reiterated, we must learn the art of coexisting with our differences in a civilized manner."[28]

For the United States, December 17, 2014, represented a fundamental shift in policy, an abandonment of coercive diplomacy aimed at forcing regime change in Havana, and adoption of a policy of coexistence and engagement—symbolized by the restoration of diplomatic relations broken fifty-four years earlier in January 1961 and Obama's trip to the island in March 2016. For Cuba, however, December 17 represented less a change in policy than a potential change in the international environment in which Cuba operated, especially the economic environment.

U.S.-CUBAN RELATIONS AND THE UPDATING OF THE CUBAN ECONOMY

When Raúl Castro assumed the presidency, the Cuban economy had yet to fully recover from the "Special Period," the deep depression that followed the collapse of the Soviet Union and loss of $3 billion in annual aid. Although the economy had been growing gradually since the 1990s, the gains had been concentrated in tourism and medical services (exported primarily to Venezuela). The actual production of goods on the island still lagged below 1989 levels, and many state enterprises operated at a loss. Hard-currency earnings, even when supplemented by more than $2 billion in annual remittances, were hardly enough to cover essential imports. Agricultural production was so poor that this agriculturally well-endowed island had to import most of its food at a cost of over $1 billion every year.

In 2011, the Sixth Congress of the Communist Party of Cuba adopted its "Resolution on the Guidelines of the Economic and Social Policy of the Party and the Revolution," a sweeping set of policies for economic reorganization embodied in 313 specific objectives. The goal was to move Cuba away from the hypercentralized planning system adopted from the Soviet Union in the 1970s to a market socialist model analogous to that in China and Vietnam, albeit without some of the social costs associated with those systems. A key aspect of this new economic policy was to integrate Cuba more successfully with the global economy by diversifying trade relations, expanding the tourist sector, attracting more foreign direct investment (FDI), and developing high value-added sectors like biotechnology and information technology.

U.S. economic sanctions represented the principal obstacle to realizing the goals of the new economic policy in the external sector. Given its proximity, the United States would be Cuba's natural trading partner: the United States was the main source of tourists traveling to the Caribbean; the United States was the main source of FDI flowing into the Caribbean; and the U.S. biotechnology and information technology sectors were global leaders with which Cuba could profitably partner. Moreover, the extraterritorial dimensions of the embargo—financial sanctions against foreign firms doing business with Cuba in U.S. dollars and potential lawsuits against foreign firms for "trafficking" in expropriated property (i.e., investing in Cuba if it involved property previously owned by U.S. citizens or naturalized Cuban Americans)—deterred many foreign firms from expanding commercial relations with Cuba.

Thus the normalization of U.S.-Cuban relations was an important component of Raúl Castro's economic strategy. From December 17, 2014, onward, Castro insisted that truly normal relations could only be achieved when the U.S. embargo was lifted since it constituted "the most serious obstacle to our economic development and the welfare of the Cuban people."[29] To Cuba's frustration, progress on relaxing the embargo proved to be slower than progress on the diplomatic front. In May 2015, the United States removed Cuba from its list of state sponsors of international terrorism, clearing the way for the restoration of full diplomatic relations in July. The two sides then established a bilateral commission to oversee negotiations taking place in some two dozen separate conversations on a wide range of issues, including migration, human trafficking, law enforcement, counternarcotics cooperation, maritime safety and coast guard cooperation, environmental protection, global health cooperation, claims, and human rights.

In 2015, Obama and Castro met face-to-face for substantive discussions at the Seventh Summit of the Americas in Panama in April and at the United Nations General Assembly in September. Then, in March 2016, Obama became the first sitting president to visit Cuba since Calvin Coolidge in 1928. By then, the two sides had reached new bilateral accords on the environment, agricultural cooperation, the restoration of direct postal service, and the establishment of regular commercial airline links.

By contrast, the development of commercial ties proceeded much more slowly, in part because of remaining U.S. economic sanctions, and in part because of the business climate in Cuba itself. While acknowledging that Obama could not unilaterally lift the embargo in its entirety, Raúl Castro nevertheless said repeatedly that Obama could do more to loosen it than he had. From January 2015 to the end of his administration, Obama approved five major packages of regulatory reforms carving out ever-widening exceptions to the embargo. The first package embodied the changes Obama announced on December 17. The Treasury Department's Office of Foreign Assets

Control (OFAC) granted a general license for travel to Cuba for all twelve categories of legal travel (so travelers no longer needed to seek OFAC's prior permission). It authorized trade and investment in the telecommunications sector. It authorized sales to Cuba's private businesses, a limited number of exports from that sector to the United States, and microfinance. It authorized exports to "human rights organizations, individuals, or non-governmental organizations that promote independent activity intended to strengthen civil society" and unlimited remittances "to directly benefit the Cuban people; to support the Cuban people through activities of recognized human rights organizations, independent organizations designed to promote a rapid, peaceful transition to democracy, and activities of individuals and non-governmental organizations that promote independent activity intended to strengthen civil society in Cuba; and to support the development of private businesses."[30]

In one way or another, all these measures were aimed at weakening the control of the Cuban state. Expanded travel and telecommunications connectivity were seen as ways to foster the diffusion of ideas. Trade with the private sector and nongovernmental organizations and support of them via microfinance and remittances were aimed at strengthening social sectors independent of—and potentially in conflict with—the government.

Announcing the new regulations, Treasury Secretary Jack Lew said that they put in place "a policy that helps promote political and economic freedom for the Cuban people."[31]

However, apart from a big jump in U.S. visitors immediately stimulated by the relaxation of travel restrictions, the practical impact of these reforms was limited by the fact that U.S. regulators had little understanding of the corresponding Cuban regulations, rendering most of their new rules inoperable. Trade with Cuba's private sector, for example, was virtually impossible because the Cuban government provided no mechanisms for private businesses to secure the necessary import-export licenses.

The most important element in the second package of regulatory changes announced in September 2015 was the authorization for U.S. businesses and nongovernmental organizations operating in Cuba to establish a "physical presence" on the island, including offices, retail outlets, and warehouses. Although the significance of this change was limited at first because only U.S. agricultural exporters and telecommunications firms were authorized to do business with Cuban state enterprises, the ensuing package of regulatory changes in January 2016 authorized sales by U.S. firms to state enterprises if they "meet the needs of the Cuban people," broadly construed. This effectively authorized the export of virtually all consumer goods to Cuba. The January reforms also authorized financing for exports to Cuba (except credits for agricultural sales, which were prohibited by the Trade Sanctions Reform and Export Enhancement Act of 2000, which first authorized agricultural sales).

The fourth package of regulatory reforms, issued in March 2016 on the eve of Obama's trip, further loosened travel restrictions by granting a general license for "people-to-people" educational travel, allowing travelers to organize their own itineraries rather than requiring that they travel on prepackaged tours with travel providers. It also authorized U.S. businesses to hire Cubans, including athletes, artists, and musicians, in the United States on nonresident visas—meaning that Cubans no longer had to abandon their homeland in order to be employed in the United States. Most importantly, the new package licensed U.S. financial institutions to process dollar-denominated international financial transactions between Cuba and third parties (so-called U-turn transactions). The prior prohibition on these transactions was a serious obstacle to Cuba's international trade and at the top of the list of issues Cuban negotiators wanted resolved.[32]

The final package of regulatory reforms was unveiled in October 2016, along with a presidential directive that included a comprehensive statement of the president's policy, its rationale, and instructions to various executive branch agencies on how to implement it.[33] The directive stated flatly, "We will not pursue regime change in Cuba. We will continue to make clear that the United States cannot impose a different model on Cuba because the future of Cuba is up to the Cuban people."

The regulatory reforms expanded opportunities for commercial collaboration to include biotechnology and infrastructure development, authorized Cubans to buy U.S. consumer goods directly online, and ended the restriction prohibiting foreign vessels from entering a U.S. port for 180 days after calling on a Cuban port. The change that received the most attention, though it was the least significant economically, was the elimination of limits on Cuban-made goods that travelers could bring back to the United States. "Obama, Cementing New Ties with Cuba, Lifts Limits on Cigars and Rum," read the headline in the *New York Times*.[34]

Yet, despite the holes punched in the embargo by Obama's regulatory reforms, two major restrictions remained in place: U.S. businesses could not invest in Cuba except in telecommunications, and Cuban state enterprises could not export goods to the United States except for pharmaceuticals. For Cuba, access to U.S. investment was more important than free trade, since Cuba could buy most things it needed elsewhere. But Cuba's goal of attracting $2.5 billion in FDI annually was unrealistic so long as U.S. investment remained prohibited. The ban on Cuban state exports to the United States meant that U.S.-Cuban trade would always be unbalanced, with Cuba running a huge balance-of-trade deficit.

Moreover, the Cubans resisted allowing Washington to dictate the rules of the game. When the U.S. government authorized the import of coffee produced by private farmers, the Cuban National Association of Small Farmers (Asociación Nacional de Agricultores Pequeños) issued a statement accusing Washington of "promoting the division and disintegration of Cuban society" and declaring that it would not allow the United States to drive a wedge between Cuban private farmers and their government.[35]

By no means were the obstacles to expanding commercial relations all on the U.S. side. Although hundreds of U.S. businesses participated in trade missions to Cuba in the two years after December 17, 2014, few signed contracts. Cuba, after all, was not an easy place to do business. Its infrastructure—roads, energy grid, and digital network—lagged behind that of most neighboring countries. Foreign companies were still required to hire labor through the state's hiring agency. Cuba's multiple exchange rates made it difficult to assess real costs. Cuba's bureaucracy was opaque and slow to make decisions. Finally, with 11 million people, many of them relatively poor, Cuba represented a small market whose limited potential profitability did not always outweigh the financial and political risks involved.

Some Cuban leaders remained wary of engagement with the United States, viewing Obama's policy as a thinly veiled attempt to lure them into complacence, while Washington quietly schemed to undermine the revolution through ideological subversion. Obama's trip to Havana catalyzed those concerns, and Fidel Castro himself gave them public expression. In a front-page article in the Communist Party daily *Granma*, Castro chided Obama for trying to "elaborate theories on Cuban politics" and warned him against "the illusion" that Cubans would renounce the achievements of the revolution for blandishments from the United States. "We do not need the empire to give us anything," he concluded defiantly.[36]

A veteran journalist followed up with an even harsher front-page attack, warning that Obama was especially dangerous because of his charisma and stage presence. "There is no doubt: Obama is the gentle and seductive face" of imperialism, whose aim was "to contribute to the fragmentation of Cuban society in order to recover U.S. hegemony."[37]

Foreign Minister Bruno Rodríguez Parrilla, the official in charge of managing the evolving bilateral relationship, called Obama's statements during his visit "a deep attack on our ideas, our history, our culture and our symbols."[38]

At the Seventh Party Congress, which convened just a few weeks after Obama's visit, Raúl Castro was more measured, noting that the period since December 17, 2014, had produced "concrete results" that were "positive but not sufficient." Hostile U.S. policies like the embargo remained in place, and the United States had not abandoned its hope of undermining Cuban socialism. "We are not naive or unaware of powerful external forces that aspire to, as they say, 'empower' non-state actors to generate agents of change in the hope of finishing off the revolution and socialism in Cuba by other means," he said, adding, "There have been no small number of statements by U.S. officials openly affirming that the goals are the same and only the methods have changed."[39]

As President Obama's second term drew to a close, the balance sheet on his policy of normalizing relations with Cuba was clearly positive albeit incomplete. Diplomatic relations had been restored, significant progress had been made on issues of mutual interest, travel to Cuba was up by over 150 percent from 2014, and there were more exceptions to the embargo in place than ever before. But the potential for trade and investment was as yet unrealized because of obstacles on both sides.

On the political front, vestiges of the old policy of regime change remained in place, despite Obama's renunciation of it. Washington was still funding "democracy promotion" programs to support Cuban dissidents and strengthen civil society in opposition to the government. Radio and TV Martí continued broadcasting to the island, even though few people were listening.

Nevertheless, the trajectory of relations was positive. Between December 2014 and January 20, 2017, twenty-two bilateral agreements were signed on issues of mutual interest, social and cultural exchanges expanded rapidly, and commercial ties were slowly growing. Just before leaving office, Obama ended the "wet foot/dry foot" migration policy that had offered Cubans preferential immigration status, stimulating a constant outward flow of young and well-educated Cubans. Public opinion in both Cuba and the United States was strongly in favor of normalization. A 2015 Bendixen & Amandi poll inside Cuba found that 97 percent of respondents thought normalization would be "good for Cuba."[40] In the United States, a series of polls found support for Obama's policy was well above 60 percent favorable, including among majorities of Republicans and Cuban Americans.[41]

COLLATERAL DAMAGE: U.S.-CUBAN RELATIONS AND THE 2016 U.S. PRESIDENTIAL CAMPAIGN

Cuba was not a major issue in the 2016 presidential campaign, but Donald Trump's stunning upset victory had major consequences for U.S.-Cuban relations. Despite the fact that the early Republican field included two Cuban Americans—Senators Marco Rubio and Ted Cruz—both of whom vehemently denounced Obama's policy,[42] Cuba was neither a priority nor a wedge issue since support for Obama's opening cut across party lines. In all the many debates during the primaries and general election, the issue of Cuba came up just once, during the primary debates held in Miami when Hillary Clinton rebuked Senator Bernie Sanders for a 1985 interview praising Cuba's free health care and education.[43]

Nevertheless, Clinton supported Obama's policy of engagement and promised to continue it. In a major speech in Miami, she echoed Obama's argument that the embargo was a "failure" that should be lifted and promised to expand on his policy of engagement. Yet her tone was noticeably sharper and more explicit about trying to catalyze internal political change. She did not shy away from arguing that engagement would weaken the Cuban regime and hasten its "day of reckoning with the Cuban people"—exactly what skeptics in Havana were warning.[44]

Donald Trump's campaign was never heavy on policy details, and Cuba was no exception. Over the course of the campaign, Trump expressed contradictory views on Obama's opening. At first, he supported it. "The concept of opening with Cuba is fine," Trump said in September 2015, "but we should have made a better deal."[45] Later, Trump returned to the more traditional Republican stance of hostility. The tougher line was foreshadowed in the Republican Party Platform adopted at the July convention. The language was reminiscent of the depths of the Cold War: "We want to welcome the people of Cuba back into our hemispheric family—after their corrupt rulers are forced from power and brought to account for their crimes against humanity. . . . The current Administration's 'opening to Cuba' was a shameful accommodation to the demands of its tyrants."[46]

In late September 2016, *Newsweek* magazine broke the story that in 1998 Trump secretly explored the possibility of opening business operations in Cuba, in violation of the U.S. embargo, and then tried to disguise the illegal activity as an allowable charitable project. Just months after Trump's representatives traveled to Cuba, as Trump flirted with running for president on Ross Perot's Reform Party ticket, he delivered a fiery speech to Cuban Americans in Miami, denouncing the Cuban regime and pledging to maintain the embargo. *Newsweek*'s exposure of Trump's hypocrisy fueled speculation that his unconsummated business proposition to Fidel Castro in 1998 might cost him Cuban American votes in 2016. Shortly thereafter, Trump pivoted, announcing his new policy via Twitter: "The people of Cuba have struggled too long. Will reverse Obama's executive orders and concessions towards Cuba until freedoms are restored."

In the final weeks of the campaign, as Florida emerged as a must-win state, the Republican ticket focused on energizing its base, including conservative Cuban Americans. Campaigning in Miami, Trump and Mike Pence both pledged to roll back Obama's policy in its entirety. "All of the concessions that Barack Obama has granted the Castro regime were done with executive order, which means the next president can reverse them," Trump said. "And that is what I will do unless the Castro regime meets our demands. Those demands will include religious and political freedom for the Cuban people and the freeing of political prisoners."[47]

Yet Trump himself was more circumspect, avoiding details when pressed on his prospective Cuba policy. Obama had negotiated "a very weak agreement," he said. "I would do whatever is necessary to get a good agreement. An agreement is fine. It has to be a strong, good agreement that's good for the Cuban people." Before developing his own approach, he told the *Miami Herald*, "I want to listen specifically to what Cuban people who came to this country and who have lived in this country—Cuban Americans—I want to hear how they feel about it."[48]

In the end, Trump's appeal to Cuban Americans had limited success. According to exit polls, he won somewhere between 52 and 54 percent of their votes, only slightly more than Mitt Romney in 2012, confirming the shifting political loyalty of the community apparent in presidential elections since 2008.[49] Yet Trump believed he owed Cuban Americans a political debt. When Fidel Castro died on November 26, 2016, President-elect Trump condemned the Cuban leader and promised Cuban Americans he would work for a free Cuba. "Today, the world marks the passing of a brutal dictator who oppressed his own people for nearly six decades. Fidel Castro's legacy is one of firing squads, theft, unimaginable suffering, poverty and the denial of fundamental human rights," Trump wrote. "Our administration will do all it can to ensure the Cuban people can finally begin their journey toward prosperity and liberty. I join the many Cuban Americans who supported me so greatly in the presidential campaign . . . with the hope of one day soon seeing a free Cuba."[50] Two days later, he tweeted, "If Cuba is unwilling to make a better deal for the Cuban people, the Cuban/American people and the U.S. as a whole, I will terminate deal."[51]

Cuban officials scrupulously refrained from commenting on the U.S. presidential election campaign, simply saying that they hoped whoever won the presidency would carry out the will of the American people, who were overwhelmingly in favor of continuing the normalization process.[52] The day after the election, Raúl Castro sent Trump congratulations on his victory.[53] Cuban media reported Trump's triumph with a factual account of the election results and quoted the olive branch Trump held out in his victory speech: "We will get along with all other nations willing to get along with us. . . . We will seek common ground, not hostility; partnership, not conflict."[54]

At the same time, the Cuban government also announced the beginning of its annual national defense exercises.[55] The message to Washington was clear: Havana was ready to continue the diplomatic dialogue, but likewise it was prepared to defend itself if necessary.

The Cuban government did not respond at all when Trump insulted Fidel Castro upon his death. Cuba's chief negotiator with Washington, Josefina Vidal, reiterated Cuba's interest in continuing to build "civilized and respectful relations" but "without concessions" on Cuba's internal affairs. "Respect is essential and has been the key to the success and results we have obtained thus far," Vidal said.[56] But in an interview a few weeks later, she also staked out the limits of Cuba's tolerance. "Aggression, pressure, conditions, impositions do not work with Cuba," she warned. "This is not the way to attempt to have even a minimally civilized relationship."[57]

Speaking shortly after Trump's inauguration to the summit of the Community of Latin American and Caribbean States (Comunidad de Estados Latinoamericanos y Caribeños, or CELAC), Raúl Castro reiterated Cuba's long-standing position:

> I wish to express Cuba's willingness to continue negotiating pending bilateral issues with the United States, on the basis of equality, reciprocity and respect for the sovereignty and independence of our country, and to continue the respectful dialogue and cooperation on issues of common interest with the new government of President Donald Trump.
>
> Cuba and the United States can cooperate and coexist in a civilized manner, respecting differences and promoting all that benefits both countries and peoples, but it should not be expected that to do so Cuba will make concessions inherent to its sovereignty and independence.[58]

THE TRUMP ADMINISTRATION'S CUBA POLICY AND HAVANA'S RESPONSE

The new administration's first step on Cuba was to launch a "full review" of policy. Although the White House had originally hoped to announce its new policy on May 20 (Cuban Independence Day), the review was not completed in time because of disagreements within the administration over what elements of Obama's policy to change.[59] Instead the president released a statement celebrating Cuba's independence, which provoked the first sharp Cuban response. An official statement read on Cuban television called Trump's statement a "controversial and ridiculous message from the ill-advised U.S. President Donald Trump to the people of Cuba about May 20, a date that the United States considers as the emergence of the Republic of Cuba, when we actually know that what was born that day was a Yankee neo-colony, which lived until on January 1, 1959."[60] Perhaps aware of Trump's inclination to escalate conflicts when personally attacked, the Cuban statement and subsequent critical comments about U.S. policy by the government and state media were always careful not to criticize Trump personally but to consistently refer to him as "ill-advised."

On June 16, President Trump announced his new Cuba policy to a cheering crowd of Cuban exiles in Miami's Manuel Artime Theater, named for the leader of the exile brigade that went ashore at the Bay of Pigs. "Effective immediately, I am canceling the last administration's completely one-sided deal with Cuba," Trump declared.[61] Despite rhetoric reminiscent of the Cold War, in which Trump called the Cuban regime brutal, criminal, depraved, oppressive, and murderous, the actual changes he announced were relatively modest. The new policy ended the ability of U.S. travelers to take "people-to-people" educational trips on their own, forcing them once again to go with organized groups, and it prohibited transactions with entities linked to the Cuban military.[62] Nevertheless, Trump's rhetoric clearly signaled that he was abandoning Obama's policy of normalizing relations and returning to a policy of hostility and regime change.

The Cuban government's official response was pragmatic but firm. A statement released shortly after Trump's Miami speech declared, "The Government of Cuba reiterates its willingness to continue respectful dialogue and cooperation on issues of mutual interest, as well as the negotiation of pending bilateral issues with the United States Government. . . . But it cannot be expected that, in order to do so, Cuba will make concessions which compromise our independence or sovereignty, nor accept conditions of any type."[63] Speaking to Cuba's National Assembly on July14, Raúl Castro said the new U.S. sanctions "represent a step back in bilateral relations." He condemned the U.S. embargo, promising that "any attempt to destroy the Revolution, whether through coercion and pressure, or the use of subtle methods, will fail." He also reiterated the position he expressed at the CELAC summit six months earlier: "Cuba is willing to continue discussing pending bilateral issues with the United States, on the basis of equality and respect for the sovereignty and independence of our country, and to continue respectful dialogue and cooperation on issues of common interest with the U.S. government. Cuba and the United States can cooperate and coexist, respecting our differences and promoting everything that benefits both countries and peoples, but it should not be expected that, in order to do so, Cuba will make concessions essential to its sovereignty and independence."[64]

Relations were strained further in late summer 2017 when the press reported that U.S. diplomats and family members (along with some Canadians) had suffered what the State Department called "health attacks" while serving in Havana, beginning in late 2016 and continuing through mid-2017. Those afflicted reported symptoms ranging from nausea and hearing loss to mild traumatic brain injury. The Cuban government stated unequivocally that it had nothing to do with the injuries, and Raúl Castro expressed his personal concerns to U.S. Ambassador Jeffrey DeLaurentis. The State Department did not accuse the Cuban government of responsibility for the injuries, and Cuba reportedly cooperated fully with the U.S. and Canadian investigations. But investigators were at a loss to explain what technology could have produced such symptoms, who could have done it, or why.[65]

Nevertheless, at the behest of five Republican senators led by Marco Rubio, Secretary of State Rex Tillerson said in mid-September that the administration was reviewing whether to close the U.S. embassy. On the same day that U.S. and Cuban diplomats were meeting in Washington for the first bilateral commission meeting since Trump's inauguration, President Trump blasted Cuba as a "corrupt and destabilizing regime" during his speech to the United Nations General Assembly.[66]

The rumors of a break in diplomatic ties brought Foreign Minister Bruno Rodríguez to Washington for an emergency meeting with Secretary Tillerson in which he reiterated the assurance that Cuba was not responsible for the health problems and urged the administration not to act hastily or to politicize the incidents.[67] His pleas went unheeded. Three days later, Tillerson announced the withdrawal of nonessential personnel (about 60 percent of the staff), suspended visa processing for Cubans seeking to enter the United States, and issued a travel warning advising Americans not to travel to Cuba. That was not enough for Senator Rubio, who denounced Tillerson's actions as "weak, unacceptable and outrageous" and demanded that Cuban diplomats be expelled.[68] On October 2, the administration gave in to Rubio and expelled 60 percent of the Cuban embassy's staff, including the entire commercial section and all but one consular officer, thereby constraining commercial relations and travel to Cuba by U.S. residents.[69] From the scope of the explusions, it was clear that the White House, at Rubio's instigation, was using the health incidents as an excuse to dismantle as much of President Obama's policy of engagement as possible.

Predictably, as the United States ratcheted up these punishments, the tone of Cuba's response became defiant. In *Granma*, Cuba's Communist Party newspaper, the Foreign Ministry on October 3 condemned the expulsion of its diplomats as "unfounded and unacceptable" and rejected "categorically" any Cuban responsibility for the incidents. Noting the absence of evidence as to perpetrator or means, Cuba for the first time questioned whether any attacks had even occurred. A few days later, First Vice President Miguel Díaz-Canel called the allegations of attacks on U.S. diplomats "tall tales."[70]

The Trump administration appeared determined to return relations to the deep freeze of the Cold War, and Cuba was likely to respond as it had in years past—by seeking alliances with other global powers capable of providing it some protection against U.S. hostility. Russia, for example, was interested in reestablishing military bases on the island, according to Deputy Minister of Defense Nikolai Pankov.[71]

Raúl Castro's Policy toward the United States and the Future

During his twelve years as president of Cuba, Raúl Castro's approach to relations with the United States was remarkably consistent in light of how dramatically U.S. policy fluctuated. From 2006 to 2008, President George W. Bush pursued a policy of regime change as aggressive as any since the John F. Kennedy administration. From 2009 to 2014, President Obama engaged with Cuba on issues of mutual interest but made no dramatic change in the policy of hostility he inherited from his ten predecessors. Then from 2014 to 2016, Cuba and the United States made rapid diplomatic progress toward normalizing relations, only to see President Trump reverse course in 2017, returning to a policy of hostility and regime change.

Through these dramatic pendulum swings in U.S. policy, Castro's position remained unchanged: Cuba was willing to negotiate with the United States to resolve conflicts and build cooperation on issues of mutual interest, but it would never make concessions on its internal political or economic arrangements that would impinge on Cuban sovereignty; nor would it yield in the face of U.S. threats. In his very first public statement as president, Castro offered to negotiate with the United States in a "spirit of equality, reciprocity and the fullest mutual respect." When Barack Obama called for a "new beginning" in U.S.-Cuban relations in 2009, Castro offered to talk about any topic Washington wanted, "but on an equal footing, with absolute respect for our sovereignty and for the right of the Cuban people to their self-determination." Announcing the decision to normalize relations with the United States on December 17, 2014, Castro began by reiterating "our willingness to hold a respectful dialogue with the United States on the basis of sovereign equality . . . without detriment to the national independence and self-determination of our people." And after Donald Trump's announcement that he was "cancelling" the normalization process, Castro responded by saying that Cuba was willing to continue a dialogue with Washington "on the basis of equality and respect for the sovereignty and independence of our country. . . . But it should not be expected that, in order to do so, Cuba will make concessions essential to its sovereignty and independence."

As Raúl Castro approached the end of his presidency in April 2018, the future of U.S.-Cuban relations was uncertain. Many of the political forces that led President Obama to normalize relations were still in play: public opinion favored normalization, including opinion among Republicans and Cuban Americans; the business community was still eager to enter the Cuban market; and U.S. allies in Latin America and Europe supported normalization. Those forces blunted proposals made to Trump by Cuban American conservatives to roll back Obama's policy in its entirety in early 2017, but they were unable to prevent the deterioration in relations following the reports of the mysterious "attacks" on U.S. diplomats.

In Havana, there was evidence of some disagreement among Cuban leaders about the relative balance of advantages and risks in engaging with the United States. Some clearly felt that the risks of subversion—the Trojan horse of U.S. soft power—outweighed the economic advantages of reducing sanctions, especially when most of the embargo remained in place. Would a new Cuban president, lacking the historical authority of those who founded the regime, be able to manage elite disagreements on how to move forward in relations with the United States? Raúl Castro set a clear and consistent course, which eventually succeeded in improving relations, but whether those gains would endure depended on the actions of new presidents both in Havana and in Washington.

NOTES

1. Lazaro Barredo Medina, "No Enemy Can Defeat Us," *Granma*, August 18, 2006.

2. On Cuba's negotiations with the United States, see William M. LeoGrande and Peter Kornbluh, *Back Channel to Cuba: The Hidden History of Negotiations between Washington and Havana* (Chapel Hill: University of North Carolina Press, 2015).

3. On Bush's policy, see William M. LeoGrande, "The United States and Cuba: Strained Engagement," in *Cuba, the United States, and the Post–Cold War World: The International Dimensions of the Washington-Havana Relationship*, ed. Morris Morley and Chris McGillion (Gainesville: University Press of Florida, 2005), 13–58.

4. "Cuba Policy," on the record briefing by Assistant Secretary for Western Hemisphere Affairs Thomas A. Shannon and Cuba Transition Coordinator Caleb Charles McCarry, U.S. Department of State, Washington, DC, August 11, 2006.

5. Tom Casey, acting spokesman, U.S. State Department Daily Press Briefing, August 18, 2006.

6. "Speech by Raúl Castro Ruz Given on December 2, 2006," *Vanguardia* (Villa Clara, Cuba), December 2, 2006.

7. Raúl Castro, "Speech on the 54th Anniversary of the Attack on Moncada and Carlos Manuel de Céspedes Garrisons, Camagüey, July 26, 2007," *Granma Internacional*, July 27, 2007.

8. Raúl Castro, remarks during the public segment of the Seventh Extraordinary ALBA Summit, Cumaná, Venezuela, April 16, 2009, http://www.cuba.cu/gobierno/rauldiscursos/2009/ing/c160409i.html.

9. President Barack Obama, "Remarks by the President at the Summit of the Americas Opening Ceremony, Port of Spain, Trinidad and Tobago," White House Office of the Press Secretary, April 17, 2009.

10. Organization of American States, "Resolution on Cuba, AG/RES. 2438 (XXXIX-O/09)," in Declarations and Resolutions Adopted by the General Assembly, Thirty-Ninth Regular Session, June 2 to 4, 2009, OEA/Ser.P AG/doc.5006/09 rev. 1, September 29, 2009.

11. Cable, from USINT (Farrar) to State, "GOC Signals 'Readiness to Move Forward,'" Havana 592, September 25, 2009, Wikileaks.

12. Secretary of State Hillary Rodham Clinton, "Remarks with Haitian President Rene Preval, Port-au-Prince, Haiti," U.S. Department of State, April 16, 2009.

13. Secretary of State Hillary Rodham Clinton, "Interview with Leopoldo Castillo of Globovision," Washington, DC, U.S. Department of State, July 7, 2009.

14. "Speech Given by Army General Raúl Castro Ruz, President of the Council of State and Ministers, at the 3rd Regular Session of the Seventh Legislature of the National Assem-

bly of People's Power, August 1, 2009, 'Year of the 50th Anniversary of the Revolutionary Triumph,'" Cuba.cu, http://www.cuba.cu/gobierno/rauldiscursos/2009/ing/r010809i.html.

15. LeoGrande and Kornbluh, *Back Channel to Cuba*, 381–97.

16. Raúl Castro, "Central Report to the 6th Congress of the Communist Party of Cuba," *Granma International*, April 16, 2011.

17. "Cuba and CARICOM Close Summit with Promise to Strengthen Integration," *EFE News Service*, December 9, 2014; see also H. Michael Erisman, "Evolving Cuban-CARICOM Relations: A Comparative Cost-Benefit Analysis," *Cuban Studies* 25 (1995): 207–27.

18. On China, see Mao Xianglin, Adrian H. Hearn, and Liu Weiguang, "China and Cuba: 160 Years and Looking Ahead," *Latin American Perspectives* 42 (November 2015): 140–52. On Russia, see Mervyn J. Bain, "'Back to the Future?': Cuban-Russian Relations under Raúl Castro," *Communist and Post-Communist Studies* 48 (2015): 159–68.

19. Peter Orsi, "Putin Kicks Off Latin America Tour with Cuba Stop," *Associated Press*, July 11, 2014.

20. Claudia Fonseca Sosa, "Cuba-China: An Alliance with Infinite Potential," *Granma*, July 30, 2015.

21. Patricia Rey Mallen, "China and Cuba: Skip the Ideology, Let's Talk about Money," *International Business Times*, April 24, 2014.

22. Jacques Lecarte, "A New Phase in EU-Cuba Relations," *European Parliamentary Research Service*, June 23, 2014.

23. Mirjam Donath and Louis Charbonneau, "For 23rd Time, U.N. Nations Urge End to U.S. Embargo on Cuba," *Reuters*, October 28, 2014.

24. Jeffrey Goldberg, "Fidel: 'Cuban Model Doesn't Even Work for Us Anymore,'" *Atlantic*, September 8, 2010.

25. LeoGrande and Kornbluh, *Back Channel to Cuba*, 421–47.

26. "Ben Rhodes Explains Where Obama Stands on Cuba," interview with Jeffrey Goldberg of the *Atlantic*, YouTube, March 11, 2016, https://www.youtube.com/watch?v=-8zL5DxNwn0&feature=youtu.be.

27. Barack Obama, "Statement by the President on Cuba Policy Changes," White House, Office of the Press Secretary, December 17, 2014.

28. Raúl Castro, "Statement by the Cuban President," *Granma*, December 17, 2014.

29. Raúl Castro, "The Blockade Is the Most Serious Obstacle to Our Economic Development and the Welfare of the Cuban People," Statement to the Press, *Granma*, March 21, 2016.

30. "Fact Sheet: Treasury and Commerce Announce Regulatory Amendments to the Cuba Sanctions," U.S. Department of the Treasury, Press Center, January 15, 2015.

31. Secretary of the Treasury Jack Lew, "Statement by Secretary Jacob J. Lew on Amendments to the Cuban Assets Control Regulations," U.S. Department of the Treasury, Office of Public Affairs, January 15, 2015.

32. Sergio Alejandro Gómez, "The Blockade Is an Outdated Policy and Must End," *Granma*, July 20, 2016.

33. U.S. Department of Commerce, "Treasury and Commerce Announce Further Amendments to Cuba Sanctions Regulations," U.S. Treasury Department, Office of Public Affairs, October 14, 2016; "Presidential Policy Directive—United States–Cuba Normalization," White House, Office of the Press Secretary, October 14, 2016.

34. Julie Hirschfeld Davis, "Obama, Cementing New Ties with Cuba, Lifts Limits on Cigars and Rum," *New York Times*, October 14, 2016.

35. "Declaración del Buró Nacional de la ANAP sobre medida del gobierno de EE.UU.," *Granma*, May 4, 2016.

36. Fidel Castro, "Brother Obama," *Granma*, March 28, 2016.

37. Dario Machado, "The 'Good' Obama," *Granma*, March 30, 2016.

38. "Cuba Minister Calls Obama Visit 'an Attack' as Communists Defend Ideology," *Reuters*, April 18, 2016.

39. Raúl Castro, "The Development of the National Economy, along with the Struggle for Peace, and Our Ideological Resolve, Constitute the Party's Principal Missions" *Granma*, April 18, 2016.

40. Joshua Partlow and Peyton M. Craighill, "Poll Shows Vast Majority of Cubans Welcome Closer Ties with U.S.," *Washington Post*, April 8, 2015.

41. See, for example, "Growing Public Support for U.S. Ties with Cuba—and an End to the Trade Embargo," Pew Research Center, July 21, 2016, http://www.people-press.org/2015/07/21/growing-public-support-for-u-s-ties-with-cuba-and-an-end-to-the-trade-embargo.

42. William M. LeoGrande, "The Last Gasp of the Cuban Collapsniks," *Foreign Policy*, February 25, 2015, http://foreignpolicy.com/2015/02/25/the-last-gasp-of-the-cuban-collapseniks.

43. Team Fix, "Transcript: The Post-Univision Democratic Debate, Annotated," *Washington Post*, March 9, 2016, https://www.washingtonpost.com/news/the-fix/wp/2016/03/09/transcript-the-post-univision-democratic-debate-annotated/#annotations:8797202.

44. Hillary Clinton, "Remarks in Miami on the Cuba Embargo," July 31, 2005, https://www.hillaryclinton.com/post/remarks-miami-cuba-embargo.

45. Jeremy Diamond, "Trump Backs U.S.-Cuba Diplomatic Relations, *CNN*, September 8, 2015.

46. "Republican Platform 2016," GOP.com https://www.gop.com/the-2016-republican-party-platform.

47. Jeremy Diamond, "Trump Shifts on Cuba, Says He Would Reverse Obama's Deal," *CNN*, September 16, 2016.

48. Patricia Mazzei and Douglas Hanks, "Trump Tries, Once Again, to Win Over Miami Cubans," *Miami Herald*, October 25, 2016; "Trump on Employees Scouting Deals in Cuba," *Naked Politics* (blog), *Miami Herald*, October 24, 2016.

49. Patricia Mazzei and Nicholas Nehamas, "Florida's Hispanic Voter Surge Wasn't Enough for Clinton," *Miami Herald*, November 9, 2016.

50. Donald J. Trump, "President-Elect Donald J. Trump Statement on the Passing of Fidel Castro," *Trump-Pence Transition Team*, November 28, 2016.

51. Patricia Mazzei, "Trump Pledges to 'Terminate' Opening to Cuba Absent 'Better Deal,'" *Miami Herald*, November 28, 2016.

52. See, for example, the comments by Josefina Vidal, Foreign Ministry director general for the United States, in Gómez, "The Blockade Is an Outdated Policy and Must End."

53. "Envía Raúl mensaje de felicitación al Presidente electo Trump," *Granma*, November 10, 2016.

54. "Trump gana las elecciones en EE.UU.," *Granma*, November 9, 2016.

55. Ministerio de las Fuerzas Armadas Revolucionaria, "Ejercicio estratégico bastión 2016 del 16 al 18 de noviembre," *Granma*, November 9, 2016.

56. "Cuba Hopes Trump Maintains Dialogue," *Havana Times*, December 9, 2016.

57. Helen Yaffe and Jonathan Watts, "Top Diplomatic Negotiator in Cuba Warns Trump," *Guardian*, January 17, 2017.

58. Raúl Castro, "Never Has It Been More Necessary to Effectively Advance along the Path of Unity," *Granma*, January 25, 2017.

59. Nora Gámez Torres, "Trump Will Not Announce Highly Anticipated Changes in Cuba Policy," *Miami Herald*, May 18, 2017.

60. Nora Gámez Torres, "Havana Lashes Out against Trump's May 20 Message to the Cuban People," *Miami Herald*, May 22, 2017.

61. Donald J. Trump, "Remarks by President Trump on the Policy of the United States towards Cuba," White House, Office of the Press Secretary, June 16, 2017.

62. "National Security Presidential Memorandum on Strengthening the Policy of the United States toward Cuba," White House, Office of the Press Secretary, June 16, 2017.

63. Government of Cuba, "Any Strategy Directed toward Changing Cuba's Constitutional Order Is Condemned to Failure," *Granma*, June 19, 2017.

64. Raúl Castro, "We Will Continue to Advance along the Path Freely Chosen by Our People," *Granma*, July 17, 2017.

65. Frances Robles and Kirk Sempleaug, "'Health Attacks' on U.S. Diplomats in Cuba Baffle Both Countries," *New York Times*, September 11, 2017.

66. Sarah Marsh, "Cuba Calls Trump's U.N. Address 'Unacceptable and Meddling,'" *Reuters*, September 19, 2017.

67. Tracy Wilkinson, "At Cuba's Urgent Request, Tillerson Meets with His Counterpart over Attacks at U.S. Embassy in Havana," *Los Angeles Times*, September 26, 2017.

68. Julia Manchester, "Rubio: US Should Kick Out Cuban Diplomats," *Hill*, September 29, 2017.

69. Gardiner Harris, Julie Hirschfeld Davis, and Ernesto Londoño, "U.S. Expels 15 Cuban Diplomats, in Latest Sign Détente May Be Ending," *New York Times*, October 3, 2017.

70. Ministry of Foreign Relations of Cuba, "Cuba Has Never Perpetrated, Nor Will It Ever Perpetrate Attacks of Any Sort against Diplomatic Officials or Their Relatives, without Any Exception," *Granma*, October 3, 2017; Nora Gámez Torres, "Cuba's Vice President Says U.S. Reports of Sonic Attacks against Diplomats Is 'Tall Tales,'" *Miami Herald*, October 9, 2017.

71. Ivan Nechepurenko, "Russia Seeks to Reopen Military Bases in Vietnam and Cuba," *New York Times*, October 7, 2016.

11

Canada and Cuba

John M. Kirk and Raúl Rodríguez

> "During the 20th century, communism's poisonous ideology and ruthless practices slowly bled into countries around the world. . . . Evil comes in many forms. . . . Whatever it calls itself, Nazism, Marxist-Leninism, today terrorism—they all have one thing in common: the destruction, the end of human liberty"
>
> —Stephen Harper, May 2014

> "Canada is back, my friends."
>
> —Justin Trudeau, November 2015

Canadian-Cuban relations have shown important elements of continuity over the past decades. Successive governments, both Liberal and Conservative, during and after the Cold War, have not questioned the legitimacy of the Cuban government. Moreover, despite ideological disagreements, Canadian governments have always opposed economic sanctions against the island and have chosen to engage, albeit within a set framework of rules, with the government of Cuba. This can be seen in the state of bilateral relations during the governments of Stephen Harper (Conservative, 2006–2015) and Justin Trudeau (Liberal, 2015–present).

Throughout the Harper years, the official Canadian position toward Cuba was extremely negative, with both Harper and government spokesmen criticizing Cuba, particularly its human rights record and approach toward democracy. Canadian foreign policy steadily moved away from its traditional liberal internationalist approach to a more Manichean worldview. At the international level this is reflected in the fact that Harper privileged bilateral relations with "key" countries like the United States.[1] Basically, then, Harper's Cuba policy entailed a de-emphasis on engagement and dialogue in favor of a policy of increasing ideological confrontation.

Then came the Liberal electoral victory in October 2015 involving a dramatic sweep (winning 184 seats and a majority government), and on November 4 the Forty-Second Parliament was inaugurated. Since then official Canada-Cuba relations have undergone a significant overhaul, with a variety of events that would have been unexpected under the Harper government. This chapter analyzes the evolution of diplomatic relations in Ottawa-Havana ties, providing examples to illustrate this remarkable recent development and suggesting reasons for this change of direction.

FROM STORMY DAYS TO "SUNNY WAYS"

There are many dramatic illustrations of this reenergized bilateral relationship, most noticeably in the increase of high-level official visits. For example, while Stephen Harper never ventured to Cuba, Justin Trudeau and his wife, Sophie Grégoire Trudeau, traveled to Cuba in mid-November 2016. Likewise, while there had never been an official visit by a Canadian navy ship in over fifty years, in November 2016 the HMCS *Fredericton* visited Cuba. Moreover, in February 2017, at the massive Twenty-Sixth International Book Fair, Canada was the guest of honor (*país invitado*), with over seventy Canadian authors and publishers—including some thirty from Quebec—participating. There were also some noticeable initiatives undertaken by the Quebec government (another significant first), with visits by International Relations Minister Christine St-Pierre during the book fair, following up on a visit by Premier Philippe Couillard in September 2016, which, among other results, produced a tentative agreement to open a Quebec trade representative office in Havana.

Indeed, within a few months of Justin Trudeau's election, Cuba's foreign minister, Bruno Rodríguez Parrilla, had visited Ottawa and Quebec City, while the Canadian minister of small business and tourism, Bardish Chagger, spoke at the 2016 Feria Internacional de Turismo, Cuba's annual tourist fair, where Canada was the guest country of honor. "Sunny ways"—as Trudeau announced on the night of his victory speech—were returning to the bilateral relationship.

Contrast that with the approach used by Stephen Harper. Speaking at the Summit of the Americas in Port of Spain, Trinidad and Tobago, in April 2009, he noted, "We can't turn a blind eye to the fact that Cuba is a communist nation, and we want to see progress on freedom, democracy and human rights, as well as on economic matters."[2] Harper was adamantly opposed to the participation of Cuba at the Summits of the Americas until all of the countries of Latin America and the Caribbean warned him and President Barack Obama that they would boycott future events unless Cuba was invited to participate. At that point the leaders of the United States and Canada acquiesced, reluctantly.

The Harper Policy on Cuba

There were consistent signals of Harper's animosity to Cuba throughout his mandate. On May 21, 2008, for instance, the government issued a statement expressing

Canada's solidarity with the struggle for freedom of the Cuban people. This was an unprecedented and uncalled-for action, on the anniversary of a historical event, welcomed by Cuban exiles but reviled by Havana (where May 20, 1902, has a rather different connotation). Moreover, in January 2009 Peter Kent, then minister of state for foreign affairs (with responsibilities for Latin America), offered the official government perspective on Cuba and explained that many Canadians "are too willing to accept a candy-coated vision of what life in Cuba really is. . . . Canadians should be realistic. . . . There certainly have been improvements in many ways, but it is still a dictatorship, any way you package it."[3]

A common theme in the Harper criticism was the question of human rights in Cuba, and on several occasions government representatives condemned the Cuban record. Showing selective indignation, however, Canada steadfastly ignored abuses carried out by its U.S. ally in Guantánamo, despite widespread reports of abuses. This inconsistency was brought into sharp relief when six former foreign ministers of Canada (both Liberal and Progressive Conservative) took Harper to task for his silence on abuses there. They (Joe Clark, Lloyd Axworthy, Flora MacDonald, Bill Graham, John Manley, and Pierre Pettigrew) condemned the abuses in the U.S. prison camp and encouraged a strong government reaction: "We urge Prime Minister Harper to speak up. He must press the U.S. government to deal with the Guantánamo detainees, and all other detainees held in the 'war on terror' in a manner consistent with international human rights standards. He should appeal to the United States to respect the rule of law and close Guantánamo."[4] The request was ignored by the Harper government.

It is worth noting, however, that in later years of the Harper period there were several visits to Cuba by Canadian government representatives. The minister for the Americas and consular services, Diane Ablonczy, visited in early 2012 and upon her return spoke positively of the potential for enhanced bilateral trade. This visit contrasted vividly with that of her predecessor, Peter Kent, which had to be postponed due to the heated (and undiplomatic) references he made to Cuba. In addition, Deputy Minister for Foreign Affairs Morris Rosenberg visited briefly, and in 2013 then foreign minister John Baird spent two days there.

Far more important than these fleeting visits by Canadian officials, however, were the close people-to-people ties between Canadians and Cubans, a relationship which had been established in the early 1990s, when Canadian tourists started to travel to Cuba in noticeable numbers. Also significant are the deeply rooted trade relations, originating in the early nineteenth century when salt fish, potatoes, and lumber were exported from the Atlantic provinces, while sugar, molasses, and rum returned to Canada. It is also worth remembering that 2015 marked the seventieth anniversary of uninterrupted diplomatic relations between the two countries.[5]

The Harper government ignored the natural advantages that Canada has in its relationship with Cuba and the potential to build upon these. In 1962, for instance, Canada and Mexico were the only two countries not to break relations with Cuba, despite tremendous pressure from Washington. In 1976 Pierre Trudeau became the first North Atlantic Treaty Organization (NATO) leader to visit Cuba—against the backdrop of the Cold War. He and Fidel Castro maintained a cordial friendship for many years, and it was no surprise when the latter was invited to be an honorary pallbearer at Trudeau's funeral in 2000. In addition, the principal foreign investor in Cuba is Sherritt International, which is involved mainly with Cuba in nickel exploration and development, as well as in oil and gas extraction and power generation—one of the few Canadian companies in Cuba.

There is also serious academic interest in Canada on the island, where there are six Canadian studies centers. Several Canadian universities also have strong academic ties with their Cuban counterparts, with well-established Study Abroad programs in Havana. Another telling illustration of Canada-Cuba ties is the annual Terry Fox run in which some 2 million Cubans participate. It is named after an unlikely Canadian hero, a one-legged runner who set out to run across Canada in order to raise money for medical research and succumbed in June 1981 after running 3,390 miles. In March 2017 Cubans ran in the twentieth annual Terry Fox run, supporting his cancer research goals. Finally, and perhaps most important of all, Canadian tourists are the single largest group of tourists to Cuba—making up almost 40 percent of the 4.1 million who visited Cuba in 2016.

Despite these natural advantages, the policy toward Cuba during the Harper years can be typified as one which placed a rather dogmatic conservative ideology before all else. The fact that bilateral trade has remained at about $1 billion annually—or about fourteen hours of one day of trade between Canada and the United States—was probably also a related factor, since it is not a particularly lucrative market for Canadian businesses. In part this is due to the punishing U.S. legislation designed to prevent foreign investment in Cuba. Sadly, during the Harper years the relationship was occasionally affected by official pettiness. Following the (rather undiplomatic) comments of Peter Kent noted earlier, the Cuban government suggested that he postpone his visit to Cuba—which was changed from May to November 2009. A few weeks after the visit was postponed, Minister of Foreign Investment Rodrigo Malmierca was scheduled to attend the annual shareholders' meeting of Sherritt International in Toronto. He was unable to do so, however, since Canadian government officials issued the visa the same day as the meeting, thereby not allowing him sufficient time to fly to Toronto.

The government in Havana also noted another relevant position of the Harper government: its lack of action in the extraterritorial application of U.S. sanctions on Cuba, despite having the instruments to counteract such external interference.[6] The case of MasterCard illustrates this.[7] In 2007 a subsidiary of the Bank of America purchased CU Electronic Transaction Services (CUETS), a major credit card service provider of MasterCard in Canada. CUETS was thus forced to comply with U.S. law, invalidating the use of MasterCard in Cuba and thus inconveniencing Canadian tourists who planned to use their credit card on vacations.

This rather churlish approach by Ottawa to Cuba continued in 2012 and 2013, when Ambassador Teresita Vicente finished her term as Cuban ambassador to Canada. As had traditionally been the case, the Cuban government sought diplomatic permission for her successor, Julio Garmendía Peña, to replace her as ambassador—a process which normally takes six to eight weeks and is—or should be—a formality. To show its displeasure with Cuba, however, the Harper government decided to delay its permission to Ambassador Garmendía for almost eight months. This apparently was in retaliation for the arrest of two Armenian Canadian businessmen in Havana, later found guilty of corruption.

This same hard-line approach by the Harper government can be seen in the position taken at the Summits of the Americas in Trinidad and Tobago (2009) and Colombia (2012). In the latter summit the prime minister made clear his opposition to the participation of Cuba in any future summits, arguing that this was based upon his government's "principled position." In Colombia, faced with the opposition of the thirty-three members of the Community of Latin American and Caribbean States, he defended his position by claiming that it was based on solid principles: "And when we take principled positions, we are prepared to argue that and discuss them. But obviously we don't have our positions dictated by any one country, or frankly, by any group of countries."[8]

Cuba responded quietly to the rather aggressive tone emanating from the Harper government, which continued to see the Cuban government as undemocratic.[9] By the time of the Seventh Summit of the Americas in Panama, Havana had already established excellent relations with all countries of the Americas, and Cuba's hemispheric prestige had increased considerably due to its role in regional organizations—especially because of its leading role as a mediator in the Colombia peace process. Moreover, as of December 17, 2014, Cuba had already agreed with Washington to move toward renewing diplomatic relations (broken by Washington in January 1961) and to open embassies in both countries. Faced with this reality, the Harper government was obliged to accept Cuba's presence in Panama City as a fait accompli.

Stephen Harper grudgingly came to accept the new reality of U.S.-Cuban relations and by extension concluded that the position which his government had staked out was now totally isolated. It was therefore in Canada's best interests—when faced with the opposition on this matter of every country in Latin America and the Caribbean—to accept the inevitable and make as brave a face as possible in light of the diplomatic reality.

The Summit of the Americas in April 2015 marks a significant stage in the decision of Stephen Harper to recognize that Cuba's participation in Panama was inevitable, after it had been demanded by all countries of Latin America and the Caribbean, including some stalwart allies of Ottawa and Washington. Speaking with journalists, Harper outlined the shift in Canada's position: "I have become convinced, our government has become convinced, that we are at a point in the hemisphere, and at a point in Cuba . . . where engagement is more likely to lead us to where we want to go than continued isolation."[10] It was clearly a significant departure from the former government position.

This was a rather safe assertion by the Canadian government since Washington and Havana had already decided to reopen diplomatic relations and had announced this in simultaneous television broadcasts on December 17, 2014. That said, it clearly went against the conservative worldview of Harper. He justified his decision by adding, "We are not, by any means, unconcerned about the lack of democratic space and human rights abuses in Cuba. We've always been clear on that. And we will continue to be clear on that."[11]

Some context is pertinent here, because the strategy employed by Stephen Harper in many ways is reflected in his government's approach to foreign relations in general. During his leadership Canada withdrew from several multilateral arrangements, as seen in its decision in 2009 to jettison the 1997 Kyoto Protocol on curbing greenhouse gases. Similarly, it opposed the conversion of the unwieldy UN Commission on Human Rights into the more pragmatic Human Rights Council. Ironically, perhaps, Cuba was elected to the council with the support of more countries than Canada. The Harper government reduced Canada's peacekeeping role, for which the Lester B. Pearson government had received the Nobel Peace Prize: whereas in 1990 Canada had 1,002 soldiers serving in this function (the largest contingent in the world), in 2015 it had just 116, ranking below Paraguay and above Mali.[12] Foreign aid dropped 14 percent between 2013 and 2016, as did the budget for international land mine clearance (from $49 million in 2007–2008 to $7 million in 2013–2014).

In general, the Harper government realigned Canadian foreign policy with that of the United States, as is particularly noticeable in the approach toward the Middle East. In 2012, for example, Ottawa broke relations with Iran, closed its embassy, and expelled Iranian diplomats—a policy which the Trudeau government has stated that it plans to reverse. The bilateral relationship with Israel and Ukraine now became particularly important for the Harper government, reflecting also the large and influential Jewish and Ukrainian populations in Canada, as well as U.S. goals. The relationship with China was particularly complex, since in his early years Harper had vociferously condemned the Beijing government over human rights matters, while toward the end of his mandate economic concerns clearly took precedence over ideology.[13] In November 2014 he made his third visit to China, underlining the clear evolution of his thoughts on dealing with Beijing.

Free trade, not development aid, was his government's priority. To a certain extent this was mirrored in his decision in 2013 to close the prestigious Canadian International Development Agency, reduce its budget, and merge it with the newly formed Department of Foreign Affairs, International Trade and Development. By contrast the incoming Trudeau government simplified the department's title to Global Affairs Canada. In the end Canada reaped few benefits from the Harper foreign policy approach, as can be seen from its failed attempt in 2010 to win a temporary seat on the UN Security Council, losing to Portugal. This was the first time in Canadian diplomatic history that it had failed to do so and clearly represented a low point in Canadian international prestige.

In many ways the dramatically changed nature of Cuban-U.S. relations since December 2014 forced Prime Minister Harper to withdraw his stern opposition to Cuba's participation in the 2015 Summit of the Americas and indeed to tone down his criticisms of Cuba in general. In providing the venues for secret U.S.-Cuban negotiations, a more pragmatic Harper emerged, since it appeared that Washington was interested in negotiations with Cuba in both the bilateral and multilateral hemispheric context. Significantly the Canadian prime minister pointed out that Canada's responsibility was only to provide a secret venue.

Much has been made of Canada's role in these negotiations. In fact there were seven meetings on Canadian soil (mainly in Ottawa but also in Toronto) over eighteen months, the objective of which was to negotiate a resumption of diplomatic relations. In congratulating both countries on the agreement, Prime Minister Harper also reiterated his own ideological perspective: "Canada supports a future for Cuba that fully embraces the fundamental values of freedom, democracy and human rights and the rule of law."[14]

The obvious question related to this is why, despite its years of fierce criticism, Ottawa apparently relented in its criticism of the Cuban revolutionary government and facilitated the reopening of diplomatic relations. There are two schools of thought on this matter. One is that officials in the Foreign Affairs Ministry convinced Harper of the need to limit Canada's isolation in regard to the official government position on Cuba and instead take advantage of the historical ties with Cuba—and to do so before Washington monopolized the North American relationship with the island. While it would be pleasing to think that Harper amended his view and saw the value of bringing Cuba into the inter-American fold, regardless of his personal deeply felt opposition, a more likely explanation is that he was requested to do so by Washington and saw the potential value of accepting the request from the Obama administration.

Whatever the explanation for the decision made by Ottawa to facilitate these high-level negotiations, there is no doubt that the actions of the Canadian government were both constructive and highly appreciated by the governments of Cuba and the United States. Common sense had finally prevailed, and Canada had played a significant role in this process. When Justin Trudeau won the next federal election, the groundwork had thus been laid to build upon this initiative.

The Approach to Cuba of Justin Trudeau

Within a few weeks of taking power, Justin Trudeau revealed a clearly different form of proactive diplomacy, attending the G20 summit in Turkey, the Asia-Pacific Economic Cooperation summit in the Philippines, a Commonwealth summit in Malta, and the UN Climate Change Conference in Paris. Since that time his activist bent has continued to be seen in many ways, ranging from the government sponsoring forty thousand Syrian refugees to come to Canada to dropping the visa requirement for Mexicans. Peacekeeping on officially sponsored UN missions is again on the agenda, probably in Africa, and clearly the significance of China has grown for the new government. Liberal internationalism, with a strong emphasis on multilateralism, is clearly a major component of the new government's foreign policy agenda. This approach to consensus building, humanitarianism, and multilateral initiatives is also seen in his fresh and quite distinctive approach to Cuba.

The visit of the HMCS *Fredericton* to Havana in November 2016 is in many ways symbolic of the distinctive new policy of Canada toward Cuba. For decades suggestions had been made by different government departments that a navy ship should visit the island. After all, navy vessels from several NATO countries had done so over the years. But all recommendations had been firmly rebuffed by the Harper government—until now. The visit was brief—just a couple of days, following a training exercise off the coast of Florida and before continuing to Cartagena, Colombia, and Veracruz, Mexico. But the visit was steeped in symbolism, and coming just a few days after Justin Trudeau had traveled to Cuba, it showed categorically Ottawa's new approach to Cuba.

The Feria del Libro in February 2017 was particularly impressive, especially since Canada was the *país invitado*, literally the "invited country," to the book fair. It should be noted that this is a massive affair, with over four hundred thousand attending the Havana portion in February 2017. The inauguration took place with the participation of famed novelist Margaret Atwood and partner Graeme Gibson, Speaker of the Senate George Furey, and Cuban minister of culture Abel Prieto. A musical group from Iqaluit, Nunavut, the Jerry Cans, gave two concerts during the first week of the festivities, including a nationally televised gala. Several Canadian authors participated in the *feria*, giving readings and participating in panel discussions. They included Giller Prize winner Madeleine Thien, Constance Brissenden, Margaret Pokiak-Fenton, Christy Jordan-Fenton, Michael Isaac, and Rawi Hage.

During the ten days of the *feria* in Havana (February 9 to 19), the Canadian presence in Havana was extremely visible. The tickets to the event bore the maple leaf imprint, and large Canadian flags were very noticeable at the two host pavilions, emphasizing the impressive presence of Canada. There were several social sciences seminars and a photo exhibit highlighting the cooperation activities of Canada. The Quebec delegation was also extremely successful, with Quebec Day on February 12 being inaugurated by the provincial minister of international relations. Just as there had been a dialogue with Margaret Atwood and Graeme Gibson, there was also a series of conversations with Québécois writers (Maya Ombasic, Louise Desjardins, Rose Eliceiry, Alexandre Belliard, Luc Chartrand, Jocelyne Saucier, and others), while folk music group Les Soeurs Boulay gave a concert that was well received. In all the Quebec group consisted of thirty-two authors, editors. and artists.

Minister St-Pierre was extremely active at the Feria del Libro, using it as a means of both promoting Québécois culture and meeting with government ministers. This is seen in her meetings with Abel Prieto, minister of culture, and Rodrigo Malmierca, minister of foreign trade and foreign investment. She also visited the National Center for the Prevention of HIV/AIDS, with which the Quebec Comité de Solidarité de Trois-Rivieres has worked since 2015. Their project has focused on the LGBTQ population in Bayamo, and government funding will allow nine young Québécois to spend time there, while ten Cubans will visit Quebec to learn about the Canadian approach to the LGBTQ population.

Overlapping with the Feria del Libro was the annual International Seminar in Canadian Studies at the University of Havana. This seminar has been in place since 2000 and brings together faculty and students from other Canadian studies programs on the island. Canadian literature was the main focus of the seminar, with masterly performances from, among others, Canadian writers Thomas King (author of the prize-winning *The Inconvenient Indian*), Helen Hoy, and Sheree Fitch. A keynote lecture was given by Hal Klepak (Royal Military College of Canada), with the participation of Karen Dubinsky (Queen's University) and several students from Dalhousie University who were spending the fall term at the Facultad Latinoamericana de Ciencias Sociales–Cuba, partner for two decades with Dalhousie's Study Abroad program.

Culture and sports are always helpful supplements to diplomatic activities, and the bilateral relationship is no exception. For many years Canadian tourists have been coming to Cuba to take classes in salsa and percussion, and countless high school bands and sports teams have been doing the same. One of the longest-running cultural programs is "Los Primos," now in its twentieth year. The Nova Scotia–based group has raised over $500,000 for music education, collected and sent over seven hundred musical instruments to Cuban schools, and organized over forty exchange trips, bringing Cuban musicians to Nova Scotia while sending young Nova Scotian musicians to the island. Well-known Cuban singer Augusto Enríquez and local musician-bandleader Jeff Goodspeed led the 2017 initiative, the goal of which was to send over seventy Nova Scotian musicians and family members for the Romerías in Holguín in May 2017. In Quebec there has also been a growing interest in cultural activities, and in October 2016 there was a particularly successful tour of Cuba by Montreal's Les Grand Ballets Canadiens, which had been invited to the island by Cuba's first lady of ballet, Alicia Alonso.

Given the passion for baseball that exists in both Cuba and Quebec, it was not surprising to see that this has also become an invaluable conduit for improving bilateral relations. In recent years Cuban baseball players have come to play in the Quebec league following an agreement in 2014 between the Cuban baseball federation and the Quebec Capitales franchise. A greater indication of Cuba's interest in "baseball diplomacy" came in June 2016 when the national baseball team flew to Montreal to play nineteen games in the Can-Am league, with games in Quebec City, Trois-Rivières, and Ottawa before moving to three locations in the United States. In addition to preparing Cuban athletes for the 2017 World Baseball Classic in Japan, the baseball tour was a confidence-building measure in strengthening diplomatic relations: "It's another example of the excellent relations between Canada and Cuba. . . . It is also a sign of the openness to improve relations between Cuba and the United States."[15]

Since the election of Justin Trudeau, there has been a striking development in the way in which both the federal government and that of Quebec have developed their relationship with Havana. In November 2015, for instance, International Relations Minister Christine St-Pierre visited Cuba, where she met several key government players in economics and politics. Cuban trade relations with Quebec are very poor; in 2014 commercial exchange was only $83 million, with $81.7 million resulting from Quebec exports.[16] The following year this increased slightly to $85.6 million, with Cuba in seventh place in terms of Quebec's exports to Latin America. Principal exports to Cuba include copper wire, pork, and automobile spare parts, while major imports from Cuba are coffee, cigars, and rum. Clearly there is room for improvement in bilateral trade.

Six months later Cuba reciprocated with the visit of Foreign Affairs Minister Bruno Rodríguez Parrilla, who spent time with ministers in Ottawa and Quebec City. He was particularly active visiting members of the Canadian government, including his counterpart at the time, Stéphane Dion, Immigration Minister John McCallum, International Development Minister Marie-Claude Bibeau, leader of the government in Parliament Dominic Leblanc, as well as Jean Lebel, president of the International Development Research Centre, and the Speakers of the House of Commons, Geoff Regan, and of the Senate, George Furey.

In Quebec City, Rodríguez was warmly received by Quebec premier Philippe Couillard (for the first time in Quebec-Cuba history) and by Minister of Foreign Relations St-Pierre. Couillard noted the political will of his government to strengthen relations with Cuba: "The government of Québec grants a great importance to the development of relations with Cuba. It is important to combine forces to develop a lasting partnership. We hope to develop a policy of diversified trade, and to take advantage of complementary interests in science and research." For her part the foreign affairs minister also referred to the potential for high-level scientific exchanges and infrastructure development.

Two bilateral political developments were also discussed. One revolves around the opening of a Quebec government office in Havana to represent and support initiatives of the province in Cuba. This is a concept which has been discussed on several other occasions, but this time the political will seems stronger. Also illustrative of the strong interest of the Quebec government in strengthening ties was the decision to extend the mandate of the general delegate of Quebec in Mexico to also now include Cuba. The official press release from the office of St-Pierre noted that "the development of partnerships and the successful establishment of projects between Québec and Cuba constituted one of the government's priorities for the following year."[17]

In September 2016 the Quebec-Cuba relationship developed further when Premier Philippe Couillard visited Havana, where he was received by President Raúl Castro. He met again with Foreign Minister Rodríguez, as well as with Minister for International Trade and Foreign Investment Rodrigo Malmierca and Ricardo Cabrisas, vice president of the Council of Ministers and minister of economy and planning. Trade and investment, along with negotiations about scientific cooperation and institutional collaboration, featured prominently in the discussions. Attention was given to the opening of the new offices of the successful Quebec transportation and heavy equipment company Terracam Équipement International.

In all, the commercial delegation headed by Premier Couillard consisted of forty-four businesses and institutions coming from fourteen regions of Quebec. Agreements were also signed between the Institute of Tourism and Hotel Management of Quebec, the Cuban Ministry of Tourism, and the national program for training personnel in the industry (FORMATUR) to train personnel in hotel management and tourism. A memorandum of understanding was also signed by the Quebec Research Institute (Les Fonds de Recherche du Québec) and BioCubaFarma, the largest biotechnology/pharmaceutical industrial group in Cuba, to work in a tripartite partnership with China exploring brain research, including brain imaging and neuroinformatics. In February 2017 Minister St-Pierre took advantage of her role at the Feria del Libro to attend the launching of this tripartite research group.

Commenting on the success of the visit, Quebec premier Couillard noted, "The friendship which united Québec and Cuba has today reached a new stage of development. The welcome which we have received again confirms that Québec has a place here in Cuba. My exchanges with President Castro have also confirmed the interest of the Cuban government in the expertise of Québec, especially in the areas of renewable energy, construction, and social economics." For her part St-Pierre noted other areas of potential cooperation, including scientific innovation, culture, education and training, energy, climate change, agriculture, and tourism.[18] In terms of the larger picture, it is striking to see how the governments of both Canada and Quebec have worked in parallel, without any criticism of the other's role or strategic interests in Cuba. During the Harper years, by contrast, there was significant tension between the governments in Ottawa and Quebec City.

In 2017 several Canadian diplomats were affected by the alleged "sonic attacks" that had also targeted their U.S. counterparts. A Royal Canadian Mounted Police investigative team traveled to Havana, and Canadian embassy personnel were examined by Canadian medical personnel. In contrast to the Donald Trump administration (which withdrew 60 percent of American embassy personnel from Havana, obliged a similar number of Cuban diplomats to leave Cuba's Washington embassy, and warned American tourists about the health dangers of traveling to Cuba), the Canadian government made clear that it saw no danger to Canadian diplomats or tourists. The normal relationship between Canada and Cuba continues, much as it has for decades.

CONCLUDING REMARKS

We can safely conclude that there is an underlying pool of goodwill and empathy between Cuba and Canada that has been unaltered, despite the highs and lows of the political relationship. It is clear that, following almost a decade of strained diplomatic relations during the Harper years, Canada-Cuba relations have entered a new era following the election of Justin Trudeau. Perhaps no greater illustration can be seen than his official communiqué on the death of Fidel Castro. The statement, issued on November 26, 2016, noted, "Fidel Castro was a larger than life leader who served his people for almost half a century. A legendary revolutionary and orator, Mr. Castro made significant improvements to the education and healthcare of his island nation. While a controversial figure, both Mr. Castro's supporters and detractors recognized his tremendous dedication and love for the Cuban people who had a deep and lasting affection for 'el Comandante.'"[19]

The statement of Justin Trudeau was also very personal, commenting on the profound friendship between Castro and his father ("I know my father was very proud to call him a friend and I had the opportunity to meet Fidel when my father passed away") and ended in mourning the death of "this remarkable leader." In many ways it is a fitting reflection of what Fidel Castro himself had noted in 1994 following a dinner with a delegation of Nova Scotian businesspeople, headed by Premier John Savage. "In this world where rich nations have intervened everywhere—especially in Africa and Latin America—the Canadians have not intervened anywhere. So what are the Canadians? And I say that they are good people, wonderful people. And for all these reasons we Cubans are proud to be their friends."[20] The potential of what Justin Trudeau has termed "sunny ways" in his government's approach to politics can perhaps be applied to bilateral relations with Cuba after almost a decade of tension and dark days.

NOTES

1. Colin Robertson, "Stephen Harper's World View," *Politics*, December 15, 2013, http://www.ipolitics.ca/author/robcolin (accessed March 26, 2017).
2. Ria Taitt, "Canada: Embargo Up to U.S., Cuba," *Miami Herald*, April 19, 2009.
3. Mike Blanchfield, "Canada Can Play a Role in Emerging Cuba: MP," *National Post*, January 6, 2009, A6.
4. Joe Clark et al., "Speak Up, Mr. Harper—Guantánamo Is a Disgrace," *Globe and Mail*, February 1, 2007, A15.
5. For a study of the historical ties between Canada and Cuba, see John M. Kirk and Peter McKenna, *Canada-Cuba Relations: The Other Good Neighbor Policy* (Gainesville: University Press of Florida, 1997).
6. The Foreign Extraterritorial Measures Act (FEMA) was enacted in 1984 to block the extraterritorial application of U.S. laws to Canadian corporations. The legislation gained more relevance after the U.S. Congress passed the Helms-Burton Act in 1996, since it added extra elements to support U.S. sanctions.
7. See Lana Wylie, *Reassessing Canada's Relationship with Cuba in an Era of Change* (Toronto: Canadian International Council, 2010), 15. In addition, several Canadian banks have yielded to U.S. pressures by rejecting business possibilities on the island and closing accounts with clients involved in business with Cuba.

8. Mark Kennedy, "Division on Cuba Ends Summit of the Americas on Frosty Note," *Ottawa Citizen*, April 16, 2012, A1. An alternative view from a Canadian journalist, Carol Goar, was more critical: "Canada has metamorphosed from a middle power that championed international co-operation and led the world in the campaign to eliminate deadly landmines into a country that seeks to be known for its military might. The Tories equate diplomacy with weakness, negotiation with naiveté. Canada's prime minister is the most bellicose member of the Group of Seven." See Carol Goar, "Stephen Harper Has Altered the Face of Canada," *Star*, June 28, 2015.

9. In 2012 he noted clearly his position about Cuba's potential role in future summits: "We do believe that the Summit of the Americas should be restricted to democratic countries and that Cuba should be encouraged to come as a democratic country in the future—It's our contention that the Canadian policy is the way to get that kind of result." Kennedy, "Division on Cuba."

10. Mark Kennedy, "Harper Sidesteps 'Principle' to Cautiously Pull Cuba Out of Isolation," *Ottawa Citizen*, April 12, 2015.

11. Ibid.

12. Data in this paragraph are taken from Mark MacKinnon, "Harper's World: Canada's New Role on the Global Stage," *Globe and Mail*, January 5, 2017.

13. "What was multilateral is far more bilateral; what was co-operative has become assertive; what was—you name it: global security, global governance, conflict resolution—is now trade before all. . . . And it meant putting economic diplomacy ahead of other concerns—in the Harper era, trade trumps everything." John Ibbitson, "How Harper Transformed Canada's Foreign Policy," *Globe and Mail*, January 31, 2014.

14. "Barack Obama Thanks Canada for Hosting Cuba-U.S. meetings," *CBC*, December 17, 2014, http://www.cbc.ca/news/politics/barack-obama-thanks-canada-for-hosting-cuba-u-s-meetings-1.2876173 (accessed March 21, 2017).

15. Grant Robertson, "Baseball Diplomacy Results in Series between Cuban and Can-Am Teams," *Globe and Mail*, March 2, 2016.

16. "Première visite d'un ministre des Relations internationales du Québec à Cuba," Radio-Canada, November 1, 2015, http://ici.radio-canada.ca/nouvelle/747478/voyage-ministre-christine-st-pierre-cuba-relations-internationales (accessed March 1, 2017).

17. "Rencontre entre le premier ministre el le ministre del Relations Extérieures: Une première dans l'histoire des relations internationales du Québec," Office of the Ministry of Relations Internationales et Francophonie, May 4, 2016.

18. "Philippe Couillard rencontre le president Raúl Castro et initle una nouvelle ere de coopération entre le Québec et Cuba," Office of the Ministry of Relations Internationales et Francophonie, September 13, 2016.

19. Justin Trudeau, "Statement by the Prime Minister of Canada on the Death of Former Cuban President Fidel Castro," Office of the Prime Minister, November 26, 2016, https://pm.gc.ca/eng/news/2016/11/26/statement-prime-minister-canada-death-former-cuban-president-fidel-castro.

20. Kirk and McKenna, *Canada-Cuba Relations*, 182.

12

Spain and Cuba

Joaquín Roy

The relationship between Cuba and Spain deserves a special place in the consideration of an analysis of the Cuban regime in today's world. This assessment is most relevant after the significant reopening of relations with the United States. However, questions may arise when evaluating the degree of importance for both actors and especially for the government of Raúl Castro.

Any analysis of the Cuba-Spain relationship should include blunt speculation based on common sense and deep historical perspective, addressing in the process such questions as: What is the level of importance of Spain in the evolution of the issues of EU-Cuba relations? How influential have the successive Spanish administrations of the democratic era been in capturing Cuba's attention? How has the alleged "very special relationship" label affected the shaping of certain Cuban actions? Are Cuba and Spain "condemned" to have a lasting common basic agreement? Would the European activity concerning Cuba in recent years have been the same without the existence of Spain, especially with an active and fully democratic regime installed in Madrid, and the European Union? For those who would respond that Cuba's activities in the wider context of Europe would be different without Spain, the problem is to evaluate exactly to what degree the relationship with Spain is worthy of special attention.

THE DEEP WEIGHT OF HISTORY

An analysis of the relationship should pay attention to certain subtopics and significant developments. The most important one is the role still played by the extremely close ties between both nations. The second should be the specific evolution of the Spanish government and most importantly its insertion into the European Union. Then the basic aspects of the economic relationship should be taken into account.

Also crucial is the consideration of the current relationship, given the challenge faced by the government of Raúl Castro in dealing with the new stage of relations with the United States. And finally, attention should be paid to changing times in Latin America.

A study of the evolution of the relationship between the two countries since Raúl took the helm of the Cuban regime reveals certain novel important trends. The most salient feature is the abandonment of the frequent outbursts of tension between the two governments that were common in the last quarter of the twentieth century, most especially during the administration of Spanish premier José María Aznar (1996–2004) but also present during previous stages.

A review of the verbal attacks by Fidel Castro includes referring to the Twelfth of October as an "infausta y nefasta" (unfortunate and ill-fated) date, considering the colonial past as a "little empire in crutches," and calling the minister of foreign affairs a "colonial corporal." He also termed the president of the Spanish Congress a "fascistoid crook," and in response to a challenge by Aznar to make a positive move and open up the Cuban system, he referred to him as *caballerito* and a "Führer with a small moustache."[1]

This animosity had also spilled over into relations with the European Union. The Spanish government took note that the bluntness used in EU messages, announcements, and demands, as well as the adoption of hard-line new policies, only served as an invitation for the Cuban government to respond by hitting back with an even higher degree of aggressive attitude and personal references.

The most obvious sign of these long-standing ties between the two countries is the fact that, in spite of the successive changes of regimes and political philosophies, Spain and Cuba never broke diplomatic relations. Tension intensified when Aznar took control in Madrid in 1996. But as later would happen under José Luis Rodríguez Zapatero (2004–2011) and Mariano Rajoy (2011–present), the breaking of relations with Havana has been a taboo, one never violated by any of the Spanish leaders. Only details of the tensions have changed, very often in colorful and spectacular ways, but never the substance. Moreover, in only one instance did the Cuban government refuse to approve the appointment of a Spanish ambassador.

This solid record is worth noting. Spain has passed through periods of contrasting changes: an authoritarian monarchy under Alfonso XIII, a military dictatorship protectorate under Miguel Primo de Rivera, the Second Spanish Republic, the Francisco Franco regime, a parliamentary democracy, and a constitutional monarchy. For its part, Cuba has faced U.S. military occupation, a controlled republic under the Platt Amendment, corrupt and unstable governments in the 1930s, 1940s, and 1950s, and finally the Castro regime. Despite these differences, neither government ever displayed any serious inclination to distance itself from the other. Indeed, even when the relationship experienced delicate moments caused by verbal personal confrontations, calm eventually always returned to preside over the general setting.

Some fundamental aspects of this bilateral relationship cannot be forgotten. First, Cuba was the last remaining outpost of the Spanish Empire in the Americas (along with Puerto Rico). Cuba's struggle for independence was the cause of the Spanish-American War, provoked by the sinking of the battleship USS *Maine*. For almost four centuries, Spain's image of Cuba was dominated by a well-established, idealized description provided centuries earlier by Christopher Columbus: "The most beautiful land that human eyes ever saw." Spain constructed its centuries-long relationship with the new land, terming it "the ever-faithful island," as the official labeling of Cuba was inscribed in the royal coat of arms. When the struggle for independence was finally seen as a dangerous threat to Madrid's control, the Spanish response was to fight "until the last man and the last peseta," as Antonio Cánovas del Castillo, prime minister of Spain, said. The trauma suffered by the Spanish establishment and the people at large is expressed in a popular saying: even today, when a family or a community is struck by a major economic loss or personal tragedy, a common reaction is to exclaim "Más se perdió en Cuba" ("Even more was lost in Cuba"). The expression is used in order to stress the relative importance of the problem, while at the same time recalling the impact of the end of the colonial relationship.[2]

Significantly, the Spanish people responded to the loss not with anger toward the former colony and newly independent state but rather by accepting that the continued dependence of Cuba was not viable. Cuba now became the destination for even greater migration from Spain than during the colonial period. In addition, thousands of Spanish soldiers decided to remain in Cuba. Life in the former colony was now seen as a more attractive option to staying in the impoverished metropole. This personal relationship between both countries has recently been reinforced by the Law of Historic Memory, granting Spanish citizenship to the descendants of Spanish immigrants.[3]

After the Spanish Civil War, the relationship was maintained. The record shows a continuous Cuban interest in retaining the links with Franco, even when Fidel Castro took the helm in 1959 and transformed the Cuban republican regime into a Marxist-Leninist state. In one of the most delicate moments of the relationship, Spanish ambassador Juan Pablo de Lojendio was expelled from Cuba. Surprisingly, both protagonists in the drama did not make any regrettable moves to endanger the relationship. Instead they only lowered the level of the diplomatic status of Madrid's representative to that of chargé d'affaires. Franco did not support his envoy and instead lectured the diplomat, "With Cuba, anything, except breaking up." As a corresponding example of the respect (if not admiration) on Castro's part, when Franco died in 1976 the Cuban government decreed a three-day period of mourning. Fidel was grateful that Franco never gave signs of following the overall U.S. doctrine of isolating Cuba.

The positive attitude toward Spain during the Franco years was also seen in Madrid's attempts to create a favorable, balanced image in Latin America. Franco wanted to avoid a repetition of the Mexican rejection of his authoritarian regime. The Spanish dictator aimed at reducing its conservative image and excessive pro-U.S. credentials. The end of the colonial struggle in Cuba and the role of the U.S. generated a negative feeling in Latin America known as *arielismo* (focused on the idealistic quality of Hispanic American thought), which was inspired by the seminal work of José Enrique Rodó and was the base of a more militant anti-U.S. attitude, a precedent of the Latin American spirit of *Bolivarismo* (based on identification with the nineteenth-century liberator Simón Bolívar), which received new strength with the Castro revolution. For Spain, the strategy was another chapter of the "foreign policy of substitution." Ironically, this plan actually matched well with the perception of the new Cuban regime in the eyes of Spanish citizens, who were attracted early on to the rather folkloric image of the *barbudos* (bearded ones) of the Sierra Maestra and the mystique of Che Guevara.

An area where the close relationship between Spain and Cuba has been reinforced involves the links with Spanish substate regions and communities, a process that provides different examples of *patria chica* (identifying with a particular place or region). None has been favored more than the Spanish region of Galicia. While *gallego* (a person from Galicia) is a synonym for "Spanish" in several Latin America countries, in Cuba it enjoys a special flavor. It is worth noting that in times of tension between the two governments, Manuel Fraga Iribarne (a Galician leader, founder of the Alianza Popular conservative party, and a former Franco minister) visited Cuba and insisted on maintaining close ties with the island. The Galician leader, who migrated briefly to Cuba with his family, placed the historical relationship above any political convenience or advantage. The father of Fidel and Raúl Castro traced his origin to a town in the province of Lugo. The latest president of Galicia, Alberto Núñez Feijoo, was the principal guest at a hemispheric congress of Galician communities in America. Fidel Castro, who never managed to make an official state visit to Madrid and only attended the ceremonies of the Olympic Games in Barcelona in 1992, did however make a special, sentimental tour of his father's region of Galicia.

CUBA'S ATTITUDE TOWARD SPAIN

After independence Cuban leaders noted the deliberate policy of the Spanish government to maintain Spain's relationship with its former colony. The rebirth of democracy in Spain accentuated this policy. This logic was strengthened with the administration of the socialist government headed by Felipe González. Fidel Castro made several moves to lure the Spanish socialist party to his side, but ironically numerous challenges emerged when the party became very active in pressuring the Cuban regime to reform. This was the time when the model of the Spanish transition was at its highest in Latin America, and in this process the socialists played a leading role.

This foreign policy strategy has been considered very useful and profitable because it has given various Spanish administrations a nonpartisan way to showcase the record of the evolution of the regime. This approach reveals pride in demonstrating the cooperation of the different political parties in strengthening the democratic process. It mirrors the reconciliation process of the European Union after the bloody confrontations of the first part of the twentieth century. The political parties of Spain put aside their differences and stressed the commonalities in approving the democratic constitutional text of 1978, demonstrating its lasting effects. The Moncloa Pacts (referring to the residence of the prime minister), as they have been known, were a standard approach provided to numerous Latin American states going through their particular evolution from the military dictatorships of the 1960s and 1970s into constitutional democracies. Cuba clearly presented a different profile; yet Spanish officials and scholars continued to insist upon using the experience as a model.

Observers claim that the essence of the differences of opinion concerning the Spanish approach stems from the fact that the Cuban regime (during both the Fidel Castro era and the ongoing administration of Raúl) did not consider the experiences comparable and does not accept the adaptability of a "one size fits all" prescription. This Cuban logic, in essence, rejects the notion that the Cuban regime is a "dictatorship" and that the resolution of the evolution of the system will end in a similar shape of "democracy."

However, both actors have shown no inclination to allow this disagreement to jeopardize their long, mutually profitable economic relationship. The importance of Spain during the worst years of Cuba's economic difficulties due to the collapse of the Soviet regime and the drastic vanishing of the subsidies supplied by Moscow and its allies was notable.[4] Traditionally, the Spain-Cuba relationship has been dominated economically by the hotel and tourism industry. Spain continues to be the leader in that sector in which the activities of the Melià chain were pioneers when the opening of joint venture investments was made possible. Spanish firms manage 80 percent of the five-star rooms and 60 percent of those below five stars in Cuba. Spanish interests expect (or hope) that the predictable invasion of U.S. investments will not take effect until the full termination of the embargo and the subsequent authorization of U.S. hotel chains by the Cuban government.

In sum, Spain has been the principal European country in terms of economic relations with Cuba. Spain is the third-largest foreign investor in Cuba, surpassed only by Venezuela and China. Moreover, trade and other economic operations between Cuba and Spain surpassed €1 billion in 2015. All this activity is set in the context of a wider agreement favoring the restructuring of the debt owed Spain by Cuba, calculated at €2.5 billion. As the historical result of long-term activity, Spain is second on the list of creditors to Cuba, with a long history of lack of repayments and often extended delays. Despite this negative factor, systematically criticized by conservative circles in Spain and hard-liners among the Cuban exile community in the United States, there are no signs indicating that this trend will be terminated.

Recent bilateral agreements include cooperation projects in the fields of road transport, maritime operations, railroad maintenance, and air and harbor services. Spanish interests are mentioned as partners in the development of the port of Mariel facilities. Among other recent cooperation activities were the financial restructuring of various projects, the training of engineers, and the promotion of technological development.[5]

SPAIN IN THE EU: THE COMMON POSITION

Spain's international relations took a decisive turn with its membership in the European Union in 1986. The result was the immediate participation of numerous (socialist, conservative, liberal) government officials, as well as academics and business leaders in European institutions. The EU then made a strategic move toward Latin America, a continent that earlier in the evolution of the organization had barely been present in the individual activities of some important member states (such as France, the United Kingdom, and Italy). In this process, Spain became an important addition to the EU's traditionally limited reach in the international scene.

Central America was the first major EU area of interest in Latin America, its entry point being the peace negotiations that sought to ameliorate the confrontational experiences of some countries. The San José Process was the result, with trend-setting programs in development, pacification, and regional integration. Cuba was to be the next stage in a wider Latin American initiative of the EU. The problem was that the notion of "transition," which was an example of the "soft power" frequently brandished by Spain, was not palatable to the Cuban regime.

Given the historical background as well as the need for new economic partners arising during the "Special Period," Spain was seen by Havana as an alternative outlet to reduce the aggressive continuation of the U.S. *bloqueo*, or embargo. This Washington reaction was implemented through the double track of the Torricelli legislation (which prohibited any dealings by Cuba with U.S. subsidiaries) and its hardening through a more serious, comprehensive program of reinforcing and codifying the embargo via the Helms-Burton Act.[6]

The Helms-Burton legislation was adopted in the beginning of 1996, thanks in large part to the lobbying exerted by the Cuban American National Foundation under the leadership of Jorge Mas Canosa and to the effective work of Cuban members of Congress. Initially approval was not totally certain, due to internal and foreign opposition. But then Fidel Castro gave the order to shoot down two planes of Brothers to the Rescue, an organization that evolved from a humanitarian enterprise to become an activist group. The tragic incident forced President Bill Clinton to give White House support for the Helms-Burton legislation.

Meanwhile, the Spanish political scene witnessed the end of the mandate enjoyed by the Spanish Socialist Workers' Party (Partido Socialista Obrero Español, or PSOE) led by Felipe González. The winner of the election, conservative José María Aznar, decided to mirror certain U.S. policies while also campaigning to obtain influence on the European scene. The centerpiece for these initiatives with respect to Cuba (which became known as the EU Common Position) revolved around imposing preconditions for an EU Cooperation Agreement with Havana. These efforts, which were a direct initiative of the Spanish government undertaken with the support of other conservative and newly reelected members of the EU, were ultimately successful. At the same time, the logic of the Common Position aimed at the twin objectives of contributing to the peaceful political transition of Cuba and the evolution of a democratic regime through what was labeled as "constructive engagement." While the traditional U.S. policy was to pressure the Cuban regime to collapse, the European strategy instead opted for a policy of preparing for the future. However, the Cuban regime systematically blamed the EU, and Spain in particular, for the maintenance of the Common Position. The Castro administration equated the European policy with the U.S. embargo, believing that Madrid and Brussels were taking instructions from Washington. Cuba then saw itself as fighting against two imperialist powers.[7]

After the change of government in Madrid in 2004, resulting in a PSOE administration led by Rodríguez Zapatero, government and diplomatic sources began to accept the convenience of a gradual change in Spain's policies toward Cuba. First they aimed at the suspension of the 2003 so-called government measures (branded as "sanctions" by Cuba) against Havana as a punishment for the imprisonment of dissidents and the execution of three hijackers who had taken control of a ferry in Havana harbor. The Cuban regime had bluntly retaliated against what it saw as an aggressive position with the freezing of high-level diplomatic communications.

Maintaining the Common Position and related measures was increasingly seen by the new PSOE government and many officials in Brussels, as well as EU member states, as "counterproductive" since they were producing results directly opposite to the goals intended.[8] The Cuban regime did not offer any signs of reform under pressure. As a result the new Spanish government insisted on a drastic policy correction and exerted influence on its colleagues to do likewise. After the two-term administration of the socialists, this logic was maintained by the government of Mariano Rajoy, with no signs of change. Few officials wished to return to an era of confrontation, one which had proved counterproductive.

Taking into account this situation, European observers often made sarcastic comments in private about the fact that the Cuba-EU relationship had become significantly a question of Spanish-Cuban relations. At one point, it seemed that the attitude of any one of the actors (be it Cuba or Spain) could in fact result in a noticeable sign of change, which could lead the rest of the partners to pay attention to that change. If, for example, Madrid were to soften its critical view in order to end the diplomatic freezing, then a number of the rest of the partners would also be likely to change gears. If, on the other hand, Madrid favored adopting a harder stance, many partners in the EU would likely side with this new attitude.[9] Aware of this relationship, Havana took advantage of its distinctive relationship with Madrid. When it was convenient for Cuba to reach Brussels through a different channel, it opted for the Havana-Madrid one. In sum, the Cuba-Spain link has been very profitable for different actors and in diverse occasions.

The expected ending of this conflict between the EU (with Spain as a decisive leader) and Cuba was the signing of the Political Dialogue and Cooperation Agreement, and the abrogation of the Common Position reinforced the sustained European efforts in contributing to a peaceful transition in Cuba. It also means that Raúl Castro's government has abandoned opposition to suggestions from European-Spanish soft-power practitioners in favor of a more pragmatic attitude.[10]

THE LATIN AMERICAN AND U.S. FACTORS

What other issues can be considered as worthy of close examination regarding the solidification of Spain's role in the stability of the Cuban regime? To answer this question, one should turn south from Havana. The factor that has increased the importance of the linkage with Europe, and most especially with Spain, is the political change experienced by several Latin American countries. Some significant actors have undergone a shift from a model based in the populist Left to a centrist pragmatic model, if not a clear tilting toward more conservative behavior. For example, the situation in Argentina has changed dramatically from the government of the Kirchners to that of Mauricio Macri. Brazil under president Michel Temer has turned out not to be the same as it was under Dilma Rousseff.

But the most dramatic reformatting of Cuba's connections has been caused by the increasing difficulties of Venezuela. During the close relationship between Havana and Caracas under President Hugo Chávez, Cuba had less need of the EU and Spain and, to a lesser extent, some other European actors. More recently, after the death of the founder of the Bolivarian Alliance for the Peoples of Our America (Alianza Bolivariana para los Pueblos de Nuestra América, or ALBA), significant problems have become evident. Economic difficulties, the defective management of the oil industry, and increased internal opposition, as well as international pressure over political abuses, have generated the weakening of the control of the country by President Nicolás Maduro, raising doubts about the future of his regime. This setting has affected the role played by Venezuela's ALBA partners. The group has reduced the activity of Cuba's role with Bolivia and to a lesser extent Ecuador and Nicaragua.

In sum, Latin America, although still in a general way displaying a pragmatic attitude toward Cuba, has shifted its approach to new and different dimensions. Raúl Castro's government has taken notice and has been forced to start seeking strategic alternatives. A subtle additional dependence on other actors has developed. As a consequence, Cuba cannot afford weakening the relationship with Europe in general, with the EU specifically, and most especially with Spain. This trend involves a need not only for investments but also for traditional political support. This has provoked a need for European endorsement, especially from Spain.[11]

However, the most dramatic challenge of this relationship has been the outstanding change of attitude by the U.S. government under President Barack Obama.[12] The decision has challenged the importance of the value of the link between the European Union (with Spain in the lead) and Cuba. Observers of this phenomenon and its consequences should raise some questions in the context of this commentary. Was there any reaction from Spain in view of the speed given to the changes with the United States? Were the EU and Spain caught flatfooted as this new policy emerged? What has been the impact of the opening of relations by the United States with Cuba upon Spain? Does the new setting constitute a challenge or even a threat for Spanish investments in Cuba? In more concrete terms, is there a clear signal for the hotel industry to expect serious competition by giant U.S. enterprises in the field? Finally, would the Cuban government increase the level of "cost-price" for the privilege of maintaining a lucrative leadership in this terrain? The initiatives under the Obama administration, overturning five decades of U.S. hostility, were extremely important. It remains to be seen, however, how the election of Donald Trump will affect bilateral relations.

This ample agenda of inquiry exceeds the limits of the present commentary. However, among the scant signs of the consequences of the U.S. move, some clear concerns can be detected. The first is that different sectors of the Cuban establishment have been expressing in private concerns about the future consequences of the new involvement of the United States. Cuban insiders consider the trend of U.S. policies in building the new relationship a cause of concern. They see a danger of burying alternative links to the U.S. that have proven very profitable during the time of the embargo. These sectors are already expressing some sort of fear that a nostalgic feeling could develop, regretting the weakening of the role of Europe and especially Spain in the evolution of the survival of the Cuban regime in the "Special Period" and beyond. Those voices call for a reinforcement of the European and Spanish involvement in Cuba. Some also warn current investors to pressure their governments to confirm their commitment in order to secure their presence in Cuba. Some act this way out of fear of losing their advantageous position, since in essence they have been serving as intermediaries in the non-U.S.-Cuban international linkages. Fear of U.S. control over Cuba in the post-Castro era is a major concern of those sectors, as is the mental framework of the Cuban government.

PROSPECTS FOR THE REMAINING TERM OF RAÚL AND HIS SUCCESSOR

In addition to the formidable number of enigmas that hang over the succession of Raúl Castro, the overall political and economic panorama presented by the prospects of Spain and the European Union in the next few years makes any prediction extremely risky. Therefore, it is safer first to review and outline some of the recorded facts and trends and then to speculate about their lasting effects.

As the previous part of this chapter has shown, the relationship between Spain and Cuba has been dominated by a combination of permanent factors and a pattern of some repetitious episodic events that have affected the political and economic links between the two nations. These historical issues have been modified by the recent evolution of events, but they cannot be considered as fundamental novelties, given the deeply rooted ties between the revolutionary regime established in Havana in the 1960s and the former metropole.

The current administration of Raúl Castro inherited many of the standing linkages consolidated during the last stages of the Franco regime in Spain and the establishment of the democratic system. Raúl took power in a situation that neither of the two actors wanted to drastically change. In reality, they could modify very little unless they wanted to run the risk of jeopardizing the advantageous framework which they had both enjoyed for decades.

The evolution of the relationship between the two countries since Raúl took the helm of the Cuban regime following the illness of his brother reveals certain important trends. As was noted earlier, the most salient feature is the abandonment of the frequent outbursts of tension between the two governments, especially during the administration of Spanish premier José María Aznar. Stridency in public declarations has vanished, most specifically on the Cuban side. The Spanish governments, under both Rodríguez Zapatero (2004–2011) and Rajoy (2011–present), have wisely accepted that the earlier bluntness used in messages and announcements of new policies only served as an invitation for the Cuban government to respond with a higher degree of aggression and personal insult.

Observers should be well aware that the complete normalization of the relationship between Spain and Cuba will not change dramatically until two facts have come to pass. One is of medium-term concern; the second is urgent. On the Cuban side, the panorama will not be better understood until the transition to a different leadership in Cuba after Raúl Castro's term ends in 2018. But before that eventuality, the political stalemate in Spain (caused by the inability to build a government as a result of the legislative elections at the end of 2015 and in mid-2016) needed to end. After a prolonged period of negotiations, a new government led by Rajoy was finally formed in October 2016, thereby allowing the international agenda to move forward.

With regard to the EU, the historical and recent record shows that Spain has apparently been forced to take the initiative in dealing with Cuba, both in a positive and in a negative way. The subtle difference in today's circumstances can be reduced to the relative importance shown by the Rajoy administration in the international scene. But Raúl Castro's government has been very careful not to dramatize this fact. While the absence of Rajoy in Cuba has been noticed, numerous European heads of government have visited Havana (with former French president François Hollande in the lead while he was still in office). King Felipe VI is also missing, in contrast to his father King Juan Carlos I, who went to Cuba within the context of an Ibero-American Community meeting. At that time, an official visit was banned by President José María Aznar. In April 2017, as result of an invitation by Cuban foreign minister Bruno Rodríguez, the Spanish government agreed on trips by Rajoy and the king to Cuba before the end of Raúl's term in April 2018.

In any event, what can be said about the relationship between Cuba and the EU, given the evolution of the different attitude of Raúl's government toward Spain? With certain exceptions, the move by the United States and the subtle reforms (mostly economic) exerted by Raúl have softened the critical attitude of certain European actors (e.g., Norway, the United Kingdom, and some of the former socialist countries of eastern Europe). This fact and the continuation of a pragmatic policy by Rajoy (avoiding unnecessary confrontations) have facilitated the situation for Raúl.

The political logic suggests that all of the speculation concerning a substantial change or reformation of Cuba's relations with Europe in general and especially with Spain will be dependent upon special changes in the overall foreign policy of Cuba. Although this fact may be denied by Cuban officials, sensible observers have agreed that such changes would not be possible until the death of Fidel Castro and substantial modifications in the island's political system. Raúl Castro's government is aware of this condition, a fact which is well known in Madrid and Brussels. Meanwhile, all actors are behaving according to their limitations and possibilities under the dictate of a shared consensus of not generating difficulties. Cuba knows that it can count on Spain for understanding, support, and subtle influence to contribute to a peaceful political evolution and economic and social progress. Indeed, any Cuban government knows that in Spain no one wants a repeat of the "Más se perdió en Cuba" syndrome.

NOTES

1. For a sample of his references, see "Fidel Castro califica a España de 'viejo imperio en muletas,'" *El País*, March 26, 2009, http://internacional.elpais.com/internacional/2009/03/26/actualidad/1238022017_850215.html. For a historical review, see Joaquín Roy, *La siempre fiel: Un siglo de relaciones hispanocubanas, 1898–1998* (Madrid: Los Libros de la Catarata/Instituto Universitario de Desarrollo y Cooperación, Universidad Complutense, 1999), chap. 3; Joaquín Roy, *The Cuban Revolution (1959–2009): Its Relationship with Spain, the European Union and the United States* (New York: Palgrave/McMillan, 2009), chap. 5.

2. Roy, *La siempre fiel*, chaps. 1 and 2.

3. In 2007 Spain passed the "Historical Memory" Law (52/2007), designed to allow the descendants of Spaniards who had sought exile after the brutal 1936–1939 Civil War to seek Spanish citizenship. A new provision was added the following year, allowing anybody whose parents or grandparents had been born in Spain and had gone overseas because of their political beliefs or economic hardship to become Spanish citizens. An estimated 180,000 to 200,000 eligible Cubans applied under this law. The Cuban government saw this as a mixed blessing. On the one hand, it reduced the population by approximately 2 percent, freeing up badly needed accommodations and reducing the need for subsidized social services, while on the other it represented an embarrassment for the government as people left to pursue their livelihoods elsewhere. That said, since so many Cubans had already left for the United States throughout the revolutionary process, and since the Spanish model was not seen as being especially politicized, this was not a major blow to the Cuban government (editors' note).

4. For samples of my research, see "The European Anchoring of Cuba: From Persuasion and Good Intentions to Contradiction and Frustration," *Miami European Union Center/Jean Monnet Chair* 2, no. 6 (May 2002), http://www.miami.edu/EUCenter/royworkingpaper_cuba.pdf; "Cuba and the European Union: Chronicle of a Dead Agreement Foretold," in *Redefining Cuban Foreign Policy: The Impact of the "Special Period,"* ed. Michael Erisman and John Kirk (Gainesville: University of Florida Press, 2006), 98–120; "From Stubbornness and Mutual Irrelevancy to Stillness and Vigil on Castro's Crisis: The Current State of European Union-Spain-Cuba Relations" (occasional paper, Jean Monnet Chair/European Union Center,

Special August/September 2006), reproduced by Real Instituto Elcano and available at http://www.realinstitutoelcano.org/documentos/253.asp; "The Attitude of the European Union and Spain towards Cuba: An Assessment, a Year after Castro's Illness (WP)," Miami-Florida European Union Center of Excellence, Vol. 4, Special, July 2007, available at http://aei.pitt.edu/8190/1/Roy_CubaSpainspecial070722edi.pdf.

5. This relationship is reflected in the websites of the embassies of Spain in Havana and of Cuba in Madrid: Embajada de España, La Habana, http://www.exteriores.gob.es/embajadas/lahabana/es/Paginas/inicio.aspx; Embajada de Cuba, Madrid, http://www.cubadiplomatica.cu.

6. Joaquín Roy, *Cuba, the United States and the Helms-Burton Doctrine: International Reactions* (Gainesville: University Press of Florida, 2000).

7. For a sample of his declarations, see Fidel Castro Ruz, "La mentira al servicio del imperio," *Granma*, March 25, 2009, http://www.granma.cu/granmad/secciones/ref-fidel/art103.html.

8. For a review of the official documents of the relationship between the EU and Cuba, see Joaquín Roy, "The Cuban Revolution (1959–2009) and the European Union: A Documentary Selection of Statements and Declarations," EUMA Special Papers, January 2009, available at http://aei.pitt.edu/11049; for general details, see also the official website of the Delegation of the European Union in Cuba (https://eeas.europa.eu/delegations/cuba_en).

9. Joaquín Roy, "Spain Takes the Lead in the EU Policy toward Cuba," in *The EU in the Global Political Economy*, ed. Finn Laursen (Brussels: Peter Lang, 2009), 261–92.

10. For a selection of analysis of the evolution of this change, see "A New Phase in EU-Cuba Relations," European Parliament Research Service, June 25, 2014, https://epthinktank.eu/2014/06/25/a-new-phase-in-eu-cuba-relations/m.EFE; European Commission, "European Commission Proposes Political Dialogue and Cooperation Agreement with Cuba," Press Release, Brussels, September 22, 2016, http://europa.eu/rapid/press-release_IP-16-3133_en.htm; Erwan Fouéré, "Winds of Change for US and EU Relations with Cuba," *CEPS*, March 21, 2016, https://www.ceps.eu/publications/winds-change-us-and-eu-relations-cuba.

11. For a comprehensive analysis, see Joaquín Roy, "Cuba: El papel de EE.UU., América Latina y la UE," in *Las relaciones triangulares Estados Unidos, Unión Europea y América Latina. Pensamiento Iberoamericano* (Madrid: Fundación Carolina), no. 8 (autumn 2011), 243–69, available at https://eulacfoundation.org/es/content/las-relaciones-triangulares-estados-unidos-uni%C3%B3n-europea-y-am%C3%A9rica-latina.

12. Joaquín Roy, "Las relaciones entre la UE y Cuba en el marco de la apertura de Barack Obama y Raúl Castro," Real Instituto Elcano, ARI 10/2015–19/2/2015, http://www.realinstitutoelcano.org/wps/portal/web/rielcano_es/contenido?WCM_GLOBAL_CONTEXT=/elcano/elcano_es/zonas_es/ari10-2015-roy-relaciones-entre-ue-cuba-en-marco-de-apertura-de-barack-obama-y-raul-castro#.VPZNJk10yb8.

13

Venezuela and Cuba

Carlos A. Romero

For many years Fidel Castro tried to encourage a revolution in Venezuela that was similar to that already established in Cuba, and some forty years later this finally occurred when Hugo Chávez was elected president in 1999. Since then Venezuela has maintained a strategic and ideological alliance with Cuba.[1] The initial years of the *chavista* experience took place in the context of globalization, a significantly less rigid and challenging background than that encountered by Cuba—which came up against greater resistance to its foreign policy and alliance with the Soviet Union. Caracas did not experience the Missile Crisis of 1962; nor was it expelled from the Organization of American States (OAS). It did not have to suffer the economic embargo imposed by the United States, and diplomatic ties between Washington and Caracas were never broken off completely. Nor did Venezuela have to face the U.S.-sponsored 1961 Bay of Pigs invasion.[2]

Within a short period, Cuba was able to eliminate the institutions of the former regime, reducing dramatically the extent of private businesses. Indeed, by 1968, in the wake of the Revolutionary Offensive there remained very few examples of a capitalist economy, and instead a centralized economy along Soviet lines was in the process of being installed. By contrast, in the Venezuelan context private enterprise has not been completely eliminated.

The Cuban Revolution followed the 1940 constitution until 1976, when a communist-based model was introduced, while one of the earliest initiatives of the Bolivarian government was to replace the 1961 version with the 1999 constitution, which was very different from the communist characteristics of the Cuban document. Parallel to the 1999 constitution, and supported by decisions of the Supreme Court of Justice, Venezuela has promulgated laws and regulations that support a socialist system. While the Venezuelan system can be described as one based upon "electoral authoritarianism," the political opposition has not been declared illegal and indeed participates actively in the electoral process. It possesses a significant majority in the National Assembly and acts with a limited degree of freedom of expression. Unlike the case in Cuba, there is not a single hegemonic party.

Between 1961 and 1990 the Cuban economy depended basically upon Soviet subsidies, resulting in a state that was economically weak and showed a decrease in production and distribution of goods and services. The Venezuelan case is different, since economic growth was based largely upon income from the petroleum industry and free enterprise. For example, more than 50 percent of imports are made by private industry. By contrast, the exportation of petroleum and its derivatives is carried out by the state petroleum enterprise Petróleos de Venezuela S.A., representing 95 percent of Venezuelan exports.[3]

Another key difference can be seen in the question of emigration. In the case of Cuba there have been several waves of migration. In particular, between 1959 and 1965 there was a major flow of middle-class emigrants, followed later by others from the working class. Estimates indicate that between 10 and 20 percent of the current population (11.2 million) has left Cuba. By contrast there has not been a massive emigration from Venezuela, although there has been a clear increase since 2014 as a result of the economic crisis faced by the country. It is estimated that 6 percent of the current Venezuelan population (33 million) now lives abroad.[4]

There are similarities in the two revolutionary processes, however. These can be seen in the brusque rupture with the past, the pushing aside of traditional elites, the growth of state control (both in economic and political spheres), the anti-U.S. tone of foreign policy, the control of the armed forces, and the search for new international alliances that seek to break with the status quo.[5]

In 2016 both countries experienced dramatically new circumstances. Cuba partially normalized its ties with the United States and the European Union as well as with some other countries. At the same time Cuban authorities warned that economic growth would not be greater than 2 percent. It had been predicted that the opening of the Cuban economy, the improvement of relations with the United States, the heightened level of remittances from the Cuban Diaspora, and increased U.S. imports, as well as the increase in visits from tourists and family members living abroad, would all help to refloat production and consumption in Cuba. The economic measures have not produced the expected results, however, and many Cubans are dissatisfied with the government. Meanwhile Venezuela has faced a severe economic crisis, political instability, and growing criticism by governments and other international actors because of the erosion, fragility, and tentative future of democracy there.

Following this general introduction to the bilateral relationship, the next section analyzes how the Cuban-Venezuelan alliance has developed since 2006. This will be followed by a study of the current state of bilateral relations. The chapter then closes with some initial conclusions and a discussion of several potential future scenarios.

The Beginning of the Friendship

In 1999 Cuba became the model for Venezuela to follow, at a moment when several countries in Latin America and the Caribbean had developed a movement in favor of less dependent international ties with the United States. At this time the ideas of a multipolar world, of developing ties with countries outside the Western orbit, of promoting socialism and a different economic model all changed the hemispheric agenda and considerably reduced the importance of the so-called Washington Consensus.

The connection between Venezuela and Cuba now largely took the place of the historical strategic relationship that had existed between Venezuela and the United States since 1999. In addition a new military doctrine arose, according to which the threat of a simultaneous attack by the United States on Venezuela and Cuba was actively considered.[6] In Venezuela, after the interest in armed struggle had been reduced by the end of the 1960s, most sectors which had earlier criticized the democratic regime then focused their demands within the framework of electoral competition and political struggle. At the same time, however, a small group maintained the armed struggle route, obtaining support from revolutionary Cuba.

As a result a political platform evolved, led by an important group of leaders and supported by members of the Venezuelan Left, for whom the Cuban Revolution came to occupy an important reference point for various forms of struggle—from military insurrection to urban and rural guerrilla struggles and even to electoral participation. While Hugo Chávez and his allies had no direct connection with Havana, given his age and military profession, his civilian political allies were able to focus their goals using their historical contacts with Havana.[7]

The relations between Venezuela and Cuba since 1999 can be divided into three stages. The first, reflecting the strong initial bilateral ties, was initiated by the first election to the presidency of Hugo Chávez in 1999 and continues until 2006. A second period can be traced from 2006 until his death in 2013, while the third goes from then until the present. The Venezuelan interest in Cuba was based upon shared interests and the defense of two political projects to promote revolution, both in Latin America and on an international level—leading Fidel Castro to claim, "Washington cannot allow Cuba and Venezuela to live in peace."[8]

There were several goals of this alliance: to overcome the U.S. economic embargo against Cuba, to reactivate and increase the supply of Venezuelan oil to Cuba, to help the Cuban government overcome the worst aspects of the "Special Period" (1989–1997) in the wake of the disappearance of the socialist common market (Council for Mutual Economic Assistance) and the USSR, to provide a united front against world circumstances, and to reactivate the international leftist movement.

From the economic and commercial perspectives, this relationship took a fundamental change in direction following the approval of an integral cooperation agreement between Cuba and Venezuela, signed in October 2000. The goal was to promote the exchange of goods and services on preferential terms for each country. As a result Venezuela agreed to send fifty-three thousand barrels of petroleum (including cost, insurance, and freight) per day for 2002, with an increase to an average of ninety-three thousand barrels daily at preferential and fixed prices ($23 per barrel) from 2005 onward. In exchange Cuba began to send to Venezuela more than thirteen thousand Cuban workers, most of whom operated in the health (doctors, nurses, and paramedics) and sports sectors. Many significant changes occurred, starting in 2003: a massive Cuban participation in the social programs (generally referred to as missions) of the Venezuelan government resulted, energy cooperation increased, visits of parliamentarians from both countries took place, the search for an anticapitalist unity among Latin American countries started, and indeed support for the international anti-imperialist struggle increased. In addition the professional exchange of armed forces personnel grew, as did the move toward socialism.

The consequences of the attempted military coup against President Chávez in April 2002 and the application of the Bolivarian Alternative for the Peoples of Our America–Treaty of Commerce between Peoples (Alianza Bolivariana para los Pueblos de Nuestra América–Tratado de Comercio de los Pueblos, or ALBA-TCP) in late 2004 made for a further development in regional relations. A joint declaration of December 14, 2004, noted, "We aspire to the development of joint positions in the world sphere," and on the same day an increase and modification in the integral cooperation agreement between Cuba and Venezuela was signed.[9] This contributed to a new stage in developing complementary economic ties, going beyond petroleum supplies and exchange of human resources, and was supported by the ALBA-TCP agreement signed by Cuba, Venezuela, and Bolivia (and Nicaragua in 2006). The goal now was to promote commerce and trade between ALBA member countries, without any taxes or tariffs, and to design projects and enterprises that would provide shared benefits for members.[10]

Venezuela is Cuba's major trading partner, exporting petroleum and its derivatives, shoes, textiles, construction materials, plastic products, and industrial supplies, while it imports from Cuba professional and technical assistance as well as medical supplies. There are also several communal projects, with a commercial balance in Venezuela's favor (see table 13.1).[11] By late 2007 Cuban authorities calculated that there were thirty-nine thousand "collaborators" in Venezuela, of whom thirty-one thousand were in the health sector—approximately 75 percent of the total number of Cubans working in the health profession abroad at that time (some fifty-two thousand). In addition the petroleum refinery in Cienfuegos was refurbished, the joint venture Cuvenpetrol was established, and several bilateral agreements related to energy were signed.[12]

In addition, the presence of Cuban officials in key posts in the Venezuelan armed forces was noted, and bilateral military agreements were signed (largely professional training of the Venezuelan military by officials of the Cuban armed forces). Technical support was given to Venezuelan institutions dealing with the identification of its citizens and the registration of property. There was also a strong Cuban presence in political intelligence organizations and military intelligence in Venezuela. In June 2007 President Chávez also suggested the creation of a Confederation of ALBA

Table 13.1. Venezuela: Foreign Trade with Cuba, 1988–2014 (millions of dollars)

Year	*Exports of Venezuelan Goods to Cuba*	*Imports of Cuban Goods to Venezuela*	*Exchange of Goods, Venezuela-Cuba*	*Payment for Professional and Technical Services*	*Imports of Professional and Technical Services from Cuba*	*Commercial Exchange of Goods and Services between Venezuela and Cuba*	*Commercial Balance between Venezuela and Cuba (Exports Less Imports of Goods and Services since 2005)*
1998			388				
1999			464				
2000	898	14	912				
2001	952	21	973				
2002	725	19	744				
2003	683	192	875				
2004	1,143	367	1,510				
2005	1,864	402	2,266	234	636	2,500	1,228
2006	2,232	409	2,641	565	974	3,206	1,258
2007	2,250	450	2,700	4,400	4,850	7,100	–2,600
2008	4,473	414	4,887	5,513	5,927	10,400	–1,454
2009	2,607	528	3,135	3,512	4,040	6,647	–1,433
2010	4,302	1,716	6,018	1,500	3,216	7,518	1,086
2011	5,902	2,273	8,175	1,932	4,205	10,107	1,697
2012	6,079	2,484	8,563	4,694	7,178	13,257	–1,099
2013	4,802	2,265	7,067	4,666	6,931	11,733	–2129
2014	5,189	2,069	7,258	3,714	5,783	10,972	594*

* Provisional figures.

Sources: Personal analysis based upon information taken from the National Office of Statistics and Information of Cuba (ONEI); *Anuario estadístico de Cuba 2014* (Havana: ONEI, 2015), found at ONEI, 2015, www.one.cu (columns 1, 2, and 3); Banco Central de Venezuela, www.bcv.org/ve and Bancoex, www.bancoex.gov.ve (column 4), and personal calculations.

States and an ALBA National Defense Organization, noting, "Now is the moment to develop a joint defence strategy, with shared equipment, military support—but not just in military matters, since we also need support in intelligence and counter-intelligence."[13]

The Maturity of the Relationship

The Venezuelan presidential election in 2006 showed how the regime had strengthened its position, for during the electoral campaign, *chavismo* had extended its revolutionary beliefs under the banner of "Socialism for the 21st Century." It was also noticeable how, despite adverse circumstances, the opposition maintained a presence in electoral, social, and media affairs as the polarization within Venezuelan society grew. In 2007 a constitutional referendum was called to vote on a series of reforms designed to open the opportunity for indefinite presidential reelection. The opposition won the referendum by a small (1 percent) margin, but the government then used the Supreme Court of Justice to ensure almost all the proposals established in the consultation process. It was an attempt to improve control of the executive branch over the remaining branches of power, with the objective not only of strengthening "Socialism for the 21st Century" but also implementing a program of nationalization and privatization of some private enterprises, thereby creating a private business sector supportive of the government. (Later these business owners would become known as *Boliburgueses*, or bourgeois of the Bolivarian model. They were largely found in the banking, commerce, and construction sectors: intermediaries, contractors, and importers working with the public sector who benefited from official credits and subsidized currency rates.[14])

Regional diplomatic relationships were also strengthened. On December 16 and 17, 2008, the two groups that would later be known as the Community of Latin American and Caribbean States (Comunidad de Estados Latinoamericanos y Caribeños, or CELAC) met in Brazil, and Cuba's incorporation into the group was formalized. Venezuela supported the initiative, which was vital for Cuba to participate fully in regional relations. At the Fifth Summit of the Americas (held in Port of Spain, Trinidad and Tobago, from April 17 to 19, 2009), the ALBA nations announced that they would not sign the summit's final declaration since there was no unanimity on issues of democracy and development and since Cuba was excluded from the summit. They also complained that no mention was made concerning the general regional consensus condemning the U.S. embargo and the isolation of Cuba.

In June 2009, at the Thirty-Ninth OAS General Assembly held in San Pedro Sula, Honduras, OAS members reached an agreement to revoke the 1962 resolution that suspended Cuba from the organization. This was followed by the February 2010 meeting in Mexico of the Second Summit of Latin American and Caribbean Heads of State and Government, where CELAC was agreed to. At the third summit, held in Venezuela in 2012, the institutional framework was agreed upon, and both Venezuela and Cuba voted in favor of the creation of CELAC.

In April 2010, President Raúl Castro visited Caracas for three days and declared, "I return to Cuba very satisfied with the advance in relations with our Venezuelan brothers and sisters. . . . [E]ach day we are exactly the same."[15] On July 26, 2010, Alí Rodríguez, then minister of energy in the Bolivarian Republic of Venezuela, gave the major address at the fifty-seventh anniversary of the attack on the Moncada Garrison in Villa Clara. He has extremely close ties with the Cuban leadership, having participated in the armed struggle more than fifty years earlier. In 2010 he was (for the second time) ambassador of Venezuela to Cuba. Summarizing the bilateral relationship at the time, he noted how "there was scarcely an ember left—the socialist hope represented by Cuba—when there resulted the breath of revolution in Latin America, and a new torch came alight in Venezuela."[16]

Nothing, however, was as important for bilateral relations as the illness of President Chávez, who was first operated on for his cancerous tumor in Cuba on June 10, 2011, and returned to Caracas on July 4, 2011. Afterward President Chávez returned to Havana on seventeen occasions between June 2011 and 2013, for a total of 225 days spent in Cuba. In all he was operated on some four times and finally returned to Caracas on February 18, 2013, following seventy-two days in Havana, in extremely poor health.

Fidel Castro wrote an emotional farewell letter to the Venezuelan president just a few days before his death, noting, "When the socialist camp collapsed and the Soviet Union fell apart, imperialism—with the weight of the embargo ready to strike—sought to drown the Cuban Revolution in blood. Venezuela, however, a relatively small country in our divided Latin America, was capable of preventing this."[17] Following the death of President Chávez, Castro wrote another letter: "On March 5, in the afternoon, the best friend that the Cuban people has had throughout its history, died."[18] For its part, on March 5, 2013, the Cuban government issued a declaration at this time: "Chávez is also Cuban! He felt very personally our difficulties and problems, and contributed all that he could, with extraordinary generosity, especially during the most difficult years of the Special Period."[19]

A Relationship with Difficulties

On April 14, 2013, Nicolás Maduro, who had assumed temporarily the presidency upon the death of Hugo Chávez, became president in a tightly contested election. On April 19, 2013, he took power as president for the 2013–2019 period. Upon his visit to Cuba in March 2013, some fifty-one new cooperation agreements, at a cost of $2 billion, were signed within the framework of the Thirteenth Intergovernmental Cuba-Venezuela Reunion. Of particular note was the continuation of Cuban support for the social programs in Venezuela and the beginning of new bilateral projects. A memorandum of understanding was signed between Caracas and Havana on May 31, 2013, according to which both parties agreed to strengthen economic and social ties between the two countries from 2013 to 2019. At the time of the CELAC summit in Havana, on January 28, 2014, a meeting took place between Presidents

Maduro and Raúl Castro, leading to a series of agreements. These included fifty-six collaboration projects in sports, electricity (through Unión Nacional Eléctrica de Cuba), agriculture, health, the economy, and education. This increased the number of Cubans working in Venezuela to sixty thousand. In addition, three joint ventures were established in Cuba to refine future deliveries of heavy Venezuelan oil so that it could then be transported to China.

After February 2014 negative public feelings toward Cuba and the participation of Cubans working in Venezuela started to grow among the Venezuelan opposition. President Maduro expressed his concern: "I am worried about the way hate is being created against the Cuban people. . . . We have 25,000 Cuban doctors here, and every day we have to look after them because many have been threatened."[20] (He also noted that the total number of Cuban professionals and technicians at the time was some forty thousand, which is twelve thousand less than in 2012.) For his part Raúl Castro, in his speech to the delegates of the Twentieth Congress of the Cuban Trade Union Central on February 22, 2014, stated, "We know from experience who the people are behind these actions, financing and supporting these brutal actions in order to overthrow the constitutional government of Venezuela."[21]

Both leaders continued to express support for each other's political autonomy and independent foreign policy. On December 14, 2014, for instance, at a meeting of ALBA members, Raúl Castro stated that Cuba "supported Venezuela, and condemned in the strongest terms the attempt by the United States to impose sanctions on Venezuela."[22] At the same time, when Washington and Havana announced the reopening of diplomatic ties, the government of Venezuela expressed "its most profound happiness for . . . the new direction being taken by Cuba and the United States."[23] A few days later, at the closing of a session of the National Assembly, President Raúl Castro referred to "the special relations that we maintain with the Bolivarian Republic of Venezuela, and which we will continue supporting."[24] Finally, on March 9, 2015, upon hearing of the state of emergency and sanctions imposed by Washington, the Cuban government condemned "the arbitrary and aggressive Executive Order issued by the President of the United States against the government of the Bolivarian Republic of Venezuela."[25]

Vocal support for Venezuela was provided again on March 17, 2015, at the meeting in Caracas of the leaders of ALBA, where Raúl Castro stated, "The United States ought to finally understand that it is impossible to seduce or buy Cuba, or indeed to intimidate Venezuela."[26] The following month, during the Seventh Summit of the Americas held in Panama, President Castro declared, "I should reaffirm all our support, in a loyal and resolved manner, for the sister Bolivarian Republic of Venezuela, as well as the legitimate government and the civil-military union headed by President Nicolás Maduro."[27]

Statements and gestures of support continued. On April 30, 2015, President Maduro visited Cuba in order to attend the May Day celebrations. The "five Cuban heroes" (accused by the United States of espionage and ultimately freed after being incarcerated) visited Caracas and other Venezuelan cities in May 2015 on their first trip abroad after being freed. Venezuelan vice president Jorge Arreaza visited Havana on August 7 and 8, and on August 14 Raúl Castro received President Maduro.

There was one significant sour note, however. In August 2015 it was announced that 720 Cuban health-care workers had deserted their medical posts in Venezuela since January of that year. Most had left illegally for Colombia and other countries, hoping to be accepted into Washington's Cuban Medical Professional Parole program, which promised them the opportunity to work in the United States. In 2014 some 603 Cuban health-care personnel defected, and it is estimated that since 2003 more than 5,000 have done the same.

Speaking at the United Nations General Assembly on September 28, 2015, Raúl Castro again stated Cuba's support for the Venezuelan government: "The Bolivarian Republic of Venezuela will always be able to count upon the solidarity of Cuba in the face of the attempts to destabilize and subvert the constitutional order, and to destroy the work initiated by Compañero Hugo Chávez Frías."[28] In early October 2015 a fresh cycle of tension between the governments of Venezuela and the United States arose. Reflecting on the situation, on October 4 President Maduro declared, "Some day we hope that this struggle for independence and dignity that Venezuela is pursuing will succeed in the same way as has happened with Cuba—and that we will have relations of respect, of equality between states, and hopefully ties of cooperation with the elites who govern in Washington."[29]

Collaboration between Cuba and Venezuela has continued. On October 6, 2015, for example, President Maduro visited Cuba to meet with Raúl and Fidel Castro. Several themes were discussed, and a decision was taken for a special development plan for the 2015–2030 period in order to ensure that the UN Millennium Development Goals were met. October 15, 2015, marked the fifteenth anniversary of the signing of the integral cooperation agreement between Venezuela and Cuba, and its accomplishments have been impressive. As a result of the exchange of petroleum for professional and technical services from Cuba, some 7,284 local clinics have been created, as well as 568 integral diagnostic centers, 585 rehabilitation centers, and 38 specialized high technology medical facilities. The Operación Milagro ophthalmology program has also been extremely successful, as have the two stages of Mission Robinson, focused on basic literacy training, whereby 2.8 million Venezuelans successfully completed their primary education. Several other bilateral agreements have resulted from the early Sandino Accord, including the work of the Bolívar and Martí Foundation and the program for Cuban professors to train Venezuelan doctors, and those from other nations, at the Salvador Allende School of Medicine in Caracas.

Opposition to the Maduro government has been increasing since 2015. In the parliamentary elections of December 6, 2015, an electoral alliance, the Table of Democratic Unity, was formed. In all, 112 of its candidates were elected, forming, in conjunction with the three deputies representing the indigenous sector, a parliamentary majority. By contrast the official party, the United Socialist Party of Venezuela (Partido Socialista Unido de Venezuela, or PSUV), had only fifty-two candidates elected and thus became the minority. Following the PSUV defeat Raúl Castro sent a message to his Venezuelan counterpart: "I am certain that there will be new victories for the Bolivarian and Chavista Revolution under your guidance. We will always be there, at your side."[30]

Following the electoral defeat of the PSUV, the Cuban government continued to express support for the Maduro government while also indicating challenges facing the relationship. In December 2015, at the closing of a session of the National Assembly, for instance, Raúl Castro commented, "Since 2015 the mutually advantageous relations with some countries—especially with the Bolivarian Republic of Venezuela—have been affected, as a result of the economic war designed to overturn the popular support for its Revolution."[31] After Washington renewed the decree of national emergency and sanctions against Venezuela, Havana reiterated its support for the government of President Maduro and, in a communiqué of March 4, 2016, stated, "The Revolutionary Government of Cuba demands the elimination of Executive Order 13692, and repeats its loyal, committed and unconditional support, as well as that of our people, for the Bolivarian Republic of Venezuela, the legitimate government of President Nicolás Maduro, and the civilian-military union of the Bolivarian nation."[32]

President Maduro visited Cuba for just a few hours on March 18, 2016, shortly before the planned visit by President Barack Obama. This was interpreted as Cuba's support for Venezuela, since it was felt in some circles that closer U.S.-Cuban ties could result in greater isolation for the Maduro government. During this visit Maduro participated in the Cuba-Venezuela High Level Joint Commission meeting with the objective of outlining the shared work plan for 2016 to 2030. He received the José Martí Order, the highest award of the Cuban government, and was received by President Raúl Castro, who reiterated "the total and unquestioning solidarity of Cuba with the Bolivarian and *chavista* Revolution and the civilian-military union of the Venezuelan population." An agreement was signed, confirming "the mutual commitment to broaden and strengthen bilateral cooperation."[33] During the visit by President Obama, Raúl Castro indicated at a press conference that "the attacks against Venezuela are counterproductive to the situation in our continent," which was seen as a clear defense of the government of President Maduro.[34]

On several occasions in 2016 the Cuban government expressed clearly its support for the Bolivarian government. On April 4, on the occasion of the Cuba-Venezuela Joint Commission, the 2016 Cooperation Program was approved, supporting several projects in the tourism, urban agriculture, pharmaceuticals and medicines, industry, and mining sectors. It was also announced that the number of Cuban doctors and other health-care personnel in Mission Barrio Adentro would increase. On April 16, 2016, on the occasion of the presentation of the central report to the Seventh Congress of the Communist Party of Cuba, Raúl Castro reiterated this support, noting, "We share the firm conviction that the Venezuelan people will defend the legacy of our dear *compañero* Hugo Chávez Frías, and will prevent the dismantling of the successes achieved to date. To the Bolivarian and *Chavista* Revolution, to President Maduro and his government, to the civilian-military union of the Venezuelan population, we ratify our solidarity and commitment, as well as the determined rejection of any attempts to isolate Venezuela at this time when the United States is involved in a dialogue with Cuba."[35]

When a controversy arose between the general secretary of the OAS, Luis Almagro, and Venezuela, the government of Cuba issued a communiqué on June 3, 2016, supporting Venezuela and its victory "against the interventionist plan of imperialism and the oligarchies." The statement continued, "Sr. Almagro has attempted to apply the Inter-American Democratic Charter, and in particular Article 20, which is supposed to condemn grave challenges to the constitutional order. Yet this was not used in 2002 when a military coup against President Chávez Frías took place, nor was it used to condemn other coups and attempted coups that have shaken the region in the last fifteen years."[36] On July 8, 2016, at the closing of the first session of the National Assembly, President Raúl Castro spoke, noting that the amount of fuel provided by Venezuela had been reduced, producing tension in the Cuban economy. In the same speech, however, he noted, "In these complex circumstances facing our national economy, there will not be the slightest weakening in our commitment, and our solidarity, with the Bolivarian and *Chavista* Revolution, or with President Maduro and his government, or the Civilian-Military Union of the people of Venezuela."[37]

Conclusions and Projections

"Cuba and Venezuela, two separate flags but one revolution" is a slogan which illustrates the close ties between the two peoples and their cooperation in ALBA, in the development of socioeconomic exchanges, in the application of a complex process of cooperation, and in shared tasks intended to develop socialism. In three distinctive areas—cooperation, commerce, and investment—bilateral relations have developed in a singular manner, to the point where it is possible to talk about how each "complements" the other. It is important to mention the immense financial investment of this experience, as well as asymmetric cooperation for which Venezuela has provided a substantial contribution. Given this context, in one interpretation the future of relations between Cuba and Venezuela can be seen, despite the current economic situation in Venezuela, as a continuation of the central aspects to date: economic complementarity, energy cooperation, and political and ideological agreements.

A second scenario rests on the possibility of an economic and political opening in Cuba, which would lead to both governments distancing themselves from each other and in turn result in Havana's revising the parameters of Venezuelan cooperation and the current relationship in terms of subsidies within future economic plans. This would be especially significant if both countries had an economic recession. It would result in Havana depending less on Caracas and controlling the negative impacts which the current level of bilateral cooperation is causing: the dislocation of Cuban society as a result of Venezuelan subsidies, corruption resulting from the nature of cooperation, the accumulation of financial debt owed Venezuela by Cuba, and the generation of inequality in income for the Cuban population, given the impact of Venezuelan aid. Another possibility is that Venezuela would have to reduce economic cooperation with Cuba, mainly the delivery of petroleum for which Cuba pays 50 percent of the cost within the first ninety days and the remaining 50 percent at 1 percent interest over a period of twenty-five years. Also significant would be the cost for Venezuela of hiring professional and technical services from Cuba and, to a lesser extent, other forms of investment and financing. This would become necessary if the economic situation in Venezuela became particularly severe and if the price of petroleum continued falling considerably. That said, the impact would be less than what Cuba felt following the implosion of the Soviet Union.

A third scenario depends upon an internal change in the direction of the political process in both Venezuela and Cuba, which would result in the need for a drastic rethinking of the basis to date of this strategic cooperation: a shared commitment to build socialism and to promote an international anti-imperialist policy. At present there is a severe political crisis in Venezuela, resulting from the economic collapse of the country, the loss of popular support for both the government and the ruling party (PSUV), an opposition majority in the National Legislative Assembly, growth in the crime rate, a dysfunctional public sector, reduction of energy production, decrease of income from the export of petroleum, and capital flight. The data are clear: the price of a barrel of oil has fallen considerably, it is estimated that inflation will reach 700 percent this year and that economic growth will be –7 percent while unemployment hovers around 12 percent. There is also a considerable official devaluation of the national currency, the bolívar. Exchange rates vary—from 6.30 to 10 bolívares to the dollar at the official rate (with limited access to a floating rate of 620) and a black-market rate of 1,100 resulting from the informal economy, which includes the drug industry, a black market in hard currency, smuggling, administrative corruption, and so forth.

This is not the first time that Cuba has encountered a crisis with a close ally in Latin America and the Caribbean, but perhaps this is the greatest to date and one with potentially the most severe consequences. Venezuela, for instance, is the major trading partner of the island, and more than 50 percent of Cuban professionals and technicians are serving in Venezuela (see table 13.1). The Venezuelan market is the principal destination for Cuban exports, while Venezuela is the largest supplier of merchandise for Cuba. In 2012, for example, trade with Venezuela represented 44.2 percent of Cuba's foreign trade in terms of goods. Because of the challenging situation of both economies, Cuba has increased trade and business with a variety of other countries, including Angola, Algeria, Brazil, Canada, China, the United States, Holland, Mexico, and Vietnam, as a means of reducing its dependency upon Venezuela. It has also renegotiated its external debt with the Paris Club, as well as with Russia, China, and Mexico, and has broadened the list of countries to which it exports professional and technical services.

Economic growth in Cuba was –1 percent in 2016, after growth of 1.3 percent in 2014 and 3 percent in 2015. This can in part—although not completely—be explained by the economic crisis in Venezuela. It is also important to bear in mind the growing problems faced by the member nations of the ALBA-TCP, an organization designed with a mandate of supporting South-South cooperation and offering an alternative to neoliberalism.

For the past five years several specialists in the area of Latin American and Caribbean integration have noted how the regional expansion resulting from the Cuban-Venezuelan alliance has shown signs of tiredness. The departure from power of Fidel Castro (2006), the illness and death of Hugo Chávez (2013), the political crises in Honduras (2009) and Paraguay (2012), the electoral victory of Mauricio Macri in Argentina (late 2015), the parliamentary victory of the Venezuelan opposition (2015), the defeat of the campaign in Bolivia to have Evo Morales reelected (2016), the ongoing economic crisis in Venezuela, and the difficulties in the Cuban economy at a time when it is opening up have all limited the development of ALBA projects.[38]

In addition, ALBA has faced many challenges of its own. The dependence upon the Venezuelan economy and on income from petroleum and the financial difficulty of developing projects fully have been major obstacles. Furthermore, the very different approaches employed by each member nation in seeking foreign investment (e.g., as is the case of Bolivia and Cuba), as well as the lack of mutual support for their respective commercial policies, have been problematic. Likewise the cases of corruption and theft, the limited institutionalization of agreements (as in the case of Ecuador and Nicaragua), and various policies (such as the social missions, the bank of ALBA, and the use of a common currency, the sucre) have all conspired to deter the normal functioning of a proper market system within ALBA.[39]

The electoral victory of Hugo Chávez in 1998 and the arrival of a "different" government in Venezuela allowed other countries to accept the "ideological package" consisting of a new foreign policy that defied Washington, an economic strategy based upon the role of the state, populist social measures, and the desire to impose a hegemonic project designed to last. While the boom in raw materials lasted, it was possible to maintain this program, thanks to sufficient public funding as well as to the leaders of the model. They had come to power bearing the standard of twenty-first-century socialism, seeing the Cuban model as the "exemplary mother" of change and the Bolivarian Revolution as the "father/benefactor." How can we weigh up the costs of these experiences, and how can we explain this process, which brought such change to Latin America and the Caribbean and indeed to other parts of the world? An approach that energized the left wing in the region and defied the United States and neoliberalism—and yet now faces a very delicate future? This chapter has sought to provide an answer to these questions.

NOTES

1. For a thorough discussion of the historical relations between Venezuela and Cuba, see Carlos A. Romero, "Cuba y Venezuela. La génesis y el desarrollo de una utopía bilateral,"

in *Cuba, Estados Unidos y América Latina frente a los desafíos hemisféricos*, ed. Luis Fernando Ayerbe (Barcelona: Icaria Editorial, IEEI-UNSP, CRIES, 2011), 159–202.

2. Carlos A. Romero, *Jugando con el globo. La política exterior de Hugo Chávez* (Caracas: Ediciones B., 2006).

3. Carmelo Mesa-Lago, "Balance económico-social de 50 años de Revolución Cubana," *América Latina Hoy* 52 (August 2009): 41–61; Omar Everleny Pérez Villanueva, "La economía en Cuba: Un balance necesario y algunas propuestas de cambio," *Nueva Sociedad* 216 (July–August 2008): 49–64; Javier Corrales and Michael Penfold, *Dragon in the Tropics: Hugo Chávez and the Political Economy of Revolution in Venezuela* (Washington, DC: Brookings Institution Press, 2011).

4. Silvia Pedraza, *Political Disaffection in Cuba's Revolution and Exodus* (New York: Cambridge University Press, 2007).

5. Brian Latell, "The Venezuelan Crisis: Implications for Cuba; Options for the U.S.," video posted to YouTube by Wenceslao Cruz, February 26, 2014, https://www.youtube.com/watch?v=JHXf9tbGtcs.

6. Susanne Gratius and Carlos A. Romero, "La proyección internacional de la Venezuela post-chavista," Policy Brief of May 27, 2013, issued by FRIDE in Madrid, http://www.fride.org/publicacion/1130/la-proyeccion-internacional-de-la-venezuela-post-chavista.

7. Germán Sánchez Otero, *Hugo Chávez y la resurrección de un pueblo* (Caracas: Vadell Hermanos Editores, 2014).

8. Fidel Castro, "Palabras pronunciadas por Fidel Castro, presidente de Cuba, el 1 de mayo de 2004," found in Alan Woods, "Los objetivos son Venezuela y Cuba. Nuevas intrigas del imperialismo estadounidense," Aporrea.org, May 26, 2004, https://www.aporrea.org/actualidad/a8277.html.

9. "Acuerdo entre el Presidente de la República Bolivariana de Venezuela y el Presidente del Consejo de Estado de Cuba, para la aplicación de la Alternativa Bolivariana para las Américas," Cuba.cu, December 14, 2004, http://www.cuba.cu/gobierno/discursos/2004/esp/a141204e.htmls.

10. Ministerio de Relaciones Exteriores de Cuba, "Gobiernos de Venezuela y Cuba celebrarán en La Habana los diez años del Convenio Integral de Cooperación, 9-11-10," www.cubaminrex.cu, 2010.

11. See República Bolivariana de Venezuela, Ministerio del Poder Popular para Relaciones Exteriores, "Síntesis de las relaciones de cooperación Venezuela-Cuba," Embajada de Venezuela en Cuba, http://www.venezuelaencuba.co.cu/venezuelacuba/sintesis.html; "Informe de gestión 2010," Petróleos de Venezuela (PDVSA), http://www.pdvsa.com/index.php?tpl=interface.sp/design/.

12. Carlos A. Romero, "South-South Cooperation between Venezuela and Cuba," in *Reality of Aid: South-South Cooperation. A Challenge to the Aid System? Special Report on South-South Cooperation 2010* (Manila: IBON Books, 2010), 107–14.

13. Hugo Chávez, "Discurso del Presidente Chávez al clausurar la primera reunión del Consejo de Ministros del ALBA, el 6 de junio de 2007," *Granma*, http://www.granma.cubaweb.cu.

14. Henry Dietz and David J. Myers, "From Thaw to Deluge: Party System Collapse in Venezuela and Peru," *Latin American Politics and Society* 49, no. 2 (2007): 61–70; Jennifer McCoy and David J. Myers, eds., *The Unraveling of Representative Democracy in Venezuela* (Baltimore: Johns Hopkins University Press, 2004).

15. Raúl Castro, "Cuba y Venezuela cada día son la misma cosa," *El Universal*, http://www.eluniversal.com/2010/04/22/pol_art_raul-castro:-cuba-y_1870989.shtml.

16. Alí Rodríguez, "Discurso pronunciado por Alí Rodríguez, ministro del poder popular para la energía eléctrica de la República Bolivariana de Venezuela, en Villa Clara, 26 de julio de 2010," ACN, http://www.acn.cu/2010/julio/26egralirodriguez.htm.

17. Fidel Castro Ruz, "Carta de despedida a Hugo Chávez," Noticiero Telemundo, Febrero 18, 2013, http://www.telemundo.com/noticias/2013/02/18/carta-de-despedida-de-fidel-castro-hugo-chavez.

18. Fidel Castro Ruz, "Carta de despedida de Fidel al Comandante Chávez," 2013, http://www.elpatagonico.cl/?p:52454.

19. For the declaration by the Cuban government, see "Declaración del gobierno revolucionario: Hasta siempre, Comandante," Cuba MinRex, March 5, 2013, http://www.minrex.gob.cu/es/declaracion-del-gobierno-revolucionario-hasta-siempre-comandante.

20. "Fear and Hope in Cuba over Venezuela Protests," *Africatime*, March 1, 2014, https://en.africatime.com/zimbabwe/db/fear-and-hope-cuba-over-venezuela-protests.

21. Raúl Castro, "Texto íntegro del discurso pronunciado por el presidente de Cuba, Raúl Castro, en las conclusiones del XX Congreso de la Central de Trabajadores de Cuba. Sábado 22 de febrero de 2014," *Telesur*, http://exwebserv.telesurtv.net/secciones/archivos/ARCH357_847.pdf.

22. See "Raúl Castro condenó a Estados Unidos por sanciones contra funcionarios del gobierno venezolano," *Noticiero Digital*, December 14, 2014, http://noticierodigital.com/2014/12/raul-castro-condeno-a-estados-unidos-por-sanciones-contra-funcionarios-del-gobierno-venezolano.

23. See "Venezuela celebra nuevo rumbo de las relaciones diplomáticas entre Cuba y Estados Unidos," Ministerio del Poder Popular para la Comunicación y la Información, December 18, 2014, http://www.minci.gob.ve/2014/12/venezuela-celebra-nuevo-rumbo-de-las.

24. Raúl Castro, "Discurso del General del Ejército Raúl Castro Ruz, Primer Secretario del Comité Central del Partido Comunista de Cuba y Presidente del Consejo de Estado y Ministros, en la clausura del IV Período Ordinario de Sesiones de la VIII Legislatura de la Asamblea Nacional del Poder Popular, en el Palacio de Convenciones, el 20 de diciembre de 2014," Cuba.cu, http://www.cuba.cu/gobierno/rauldiscursos/2014/ing/r201214i.html.

25. For his remarks, see "Cuba califica de agresiva sanciones de Obama contra Venezuela," *La Prensa*, March 10, 2015, http://www.laprensa.hn/mundo/820900-410/cuba-califica-de-agresiva-sanciones-de-obama-contra-venezuela.

26. See "Raúl Castro a EEUU: Entienda que es imposible comprar a Cuba e intimidar a Venezuela," *Noticiero Digital*, March 17, 2015, http://www.noticierodigital.com/2015/03/raul-castro-a-eeuu-entienda-que-es-imposible-comprar-a-cuba-e-intimidar-a-venezuela.

27. See "Palabras de Raúl Castro la Cumbre hemisférica de Panamá. 11/04/2015," *La Pupila Insomne*, April 11, 2015, https://lapupilainsomne.wordpress.com/2015/04/11/el-discurso-mas-aplaudido-en-la-cumbre-de-las-americas.

28. See "Discurso del Presidente cubano Raúl Castro en el segmento de alto nivel del 70 Período de la ONU," *Juventud Rebelde*, September 28, 2015, http://www.juventudrebelde.cu/internacionales/2015-09-28/discurso-del-presidente-cubano-raul-castro-en-el-segmento-de-alto-nivel-del-70-periodo-de-la-onu.

29. See "Maduro: Nuevos funcionarios de la embajada de EEUU son peores que los anteriores," *Noticiero Digital*, October 4, 2015, http://www.noticierodigital.com/2015/10/maduro-nuevos-Funcionarios-de-la-embajada-de-eeuu-son-peores-que-los-anteriores.

30. See "Acá el Mensaje Corto, Preciso y Contundente de Raúl Castro a Nicolás Maduro," *La Iguana*, December 7, 2015, http://laiguana.tv/articulos/18378-raul-castro-niclas-maduro-mensaje-parlamentarias.

31. See "Jamás aceptaremos condicionamientos que laceren la soberanía y dignidad de la Patria," *Granma*, December 30, 2015, http://www.granma.cu/cuba/2015-12-30/jamas-aceptaremos-condicionamientos-que-laceren-la-soberania-y-dignidad-de-la-patria-30-12-2015-00-12-10.

32. "Cuba rechaza renovación del decreto ejecutivo de EEUU contra Venezuela," *Globovision*, March 5, 2016, http://globovision.com/article/gobierno-de-cuba-rechaza-renovacion-del-decreto-ejecutivo-de-eeuu-contra-venezuela.

33. See Ismael Francisco, "Recibió Raúl al Presidente Nicolás Maduro Moros," *Cuba Debate*, March 18, 2016, http://www.cubadebate.cu/noticias/2016/03/18/recibio-raul-al-presidente-nicolas-maduro-moros/#.WmePdjdOk2w.

34. See "Transcript of Obama-Castro News Conference," *USA Today*, March 21, 2016, https://www.usatoday.com/story/news/politics/2016/03/21/transcript-obama-castro-news-conference/82098056.

35. See "Hemos continuado avanzando con paso seguro, sin prisas, pero sin pausas, o sea, con la gradualidad e integralidad necesarias para alcanzar el éxito," *Juventud Rebelde*, April 17, 2016, http://www.juventudrebelde.cu/cuba/2016-04-17/hemos-continuado-avanzando-con-paso-seguro-sin-prisas-pero-sin-pausas-o-sea-con-la-gradualidad-e-integralidad-necesarias-para-alcanzar-el-exito.

36. See "Declaración del Ministerio de Relaciones Exteriores," *Juventud Rebelde*, February13, 2016, http://www.juventudrebelde.cu/cuba/2016-06-03/declaracion-del-ministerio-de-relaciones-exteriores-27.

37. See the July 8, 2016, speech of Raúl Castro to the Cuban National Assembly: "The Revolutionary Cuban People Will Again Rise to the Occasion," *Granma*, July 13, 2016, http://en.granma.cu/cuba/2016-07-13/the-revolutionary-cuban-people-will-again-rise-to-the-occasion.

38. Daniela Benzi, "El exitoso ocaso del ALBA. Requién para el último vals tercermundista," *Nueva Sociedad* 261 (January–February 2016): 77–91.

39. Ibid., 90.

14

Brazil and Cuba

Regiane Nitsch Bressan

This chapter seeks to present and discuss the relations between Brazil and Cuba during Raúl Castro's government (2008–2018). The study covers the principal advances in this bilateral relation, most of which occurred while Dilma Rousseff (2011–2016) held office in Brazil.

The government of Luis Inacio Lula da Silva (2003–2010) was instrumental in intensifying Brazil's relations with other countries in the region, including Cuba.[1] At his inauguration speech in 2003, Lula stressed the importance of turning Latin America into a politically stable, prosperous, and just region, arguing that this goal could only be reached if other countries in the region cooperated. Against this background, Brazil was one of the proponents of the Community of Latin American and Caribbean States (Comunidad de Estados Latinoamericanos y Caribeños, or CELAC), which joined the Rio Group and the Summit of Latin America and the Caribbean and was aimed at promoting integration and development in Latin American and Caribbean countries.[2] CELAC provided Cuba with a new platform to participate in regional integration, as opposed to the Organization of American States (OAS), of which Cuba is not a part.[3]

During the Rousseff government, bilateral relations between Cuba and Brazil developed in a positive and prosperous manner. Politically, both countries were aware of the importance of regional integration and cooperation regarding relevant issues addressed at other international platforms. During her time in office, Rousseff made two official visits to Cuba, the last one in 2014 when she and Raúl Castro inaugurated the Mariel port renovation project financed by the Brazilian National Bank for Economic and Social Development (BNDES). The project involved the construction of the country's first container terminal and is considered an essential element for the insertion of Cuba into the world economy. The proposal to create an export-oriented free trade zone in Mariel has also attracted several private-sector investments from Brazil.

At the same time, commercial relations have increased significantly. Brazilian exports to Cuba grew from US$73 million in 2002 to US$568 million in 2012, while exports from Cuba to Brazil grew from US$10 million to US$96 million between 2001 and 2013. During this period export products also diversified.[4] Finally, the intensification of bilateral relations is also expressed through the participation of Cuban professionals in the Brazilian Mais Médicos (More Doctors) program, which started in 2013 and involved the recruitment of 11,429 Cuban doctors hired to work in poor, underserved regions, on indigenous reservations, and in other remote areas in the country.[5]

Although changes have occurred in the foreign policy of the Rousseff government, a pragmatic course was followed, aimed at maintaining Brazilian interests in the Caribbean country, which is an indication of the importance of Cuba for Brazil and the entire region.[6] However, after the appointment of Michel Temer as president (2016–2018) following the impeachment of Dilma Rousseff, there has been a reorientation in Brazilian foreign policy away from the Latin American region, including Cuba, and toward northern industrialized countries. Nevertheless, the pragmatic gains of the policy toward Cuba, particularly those of an economic and commercial nature, have been retained.[7]

Relations with Cuba under Rousseff

During the Rousseff government, Latin America remained a priority on the Brazilian foreign policy agenda. However, in comparison with the previous government, a slight decline can be noted.[8] In the domestic arena, there was friction between the main actors—the government, the private sector, and nongovernmental organizations—that determine Brazil's foreign policy and its capacity to realize its ambitions as a regional power. At the regional level, two diplomatic incidents affected Brazilian relations with Latin America, namely, the suspension of Paraguay from Mercosur and the flight to Brazil of Bolivian senator Roger Molina Pinto. Generally speaking though, it can be said that positive Brazilian-Cuban relations with a predominantly economic focus continued and in fact developed significantly under Rousseff.[9]

During her first term, Rousseff traveled to Cuba twice, in 2012 and 2014. In 2012, the objective was to give an impulse to economic projects and other types of cooperation, and the visit coincided with the last instalment of the Brazilian loan to construct a new port terminal in Mariel, near Havana. When asked about the human rights situation during that visit, she steered away from the subject by alleging that this theme should be addressed in a multilateral context, thereby maintaining a neutral posture.[10] In addition, two sensitive events from a human rights perspective took place around the time of her visit to Cuba: the death following a hunger strike of the Cuban dissident Wilman Villar after he had been sentenced to four years in prison and the visit to Brazil of the blogger Yoani Sánchez, one of the Cuban regime's most prominent critics.

The 2014 visit centered on the inauguration of the port of Mariel and a meeting of CELAC, where thirty-two heads of state gathered to discuss the U.S.-imposed trade embargo against Cuba.[11] This visit also included a historic meeting with Fidel Castro, to whom Rousseff expressed her gratitude for the participation of Cuban physicians in the Brazilian Mais Médicos program. They also discussed Brazilian investments in Mariel and other infrastructure projects. Rousseff declared her country's support for Cuba's human and economic potential and criticized the American trade embargo.

However, Brazil's position in CELAC weakened during Rousseff's time in office, and a deepening of relations with Cuba was not realized. Created in 2011 with the intention of providing an alternative for the OAS, which includes the United States and Canada, CELAC has followed a pattern that characterizes initiatives for regional integration in Latin America: ambitious goals are formulated at summit meetings, but in practice the organization has little power to realize these ambitions.[12]

In essence, Rousseff promoted an economic strategy that was extremely pragmatic, an approach that led to a decrease of Brazilian interests in this predominately political organization. In the January 2015 business forum of CELAC, for example, the Brazilian president outlined her support for a "diplomacy of results," which prioritized national economic growth. Her approach guided other external initiatives of her government, among them the plans to employ the Brazilian Cooperation Agency to stimulate the export of Brazilian products. As a result, the relations between Brazil and Cuba have taken place mainly at the bilateral level, focusing on economic and commercial cooperation as well as the social goal of recruiting Cuban health professionals for underdeveloped regions in Brazil.[13]

Cuban Physicians in Brazil: The Mais Médicos Program

The arrival of Cuban physicians is a key factor in the Brazilian social program called Mais Médicos, or More Doctors. Started in 2013, it was intended to tackle the chronic lack of physicians in parts of the country by bringing basic health-care services to poor and/or remote areas as well as indigenous reservations. It is a program in which the federal government works with states and municipalities to provide physicians to areas where these professionals are scarce or not present.[14]

Upon its creation, Mais Médicos announced 18,240 job vacancies for physicians in a total of 4,058 municipalities all over the country, covering 73 percent of Brazilian towns and settlements, as well as thirty-four special indigenous health districts. Prior to the program, Brazil had 1.8 physicians per one thousand inhabitants, compared to 3.5 in Argentina and Uruguay and 6.7 in Cuba.

In Brazil, the contracting of physicians willing to work in underdeveloped regions is conducted through public competitions, which prioritize Brazilian physicians. However, if after this procedure vacancies are still open, Mais Médicos states that they can then be filled by foreign professionals. Those can be contracted individually or through an arrangement established in 2013 between Brazil and the Pan-American Health Organization (PAHO). It was through PAHO that the Cuban doctors were hired.

According to the Ministry of Health, in 2016 Mais Médicos hired a total of 5,274 Brazilian physicians, 11,429 Cubans, and 1,537 doctors from other nationalities, with Cubans making up 62.6 percent of the total. Among the non-Brazilian physicians, the Cubans are best equipped to deal with the Brazilian reality, due to the fact that Cuban medical training puts a strong emphasis on family medicine. This allows Cuban doctors to live in the communities where they serve, working as family doctors for all members of the local community and as active participants in the family health program.

The Brazilian health authorities claimed that without Cuban doctors, it would not have been possible to fill all the vacancies offered by Mais Médicos. With ample experience in overseas missions, Cuban physicians are now working in Brazil for the second time; the first time was as part of a local social program in 1998.[15] Mais Médicos' impact on Brazilian public health services has been very positive in both human and economic terms, considering that 80 percent of all medical issues can be resolved at the local level by the family doctor, using a preventive medicine approach.

In 2016, the 18,240 physicians contracted by Mais Médicos worked in 4,058 municipalities, of which 700 possessed no prior public health care, as well as on thirty-four indigenous reservations, reaching a total of 63 million people. Considering the impact felt across the country, the presence of Cuban physicians has strengthened and deepened relations with Cuba, according to ex-president Rousseff.

Despite Mais Médicos' successes, there was opposition to the program from within the medical sector and opposition parties. When the recruitment of Cuban doctors began, medical associations represented by the Federal Council of Medicine released a Declaration in Defense of the Health of Brazilians. Among the forty-four demands stated in this document was the abolition of Mais Médicos. Nevertheless, in 2016 the Temer government extended the program for another three years, including the controversial practice of employing Cuban physicians. There was, however, a reduction in the number of vacancies, from eighteen thousand to fourteen thousand.[16]

In November 2016, the three-year contracts of thirty-five hundred Cuban medical personnel expired. With the exception of those who had started families while working in Brazil, they returned to Cuba, in accordance with the terms of the bilateral agreement. In the face of the departure of these professionals, the Brazilian authorities determined to offer one thousand potentially more attractive posts to Brazilian candidates. The target set by the Ministry of Health is to replace four thousand foreign doctors with Brazilians by the end of 2019.

Following the renewal of the agreement, the Cuban deputy minister of public health raised a number of concerns. Among these were the devaluation of the Brazilian currency, the absence of any wage indexation for the doctors working in the program, and the need for extra allowances for those working in risk sectors or isolated regions. Nevertheless, the Cuban government remains committed to the project, which is up for renewal every three years. Since these issues were raised, there have been some related developments. Cuban demands regarding wage adjustments were met by Brazil following negotiations with the PAHO. At present, Mais Médicos is expected to continue employing foreign professionals for as long as it is unable to fill all vacancies from the domestic labor pool.

It is worth noting that when the congenital Zika syndrome epidemic struck Brazil (reaching its peak in 2016), the Cuban doctors were actively engaged in treating patients with this condition. As employees of the PAHO, they followed instructions in terms of accepted treatment, employing specialized diagnostic kits and promoting insecticides. PAHO was particularly vigilant both in developing a methodology of analysis of microcephaly and in the diagnosis and treatment of patients. Given the emphasis on prevention in the medical training of the Cuban physicians, they used this approach in actively seeking to prevent the spread of the Zika virus, as well as dengue and chikungunya, in the largely underserved areas where they worked.

Investments in Infrastructure and the Port of Mariel

The biggest Brazilian investment in Cuba has been the modernization and expansion of the port of Mariel. Its terminal, which can service post-Panamax vessels, is highly sophisticated and comparable with those in other major Caribbean ports like Kingston, Jamaica, and Freeport, Bahamas. The Mariel project is the biggest of its kind in Cuba, with a total cost of US$957 million, of which US$682 million was financed by the Brazilian development bank, BNDES.[17] It was executed as a joint venture by the Brazilian private company Odebrecht and the Cuban company Quality. Of the invested amount, some US$800 million was spent in Brazil on goods and services, generating 156,000 direct and indirect jobs. This huge investment illustrates several Brazilian interests in the Caribbean region.

Brazil wishes to become one of Cuba's principal trade partners. But in order to achieve that goal, heavy investments in the Cuban infrastructure are needed. The modernization of Mariel and the subsequent creation of a special economic zone in that area will play a key role in this process, because the investment of private capital will be allowed. This will provide Brazilian companies with access to the Cuban market. Keen on intensifying the economic relations with Cuba, the Brazilian government has offered a US$290 million loan to set up the special economic zone in Mariel.

At the inauguration of the Mariel building site, President Rousseff stressed the strategic importance of Mariel for Brazil's external trade, as it involves the creation of a logistical system to process Brazilian export goods. In addition, at a distance of less than ninety-three miles from the United States, Mariel is a geographically significant location for Brazilian companies to establish a base. Moreover, the region has an ample supply of qualified and cheap labor. Finally, by investing in Cuba, Brazil has a chance to increase its influence in a part of the Americas that lies outside the U.S. sphere of influence. The fact that President Donald Trump, influenced by the powerful lobby of Cuban exiles in the United States, has shown little interest in normalizing American relations with Cuba means that Brazil will be able to operate in Cuba without American competition for some time to come.

The governments of Lula and Rousseff, however, were not unique in cultivating relations with Cuba. During Brazil's history, many governments have cooperated with Cuba.[18] But with the significant investments in Mariel, these relations have become more pragmatic in nature than ideological, opening the way for other investments.[19] Following the inauguration of Mariel, representatives of both countries have signed an agreement allowing the Brazilian conglomerate Odebrecht to carry out other infrastructure projects in Cuba.[20] Among these are the expansion and modernization of the airports of Havana, Santa Clara, Holguín, Cayo Coco, and Cayo Largo. The most important of these is the construction of a new terminal at José Martí International Airport in Havana, at a cost of US$207 million. Again, BNDES is taking on the role of financier, underscoring the internationalization tendency that benefits many Brazilian businesses and increases their competitiveness, in addition to strengthening economic relations between Brazil and Cuba.

Commerce and Bilateral Trade

Brazilian exports to Cuba have grown fivefold since the beginning of the century, reaching an all-time high in 2012 of US$568 million. Data from the Ministry of Industrial Development and Commerce show that in 1989 Brazil exported goods to Cuba valued at US$76.6 million, while it imported US$31.9 million, small numbers in comparison with the present. The governments of Lula and Rousseff were instrumental in this increase by forging political relations as a basis for trade relations.[21] In this process, Brazil has become Cuba's third-largest trading partner, surpassed only by Venezuela and China. According to the Brazilian Agency for the Promotion of Exportation and Investments (APEX), if this trend continues, Brazil has a good chance of becoming Cuba's leading trade partner.

Commerce between the two countries has intensified with the investment in Mariel and the consolidation of economic and political relations. Figure 14.1 demonstrates a growth in exports to Cuba after 2008, a favorable year for the commodities trade. Despite a decrease in 2009, there was a sustained growth, peaking in 2012, when Brazilian exports reached US$568 million. This trend continued, and up to 2015 exports were in excess of US$500 million.

Imports from Cuba have followed a similar trend (see figure 14.2). Since 2000, there has been a significant increase, accelerating in 2008, and between 2010 and 2013, when the Mariel project was being carried out, the total value of imports almost reached US$100 million. Nevertheless, imports from Cuba represent a mere fifth of the total bilateral trade.

Although this trade balance has been favorable for Brazil, trade started to decline in 2015 when Brazil entered an economic and political crisis (see figure 14.3). Key factors behind the decline are the fall of commodity prices, difficulties in Brazil's economic recovery, the overthrow of the government, and changes in Brazilian foreign policy by Rousseff's successor, Michel Temer. The decline is expected to last until 2018, when Raúl Castro's and Michel Temer's terms in office come to an end.

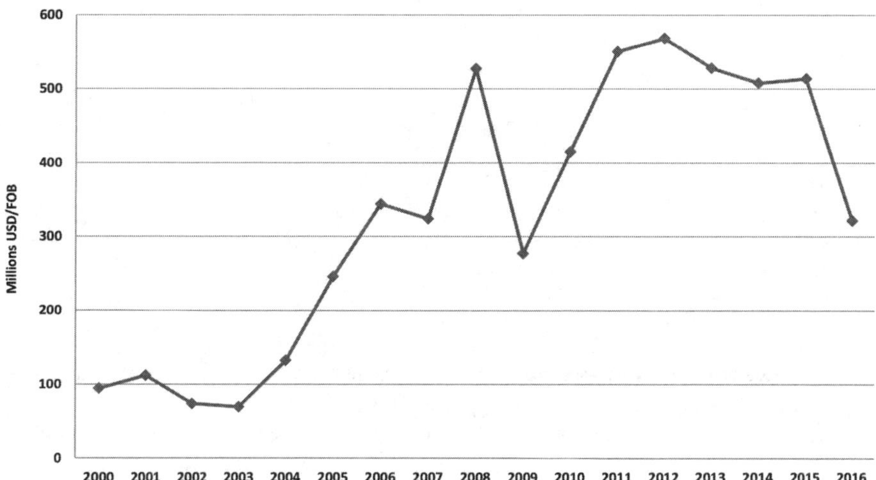

Figure 14.1. Brazilian exports to Cuba (US$/FOB).
Source: Ministério da Indústria, Comércio Exterior e Serviços (MDIC), "Estatísticas de comércio exterior," Brasília, November 1, 2016. Available from http://www.mdic.gov.br

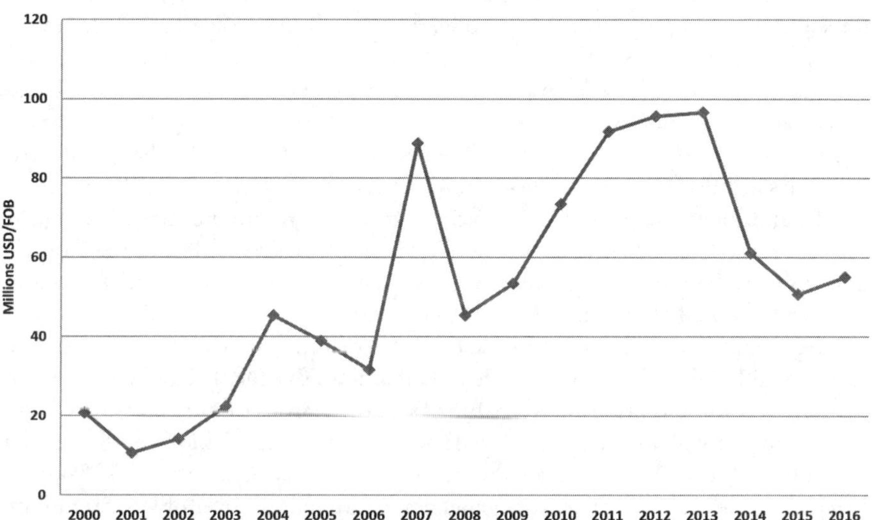

Figure 14.2. Brazilian imports from Cuba (US$/FOB).
Source: MDIC, "Estatísticas de comércio exterior," Brasília, November 1, 2016. Available from http://www.mdic.gov.br.

Nonetheless, the strong foundation that has been laid guarantees a lasting commercial relationship.

Over half of Brazil's exports to Cuba consist of commodities like meat, chicken, soy oil, corn, rice, and coffee. Manufactured items such as machines, shoes, and carpentry products have also gained in importance. Several other products are also

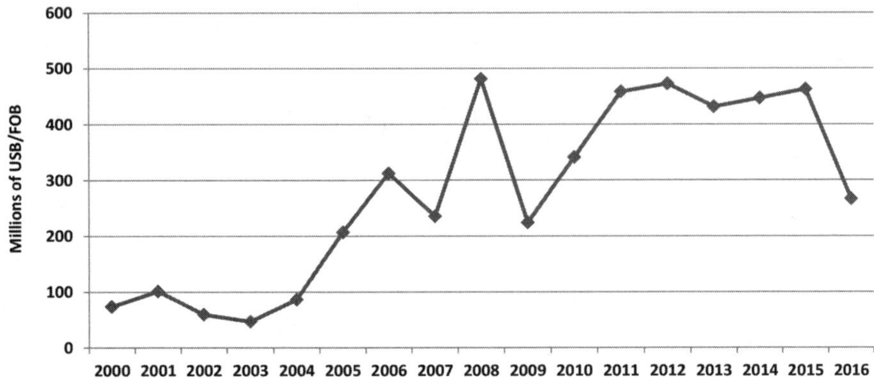

Figure 14.3. Brazil-Cuba trade balance (US$/FOB).
Source: MDIC, "Estatísticas de comércio exterior," Brasília, November 1, 2016. Available from http://www.mdic.gov.br.

exported, notably cereals, cellulose, milk, soap, cars and car parts, rubber, iron, textiles, and furniture. Brazilian meat (chicken, beef, and pork) has become very important for the Cuban consumer market in the last decade. The same can be said for soy derivatives. Together, these products make up more than half of the Brazilian exports to Cuba. Brazil, in turn, also imports Cuban products, albeit in lesser quantities. The focus here is on pharmaceuticals (medicines and vaccines), tobacco, beverages, and chemicals.

Brazilian companies have invested increasingly in Cuba over the last decade. Examples of this are large businesses from the food industry, such as JBS and Brazil Foods, and logistics operator Surimpex. In addition, traditional Brazilian companies have participated in trade missions organized by APEX during the Rousseff government: Bauducco, Asa Alimentos, Globoaves, and Vilheto from the food industry; Cosil and TendTudo from the construction sector; IT equipment manufacturer Oberthur; and truck and tractor parts manufacturer Eletroflex. There are also several key Brazilian investments in Cuba. For example, BRASCUBA Cigarillos S.A. is a joint venture between Brazil's leading cigarette manufacturer, Souza Cruz, and the Cuban state company Tabacuba. From its creation in 1995, it has expanded capacity and doubled the production of its main product, "Popular" black cigarettes. This joint venture generates an annual turnover of US$50 million, selling 3 billion cigarettes per year. The original agreement will expire in 2020, but due to its success and government incentives, Souza Cruz wants to extend the partnership until 2070.

Fanavid, a manufacturer of automotive safety windows and civil construction materials, has reached an agreement with the Cuban authorities to open a plant in Cuba, focused on the production of construction materials, involving an initial investment of US$250 million. The plant will supply the local market and export 80 percent of its production to other Caribbean countries and Brazil.

The Compañía de Obras en Infraestructura, an Odebrecht subsidiary in Cuba, signed a contract with the Cuban sugar company Azcuba to take over the management of the "5 de Septiembre" sugar factory in the province of Cienfuegos for a period of ten years, during which time Odebrecht will apply its experience in the sugar industry to increase the plant's production and revitalize the sugar sector. This investment is a welcome relief for the Cuban sugar sector, which is operating at an eighth of its capacity in the early 1970s, and could well use the Brazilian expertise in that area. Furthermore, as part of an initiative to reduce the country's reliance on fossil fuels and to promote sustainability, Odebrecht will invest in the production of ethanol made from sugarcane so that in due course the sugar sector can become Cuba's main energy supplier.[22]

Despite the fact that ex-president Fidel Castro was opposed to agroenergy due to its being at odds with food production, Cuba has the potential to become the world's third-largest producer of biofuels, surpassed only by the United States and Brazil. Although it will take years to set up a modern ethanol production system in Cuba, the Brazilian technical assistance does offer the perspective of reducing Cuba's dependence on fossil fuel imports in the long term.

In synthesis, it can be said that the cooperation agreements and presence of the Brazilian private sector in Cuba are the result of reforms in the Cuban economic policy implemented by Raúl Castro. Gradually, the door is being opened for private initiatives, and the fact that Brazil is among the first to capitalize on these new opportunities further consolidates the relations between the two countries.

CONCLUSION: THE COUP BY MICHEL TEMER AND ITS REPERCUSSIONS FOR RELATIONS WITH CUBA

Since the beginning of the twenty-first century, Brazilian foreign policy has focused on intensifying diplomatic relations with Latin American countries.[23] Under the government of Lula, the country took on a leadership role in the region, giving impulse to platforms for regional cooperation such as Mercosur, the Union of South American Nations, and CELAC.[24] The expectation was that Rousseff would continue this policy, but in reality her government experienced some difficulty in maintaining the same level of intensity in its relations with Latin America.[25] Nevertheless, the fruitful bilateral cooperation with Cuba was continued and expanded, resulting in the successes of Mariel, the Mais Médicos program, and growing trade, among others.

The government led by Michel Temer (2016–2018), on the other hand, has very different views on regional relations, particularly with regard to Cuba. The conservative forces in Brazilian society that supported the ousting of Rousseff in favor of Temer have always criticized the pursuit of relations with Cuba, which they describe as a dictatorial state with no respect for human rights. This argument is strictly ideological and is not based on any analysis of the actual cooperation that exists between the countries. However, because several powerful actors in the Brazilian private sector stand to gain from undisrupted relations with Cuba, this criticism was quickly silenced. Cuban president Raúl Castro, in turn, has expressed support for ousted president Rousseff, describing her removal as a "parliamentary coup."

Overall, then, during the Temer government a decrease in Brazil's commitment to regional relations and integration projects can be observed, including those with Cuba. The first speeches by Temer's minister of foreign relations, José Serra, point to a reorientation of Brazilian foreign policy toward the major industrialized powers of the world, to the detriment of South-South relations.[26] What Serra proposes is essentially a return to economic and political relations aligned with the developed countries, and the United States in particular, a process which implies a subordinate position for Brazil. In this way, the government aims to dismantle the alternative foreign policies constructed by the previous governments.

Although the political relations between Brazil and Cuba have deteriorated since Temer took office, it is to be expected that the economic aspects of the relation will be maintained, considering the advantages for both countries. Recently, bilateral trade has decreased, but this was more a result of the Brazilian economic crisis than of any deliberate government policy changes. The tendency of reducing ties at a political and ideological level but conserving economic relations is expected to last until the terms of both Raúl Castro and Temer end.

NOTES

1. C. Amorim, "Sem medo de decidir," in *A nova política externa. 2003–2010*, vol. 4 of *O Brasil em transformação*, ed. Kjeld Jakobsen and Elói Pietá (São Paulo: Editora Perseu Abramo, 2010).

2. Tullo Vigevani and Gabriel Cepaluni, "A política externa de Lula da Silva: A estratégia da autonomia pela diversificação," *Contexto Internacional* 29, no. 2 (2007): 273–335.

3. Samir Perrone de Miranda, "A integração da América do Sul no discurso da política externa brasileira (1992–2010)" (PhD thesis, Universidade Federal do Rio Grande do Sul, 2013).

4. Ministério da Indústria, Comércio Exterior e Serviços (MDIC), *Estatísticas de comércio exterior* (Brasília: MDIC), http://www.mdic.gov.br/comercio-exterior/estatisticas-de-comercio-exterior.

5. Marina Dias and Natália Cacian, "Mais Médicos 'estreitou' relações entre Brasil e Cuba, diz Dilma," *Folha de São Paulo*, August 4, 2015, http://www1.folha.uol.com.br/cotidiano/2015/08/1664328-mais-medicos-estreitou-relacoes-entre-brasil-e-cuba-diz-dilma.shtml.

6. Samir Perrone de Miranda and Camille Amorim Leite Ribeiro, "A América do Sul na política externa de Dilma Rousseff: Continuidades e rupturas," in *Anais do I Seminário Internacional de Ciência Política. Estado e Democracia em Mudança no Século XXI* (Porto Alegre: UFRGS, 2015), https://www.ufrgs.br/sicp/wp-content/uploads/2015/09/PERRONE-MIRANDA-2015-A-América-do-Sul-na-política-externa-de-Dilma-Rousseff.pdf.

7. Renato Xavier, "Análise—a política externa brasileira à la Temer," *Estadao*, May 13, 2016, http://www.estadao.com.br/noticias/geral,analise—-a-politica-externa-brasileira-a-la-temer,10000051104.

8. Cristina Soreanu Pecequilo and Corival Alves do Cormu, *O Brasil e a América do Sul—Relações regionais e globais* (Rio de Janeiro: Altabooks Editora, 2015).

9. "Dilma: Maior contribuição do Brasil a Cuba é econômica," *Exame*, July 12, 2012, http://exame.abril.com.br/economia/dilma-maior-contribuicao-do-brasil-a-cuba-e-economica.

10. "Em Cuba, Dilma diz que violações de direitos humanos ocorrem em todos os países," *Noticias r7*, January 31, 2012, http://noticias.r7.com/brasil/noticias/em-cuba-dilma-diz-que-violacoes-de-direitos-humanos-ocorrem-em-todos-os-paises-20120131.html.

11. Afonso Benites, "A relação entre o Brasil e Cuba vai além de turismo e Mais Médicos," *El Pais*, March 26, 2014, http://brasil.elpais.com/brasil/2014/03/27/economia/1395877329_050738.html.

12. Amado Luiz Cervo and Antonio Carlos Lessa, "O declínio: Inserção internacional do Brasil (2011–2014)," *Revista Brasileira de Política Internacional* 57, no. 2 (2014): 33–151, http://www.scielo.br/scielo.php?script=sci_arttext&pid=S0034-73292014000200133&lng=en&tlng=pt.10.1590/0034-7329201400308.

13. Dias and Cacian, "Mais Médicos 'estreitou' relações."

14. Governo Federal, *Programa Mais Médicos* (Brasilia: Government of Brazil, 2016), http://maismedicos.gov.br.

15. "Para médicas cubanas, sistemas de saúde de Cuba e do Brasil se parecem," *O Globo*, August 30, 2013, http://g1.globo.com/pernambuco/noticia/2013/08/para-medicas-cubanas-sistemas-de-saude-de-cuba-e-do-brasil-se-parecem.html.

16. Manoel Ventura, "Temer quer manter médicos cubanos no Brasil," *O Globo*, July 21, 2016, http://oglobo.globo.com/brasil/governo-temer-quer-manter-medicos-cubanos-no-brasil-19761775.

17. Vera Rosa, "O Estado de São Paulo. Brasil financia mais US$ 290 milhões para Cuba ativar seu principal porto, Havana," *Estadao*, January 27, 2014, http://internacional.estadao.com.br/noticias/geral,brasil-financia-mais-us-290-milhoes-para-cuba-ativar-seu-principal-porto,1123505.

18. Marcos Alan Shaikhzadeh V. Ferreira, "La política exterior de Brasil hacia Cuba: Un análisis histórico desde el gobierno de José Sarney hasta los dias actuales," in *Cuba, Estados Unidos y América Latina frente a los desafios hemisféricos*, ed. Luis Fernando Ayerbe (Barcelona: Icaria, 2011), 203–28.

19. Afonso Benites, "A relação entre o Brasil e Cuba vai além de turismo e Mais Médicos," *El Pais*, March 26, 2014, http://brasil.elpais.com/brasil/2014/03/27/economia/1395877329_050738.html.

20. "Brasil dará crédito de U$176 milhões a Cuba para modernizar aeroportos," *Em.com.br*, May 7, 2013, http://www.em.com.br/app/noticia/internacional/2013/05/07/interna_internacional,383319/brasil-dara-credito-de-u-176-milhoes-a-cuba-para-modernizar-aeroportos.shtml.

21. MDIC, *Estatísticas de Comércio Exterior*.

22. Roberto Salomón, "Biomassa, fonte de eletricidade inesgotável para Cuba," *Granma*, March 3, 2016, http://pt.granma.cu/cuba/2016-03-03/biomassa-fonte-de-eletricidade-inesgotavel-para-cuba.

23. Amado Luis Cervo, *Inserção internacional: Formação dos conceitos brasileiros* (São Paulo: Editora Saraiva, 2008).

24. Regiane Nitsch Bressan, "*A integração sul-americana e a superação da pobreza. Uma abordagem pela percepção das elites*" (PhD thesis, University of São Paulo, 2012), http://www.teses.usp.br/teses/disponiveis/84/84131/tde-18122012-104158/publico/2012_RegianeNitschBressan.pdf.

25. Joao Marcelo Conte Cornetet, "A política externa de Dilma Rousseff: Contenção na continuidade," *Conjuntura Austral* 5, no. 24 (January–July, 2014): 111–50.

26. Chico Dênis and Alexandre Andreatta, "José Serra afasta o Brasil da América Latina," *Rede Latinamerica*, May 24, 2016, http://redelatinamerica.cartacapital.com.br/jose-serra-afasta-o-brasil-da-america-latina.

15

Russia and Cuba

Mervyn Bain

Since Raúl Castro became the permanent president of Cuba in early 2008, Havana's relationship with Moscow is at its most robust politically since the end of Cuban-Soviet relations, as evidenced by Dmitry Medvedev's having visited Cuba twice since February 2008, Raúl Castro's traveling to Moscow three times in the same period, and Vladimir Putin's visiting Cuba in July 2014. This is very different from the early 1990s, when the absence of such visits was highly symbolic of the downturn in the bilateral relationship in the years following the disintegration of the USSR. Moreover, the historic change in Cuba's relationship with the United States since December 2014 has not had any apparent negative repercussions for the island's rejuvenated relationship with Russia. It could also be thought that the perception of Raúl Castro as having been the Cuban revolutionary leader who had enjoyed the most cordial relationship with the Soviet leadership may be significant for the present robust state of the relationship.[1]

This chapter examines contemporary Cuban-Russian relations to ascertain the processes and pressures evident within this relationship and therefore the foundations of the rejuvenated alliance. It starts by charting the robust nature of the multifaceted relationship in the middle of the second decade of the twenty-first century and examines its theoretical foundations before analyzing how these theoretical underpinnings have impacted the bilateral relationship.

THE REJUVENATED RELATIONSHIP

The relationship retains political significance for both Cuba and Russia, with the frequency of visits to each other by the political elites of both countries, which will be detailed throughout this chapter, being a manifestation of its importance. Moreover,

Cuba and Russia share a desire for a multipolar world, evidenced by the joint memorandum that was issued at the end of Raúl Castro's January 2009 trip to Moscow, which stated, "Raúl Castro and Dmitry A. Medvedev noted with satisfaction the need for a multipolar and stable system, which will ensure sustainable development and ways to achieve peace and welfare for the global community."[2] In July 2014, while in Havana, Putin stated, "Today, Cuba is one of Russia's leading partners in the region. Our cooperation is strategic and long-term oriented. We closely coordinate our foreign policy, including within multilateral organizations. Our positions coincide on many global and regional issues."[3]

In 2008 at the United Nations, Cuba supported Russia regarding the Georgian situation, with Raúl Castro having described Georgia as the "aggressor."[4] This was repeated with the situation which unfolded in Syria throughout 2013. In September 2013 *Granma* published a Cuban Ministry of Foreign Affairs statement, which said,

> The Ministry of Foreign Affairs of the Republic of Cuba has learned of, with profound concern, the statement made on August 31 by Barack Obama, President of the United States, in which he announced his decision to launch a military action against the Syrian Arab Republic.
>
> Without leaving any margin whatsoever for attempts underway to reach a political solution to the conflict, or presenting any kind of evidence, and with total disrespect for the opinions of many countries—including some of its principal allies—and the United Nations, the President of the United States has announced his intention to engage in actions in violation of international law and the UN Charter. These will inevitably provoke more death and destruction and will unavoidably lead to an intensification of the existing conflict in this Arab nation.[5]

Moreover, on March 27, 2014, Cuba was one of eleven countries to vote against the UN resolution condemning Russia for the referendum held in the Crimea.[6] In April 2016, during his address to the Seventh Congress of the Communist Party of Cuba, Raúl Castro criticized expansion of the North Atlantic Treaty Organization (NATO) to the edge of Russia's borders.[7] This criticism is important in itself, but interestingly such Cuban sentiments have only recently become apparent in speeches by the Cuban ruling elite, illustrating the political robustness of the contemporary bilateral relationship.

This Cuban support for Russia has been reciprocated by Moscow, with the Russian government repeatedly criticizing the U.S. embargo against Cuba, as demonstrated in February 2013 when Medvedev was in Cuba and called the embargo "outrageous and outdated."[8] The impact of the United States on Cuban-Russian relations will be examined more fully later in the chapter, but significantly Moscow has continued to call for the embargo's end even after December 2014 and the start of a normalization process between Havana and Washington. In September 2015 Sergey Lavrov, Russian foreign minister, called for the embargo to be lifted while addressing the United Nations in New York City.[9]

Closely linked to the relationship and retaining political significance for both countries is the existence of the political will for the level of bilateral trade to increase. This has been evident for some time, with Ricardo Alarcón, president of the National Assembly, and Boris Gryzlov, Speaker of the Russian State Duma, signing an interparliamentary agreement in December 2010 to boost bilateral trade.[10] Moreover, in February 2013 Medvedev stated, "Regrettably, trade between Russia and Cuba is not high as it should be. . . . There are good investment plans, and investment is developing despite its small volume. I am sure it will grow and our cooperation will expand to many new areas."[11]

This desire to increase bilateral trade was repeated in May 2013 by Valentina Matvienko, president of the Council of Federations of the Russian Federation's Federal Assembly, in an interview with *Granma* during her trip to Cuba. During this interview she said, "Despite the fact that trade relations have grown recently, they still do not reflect the potential and possibilities of our two countries. The value of our trade exchange is approaching $270 million, according to 2012 figures, which is insufficient. We are currently negotiating a broad range of projects relating to energy, and Russian companies such as Zarubezhneft are actively involved in oil prospecting in Cuban waters, and this work is going to continue."[12]

The talks between Raúl Castro and Dmitry Rogozin, Russian vice president, when Rogozin visited Havana in December 2014, were dominated by the topic of trade.[13] This was repeated in May 2015, when Raúl Castro met both Putin and Medvedev while in Moscow for the seventieth anniversary of the end of the Great Fatherland War.[14]

The existence of the political will for trade to increase is highly important because the level of bilateral trade has remained low for a number of years. In 2000 bilateral Cuban-Russian trade turnover was 435,877,000 pesos, with this figure falling below 200 million pesos from 2003 to 2005. However, in the period from 2005 to 2012 bilateral Cuban-Russian trade increased, with 341,228,000 pesos worth of trade being conducted in 2012, which made Russia the island's ninth most important trading partner.[15] In 2014 bilateral trade fell to 193,265,000 pesos.[16] The low level of trade makes the existence of the political will for it to increase imperative as the level of trade conducted in 2014 is less than 0.05 percent of the trade conducted in 1991, the final year of Cuban-Soviet relations.[17]

However, it is not just these public statements which demonstrate the existence of this political will for trade to increase as it is also evident in a number of agreements which have been signed between the two countries. In April 2013 an agreement was signed for a collaborative project to build by 2020 a new international airport at San Antonio de los Baños, thirty kilometers from the Cuban capital.[18] In July 2014, when in Havana, Putin commented upon the importance of both the building of this airport and the construction of deepwater maritime facilities at Mariel when he said, "The construction of a major transport hub is another large-scale project currently under development with Russia's and Cuba's involvement, as well as the possibility of attracting investment from third countries. It involves upgrading the port of Mariel and building a modern international airport with a cargo terminal in San Antonio de los Baños."[19] Furthermore, during Medvedev's February 2013 trip to Cuba, a number of agreements were signed, including one for the Cuban purchase of Ilyushin aircraft. Medvedev also iterated the wish for an increase in scientific links, especially with regard to Cuba's biotechnology industry.[20] This wish was realized in July 2014 when Putin traveled to Cuba with ten new cooperation accords being signed, which concentrated both on the areas detailed above and also on others, including energy, transportation, and industry.[21] In 2015 the two countries signed a contract for the erection of four two-hundred-megawatt power units on the island.[22] Also in 2015 Mikhail Kamynin, Russian ambassador to Cuba, spoke of interest in Cuba on the part of the Russian oil companies Zarubezhneft and Rosneft, while Russia was also heavily represented at the Thirty-Third International Trade Fair "FIHAV-2015," held in November 2015 by companies such as KAMAZ, Helicópteros de Rusia, Grupo GAZ, and Zarubezhneft.[23] In June 2016, while in Moscow, Ricardo Cabrisas, vice president of the Council of Ministers, and Rogozin signed an agreement for experimentation and collaboration in energy, metallurgy, transport, biotechnology, and education.[24] Moreover, at the start of 2017 media reports began to surface that indicated that the Russian Ministry of Energy was exploring the possibility of Russian oil companies supplying oil to Cuba.[25]

An agreement has also been reached regarding Cuba's Soviet-era debt, which has been a bone of contention between the two countries throughout the post-Soviet era. First, during Medvedev's February 2013 visit it was agreed that this debt should be partially written off with the remainder being refinanced over a ten-year period.[26] However, one of the agreements signed during Putin's July 2014 trip superseded the February 2013 agreement; in it the Kremlin wrote off 90 percent of this debt, with the remaining 10 percent to be "paid" with Russian investments in the Cuba economy.[27] This is highly significant because it could have been thought that Cuba's Soviet-era debt had "blocked" increases in trade as the latter had remained at a low level for a number of years. However, with this "block" removed, it could be assumed that bilateral trade will increase. The fact that part of the debt is being "paid" by Russian investment in the Cuban economy provides further evidence of both Moscow's interest in the island's economy and also the political will for bilateral trade to increase.

Joint collaborations are not just in the civil field as they also extend to military cooperation, evidenced by Russian army general Valeri Guerasimov's verifying in May 2013 that Cuban-Russian military cooperation would continue. This could seem to be a throwback to the Cold War period of the relationship, but Cuba's possessing Soviet-era hardware appears to have underpinned this situation, as Alexandr Fomín, vice president of the Russian Federal Service of Military and Technological Cooperation, indicated when he said, "We will not supply Cuba with the most modern armaments, but rather it will be of a level to maintain Cuban defense."[28] Further demonstrating joint military collaboration was the arrival in Havana in August 2013 of a Russian naval task force led by the missile cruiser *Moskva*.[29] On

January 20, 2015, the Russian spy ship *Viktor Leonov* visited the Cuban capital, with the significance of this visit increasing as it was the day before the commencement of bilateral Cuban-U.S. talks after the start of a normalization process in December 2014.[30] In February 2015 army general Serguey Shoigu, Russian defense minister, visited Cuba and thanked the island for "the warm welcome the Russian navy receives in the port of Havana," which Shoigu said was representative of the bilateral relationship in general.[31]

The continuation of military collaboration may be highly symbolic and connote the relationship's Soviet past, but since 2008 there has been a general increase in symbolism within the relationship. In January 2009 Raúl Castro officially visited Moscow for the first time in more than twenty years, which is important in itself as he had not visited the Russian capital since the end of Cuban-Soviet relations in late 1991. Moreover, in his April 19, 2011, closing address to the Sixth Congress of the Communist Party of Cuba on the fifty-first anniversary of the failed Bay of Pigs invasion, Raúl thanked the Kremlin for its aid and support for the revolution's infancy when he said, "It is appropriate on a day like today to remember that without the help of the peoples who made up that immense country, especially the Russian people, the Revolution would not have been able to survive in those initial years facing growing and continuous imperialist attacks and for this reason we are eternally grateful to them."[32] Not only does this demonstrate the current robust nature of the relationship, but the reference to the Soviet era is also important, which will be detailed more fully below.

While in Moscow in July 2012, Raúl Castro placed a wreath at the Tomb of the Unknown Soldier in Red Square and also visited the Lenin Mausoleum.[33] Interestingly, during his 2009 trip to Moscow, Raúl had not visited this mausoleum. Furthermore, in May 2016 the "Cuban Five" were in Moscow to attend the celebrations for the anniversary of the end of World War II.[34] Due to the significance of the "Cuban Five" and the Great Fatherland War in the Cuban and Russian societies, respectively, the symbolic importance of this visit is hard to overestimate.

An increase in a number of cultural events has also occurred since 2008. Russia was the "guest of honor" at the 2010 Havana International Book Fair, which Lavrov visited while on the island. In the months immediately afterward, a permanent Russian exhibition was opened in the José Martí National Library in Havana, partly funded by the Russian "Mir" Fund. In October 2012 performances by the Moscow theater company Et Cetera were staged during a four-day stay in Havana. On June 15, 2015, in the Russian Foreign Ministry in Moscow, Lavrov gave the address at the launch of the book by Russian author Nikolay Leonov, which focused on Raúl Castro, published to celebrate the fifty-fifth anniversary of the restoration of diplomatic relations between Havana and Moscow. Moreover, from September 21 to 27, 2015, the Charles Chaplin Cinema in Havana hosted "Russian Cinema Week in Cuba." On March 6, 2016, the orchestra of Mariinsky Theatre in Saint Petersburg, directed by Valery Gergiev, played in Havana.[35]

At the start of 2008 the Our Lady of Kazan Russian Orthodox Cathedral was opened in Havana and visited by Medvedev during his November 2008 trip to

Cuba. Both Fidel and Raúl Castro subsequently received awards from the Russian Orthodox Church, and during his May 2015 trip to the Russian capital, Raúl met Kirill, patriarch of Russian Orthodox Church.[36] Subsequently, in February 2016, Patriarch Kirill visited the Russian Orthodox Church in Havana and met Raúl Castro.

Since 2008 the longevity of the relationship between Havana and Moscow has been highlighted by both governments, with this being evident in May 2016 when Miguel Díaz-Canel, Cuban first vice president, traveled to Russia. During this visit he met Putin, Medvedev, and Rogozin, and the Cuban newspaper *Juventud Rebelde* spoke of the "indestructible friendship since the reestablishment of diplomatic relations on 8 May 1960."[37] Both Havana and Moscow have begun to comment on the relationship which existed between the two countries before the Cuban Revolution.[38] This was demonstrated by Raúl Castro in January 2009 when, during his tour of the Museum of the Great Patriotic War in Moscow, he visited the permanent exhibition to Jorge and Aldo Vivo and Enrique Vilar, who fought for the Red Army during World War II. On August 7, 2015, Kamynin visited the new permanent exhibition in the Museo de la Revolución in Havana dedicated to Marina de Gontich, the Russia ballerina who had lived in Havana in the early twentieth century.

During his January 2009 trip Raúl described Cuban-Russian relations as "magnificent" and said that the two countries are "inextricably" linked in an interview with the Russian journal *América Latina*.[39] When Raúl returned to the Russian capital in July 2012, Putin said, "Cuba is not only an old ally, but remains a great friend." He continued, "All that we have achieved during these past years, it's our common treasure."[40] Moreover, in the aftermath of Fidel Castro's passing in November 2016, Medvedev said, "I would like to emphasise Fidel Castro's significant personal contribution to the development of friendly and brotherly partnership relations between the Russian Federation and Cuba. We will cherish the memory of this remarkable man and a true friend of our country."[41] In February 2013 these sentiments were repeated by Medvedev when he said in an interview with *Prensa Latina*, "Our relations with Cuba rest on a formidable basis that had been laid previously. I think it is essential not to squander our past achievements but to build on them."[42]

These actions and comments are highly interesting as they evidence not only the longevity of the relationship but also that the Soviet and post-Soviet eras are being treated as one entity. This reconceptualization of the relationship appears to be an attempt to demonstrate to the younger population in both countries, where a whole generation has come of age since the end of Cuban-Soviet relations in 1991, the longevity of the relationship. This is important because due to the geographical distance between the two countries, questions could arise over the relationship's continuing existence.

At the nongovernmental level, the number of Russians holidaying in Cuba increased in the late 1990s and the first decade of the twenty-first century. In 2003, 10,653 Russians vacationed in Cuba, with the flow increasing to 78,472 in 2011. In 2012 the figure rose to 86,944 before falling to 69,237 in 2014.[43] This 2014 figure may be dwarfed by the more than 1 million Canadians who travel to Cuba each year, but it still makes Russia the tenth-largest source of visitors to Cuba. This influx is facilitated by the fact that travel to Cuba is made easier because Russians do not need entry visas. The significance which the Caribbean island attaches to attracting Russian tourists also is illuminated by Russian being one of four language options on the official tourism website (Cubatravel.cu). Furthermore, Cuba was present at the Seventh International Tourist Fair held in March 2012 in Moscow, demonstrating the importance which Cuba attaches to attracting Russian tourists to the island.[44]

THE FOUNDATIONS OF THE REJUVENATED RELATIONSHIP

As detailed above, Cuban-Russian relations have been very robust since 2008, but the foundations of the relationship were created before Raúl Castro became the permanent president of Cuba, with the changes which took place in both Cuban and Russian foreign policies in the early to mid-1990s being of paramount significance.

At the start of the final decade of the twentieth century, Cuba faced great uncertainty from the new world order that emerged from the Cold War era, especially since it was now bereft of its socialist trading partners and U.S. animosity toward the Caribbean island endured. Consequently Havana's foreign policy underwent some radical changes. On this, John Kirk has written, "The greatest single task in terms of foreign policy facing the Cuban government in the early 1990s, however, was how to keep the traditional (self-declared) enemy at bay."[45] Michael Erisman has stated that Cuba accomplished this by creating greater economic and political space, which resulted from the island diversifying its foreign policy.[46] Additionally, Julie Feinsilver has written, "Cuba's foreign policy initiatives have been geared toward ensuring Cuba's security in an adverse geopolitical situation through support of progressive governments and the creation of a Third World constituency, to gain not just diplomatic support in international organizations but also economic or trade benefits."[47] Jorge Domínguez believes that Havana achieved this by utilizing a four-part strategy. First, due to a neorealist perspective Cuba endeavored to balance the United States internationally; second, the diversification of economic policy abrogated the possible appearance of economic dependence; third, Cuba desired cooperation with the United States regarding common security issues; fourth, Havana strove to create a "constituency abroad," particularly in the Global South.[48]

The above changes to Cuban foreign policy are ultimately underpinned by the principles of realist pragmatism which have been paramount in the Cuban revolutionary elite's thinking since January 1959 and will be detailed here later. However, at various times during the revolutionary era, other concepts have also been evident in Cuban foreign policy. In *Cuba's Foreign Relations in a Post-Soviet World*, Michael Erisman has specified five concepts that have been prevalent in revolutionary Cuba's foreign policy. Many believed that during the Cold War the notion of a revolutionary crusade—that the Cuban government desired to instigate other revolutions around the world—and the superclient/surrogate thesis, which theorizes that Cuba merely acted on Moscow's orders, were preeminent in Cuban foreign policy. However, Erisman has written that the island's foreign policy was too nuanced and complex to be monopolized by just one of these concepts. Furthermore, the end of the Cold War reduced the significance of both ideas.[49] *Fidelista personalismo*, the distinct Cuban version of the great man theory,[50] has also receded in importance since Raúl Castro replaced Fidel Castro as the president of Cuba, first temporarily in August 2006 and then permanently in February 2008.

From the time of the Spanish conquest in the late fifteenth century, Cuba has been subjugated by outside powers. First came Spain and then, from 1898 until 1959, the United States, with some believing that subsequently Cuban dependence on the Soviet Union appeared.[51] This prompted Erisman to write of the importance of dependency in Cuban history, but Erisman has written that after 1959, due to repeated Cuban attempts to reduce dependence on the Soviet Union, what evolved was counterdependence. The preeminence of nationalism within the revolution was fundamental for this.[52]

Moreover, realism has had, and continues to have, salience in both Cuban and Russian foreign policies. The central assumptions of realism are that sovereign states are the preeminent actors in international relations, the international system is intrinsically anarchic and consequently antagonistic, states are unitary rational actors whose focus is their own fixed self-interest, and consequently states strive to maximize power due to their principal goal being their own survival. Regarding this Hans Morgenthau has written, "International politics, like all politics, is a struggle for power."[53] This can be economic dominance or political control of one country over another, among a number of different forms. Consequently, realism is materialist in nature and concentrates on the distribution of material power within the parameters of a self-help system, with states' behavior being determined by the nature of the international system.

A number of different forms of realism have emerged over time, with Kenneth Waltz in *Theory of International Politics* elucidating the idea of defensive realism, which hypothesizes that, due to the international system's being intrinsically anarchic, states perceive all other states as potential threats and consequently their preeminent goal is security. The result is that states are security maximizers rather than power maximizers, with Waltz having written, "The ultimate concern of states is not power, rather security."[54]

Conversely, in *The Tragedy of Great Power Politics* John Mearsheimer details the tenets of offensive realism, which is founded on a divergent perception of power dynamics in the anarchic international system. State security remains key, but Mearsheimer believes that security is achieved by a different means when compared to defensive realism, and he has written, "Offensive realism parts company with defensive realism over the question of how much power states want."[55] The primary action remains self-help, but security is achieved by states' maximizing their power at the expense of other states. The most extreme variant of this is a state's desire to become a hegemonic power.[56]

Both offensive and defensive realism have had resonance for Cuban-Soviet relations, but realism, or more precisely realist pragmatism, has underpinned the actions of the Cuban government throughout the revolutionary period because the survival of the revolution has predicated all policy decisions.[57] More precisely, this exhibits the principles of defensive realism, which has impacted Cuba's relationship with the Kremlin considerably since the late 1950s and early 1960s, which will be detailed, as have counterdependency and nationalism.[58]

In the mid-1990s Russian foreign policy began to move away from the pro-Western outlook of the immediate post-Soviet years,[59] as evidenced in December 1995 when Yevgeny Primakov replaced Andrei Kozyrev as Russian foreign minister. Kozyrev had been closely linked to the pro-Western foreign policy of the early to mid-1990s, but in comparison Primakov believed much more in "spheres of influence."

The key for this policy change was a revival of nationalism within Russian society in general, which impacted on the composition of the State Duma and led Stephen White to write regarding Kozyrev's removal as Russian foreign minister, "In the end he became a 'virtual sacrifice' to the new Duma."[60] A number of reasons underpinned this resurgence in Russian nationalism, which included many within Russia believing that Moscow's pro-Western foreign policy had been a failure. They also believed that the West and organizations such as the International Monetary Fund and World Bank were responsible for the economic problems that continued to blight the country.[61] Additionally, NATO's expansion to the east and treatment of their fellow Serbs in the former Yugoslavia deeply offended Russian nationalists. In March 1999 Boris Yeltsin called the NATO bombing of Belgrade "undisguised aggression,"[62] and he would later comment, "The Kosovo crisis increased the anti-Western sentiment in society."[63]

This change in Russian foreign policy manifested itself in Moscow's desire to be more prominent in global politics after having been marginalized by the disintegration of the Soviet Union. This desire was closely linked to Moscow's wish for a more multipolar world in comparison to the one that had emerged in the 1990s. Since 2000 this wish endures, with Putin having strengthened ties with a number of former Soviet allies. The result is that some believe that within Russian foreign policy a "Putin Doctrine" has emerged.[64] The "Putin Doctrine" seeks Russia's return to great power status, desires a multipolar world, and by nature is expansionist. But ultimately defensive realism is key as Moscow's perceived assertiveness results from the Russian government's striving to garner support for itself.[65]

The Foundations in Practice

The changes that took place in both Cuban and Russian foreign policies in the mid-1990s, detailed above, have been key for the rejuvenated relationship since

2008. Feinsilver's previously cited quote about the Cuban desire for "the creation of a Third World constituency,"[66] Erisman's idea that Cuban foreign policy aimed to create greater political space for the island, and Domínguez's first point outlined above that Havana attempted to balance the United States are imperative for Cuban-Russian relations. These ideas may have helped the revolution to survive the loss of its socialist trading partners in the early 1990s, and Russia may not constitute part of the developing world, but the upturn in Havana's relationship with Moscow was not contrary to this process. Significantly Russia has provided important backing for the Cuban government in various UN forums. From 1995 onward Moscow has returned to its traditional voting practice at the conventions on human rights held in Geneva and voted with Cuba, which had not been the case in the years from 1992 to 1994. Moscow continues to support Cuba in these forums and calls for the end of the U.S. embargo against the island at the United Nations. Ultimately defensive realism is fundamental to Havana's desire for its relationship with Moscow to be politically robust. Russia's political support has been an integral part of the process of the Cuban government's garnering international support as it continues to safeguard both Cuban state security and also the survival of the revolution.

The alteration in the Kremlin's foreign policy in the mid-1990s resulted in an improved relationship with Havana, which demonstrated to Washington that Moscow once again had influence on a global scale and was no longer marginalized in international relations, as had been the case in the years immediately after the disintegration of the Soviet Union. It appeared that the geostrategic significance of Cuba for Russia was increasing. It has not returned to the level of the Cold War, but the Kremlin did wish to "tickle the Americans' underbelly," with closer relations with Havana achieving this aim.[67]

In the twenty-first century this wish has continued, particularly due to the emergence of the "Putin Doctrine." Russian foreign policy may seem assertive under this doctrine, which could result in it appearing that offensive realism was important to the Russian desire for improved Cuban-Russian relations. However, it is really defensive realism that is the key due to these Russian actions being part of the process of the Russian government's striving to amass support for itself, which ultimately underpinned this doctrine.[68] Furthermore, the geostrategic significance of Cuba has increased still further with Russia's increased interest in Latin America in the twenty-first century. Cuba's considerable regional influence has helped facilitate the Russian desire to increase its influence in Latin America. Moreover, as detailed, these changes in Cuban and Russian foreign policies have also led to a convergence in the goals of Havana's and Moscow's foreign policies, most noticeably in a desire for a multipolar world.

In the immediate future the significance of Latin America for Moscow is only likely to increase as the Kremlin's relationship with the West deteriorates. Russia's reinsertion into Latin America since 2000 has been predominantly driven by commerce, but a belief exists that the Russian government is striving to garner international support for itself as it attempts to counter possible political isolation resulting from its deteriorating relationship with the West.[69] Russian interest in the region was demonstrated in May 2013 when the ambassadors to Moscow of the members of the Community of Latin American and Caribbean States met the Russian and Cuban foreign ministers Sergey Lavrov and Bruno Rodríguez Parrilla during Rodríguez's visit to the Russian capital.[70] As stated, due to its regional influence Cuba is important in these Russian attempts to acquire political allies in Latin America.

The previously cited ideas of Domínguez, Erisman, and Feinsilver are once again keys for bilateral Cuban-Russian trade. In short, Cuba needs to acquire trading partners. The continuing U.S. embargo may predicate this desire, but it is not the only reason for Havana's wishing to find other trading partners. A conceivable level of Cuban dependence on Venezuela may have appeared under the presidency of Raúl Castro. In 2006 Cuban-Venezuelan trade represented 21.3 percent of Cuba's total global trade; this increased to 27.3 percent in 2008 and 41.7 percent in 2011; in 2014 it was 40.5 percent. This made Venezuela Cuba's most important trading partner, graphically illustrated in 2014 when the level of Cuban-Venezuelan bilateral trade exceeded Cuba's trade with its second-largest trading partner, China, by over 400 percent.[71] Potential Cuban dependence on Venezuela is given further credence by the composition of the bilateral trade that is taking place as it is predominantly the Cuban import of Venezuelan goods. In 2006, 84.5 percent of Cuban-Venezuelan trade comprised Cuban imports of Venezuelan goods, with the figures for 2008, 2011, and 2014 being 91.5, 70.8, and 71.5 percent, respectively.[72]

The result is that Cuba's wish for increased trade with Russia can be perceived as Havana's striving to diversify the number of countries with which it is trading, thus reducing a possible economic reliance on Venezuela. Cuba's wish to diversify its trading partners may be somewhat astute due to the doubt which surrounds both Cuban-Venezuelan trade and Venezuela's internal political situation since Hugo Chávez's death in January 2013. In short, the previously detailed ideas of Domínguez, Erisman, and Feinsilver for Cuba to acquire greater economic space are fundamental, as is the revolutionary Cuban elite's traditional wish to avert the appearance of possible dependency resulting from the principles of defensive realism and realist pragmatism.

Cuba's global trade may be dominated by Venezuela, but with respect to tourism Cuba is heavily reliant on Canada. Over 1 million Canadians travel to Cuba each year, which in 2014 represented over 39 percent of the island's total tourists. Further illuminating the importance of Canadian tourists is that this 2014 figure exceeded by 800 percent the number of Germans vacationing on the island, the country which provides the second-largest number of tourists.[73] The upshot is that Cuba's efforts to attract more Russian visitors can be perceived as an attempt to find alternative sources of tourists, thus reducing a possible dependency on Canada for tourism. Such considerations are consistent with the traditional revolutionary Cuban desire, rooted in the ideas of realist pragmatism and defensive realism, to avoid possible dependency.

Furthermore, these reasons of trying to avoid possible dependency are also applicable to the various agreements between Cuba and Russia, as their signing has enabled Havana to expand its portfolio of countries with which it has cooperative ties. This also applies to the military links which continue to exist between the two countries. Legacies from the 1959–1991 years of the relationship are also important for the resolution of Cuba's Soviet-era debt and for the increase in symbolism which now exists in the relationship. This symbolism is significant with respect not just to the years from 1959 to 1991 but even to those before this. As detailed, both governments are highlighting the longevity and considerable heritage of the bilateral relationship to their respective young populations.

As alluded to throughout this chapter, the United States has cast a long shadow over Havana's relationship with Moscow since the Cuban Revolution, with some believing that the burgeoning relationship between Havana and Moscow in the aftermath of January 1959 was partly driven by a Cuban desire to acquire increased security guarantees from the Kremlin in the face of increasing animosity from Washington.[74] Again, this demonstrates the prevalence of defensive realism and realist pragmatism within the Cuban ruling elite, but other reasons also underpinned the fledgling relationship between Cuba and the Soviet Union.[75] As argued throughout the chapter, defensive realism, realist pragmatism, and the role of the United States have constantly impacted Havana's relationship with Moscow since January 1959. Since December 2014 historic change is taking place in Cuban-U.S. relations as a normalization process has begun. This has seen both the return of diplomatic relations between the two countries and President Barack Obama's visit to Cuba in March 2016.[76] What impact could this have for Cuban-Russian relations if this one constant factor in the relationship for the last fifty years begins to recede in importance?

The U.S. economic embargo remains in place, with Moscow continuing to call for it to be lifted while supporting the improvement in Cuban-U.S. relations.[77] However, even if the embargo was removed, this does not mean that subsequently Cuba's relationship with Russia would deteriorate and return to one which may be expected to exist between a Caribbean island and a large Eurasian country. This stance is rooted in realist pragmatism and defensive realism because it would be completely contrary to the Cuban government's decision-making process since January 1959 to "throw all its eggs in one basket" if, as its relationship with Washington improved, its relationship with Moscow became less important. Cuba's "not turning its back on" Russia was made abundantly clear to Washington with the arrival of the *Viktor Leonov* spy ship in Havana on January 20, 2015, the day before the commencement of bilateral Cuban-U.S. talks after the start of a normalization process in December 2014.[78]

Again, realist pragmatism, defensive realism, and the wish to avoid dependency are likely to continue to impact positively on Cuban-Russian relations in the years after 2018. This is crucial due to Raúl Castro's proposed 2018 retirement, which makes it highly probable that a generational change will occur in the Cuban leadership. The new Cuban leaders are likely to have been born after the onset of the Cuban Revolution. However, their political careers will have been constructed within a system where realist pragmatism, defensive realism, and the wish to avoid dependency have been paramount, thereby increasing the probability that these concepts will remain fundamental in Cuban foreign policy in the post-2018 era.

The outcome is that Cuban-Russian relations are likely to remain similar to their present form in the short to medium term due to the importance of the above concepts in the relationship both since 2008 and in the years before. The likelihood of Cuban-Russian relations remaining politically robust increases further due to the longevity of the bilateral relationship between Havana and Moscow and particularly the legacy from the 1959–1991 period. The result is that Cuban-Russian relations will always be different from Moscow's relationship with the rest of the region and not resemble the relationship which the Kremlin has with other Caribbean islands.

CONCLUSIONS

Since 2008, when Raúl Castro became president of Cuba, Havana's relationship with Moscow has been at its most robust politically since the end of Cuban-Soviet relations. This has been evidenced by the number of visits by the elites from one country to the other, the political will for trade to increase, and the number of bilateral agreements that have been signed, among other things. Moreover, the relationship continues to be politically important for both countries, with this being aided by their similar positions on a number of global issues, not the least being a desire for a multipolar world.

However, the foundations of this rejuvenated relationship between Havana and Moscow are much older than the duration of Raúl Castro's presidency, representing the thinking that has been prevalent in the Cuban ruling elite since January 1959. Of fundamental significance has been the existence of realist pragmatism and its close association with defensive realism, along with the desire to avoid forms of dependency. These concepts also underpinned the changes which took place in Cuban foreign policy in the last decade of the twentieth century and remain of utmost significance in contemporary Cuban foreign policy. When they are combined with the changes which took place in Russian foreign policy in the mid-1990s, the result is that Cuban-Russian relations remain mutually beneficial for both countries. Additionally, contemporary Cuban-Russian relations continue to be impacted positively by a legacy from the 1959–1991 period of the relationship. Historic change may be taking place in Cuban-U.S. relations, and future change in Cuba is highly probable, but due to its deep-rooted foundations, Havana's relationship with Moscow is likely to continue in its present form for the foreseeable future.

NOTES

1. This can be illustrated by the twenty-three official trips that Raúl Castro made to the Soviet Union during the Soviet period compared to the four that Fidel Castro made. G. E.

Mamedov and A. Dalmau. *Rossiia-Kuba, 1902–2002, dokumenty i materialy* (Moscow: Mezhdunarodnye otnosheniia, 2004), 628–58.

2. "Sobre los principios de la colaboración estratégica entre la República de Cuba y Federación de Rusia," *Granma*, January 31, 2009, http://www.granma.cu/espanol/2009/enero/sabado31/memorando.html.

3. Vladimir Putin, "Cooperation with Latin America is key to Russia's foreign policy," July 14, 20014, http://rt.com/politics/official-word/171900-putin-interview-latin-america/

4. Raúl Castro Ruz, "Official Statement from the Government of Cuba," August 10, 2008, http://www.cubaminrex.cu.

5. "Statement by the Ministry of Foreign Affairs," Cuba MinRex, September 1, 2013, http://www.minrex.gob.cu/en/statement-ministry-foreign-affairs-7.

6. "Backing Ukraine's Territorial Integrity, UN Assembly Declares Crimea Referendum Invalid," United Nations, March 27, 2014, http://www.un.org/apps/news/story.asp?NewsID=47443#.VIHiSHNFAdU.

7. Raúl Castro Ruz, "The Development of the National Economy, along with the Struggle for Peace, and Our Ideological Resolve, Constitute the Party's Principal Missions. 7th PCC Congress Central Report, Presented by First Secretary Raúl Castro Ruz," *Granma*, April 18, 2016, http://en.granma.cu/cuba/2016-04-18/the-development-of-the-national-economy-along-with-the-struggle-for-peace-and-our-ideological-resolve-constitute-the-partys-principal-missions.

8. Dimitri Medvedev, "Interview with Prensa Latina, Russian Foreign Ministry," *Russian Government*, February 23, 2013, http://www.government.ru/docs/22956.

9. Sergey Lavrov, "Statement by H. E. Mr Sergey Lavrov, Minister of Foreign Affairs of the Russian Federation, at the UN Summit for the Adoption of the Post-2015 Development Agenda," REX, September 28, 2015, http://www.rexfeatures.com/livefeed/2015/09/28/united_nations_sustainable_development_summit,_new_york?celeb=SergeyLavrov.

10. "Russia, Cuba Sign Inter-parliamentary Cooperation Pact, 2010," *RIA Novosti*, December 31, 2010, http://en.rian.ru/russia/20101231/162003225.html.

11. Medvedev, "Interview with Prensa Latina."

12. Interview with Valentina Matvienko: Aliana Nieves Quesada, "President of the Russian Federation Council: 'We Are Living in a New Era of Friendship and Collaboration with Cuba and Latin America,'" *Granma*, May 22, 2013, http://www.granma.cu/idiomas/ingles/international-i/30may-Valentina.html.

13. "Recibió Raúl al Vicepresidente del Gobierno ruso," *Juventud Rebelde*, December 20, 2014, http://www.juventudrebelde.cu/cuba/2014-12-20/recibio-raul-al-vicepresidente-del-gobierno-ruso.

14. "Raúl se reúne hoy con Putin" *CubaDebate*, May 7, 2015, http://www.cubadebate.cu/noticias/2015/05/07/raul-se-reune-hoy-con-putin/#.VUzrHHNwYdW.

15. Oficina Nacional de Estadísticas, *Anuario estadístico* (Havana, 2012), 8.4.

16. Oficina Nacional de Estadísticas, *Anuario estadístico* (Havana, 2015), 8.4, http://www.one.cu/aec2015/08%20Sector%20Externo.pdf.

17. *Vneshiaia Torgovliia v 1989–1990* (Moscow: Mezhdunarodnye otnosheniia, 1991), 5.

18. "Rusia y Cuba construirán un aeropuerto internacional en La Habana," *Correo del Orinoco*, April 19, 2013, http://www.correodelorinoco.gob.ve/multipolaridad/rusia-y-cuba-construiran-un-aeropuerto-internacional-habana.

19. Vladimir Putin, "Putin por una América Latina India, sostenible e independiente," *Granma*, July 11, 2014, 8. Additionally, Cuba could become a regional hub for both increased

commercial links with Latin America and the Russian national air carrier Aeroflot. This would result in Cuba's strategic importance for Russia increasing further.

20. Medvedev, "Interview with Prensa Latina."

21. "Fidel Receives President Putin," *Granma*, July 14, 2014, http://en.granma.cu/cuba/2014-07-14/fidel-receives-president-putin.

22. Taras Litvinenko, "Russia Ready to Invest $1.35Bln in Cuba's Thermal Power Plants," *Sputnik News*, March 29, 2016, http://sputniknews.co./business/20160329/1037170966/russia-cuba-power-investments.html.

23. "El embajador de la Federación de Rusia en Cuba: Los cubanos continúan siendo aliados leales de Rusia," *Edición de la Embajada*, no. 17 (2015): 14; "Rusia en la Internacional de la Habana 'FIHAV-2015," *Edición de la Embajada*, no. 17 (2015): 25.

24. "Cabrisas y Rogozin presiden reunión de Comisión Intergubernamental Cuba-Rusia," *CubaDebate*, June 14, 2016, http://www.cubadebate.cu/noticias/2016/06/14/cabrisas-y-rogozin-presiden-reunion.

25. "Russia May Supply More Oil to Cuba," *Sputnik News*, January 13, 2017, http://www.sputniknews.com/worl/201701131049549066-russia-cuba-oil.

26. An agreement regarding Cuba's Soviet-era debt had been signed in September 2005, which deferred its payment. ITARR-TASS News Agency, September 15, 2005. Medvedev, "Interview with Prensa Latina."

27. "Putin anuncia incremento de la colaboración con Cuba," *Granma*, July 12, 2014, 5.

28. "Rusia constata los 'modestos recursos' de Cuba en su cooperación militar con Moscú, 2013," *eldiario.es*, May 14, 2013, http://www.eldiario.es/politica/Rusia-recursos-Cuba-cooperacion-Moscu_0_132287413.html.

29. "Russian Warships Arrive in Cuba on Official Visit," *RIA Novosti*, August 4, 2013, http://en.rian.ru/military_news/20130804/182571697/Russian-Warships-Arrive-in-Cuba-on-Official-Visit—-Report.html.

30. "Russian War Ship in Cuba to Greet US Government Delegation," *eTN Global News*, January 21, 2015, http://www.eturbonews.com/54733/russian-war-ship-cuba-greet-us-government-delegation.

31. "Visita Cuba el General de Ejército Serguey Shoigu, Ministro de Defensa de Rusia," *Edición de la Embajada*, no 17 (2015): 12.

32. "Central Report to the 6th Congress of the Communist Party of Cuba," *Granma*, April 16, 2011, http://www.granma.cu/ingles.cuba-i/16-abril-central.html.

33. Yaima Meneses Puig, "Mañana de homenaje y recordación," *Juventud Rebelde*, July 12, 2012, http://www.juventudrebelde.cu/internacionales/2012/07/-12.

34. "Triunfo soviético contra el fascismo inspiró a antiterroristas cubanos," *Juventud Rebelde*, May 9, 2016, http://www.juventudrebelde.cu.internacionales/2016-05-09/triunfo-soviético-contra-el-fascismo-inspiro-a-antiterroristas-cubanos.

35. "El Primer Concierto en La Habana de la Orquesta del Teatro Mariinski bajo la dirección de Valery Gergiev" *Edición de la Embajada*, No.18 (2016): 19.

36. "Patriarch Kirill Meets with President of the Council of State and Council of Ministers of Cuba Raul Castro Ruz," *Russian Orthodox Church*, May 8, 2015, https://mospat.ru/en/2015/05/08/news118856.

37. "Presidente Putin recibe a vicepresidente Miguel Díaz-Canel," *Juventud Rebelde*, May 25, 2016, http://www.juventudrebelde.cu.internacionales/2015-05-25/president-putin-recibe-a-vicepresidente-miguel-diaz-canel.

38. Mervyn J. Bain, *From Lenin to Castro, 1917–1959: Early Encounters between Moscow and Havana* (Lanham, MD: Lexington Book, 2013).

39. Raúl Castro Ruz, "Hoy las relaciones entre Rusia y Cuba son excelentes. Entrevista al Presidente del Consejo de Estado de Cuba," *América Latina* no. 3 (2009): 6.

40. Yaima Meneses Puig, "Intensa y muy útil visita de trabajo," *Juventud Rebelde*, July 12, 2012, http://www.juventudrebelde.cu.

41. "Dimitry Medvedev Offers His Condolences to Raúl Castro, President of the Council of State and the Council of Ministers of Cuba," Russian Government, November 26, 2016, http://www.government.ru/en/news/25417.

42. Medvedev, "Interview with Prensa Latina."

43. Oficina Nacional de Estadísticas, *Anuario estadístico* (2015), 15.3.

44. Antonio Rondón García, "Cuba presente en feria de turismo rusa Inturmarket-2012," *Prensa Latina*, March 19, 2012, http://www.prensalatina.cu/index.php?option=com_content&task=view&id=488940.

45. John M. Kirk, "Defying the Odds: Five Conclusions about Cuban Foreign Policy," in *Redefining Cuban Foreign Policy: The Impact of the "Special Period,"* ed. H. Michael Erisman and John M. Kirk (Gainesville: University Press of Florida, 2006), 334.

46. H. Michael Erisman, "Between a Rock and a Hard Place: Survival Strategy in Cuba's New Foreign Policy," in Erisman and Kirk, *Redefining Cuban Foreign Policy*, 3–5.

47. Julie M. Feinsilver, *Healing the Masses: Cuban Health Politics at Home and Abroad* (Berkley: University of California Press, 1993), 13.

48. Jorge Domínguez, "Cuba and the Pax Americana," in *A Contemporary Cuba Reader: Reinventing the Revolution*, ed. Philip Brenner et al. (Lanham, MD: Rowman & Littlefield, 2008), 203.

49. H. Michael Erisman, *Cuba's Foreign Relations in a Post-Soviet World* (Gainesville: University Press of Florida, 2000), 3, 33–36.

50. The great man theory postulates that at times a country's political system has become dominated by one person, with the examples often provided being Nazi Germany with Adolf Hitler and the Soviet Union under Joseph Stalin's leadership.

51. Cole Blasier, "The End of the Soviet-Cuban Partnership," in *Cuba after the Cold War*, ed. Carmelo Mesa-Lago (Pittsburgh, PA: University of Pittsburgh Press, 1993), 60; Carmelo Mesa-Lago, "Introduction: Cuba, the Last Communist Warrior," in ibid., 603–4; Brian H. Pollitt, "Sugar, 'Dependency' and the Cuban Revolution," *Development and Change* 17 (1986): 196.

52. Erisman, *Cuba's Foreign Relations*, 43–47.

53. Hans Morgenthau, *Politics among Nations* (New York: Knopf, 1972), 25.

54. Kenneth Waltz, *Theory of International Politics* (Reading, MA: Addison-Wesley, 1979), 4.

55. John Mearsheimer, *The Tragedy of Great Power Politics* (New York: W. W. Norton, 2001), 21.

56. Ibid, 2.

57. Mervyn J. Bain, "'Back to the Future?': Cuban-Russian Relations under Raúl Castro," *Journal of Communist and Post-Communist Studies* 48, no. 2–3 (September 2015): 159–168; Erisman, *Cuba's Foreign Relations*, 25–26.

58. Erisman, *Cuba's Foreign Relations*, 30–47.

59. Margot Light, "Foreign Policy Thinking," in *Internal Factors in Russian Foreign Policy*, ed. Alex Pravda, Roy Alison, and Margot Light (Oxford: Oxford University Press, 1996), 33–100; Bobo Lo, *Russian Foreign Policy in the Post-Soviet Era: Reality, Illusion and Mythmaking* (London: Palgrave Macmillan, 2002), 8.

60. Stephen White, *Russia's New Politics: The Management of a Postcommunist Society* (Cambridge: Cambridge University Press, 2004), 229.

61. Roger E. Kanet, "From 'New World Order' to 'Resetting Relations': Two Decades of U.S.-Russian Relations," in *Russian Foreign Policy in the 21st Century*, ed. Roger E. Kanet (New York: Palgrave Macmillan, 2011), 204–6.

62. *Rossiiskaya gazeta*, March 26, 1999, 2.

63. Boris Yeltsin, *Midnight Diaries* (New York: Public Affairs, 2000), 271.

64. Leon Aron, "The Putin Doctrine: Russia's Quest to Rebuild the Soviet State," *Foreign Affairs*, March 8, 2013, http://www.foreignaffairs.com/print/136255 (accessed March 3, 2015).

65. Aron, "The Putin Doctrine," 2; Lilia Shevtsova, "The Kremlin Is Winning," Brookings Institution, February 12, 2015, http://www.brookings.edu/research/articles/2015/02/12-kremlin-is-winning-shevtsova, 3.

66. Feinsilver, *Healing the Masses*, 13.

67. A. Sosnovsky, "On the Benefit of Routine Professionalism," *Moskovskiye novosti*, no. 21 (May 26–June 2, 1996), 5.

68. Aron, "The Putin Doctrine," 2; Shevtsova, "The Kremlin Is Winning," 3.

69. Benedict Mander, "Russia Is Looking for Allies, Not Deals, in Latin America," *Financial Times*, April 26, 2015, http://www.ft.com/cms/s/0/5ca9fb9c-ea86-11e4-a701-00144feab7de.html#axzz3ZC2o8ry5.

70. "Rusia y CELAC fomentan espacios multilaterales de diálogo, 2013," *Granma*, May 31, 2013, http://www.granma.cubaweb.cu/2013/05/31/interna/artic11.html.

71. Oficina Nacional de Estadísticas, *Anuario estadístico* (Havana, 2014), 8.3–8.4.

72. Ibid, 8.6. Possible Cuban dependence on Venezuela was highlighted on July 8, 2016, by Raúl Castro in his address to the National Assembly of People's Power. In this speech he detailed that the Cuban economy had not grown at the rate that was hoped for and said, "Added to the above is a certain reduction in the supply of fuel contracted with Venezuela, despite the intention of President Nicolás Maduro and his government to fulfill this commitment. Of course, this has caused additional tensions in the functioning of the Cuban economy." Raúl Castro Ruz, "The Revolutionary Cuban People Will Again Rise to the Occasion," *Granma*, July 13, 2016, http://en.granma.cu/cuba/2016-07-13/the-revolutionary-cuban-people-will-again-rise-to-the-occasion.

73. Oficina Nacional de Estadísticas, *Anuario estadístico* (2014), 15.3.

74. Peter Shearman, *The Soviet Union and Cuba* (London: Routledge & Kegan Paul, 1987), 11.

75. Mervyn J. Bain, *Russian-Cuban Relations since 1992: Continuing Camaraderie in a Post-Soviet World* (Lanham, MD: Lexington Books, 2008), 21–24.

76. "Remarks by President Obama and President Raúl Castro of Cuba in a Joint Press Conference," White House, March 21, 2016, http://www.whitehouse.gov/the-press-office/2016/03/21/remarks-president-obama-and-president-raul-castro-cuba-joint-press.

77. During Raúl Castro's trip to Moscow in May 2015, a TASS spokesmen stated, "Moscow welcomes the process of normalizing relations between Havana and Washington, as . . . the full restoration of bilateral dialogue is in the interests of both countries and of international security." "Raúl se reúne hoy con Putin," *CubaDebate*, May 7, 2015, http://www.cubadebate.cu/noticias/2015/05/07/raul-se-reune-hoy-con-putin/#.VUzrHHNwYdW.

78. "Russian War Ship in Cuba."

16

China and Cuba

Adrian H. Hearn and Rafael Hernández

During his 2014 visit to Cuba, Chinese president Xi Jinping declared, "I feel that as socialist countries, China and Cuba are intimately united to fight for the same missions, ideals and goals."[1] While they may be united in their socialist ideals, both governments have practiced what they call "socialism with local characteristics," leading to political and economic divergences. In the post-Soviet era of global trade, investment, and market reform, political ideology does not single-handedly determine the course of Sino-Cuban engagement.

According to a former Cuban diplomat in Beijing, "We can no longer knock on China's door and ask for favors the way we used to. Political trust is still important in our relationship, but now it's a matter of pragmatism, because the Chinese insist that the numbers have to add up" (interview, May 28, 2012). Similarly, Cuba's de facto ambassador to China during the Cultural Revolution, Mauro García Triana, notes the difference with earlier Soviet forms of cooperation: "The Chinese are very clear about one thing: they're not going to be benefactors for Cuba like the Soviets were. I was once told in no uncertain terms by a Chinese diplomat: 'Our relations with Cuba have to be mutually beneficial or they will not work'" (interview, January 11, 2007).

Political solidarity continues to shape the contours of Sino-Cuban cooperation, but the ideological foundations of the relationship are shifting away from doctrines of top-down control. This shift reflects a common trajectory: centralized governance once sought to command economic development and the social interactions it entails. As Lenin put it, "Trust is good, but control is better." More recently, appropriately regulated private sectors are gaining credibility in both nations as experimental policies cede ground to small businesses and the independent exchanges they require. Both nations are grappling with this transformation in their own ways, in the process updating and inflecting the concept of socialism to reflect "local characteristics."

This chapter analyzes how Cuban and Chinese conceptions of socialism have sometimes united, other times divided, and in general created common opportunities and challenges for the two nations. Ideological convergences, tensions, and negotiations continue to the present day, revealing complex interactions behind the scenes of official declarations about socialist brotherhood. The dynamics of these interactions reflect the internal transformations underway within both countries as they forge a new balance of state, market, and civil society forces. China under President Xi Jinping is applying lessons learned from the Shanghai Free Trade Zone, progressively rolling out a national plan that permits foreign investors national treatment and access to a wider scope of sectors.[2] Meanwhile, as Rafael Hernández writes, Cuba's reforms "represent only one of the dimensions of a deeper and broader process, not fully restricted to a single plan, which precedes and surpasses it: the transition towards a new socialist stage."[3] Underpinning these transformations is the long-standing need to renew and refresh the meaning of socialism in relation to changing conditions.

The chapter begins with an overview of Sino-Cuban trade and investment relations and then considers how these interactions reflect the changing context of world politics, from ideologies of state control during the Cold War to market exchange in the twenty-first century. It then presents a 2016 survey we conducted at Renmin University in Beijing to assess attitudes toward the realities and potentials of socialism as an overarching framework to advance national interests and facilitate Sino-Cuban cooperation. We find that Chinese appraisals of the bilateral relationship identify opportunities for Cuba to learn from China's prior development experiences but also to avoid the inequalities associated with China's rapid growth. Indeed, some in China view Cuba as a source of inspiration in the pursuit of a socialist model that is more just and egalitarian than their own.

SINO-CUBAN TRADE AND INVESTMENT IN GLOBAL CONTEXT

As other chapters in this volume demonstrate, China is one among many nations influencing Cuba's development trajectory. This is evident in the energy sector, into which Cuba has invited foreign firms to prospect for onshore and offshore oil. As of mid-2016, Angola's Sonangol has stated it will proceed with deepwater drilling in Cuba's Gulf of Mexico special economic zone despite the difficulties encountered there by Brazilian, Spanish, Russian, and Venezuelan oil companies. Russia's state enterprise Zarubezhneft continues to prospect in the zone with the support of another Russian state enterprise, Rosneft, and in 2014 Russian president Valdimir Putin forgave 90 percent of Cuba's $35 billion debt to Moscow. Onshore, east of Varadero, Australia's MEO claims to have discovered 8.183 billion barrels of oil, which would cover Cuba's needs for more than six years. Foreign oil and gas prospecting in Cuba strengthen the case of U.S. business lobbies against the embargo because, as an article in *Havana Times* puts it, "the United States would find it difficult to accept being sidelined without a piece of the pie, especially with regard to gas reserves that could reduce energy costs in some southern states."[4]

There are signs that the bilateral accords pursued by the Barack Obama administration will bear fruit under President Donald Trump. For one thing, Fidel Castro's death meets the long-standing demand of his foes in the United States that the United States not engage in business with Cuba as long as Fidel was on the scene. Should the new U.S. administration wish to promote trade and investment with the island, or should Trump wish to open a hotel there (as he has openly ruminated), an important political obstacle has now been removed. Trump's threat to roll back Obama's agreements if the Cuban government does not offer a "better deal" rings opportunistic. Sources in Havana report that Trump envoys were spotted meeting with Cuban officials prior to the U.S. election. This is logical, they say, because President Obama spent his political capital to make such meetings possible. The business-friendly Republican legislature owes a debt to Trump and will be more disposed to support his policies than would have been the case with Hillary Clinton as president. Cuban political analyst Carlos Alzugaray sums up the situation nicely: "Obama has opened the door. All Trump has to do is walk through" (personal communication, November 21, 2016).

At a time when U.S.-Cuban relations are warming, it is logical that other countries should reinvigorate and assess new prospects for cooperation with the island. UK ambassador Antony Stokes sees potential for cooperation in financial services: "The UK has strengths that fit Cuba's needs unusually well. For example, if the Cuban economy is going to become more efficient, it will need to be managed smartly. That means know-how on the practical business of accounting, auditing, tax collection, fraud prevention, and online payments. The City of London has a world-leading reputation in financial and professional services, and we are uniquely placed to work with Cuba in these areas" (personal communication, December 7, 2016).

Also seeking wider forms of engagement, Iranian president Hassan Rouhani visited Havana in September 2016 after attending the Non-Aligned Movement summit in Venezuela. Rouhani signed agreements on health, education, science, medicine, and banking with Raúl Castro; discussed global food security with Fidel; and substantiated the promise of his foreign minister to open a "new chapter" in bilateral relations.[5]

The same week as Rouhani's visit, Chinese premiere Li Keqiang conducted the highest-ranking Chinese mission to Cuba since Obama's visit in March 2016. Approximately thirty agreements covering science, environment, industry, oil and gas, public health, and agriculture will underpin the transfer of Chinese credits and sustain bilateral trade. China is Cuba's second-largest trade partner: from a base of just $314 million in 2000, bilateral trade peaked at $2.3 billion in 2007, fell sharply to $1.6 billion in 2009 during the global financial crisis, improved somewhat over the subsequent four years, fell again to $1.39 billion in 2014, and recovered once more to $2.2 billion in 2015 (see figure 16.1).

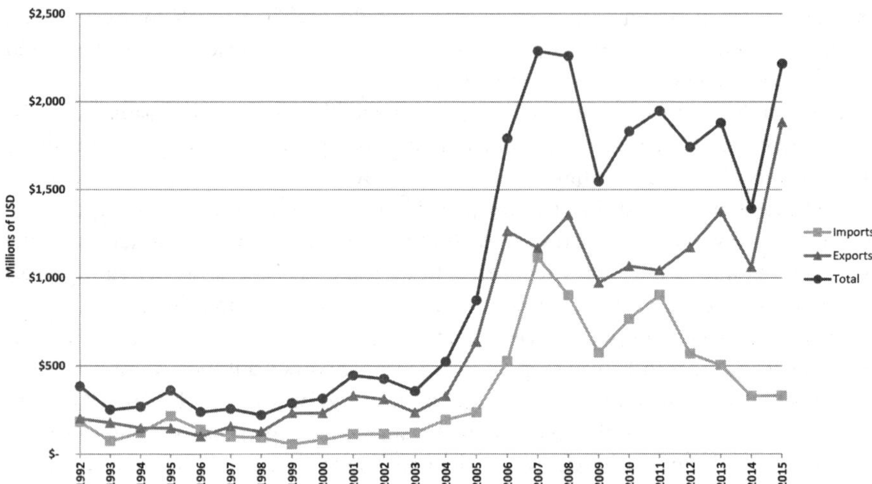

Figure 16.1. Cuba's trade with China as reported by China, 1992–2015.
Source: UN-Comtrade 2016.

The easing of U.S. restrictions on remittances to Cuba carries implications for the island's consumption and production of Chinese-brand consumer and capital goods. By 2012 annual remittances sent by Cuban Americans exceeded $500 million and in 2016 were estimated by the U.S. State Department to surpass $3 billion. This injection of capital has been critical for Cuba's emerging self-employed entrepreneurs, whose numbers grew from approximately 150,000 in 2010 to 500,000 in 2015. The Cuban government has responded by permitting public access to consumer goods whose direct sale was previously restricted. Chinese exporters have benefitted from this development since electronic and other products carrying Chinese brand names are prominent in Cuban stores and relatively inexpensive. The 2015 spike in Sino-Cuban trade reflects a sharp increase in Cuban imports of Chinese consumer goods.

To expand the range of goods and services they provide to Cuba, Chinese exporters wish to see the island's private sector grow and a broader range of projects made available for foreign investment. Conversely, to attract foreign finance while maintaining regulatory oversight, the Cuban government is promoting the port of Mariel and its associated special development zone as a secure manufacturing hub for foreign investors. In an attempt to attract Chinese investment, Cuban foreign trade and investment minister Rodrigo Malmierca has spoken of Mariel's relevance for Chinese exporters, which he hopes will use it as a distribution hub for markets in the Caribbean, Central America, and Mexico. No other Caribbean Basin port can currently accommodate the "post-Panamax" (extra-large) cargo vessels that will pass through the Panama Canal when it has been widened. The revamped port could therefore become a way station for vessels bound for the Americas, as well as for those on their way to Europe and elsewhere.

The China Communications Construction Company Limited is experienced with Cuban maritime infrastructure, as it is currently upgrading the port of Santiago de Cuba, the island's second-largest port after Mariel. Financed by a $120 million line of credit provided during Xi Jinping's 2014 visit, the project is scheduled for completion in 2018. The renovated docking facility will have a depth of eleven meters, accommodating vessels carrying loads up to fifty thousand tons (double the current cargo limit). Featuring a two-hundred-meter multipurpose quay, three gantry cranes, and two cargo warehouses, the port of Santiago de Cuba will employ approximately five hundred people in construction and operations.

Dwarfing the port of Santiago de Cuba, Mariel's renovation and expansion will make it a serious competitor to existing Caribbean transshipment hubs in Kingston (Jamaica), Caucedo (Dominican Republic), and Manzanillo (Panama). Mariel is projected to handle more than 2 million cargo containers annually, more than doubling its present capacity and significantly augmenting Cuba's foreign trade.

According to Ricardo Cabrisas, vice president of Cuba's Council of Ministers, Mariel's scale and ambition were inspired by the Chinese port of Shenzhen and its associated special economic zone. Mariel's first phase was completed in January 2014 and inaugurated by Raúl Castro and Brazilian president Dilma Rousseff, whose government loaned Cuba $682 million for the $950 million project. Phase one featured a 702-meter berthing facility, an 18-meter quayside draught, four post-Panamax cranes, and a 27.5-hectare container yard capable of accommodating 820,000 TEUs (twenty-foot equivalent units). When finished, the port's linear quay will extend to 2.4 kilometers. Cuba's commitment to the project is evident in the associated infrastructure and facilities already installed, including a sixty-five-kilometer railway, completed in 2014, connecting the Mariel port to Havana. Raúl Pérez Ramos, vice minister of transport, has stated his intention to acquire 240 additional train cars from China at an estimated cost of $150 million.

The Cuban government is seeking Chinese participation in the special development zone adjacent to the revamped Mariel port. In September 2013 Raúl Castro signed a decree permitting foreign firms to import goods duty-free into the zone and to remain exempt from taxation on profits for ten years. Unlike previous regulations that required external investors to form joint ventures with the Cuban state, the new framework permits 100 percent foreign ownership and contracts of up to fifty years. Spanning 465 square kilometers, the zone is expected to generate eight thousand jobs, one-third of them in ongoing duties within the zone. In the Chinese pavilion at the 2013 Havana International Trade Fair, Minister Malmierca told representatives from sixty-five Chinese enterprises, "The Chinese companies that today produce in China and bring their goods here could produce here in Cuba, in this special zone . . . with many incentives."[6]

The Mariel decree resonates with the 2014 Foreign Investment Law No. 118, which was last updated in 1995. Law No. 118 asserts protection of investors against the nationalization of their assets, exemption from personal income and labor taxes, and a profits tax ceiling of 15 percent preceded by an eight-year grace period. Like its

1995 predecessor, the new law requires Cuban staff to be contracted through a local employment agency while permitting foreign firms to bring in their nationals for supervisory and administrative roles. Article 28.2 of Law No. 118 states that mixed or fully foreign enterprises may employ foreign nationals in a range of managerial and technical positions without securing their Cuban residency status, and in such cases the foreign investor may determine staff responsibilities and rights. Chinese enterprises have long requested labor force flexibility, particularly for construction projects. The architect of Cuba's new investment regulations, Marino Murillo, was reappointed as minister of the economy in 2014, affording him the executive authority to supervise implementation.

According to Omar Pérez from the University of Havana, Chinese firms have expressed interest in establishing an automotive plant in the Mariel zone. This assertion corresponds with reports of enquiries from the China Development Bank about financing automotive, pharmaceutical, and biotechnology production facilities in the zone. These initiatives would mark a new chapter in Sino-Cuban exchange, appropriate to the evolving nature of the nations' relations. As the next section shows, modes of cooperation between the two have never been static; rather, they reflect conceptions of socialism that have adapted to more than fifty years of changing conditions.

FROM IDEOLOGY TO PRAGMATISM

Sino-Cuban trade was initially regulated through a system of annual quotas, codified in 1960 in the first five-year trade and payment agreement. The agreement was eminently political, with Premier Zhou Enlai proposing that China would buy 1 million tons of sugar from Cuba (at the inflated price of $100 million) and pay for it with industrial equipment. Ernesto "Che" Guevara recognized the added value of Zhou's offer: "This is not tenable from the economic point of view, but we raised it from the political point of view."[7]

Ideological differences and rivalry between the communist parties of China and the Soviet Union (known as the Sino-Soviet split) produced tensions—though never a rupture—in Sino-Cuban relations from the middle of the 1960s to the early 1980s.[8] To remain economically viable in the face of pressure from the United States, Cuba sided with the Soviet Union, and in 1967 the Chinese ambassador was recalled from Havana after Castro called Mao Zedong "a senile idiot."[9]

The disintegration of the Soviet Union at the end of the 1980s precipitated a 75 percent reduction in Cuba's import capacity and a 35 percent decline in gross domestic product (GDP). China played an important but little-known role in seeing Cuba through this tumultuous period. The Chinese Communist Party had also come under domestic pressure for change at this time, but it emerged intact in part through its 1989 crackdown in Tiananmen Square and in part through a decade of sincere commitment to opening the economy, improving living standards, and creating jobs. Arriving in Havana in June 1989, just days after the Tiananmen incident, Chinese foreign minister Qian Qichen was warmly received by Castro. The gesture was deeply appreciated in Beijing, since every other country on Qian's itinerary had canceled his visit. As Cheng Yinghong notes, China's relationship with Cuba became "one of the most important Sino-foreign relations in the eyes of the post-Tiananmen Chinese leaders."[10]

The show of solidarity was mutually beneficial: in 1993, a time when most of the world believed the downfall of the Cuban Revolution was imminent, Chinese president Jiang Zemin broke the island's isolation with a state visit and an offer of financial assistance. According to a Chinese official in Beijing, Jiang conducted the visit to "save Cuba's revolutionary project," expressly against the advice of China's increasingly pragmatic Communist Party.

As Cuba's vice president, Raúl Castro showed more interest than his brother in effecting domestic economic reforms and in building a pragmatic relationship with China. According to a former employee of the Cuban embassy in Beijing, Raúl's 1997 "weeklong learning trip" to China actually consisted of a month of research into Chinese approaches to industrial reform, privatization, and urban development. As the evidence collected by Hal Klepak shows, the military institutions Raúl crafted on his return to manage operations in tourism and agriculture were subjected to essentially the same pressures as Chinese firms: to produce, be accountable, and make a profit.[11] Raúl's efforts to this end were assisted by visiting Chinese advisors, such as a specialist appointed by Zhu Rongji, the future premier, to share insights into China's experience with foreign investment and outreach to expatriates.

Another visitor was Mao Xianglin, a special envoy of the Central Committee of the Chinese Communist Party, who developed action plans for expanding Cuban consumer markets. This involved the establishment in 1997 of a bicycle factory with Chinese capital and technical expertise and a facility for producing electric fans and household consumer goods. Mao described this strategy as an incremental process: "I would hesitate to say that our Cuban manufacturing operations are entirely commercial, because what we're doing is broader than that. We're trying to help Cuba to incrementally upgrade its technical ability. If our products prove popular and useful then we assist by setting up factories. . . . It is interesting that China learned from the United States how to manage its economy, and now Latin America looks to China as a teacher of socialism!" (interview, December 14, 2007). Mao Xianglin's mission in Cuba was driven not by orchestrated quotas and artificial prices but by the goal of modernizing Cuba's infrastructure to enable the country's integration into international markets.

As noted, the Chinese Communist Party elite was privately less enthusiastic about Cuba than Jiang Zemin was, not least because the slow recovery of the Cuban economy had delayed the repayment of loans. Although the amount of Cuba's debt to China is not published, announced loans exceed $6 billion, largely in the form of trade credits bestowed during high-level Chinese visits. According to Chinese officials quoted by a U.S. diplomat in Havana, discussions between China and Cuba about carrying through Chinese-style reforms to kick-start the economy and permit foreign investment have become "a real headache."[12] China nevertheless continues to financially and politically support the Cuban government, indicating Beijing's confidence that the latter's reforms will eventually yield economic results, among them the repayment of loans.

Bilateral relations thus reflect a blend of political and economic factors, evident during President Xi's visit to Havana in 2014. Xi committed China Minmetals Corporation to purchasing $600 million in Cuban nickel and commended Cuba for "persisting on the socialist path, firmly safeguarding the sovereignty of the state."[13] Such statements have become an expected ceremonial feature of presidential visits between the two nations, equally prominent during Raúl Castro's 2012 visit to Beijing, when he praised China's scientific progress, humanitarianism, economic stability, and faithful pursuit of socialism. Cheng Yinghong argues that these rhetorical endorsements carry genuine value for the Chinese state: "Cuba has been perceived as the most unyielding and thus the most admirable anti-American hero who, as the Chinese government has introduced to its people, sets an example of the defiance of 'international pressures' and of survival against all odds. In this way the image of Cuba has facilitated China's newly emerging nationalism. The hardliners, old Maoists and new leftists have looked upon Cuba as the example of the socialism purer than China's."[14]

Cheng's argument raises questions about how socialism is understood in Cuba and China and how these visions coincide or diverge. For two decades Chinese officials have been advising their Cuban counterparts to liberalize markets and empower private actors, while at the same time extolling the virtues of assertive state leadership as a fundamental principle of socialist development. It is only since Raúl Castro assumed the presidency in 2008 that the Cuban government has shown genuine interest in formulating and applying such a blended approach at home.

Although leaders from both countries acknowledge that liberalization implies a greater role for the private sector and civil society, it is noteworthy that bilateral exchanges remain devoid of contact between nonstate actors. Nearly all aspects of formal engagement are designed and managed through governmental accords, limiting the potential for cooperation between the two nations to keep pace with developments within them. Interactions between emerging Cuban small businesses, cooperatives, and nongovernmental organizations and their more established Chinese counterparts could provide a broader basis for building trade, understanding, and trust. The formulation of legal guidelines for regulating such exchanges would also enable both sides to more effectively contain informal connections.[15]

A prerequisite for the emergence of more heterogeneous forms of Sino-Cuban engagement is legal authorization and economic capacitation to develop autonomous partnerships, conduct trade, and host independent meetings, conferences, and forums. As the Cuban private sector gains strength, to forbid such activities is to invite unregistered trade, clandestine negotiations, and political dissent. The Cuban government is moving toward a more flexible and tolerant style of governance that accommodates a broader range of socioeconomic voices. As Rafael Hernández writes,

"The policy of naturalizing dissent formulated by Raúl Castro responds to a diverse and vibrant socialist society. In order to implement it, new visions and practices are needed, that integrate it into the critical confrontation with the problems and deficiencies of the system."[16]

As Raúl's policies gain momentum and as China advances its own forms of openness, cooperation between independent Cuban and Chinese actors will become more likely.[17] State authority has historically been an important feature of both nations' visions of socialism, but "socialism with Chinese characteristics" has been evolving for decades in step with China's economic integration with the United States. With the prospect of normalized trade and investment with the United States potentially on Cuba's horizon (depending on the approach taken by the Trump administration), China's prior experiences may harbor useful insights.

According to twelve Chinese officials interviewed in Beijing, the main impediment to improving China's relations with the United States has been mistrust. This sentiment permeates everything from U.S. attempts to promote "good governance" and democratization in China to incompatible military strategies in the South China Sea. Despite these sources of distrust, political determination on both sides has over time moved bilateral relations away from confrontation toward dialogue, negotiation, and cooperation, particularly in the economic sphere. When asked how Cuba might apply Chinese experiences to its own relationship with the United States, the officials emphasized the importance of strengthening business exchanges, expanding dialogue with U.S. corporations nationalized in the 1960s, deepening market reforms, and reengaging with those who have moved overseas. China's experiences of rapprochement with the United States and of development more broadly are clearly relevant to Cuba. However, as the next section shows, respondents to a survey we conducted in Beijing believe that Cuba would do well to avoid the inequalities and injustices that have accompanied China's rapid economic growth.

CHINESE PERSPECTIVES: A PRELIMINARY SURVEY

In July 2016 we conducted a survey at Renmin University of China to gauge students' perceptions of Sino-Cuban relations and their understandings of socialism. We asked fifty-six English-speaking respondents to anonymously indicate strong agreement, agreement, neutrality, disagreement, and strong disagreement with sixteen statements. As discussed below, they were also invited to answer an open-ended question in their own words. Piloting a broader study we intend to conduct in China, Cuba, and the United States, our sample furnished preliminary insight into the views of educated young people. Our intention was to gain a sense of how emerging thought leaders understand connections between models of domestic governance—socialism in particular—and approaches to foreign affairs.

The survey results confirmed some of our expectations and challenged others. As expected, the sample recognized shared political ideology as an encompassing feature of Sino-Cuban relations. In all, thirty-nine agreed with the statement "Differences among socialist countries, such as China and Cuba, are a consequence of their different histories and cultures, but they share the same ideologies." More than two decades of diplomatic differences over relations with the Soviet Union, accompanied by the slower pace of market reform in Cuba compared to China, have apparently not shaken the impression that ideological solidarity remains a linchpin of bilateral exchange. The statements of President Xi and others about the two countries' "fight for the same missions, ideals and goals" (quoted above) have likely strengthened perceptions of socialist affinity.

Despite respondents' consensus about the importance of ideology, the statement "A strong public sector and a dynamic market economy can coexist better in a socialist than in a capitalist system" drew a mixed response: five strongly agreed, twenty agreed, fifteen neither agreed nor disagreed, ten disagreed, and one did not answer. Our sample was thus undecided on the capacity of socialism and capitalism to attain a successful blend of state and market forces. Achieving this blend has been a central goal of China's reforms since the early 1980s, evident most strikingly in the introduction of special economic zones in Shenzhen and other southeastern port cities, the recent expansion of economic freedoms in the Shanghai Free Trade Zone, and the current application of successful results (negative lists, national treatment for investors, etc.) to other industrial sectors.

Given China's success in this regard, the respondents were less united than we expected behind the view that socialism provides the best platform for achieving a mixed economy. Their varied responses may reflect the scarcity of counterexamples: barring outright revolutions, few capitalist countries have explicitly sought to become more socialist. The result may also emulate the view of senior Chinese commentators that Latin America's "pink tide" or "left turn" in the first decade of the 2000s was a positive development but lacked a clear social and economic strategy. In the words of senior Latin America specialist Jiang Shixue, Latin America's left-leaning leaders during this period were "full of new ideas about socialism but lacking any coherent, guiding, and long-term principles. In China the approach to socialism has been more carefully thought out over decades" (interview, December 10, 2007).

The respondents viewed China's approach to resolving the tensions of a mixed economy as exemplary: nineteen strongly agreed and thirty-four agreed with the statement "Cuba can learn from China how to balance state control with market forces." This is perhaps not surprising for a cohort of students familiar with China's developmental achievements: 680 million people lifted out of poverty since 1980, reduction of extreme poverty from 84 to 10 percent over the same period, average GDP growth of more than 9 percent since the mid-1980s, and so forth. The students were also aware that Cuba is currently introducing reforms that China has been trialing and refining for more than three decades.

The cohort's confidence that China has paved the way for Cuba to emulate some of its achievements contrasts with more ambivalent responses to our open-ended question: "Describe in a few sentences your vision of China's socialist development today." Common themes in response to this question were the need to strengthen individual rights and to overcome growing inequality, evident in answers like these:

"China's government has made projects to develop our country quickly and reduce poverty. . . . China's future has to find a better way to listen to normal people because they often are forgotten and left behind."

"People who work in big factories like the ones in Shenzhen sometimes suffer a lot and do not see their families. We are the 'factory of the world' because we have the most efficient and cost effective way. Cubans can learn from China about efficiency and economic growth but we are not an equal society. We have to try not to teach Cuba to be unequal like us."

Such responses indicate a belief that China's pursuit of socialist development has been uneven and at times unjust. The subordination of personal interests to large government-mobilized development projects was recognized not as a necessary sacrifice for the greater good but as a contradiction of the core values of socialism. How Cuba might emulate China's industrial achievements while avoiding the injustices that have accompanied them was identified as a challenge for the future of bilateral relations. Practical expression of this challenge will likely emerge in the Mariel Free Trade Zone, which, like that in Shenzhen, is prioritizing "efficient and cost-effective" production. But labor conditions in the processing plants of southern China are a far cry from Cuban experiences of work and visions of socialism. As Cuban anthropologist Yenisel Rodríguez writes, "We are not so economically desperate that a *maquiladora* can bring us the taste of liberation."[18] Cuban socialism, it seems, may yet improve on China's example.

In 2016 China's leading newspaper, *Xinhua*, appointed prominent journalist Ma Guihua as its chief correspondent in Cuba. We asked Ma about Chinese perceptions of Cuba and the media's role in shaping these. Her response resonates with the finding of our survey that Cuba is seen by many as an unspoiled nation that can learn from China's developmental advances, avoid its mistakes, and even inspire fresh Chinese visions of socialism:

> China's economy is now transitioning, with abundant manufacturing capacity searching for an outlet to benefit other countries that want to modernize. Cuba could take advantage of China's expertise to jumpstart its economy and develop its own national industries. But China's remarkable development has not come without costs. Environmental pollution is a case in point, which Cuba, whose economy relies on tourism and sustainability, should steer away from. Also, China has witnessed huge disparities between rich and poor owing to market-oriented reforms of the education and health systems. Through our reporting we tell the Chinese people Cuba's story of cultural preservation, social justice, free education and health, and innovations in drugs and medicine. Cuba's story inspires Chinese people to improve their own circumstances. (personal communication, December 4, 2016)

As noted above by Cheng Yinghong, many Chinese people view Cuba as an example of "socialism purer than China's." Cheng argues in a later article that Cuba has come to function as "a mirror for China's own reflection" because sensitive topics such as inequality and political dissent are not easily broached within China unless projected onto a foreign "other."[19] This discursive tactic has opened spaces for debate about governance models that could overcome the contradictions of socialism as practiced in China and elsewhere.

CONCLUSION

Since the inception of their diplomatic relations in 1960, Cuba and the People's Republic of China have worked to define a consensual political framework for cooperation. Despite their apparent ideological affinity, the 1960s and 1970s were fraught with differences over the broader leadership of the Communist movement, Cuba's close relationship with the Soviet Union, and competing Cold War interests. The Soviet collapse favored Sino-Cuban rapprochement, which set in motion what one Chinese newspaper called a "period of completely new and steady development" that saw China become Cuba's second-largest trade partner.[20] Marked by a shared commitment to "socialism with local characteristics," this post–Cold War period has seen both nations shore up political stability through the gradual liberalization of their economies.

As the two countries pursue market reforms, questions have arisen about the capacity of socialism to provide an overarching framework for blending state and market inputs and for serving citizens' interests. For Cuba, updating the socialist model means not simply catching up with China (and Vietnam) but also assessing past practices to inform new ones that facilitate civic participation, the expansion of the public sphere, and institutional revitalization.

Our survey helped to clarify how Chinese students understand socialism as a platform for national development and international cooperation. It illuminated the attitudes of a demographically specific but potentially influential cohort. While the results cannot be generalized, they suggest that visions of socialism are far from uniform. Responses on the capacity of socialism to blend state and market forces were mixed, but there was consensus that ideological ties with Cuba are strong and therefore provide a framework for communicating best practices.

Judging from the ambivalent responses to the open question, it seems that these best practices may be drawn as much from China's mistakes as from its successes. While Cuba may draw insights from China to better coordinate development planning, there appears to be an emerging consensus in China that Cuba should avoid the socioeconomic inequalities generated by rapid growth. Local solutions to local challenges will be at least as important for Cuba as insights from afar and may ultimately generate fresh approaches to reconstructing socialism both at home and overseas.

NOTES

1. Quoted in Nigel Wilson, "China's Xi Meets Fidel Castro and Praises Socialist Bond with Cuba," *International Business Times*, 23 July 2014, http://www.ibtimes.co.uk/chinas-xi-meets-fidel-castro-praises-socialist-bond-cuba-1457904.

2. Jianmin Jin, "Chinese Visions of Transpacific Integration," in *The Changing Currents of Trans-Pacific Integration: China, the TPP, and Beyond*, ed. Adrian H. Hearn and Margaret Myers (Boulder, CO: Lynne Rienner Publishers, 2016), 35–48.

3. Rafael Hernández, "Socialist Transition in Cuban Political Institutions and Leadership: A Few Notes on Power Structures and Politics" (forthcoming).

4. Fernando Ravsberg, "Cuba Plans to Drill as Oil Rig Arrives," *Havana Times*, January 20, 2012, http://www.havanatimes.org/?p=60134.

5. Sarah Marsh, "Iran's President Meets Castros in Cuba to Reaffirm Friendship," *Reuters*, 19 September, 2016, http://www.reuters.com/article/us-cuba-iran-rouhani-idUSKCN11Q06I.

6. "Cuba Seeks Chinese Investment," *China Daily* (November 4, 2013).

7. Ministry of Foreign Affairs of Cuba, "Memorandum of the Conversation between Premier Zhou Enlai and Cuban Revolutionary Government Economic Delegation, November 18, 1960" (1960), trans. Zhang Qian, Wilson Center History and Public Policy Program Digital Archive, PRC fma 204-00098-02,1-16, http://digitalarchive.wilsoncenter.org/document/115156.

8. Zhu Wenchi, Mao Xianglin, and Li Keming, *Communist Movements in Latin America* (Beijing: Contemporary World, Press, 2002), 319.

9. Mauro García Triana, Pedro Eng Herrera, and Gregor Benton, *The Chinese in Cuba: 1847–Now* (Lanham, MD: Lexington, 2009), xxi.

10. Cheng Yinghong, "Sino-Cuban Relations and Cuba's Future after Fidel Castro," *History Compass* 5, no. 2 (2007): 725–36.

11. Hal Klepak, *Raúl Castro: Estratega de la defensa revolucionaria de Cuba* (Buenos Aires: Capital Intelectual, 2010).

12. "Key Trading Partners See No Big Economic Reforms," U.S. Embassy Cables (Reference 10HAVANA84, November 28, 2010), *Wikileaks*, https://wikileaks.org/cable/2010/02/10HAVANA84.html.

13. Ladyrene Pérez, "Presidente chino inicia visita a la Isla: 'Cuba es un país de peso,'" *CubaDebate*, July 2, 2014.

14. Cheng, "Sino-Cuban Relations and Cuba's Future after Fidel Castro."

15. Adrian H. Hearn, "Harnessing the Dragon: Overseas Chinese Entrepreneurs in Mexico and Cuba," *China Quarterly* 209 (2012): 111–33.

16. Hernández, "Socialist Transition in Cuban Political Institutions and Leadership."

17. Adrian H. Hearn, *Diaspora and Trust: Cuba, Mexico, and the Rise of China* (Durham, NC: Duke University Press, 2016).

18. Rafael Hernández, Yenisel Rodríguez, and Juan Triana, "Dossier," *Espacio Laical* 1 (2011): 24–47, http://espaciolaical.org/contens/25/2447.pdf.

19. Cheng Yinghong, "The 'Socialist Other': Cuba in Chinese Ideological Debates since the 1990s," *China Quarterly* 209 (2012): 198–216.

20. "Chairman Qiao Shi Met with Chairman Alarcon," *People's Daily*, April 10, 1996.

IV

RETROSPECTIVE AND PROSPECTIVE VIEWS

17

Conclusion

H. Michael Erisman and John M. Kirk

As many expected, Raúl Castro took over the presidency from his brother first on a temporary basis in 2006 and subsequently, in 2008, as the country's legally appointed leader after Fidel's medical condition made his role as president untenable. Since that time there have been significant changes in many aspects of Cuban society.[1] This collection of essays has focused on a clear path of evolutionary change in foreign policy that has occurred during the years that Raúl Castro has been president of Cuba, and the objective has been to provide an overview of the past decade. It is important to note the significance of these changes, which in some cases have been substantial.

For instance, at the start of his presidency in 2008, who would have predicted that Barack Obama would have traveled to Havana, appeared on national television with Cuba's leading comedian, and then attended a baseball game featuring the Tampa Bay Rays? Or that Cuba's extremely close economic relationship with Venezuela would be decimated, leaving Cuba to scramble to source oil supplies elsewhere? China's increasing role was perhaps predictable (given its significant investment projects throughout Latin America), but the increasingly warm relations with the European Union probably were not, given the critical Common Position that had been in place since 1996. In sum, while the essential pragmatism of any government headed by Raúl Castro was not in itself surprising, the significant evolution of Cuba's international relations is noteworthy.

So where does that leave us now, and what should we expect in terms of Cuba's future foreign policy? As we write (in January 2018) there are so many loose threads on both the international and Cuban scenes that any one of these could have a major impact on Havana's policies and change the direction of Cuba's foreign policy. If the Nicolás Maduro government in Venezuela falls, for example, the economic impact on Cuba (which has depended on Caracas for up to half of its fuel needs) would be extremely severe. Cuba has tremendous political capital invested in the Bolivarian Revolution, and the economies are heavily intertwined, which means that the fall of the government in Caracas would be a major political and economic blow for Havana, which is already suffering from losing important allies in Argentina and Brazil.

In terms of the key question of Cuba's future leadership, to take an example in domestic politics, who will replace Raúl Castro as president of Cuba? Will it be First Vice President Miguel Díaz-Canel? Or perhaps Foreign Minister Bruno Rodríguez Parrilla? What exactly will Raúl's successor's role be? Equally important is the question of how Cubans will react to having the first post-Castro leader since 1959. And, specifically with respect to this collection of essays, in which future direction will Cuba's foreign policy head? But before addressing such issues, it would seem useful to provide some contextualization by proposing, admittedly in rather general terms, a summary foreign relations track record for the Raúlista era.

A RETROSPECTIVE ON RAÚL'S FOREIGN POLICIES

Postmortem evaluations of leadership can be extremely tricky, especially when one does not have the luxury of considerable historical hindsight. Consider, for example, the fact that presidential rankings initially slotted Dwight D. Eisenhower at a mediocre #22 (1962) in terms of leadership and then recently elevated him to a lofty #5 (2017).[2] Such fluctuations serve as a red-flag warning that first impressions often cannot survive the test of time. In any case, while recognizing the danger of such pitfalls, what can we say about Raúl's stewardship of Cuba's foreign relations?

Several fairly obvious observations about Cuba under Raúl's tutelage quickly move to the fore. First, there has been a much more pragmatic approach to the management of Cuba's foreign relations, particularly when compared to Fidel's flamboyant, high-intensity style. This characteristic should not be particularly surprising when one considers that Raúl spent most of his professional career in the military, where fact-driven, risk-/cost-benefit analysis tends to be the decision-making norm.[3]

Second, there has also been a devaluation of hard power as an instrument in Havana's foreign affairs toolbox. During the Fidel era there were numerous instances in which Cuba flexed its military muscles in one form or another, the most dramatic examples being Havana's involvement during the 1970s and 1980s in the Ethiopian and especially the Angolan/Namibian conflicts in Africa. It was this audacity that led Secretary of State Henry Kissinger to ask, his question laced with both anger and incredulity, "Whoever heard of the Cubans conducting a global foreign policy?" Yet that is exactly what the Cuban Revolutionary Forces (Fuerzas Armadas Revolucionarias de Cuba, or FAR) were doing. Moreover, in addition to these conventional military campaigns, throughout the Cold War Havana was extending material as well as moral support (especially in sub-Saharan Africa and Latin America) to the armed struggles being waged by various guerrilla movements in their efforts to seize power.

However, by the time Raúl became president, the situation had changed dramatically. The FAR, as noted in Hal Klepak's chapter, experienced shrinkage in terms of its budget, its equipment, and its manpower, which meant that it no longer had the capacity to project significant power overseas. A similar process unfolded in the arena of unconventional armed conflicts, where Havana shifted its priority to political/diplomatic solutions, with Raúl's greatest achievement being the key role that Cuba played in the peace negotiations between the Colombian government and the guerrillas of the Revolutionary Armed Forces of Colombia (Fuerzas Armadas Revolucionarias de Colombia, or FARC), which ended the brutal war that had been raging in that country for more than fifty years. (This was of enormous importance, since the civil war had resulted in 220,000 dead and over 5 million displaced. The peace negotiations were held in Havana for almost four years before a truce was negotiated.)

Third, there has been a de-emphasis on playing a South-South leadership role. Fidel's tenure was characterized by very high-profile Third World initiatives, two excellent examples being that (1) Cuba was twice chosen to serve as the head of the Non-Aligned Movement (1979 and 2006),[4] and (2) Fidel and Venezuela's Hugo Chávez were the driving forces behind the 2004 creation of the Bolívarian Alliance for the Americas (Alianza Bolivariana para los Pueblos de Nuestra América, or ALBA), one of the hemisphere's most ambitious integration projects.[5] Today ALBA's political influence has been substantially reduced in the region.

In recent years, however, one hears little about Havana playing a leading role in such South-South organizations.[6] Cuba remains, of course, a member, but it is rather clear that leadership has not been a high-priority item on Raúl's foreign relations agenda.

Raúl and Key Areas of Cuba's Foreign Policy Concerns

A constant theme in international affairs stresses the need for, as well as the responsibility of, governmental leaders to protect and promote their countries' vital national interests. Specific interests and the means to achieve them will vary from country to country and sometimes change for an individual nation (due, for example, to developments in the internal and/or external environments). But in general, and certainly in Cuba's case, most of these specific interests can be grouped into three broad categories or fields of concern: (1) the "economic security" dimension, (2) the "international stature" dimension, and (3) the "effective sovereignty/security" dimension. These issue areas do not, of course, function independently of one another but rather are often mutually reinforcing. For example, maximizing one's economic security and/or international stature can contribute significantly to a greater degree of effective sovereignty.[7] In any case, based on material in the preceding chapters and utilizing this tripartite conceptual framework, we can now offer some general concluding observations regarding Raúl's stewardship of Cuba's foreign relations.

The Economic Security Dimension

For much of Fidel's tenure, this dimension was managed quite effectively via the very preferential trade/aid relations that Havana was able to arrange with the USSR and the Soviet Bloc. To cite but one admittedly dramatic example of the generosity that Cuba enjoyed, the oil that Russia was supplying was not only sufficient to meet the island's needs but sometimes flowed so profusely that the island actually became a petroleum exporter. This relationship served not only to enhance the standard of living in Cuba but, perhaps more importantly, was also crucial to the revolution's struggle to survive by insulating it against the economic warfare that Washington was waging via trade and other sanctions in an effort to create such chaos that the government and the revolution would collapse under the pressure. The disintegration of the Soviet Bloc, which during the Cold War had comprised approximately 85 percent of Cuba's foreign trade profile, raised hopes in Washington that the revolution would follow its Eastern European compatriots into oblivion. These expectations were, of course, frustrated as Fidel and later Raúl were able to radically restructure the island's shattered web of international economic relations.

Recently, however, turmoil has reappeared, flowing from the economic and political instability sweeping through Venezuela (which had become under Raúl the island's dominant trading partner and the main supplier of its crucial petroleum imports). As the Venezuelan economy imploded and its ability to export oil was undermined, the ripple effects raised the specter of recession in Cuba as its 2016 gross domestic product (GDP) growth rate (–1.0 percent) sank into the negative range for the first time since the worst days of the "Special Period" in the early 1990s (–14.9 percent in 1993).[8] The impact of Hurricane Irma along the north coast in September 2017 will also have a negative impact upon tourist receipts for the year.

The economies of small countries, especially island nations like Cuba, tend to be heavily dependent on foreign trade, especially with regard to imports. It is, therefore, extremely risky for them to become too dependent in their relations with a very limited range of partners/suppliers, a fact which surely was known to Raúl. Nevertheless, probably for short-term pragmatic reasons, he chose to roll the dice and enter into such an arrangement with Caracas. Certainly this unsuccessful gamble represents his biggest mistake in what otherwise has been a solid record in terms of promoting Cuba's economic security. It appears that Raúl has, in the waning days of his presidency, looked to two options, currently in their infancy, as possible international remedies to the unravelling of Havana's Venezuelan connection.

The first involves, somewhat ironically, closer ties with Russia. Summarizing the broad outline of this rapprochement, William LeoGrande noted in October 2016,

> Russia's resurgence in the Caribbean traces back to Putin's 2000 trip to Cuba, which resulted in expanded trade deals, followed by Castro's 2009 visit to Moscow, the first by a Castro since the end of the Cold War. Prime Minister Dmitry Medvedev traveled to Cuba in February 2013, signing a number of agreements on trade and scientific cooperation. In July 2014, Putin visited the island and agreed to forgive 90 percent of Cuba's

$32 billion in Soviet-era debt, with the remainder to be retired through debt-equity swaps linked to Russian investments. By the time Castro traveled to Moscow again in 2015, Russia had signed agreements to invest in airport construction, development in the port of Mariel, metallurgy and oil exploration. It also agreed to lend Cuba more than $1.3 billion to develop thermal energy plants.[9]

But what has probably been Moscow's most important initiative, at least from Cuba's viewpoint, was launched in May 2017 when Russia once again began shipping large quantities of oil to the island to help replace its Venezuelan losses. The first tanker to arrive contained 240,000 barrels, with much more on the way according to an agreement that provided for Rosneft, the Kremlin's state oil company, to supply 250,000 tons of various petroleum products, which was estimated to be the equivalent of approximately 1,865,000 barrels worth $105 million at current prices.[10]

Exactly what may be the potential for the future development of this resuscitated Havana-Moscow link remains to be seen. Putin has evidenced increased interest in expanding the Russian presence in Latin America,[11] and Cuba is an obvious place to start, given the two countries' history of Cold War ties. Indeed, as Richard Feinberg has noted, "Putin longs to regain the past imperial glory and relations with Cuba follow that same pattern."[12] A number of high-level meetings between Cuban and Russian ministers have taken place, in December 2016 Russia and Cuba agreed for Moscow to modernize the Cuban army, agreements in the energy and transportation sectors have been made, and for the first six months of 2017 bilateral trade increased 72 percent over the same period in 2016. On the other hand, Havana often viewed its Moscow connection with considerable skepticism, and its rupture in the early 1990s was extremely traumatic for the island. As such, despite the obvious pragmatic reasons to do so, Havana might be leery about going very far down this road again.

Raúl's second remedial option is rooted in Cuba's improved relations with Washington during the Obama administration. Although most media attention focused on the resumption of diplomatic ties, the rapprochement produced some significant advances in economic relations between the two countries. In particular, Obama began to interject an important element that had heretofore been missing from the equation: reciprocity with respect to the sale of goods and services. Previously any deviation from Washington's trade restrictions involved one-way transactions that allowed U.S. entities such as agricultural companies make sales to Cuba (see table 17.1) but did not provide similar opportunities for Havana in the U.S. market. One could not, for example, find Cuban cigars or rum on the shelves of U.S. stores.

Table 17.1. U.S. Agricultural Exports to Cuba (millions of dollars)

2005	*2006*	*2007*	*2008*	*2009*	*2010*	*2011*	*2012*	*2015*	*2016*
346	321	431	685	525	349	353	459	350	286

Source: Mark A. McMinimy, "U.S. Agricultural Trade with Cuba: Current Limitations and Future Prospects," *Congressional Research Service*, September 21, 2016.

Slowly, however, this imbalance began to be rectified, with travel being the most dynamic area as more U.S. citizens were allowed to visit the island and in the process to provide (in return for Cuban services) hard currency, which Havana needs to pay for various imports. In 2016, for example, there was a 34 percent growth in U.S. arrivals over 2015, the total being 614,433. Most interesting, however, was the fact that the increase of those who did not have a Cuban background rose 74 percent.[13] This continued to increase throughout 2017. In all some 619,000 American citizens traveled to the island in 2017.[14] Cuban officials also note that this did not include a further 450,000 Cubans resident in the United States.

The medical arena represents another area of great growth potential for Havana. Cuba has made remarkable strides in pharmaceutical research and development, operating at a world-class level that has drawn serious attention from its U.S. counterparts. The Obama administration responded by relaxing restrictions on collaborative clinical trials that could eventually open the highly lucrative domestic market to Cuban-developed drugs. The first U.S. institution to take advantage of this initiative was the Roswell Park Cancer Institute in Buffalo, New York, which received authorization from the U.S. Food and Drug Administration (FDA) to begin clinical trials in late 2016 of a Cuban lung-cancer vaccine called CIMAvax. The drug would, of course, need FDA approval and a distributor before it could be sold in the United States, but as one observer noted, "Regardless of how well CIMAvax itself works, it will blaze a path for medical collaborations with Cuba. Behind CIMAvax, Roswell has prepared paperwork for clinical trials on a second cancer immunotherapy candidate from Cuba, and it's interested in several more. Cuba also has developed other cost-effective treatments that are currently unavailable in the U.S., such as injections for diabetes-related foot ulcers and the meningitis vaccine that predated CIMAvax."[15] Indeed one can confidently assume that the giant U.S. pharmaceutical companies are closely watching these developments and evaluating their options.

Despite the potential benefits offered by both the Russian and U.S. "insurance policies" to Havana's fragile economic ties with Venezuela, these two relationships have yet to demonstrate to Cuba both a high level of viability (i.e., producing significant contributions to its economic health) and reliability (i.e., staying power). In particular, it appears that the U.S. option has been removed from the equation, at least for the time being, given Donald Trump's June 2017 reversion to a Cuban policy characterized by hostility and demands for regime change. At that time he announced in Miami his clear opposition to the Obama policy of improved relations: "America will expose the crimes of the Castro regime and stand with the Cuban people in their struggle for freedom. . . . Effective immediately, I am canceling the last administration's completely one-sided deal with Cuba."[16] Since then he has clearly targeted the Cuban tourist industry, stating that the initial self-reporting travel strategy introduced by the Obama administration would be abolished and that American visitors to Cuba would now have to travel with tour operators that followed the strict requirements of the U.S. Office of Foreign Assets Control. Moreover, American citizens would not be allowed to have any business relations with companies controlled by the Cuban military—which has a leading role in the tourist economy, owning hotels, transportation, and stores.

The "acoustic attack" incidents, which resulted in some two dozen U.S. diplomats being sent home for medical treatment, are another aggravation to the bilateral relationship. A travel advisory was subsequently issued by the U.S. government, warning American tourists of the health risks of traveling to the island. Secretary of State Rex Tillerson then reduced the number of American employees at the embassy in Havana and in October 2017 ordered a reciprocal reduction in diplomats at Cuba's Washington embassy. In addition, in a major blow to Cuban families on both sides of the Florida Strait, Washington insisted that all requests for visas were now to be processed by the consular section of the U.S. embassy in Bogotá. As such, the international dimension of the island's economic security agenda remains highly challenging as the country moves into the post-Raúl era. The heady days of December 2014 (when Presidents Obama and Raúl Castro announced the renewal of diplomatic relations) and August 2015 (when the U.S. and Cuban embassies were reopened) clearly belong to another era.

The International Stature Dimension

The Cuban Revolution has always enjoyed a high degree of international prestige, admittedly not always at the governmental level, but certainly with the people. Fidel's charisma (as well as that of Che Guevara) was a major factor in this phenomenon, but equally important were Cuba's anticolonial/anti-imperialist policies in general and in particular its astonishing ability to play the Caribbean David to Washington's Goliath. These exploits were most evident in what is often called the "heroic" period of the revolution in the 1960s and 1970s as Havana supported armed insurgencies throughout the world (especially in Latin America) and even dispatched regular military forces to fight successfully in Africa. In short, many people who were just emerging from colonialism or who, in the case of Latin America, had a long history of conflict with the colossus to their north viewed Cuba as their champion.

Raúl's "stature strategies," while remaining true to the revolution's internationalist principles, have focused more on conventional state-to-state relations, with Latin America tending to overshadow Africa as a regional center of Havana's attention as a "pink tide" of elected progressive, leftist governments swept through the hemisphere in the early twenty-first century.[17] Accompanying this geographic reorientation was a shift in programmatic focus to a less confrontational approach centered on various cooperative initiatives to address developmental and human needs issues plaguing many countries of the world. Such stature/influence seeking can, says Joseph Nye, be best understood in terms of the acquisition of "soft power," which he explains as follows: "Power is the ability to alter the behavior of another to get what you want. There are basically three ways to do that: coercion (sticks), payments (carrots), and attraction (soft power). . . . A country's soft power can come from three resources: its culture (in places where it is attractive to others), its political values (when it lives up to them at home and abroad), and its foreign policies (when they are seen as legitimate and having moral authority)."[18]

At the epicenter of this scenario is Havana's unparalleled role in medical internationalism, whose humanitarian ethos represents the epitome of Nye's moral-authority criterion. Advances in public health, which required Havana to develop a cadre of highly trained and highly dedicated medical professionals, have been one of the crown jewels of the revolution's domestic accomplishments (education being the other priority area). Drawing on this extensive personnel pool, Cuba quickly developed a deserved reputation as a trailblazer in medical internationalism. To put this in context, approximately one-quarter of Cuban medical personnel are working abroad, mainly in developing countries.

Although Havana had already established its medical aid leadership, there was a brief hiatus in its activity at the height of the country's traumatic Special Period. Subsequently, however, its efforts reemerged stronger and more ambitious than ever. This has been particularly true during Raúl's tenure, when the number of Cuban medical personnel dispatched abroad increased 92 percent from 2006 to 2015 and in the process generated immense prestige for Havana. No less an observer than President Obama conceded this fact when in a press conference at the 2009 Summit of the Americas meeting in Trinidad, he said,

> One thing that I thought was interesting—and I knew this in a more abstract way but it was interesting in very specific terms—was hearing from these leaders who when they spoke about Cuba talked very specifically about the thousands of doctors from Cuba that are dispersed all throughout the region, and upon which many of these countries heavily depend. And it's a reminder for us in the United States that if our only interaction with many of these countries is drug interdiction, if our only interaction is military, then we may not be developing the connections that can, over time, increase our influence and have a beneficial effect when we need to try to move policies that are of concern to us forward in the region.[19]

Basically these comments represented an acknowledgment on Washington's part that Havana's medical internationalism constitutes a major source of competition in the realm of soft-power politics.

Overall, then, it seems accurate to say that Cuba's international stature has remained high under Raúl's stewardship. The major area of ambiguity, at least in terms of the prestige and influence accorded to Havana at the governmental level, is the future of Latin America's "pink tide." It has already been rolled back in such key countries as Argentina, Ecuador, and Brazil, with Venezuela teetering on the brink. Reversals like this can have a negative impact not only on Cuba's reservoir of soft power but also on its economic security since the new governments emerging on the scene may very well be less inclined to embrace Havana as a trading partner or to pursue developmental projects with it.

But even with these uncertainties looming on the governmental horizon, Cuba continues to enjoy strong admiration at the popular level, which, not coincidentally, represents ground zero for Havana's medical aid programs. Cuba's doctors are dispatched to those areas of their host countries where decent health care has long been scarce to nonexistent, and they provide it at no cost to their dispossessed patients. Their track record is astonishing, as illustrated by just a few statistics: they have served over 1.1 billion people, have performed over 9.8 million surgeries, and have in the process saved 5,146,977 lives.[20] It is such grassroots initiatives which provide a firm foundation for Cuba's ongoing international stature.

The Effective Sovereignty/Security Dimension

Many observers of international affairs, especially those influenced by the realist school, tend to be rather skeptical about the status of small countries (like Cuba) on the world stage, often seeing them as political casualties of the stark differentials that exist in national power. This perspective was eloquently explained by William Demas when he wrote regarding the Caribbean, "Many people in the region . . . hold pessimistic and deterministic positions regarding our prospects for any degree of effective independence vis-à-vis the outside world. They believe that we are doomed to abject subordination because of our small size . . . and because of our long colonial history as mere political, economic, military, and cultural appendages of the metropolitan countries. They consider that we . . . [are] impotent, unable to control our destiny . . . and invariably subject to the decisions, and indeed the whims, of outside countries."[21]

Stated somewhat differently, what Demas is doing here is calling attention to the difference between formal and effective sovereignty. The former is in many respects of symbolic importance, involving such attributes as admission to the United Nations and other similar badges of acceptance into the international community. Effective sovereignty is much more substantive, for it is characterized by a country's maintaining a firm grip on its destiny by minimizing the political system's susceptibility to external penetration and thereby maximizing control over its decision-making processes.

The architects of the Cuban Revolution, well aware of the island's vulnerabilities (both historical and contemporary) to foreign domination, have made defending the country's effective sovereignty their highest priority. Indeed this pursuit, fueled by nationalistic aspirations that are not only an integral element of the revolution's ethos but likewise deeply embedded in the larger society's political culture, represents the leitmotif underlying much of Havana's foreign policies. This sentiment can trace its roots to the very beginning of the Cuban independence struggle, and its resonance continues to this very day.

Not surprisingly, the pyrotechnics that can be sparked by these sensitivities have often erupted within the context of U.S.-Cuban relations, for it has been Washington's hostility that has posed the greatest threat to the revolution. As such, the litmus test for Cuba's leadership with respect to maximizing the country's effective sovereignty has always revolved heavily around managing its relationship with the United States.

During the Cold War the island's Soviet connection played a major role in protecting its national security and enhancing its effective sovereignty by insulating it against U.S. military threats and economic warfare. But ultimately this buffer would disappear, requiring Fidel and then later Raúl to confront the daunting task of adjusting Havana's foreign relations to the new international environment, which many felt contained serious security threats for Cuba by giving Washington a freer hand to pursue its efforts at regime change. Both men proved up to the challenge, with Raúl orchestrating a breakthrough in the management of U.S. relations by negotiating a resumption of diplomatic relations followed by cooperative agreements in various fields (see William LeoGrande's chapter for details).

Throughout this rapprochement drama, Raúl was, like Fidel before him, extremely sensitive to protecting and indeed exercising Havana's effective sovereignty, successfully demanding that the process move forward on the basis of mutual respect, which included what were traditional Cuban terms of no U.S. preconditions (i.e., domestic and/or foreign policy concessions by Havana) as the "price" for launching negotiations. Raúl made this quite clear when he eloquently stated in January 2014,

> We have expressed on many occasions our willingness to hold a respectful dialogue with the United States without compromising the independence, sovereignty and self-determination of our nation. We make no demand on the United States that it change its political system, nor do we agree to negotiate ours. If we really want to make any progress in our bilateral relations, we must learn to mutually respect our differences and get used to living peacefully with them. This is the only way; otherwise, we are ready to endure another 55 years in the same situation.[22]

Raúl not only prevailed in a political sense by achieving full diplomatic recognition from Washington but moreover (as noted previously) was able to gain, admittedly on a limited scale, something that had eluded Havana in the past—economic reciprocity, which allowed Cuba to establish agreements with the United States wherein it serves as a supplier rather than just as a consumer of U.S. goods and services.

Recognize, however, that this U.S./Cuban détente is far from complete, for most of Washington's sanctions remain in place and can only be lifted by an act of Congress. Obama in many instances was able to circumvent this obstacle by using executive agreements as the tool to pursue better relations, but they can be revoked with the stroke of a presidential pen.[23] (Indeed Obama's successor in the White House has hinted that he might well pursue such a course of action.) Nevertheless most observers would probably agree that Raúl passed the test of managing U.S. relations with flying colors, reinforcing this performance with achievements in the areas of economic security and international stature, which likewise served to help protect and enhance the country's crucial effective sovereignty.

CONCLUSION

Within the three key dimensions of Cuba's foreign affairs agenda, Raúl's fairly conventional, pragmatic state-to-state approach, combined with a low-profile style, has worked quite well. Under his stewardship the county's network of international economic relations, whose decimation during the Special Period posed a lethal threat to the island's economic security, has continued to be restructured and strengthened, although the deteriorating situation in Venezuela has become an increasingly dangerous storm cloud on the horizon; the revolution's international stature is as strong as ever; and Havana continues to display a high degree of effective sovereignty, as exemplified by Raúl's success in negotiating the inception of a new relationship with the United States characterized (finally) by respect for, and recognition on Washington's part of, Cuba's status as a fully independent member of the global community.

But with the remarkable Castro era coming to an end as Raúl departs the presidency in 2018, questions abound regarding the future of Cuba's foreign relations.

Cuban Foreign Policy: The Future

Futurology is of course a dangerous field of research, and the study of Cuba (with its many examples of logic-defying magical realism, where policies adopted there have often confused Western politicians and analysts alike) is clearly no exception. Nobody knows this better than the Pulitzer Prize winner and *Miami Herald* journalist Andrés Oppenheimer, author of the unfortunately titled *Castro's Final Hour: The Secret Story behind the Coming Downfall of Communist Cuba*, published fully a quarter century ago (in 1992).[24] That said, it is important to draw some pertinent conclusions about the evolution of Cuban foreign policy in recent years and offer some thoughts on probable future developments.

The first conclusion is that, as has been the case for nearly two centuries, by far the most significant factor that will influence future Cuban foreign policy will result from developments on the Washington-Havana axis. The United States has been significantly involved in Cuba in many different ways since it became the island's leading trading partner in the mid-nineteenth century when it was still a colony of Spain. Besides its role as Cuba's leading trading partner and foreign investor in prerevolutionary times, the United States has actually governed the island in the immediate postindependence period (under Generals John Brooke and Leonard Wood), has sent in U.S. military forces to shore up unpopular governments (and protect U.S. economic and political influence), has maintained a military base at Guantánamo since 1902, has at times been involved in attempts at regime change in Cuba, and has been a major target for migration.

The difference at the present juncture, however, is the highly unpredictable approach to foreign affairs of President Donald Trump, who within his first hundred days in office changed his mind several times on key foreign policy questions—on

Syria, China, North Korea, Mexico, and Canada. Typical of his rather superficial and changeable appreciation of foreign policy was his position on the North American Free Trade Agreement (NAFTA), which changed from wanting to tweak some of its clauses to threatening to tear up the tripartite agreement to then offering to renegotiate it.[25] Where his mercurial grasp of foreign affairs will lead with regard to the Cuban question is open to many (and often conflicting) interpretations.

Trump's approach to the Cuba question follows a tortuous, confusing, and often contradictory path. Initially during in his presidential campaign, for instance, he noted how President Barack Obama was right to move toward establishing a dialogue with the Cuban government, since five decades of hostility from Washington had resulted in bringing about little change in Havana. Then, while campaigning in southern Florida among Cuban exiles, he radically altered this perspective and instead committed to overturning the reforms on Cuba made by Obama.[26] The third (and so far most recent) stage of his interpretation of U.S.-Cuban relations revolves around getting a "better deal" from the Cubans. On November 28, 2016, he tweeted, "If Cuba is unwilling to make a better deal for the Cuban people, the Cuban-American people and the U.S. as a whole, I will terminate the deal."[27] Since then the tone of his pronouncements on Cuba has become significantly more aggressive.

The reduction in State Department staff and the disappearance of their knowledge and expertise regarding the Cuba file is a major lacuna—the historical memory has thus been severely weakened. This situation is aggravated by the growing influence of conservative, influential Cuban Americans and congressional representatives, on the one hand, and the significant business lobby keen to do business in Cuba, on the other. As a result of these conflicting pressures upon the president, it is unclear what the future holds for the Trump position in terms of the final U.S. policy toward Cuba. The oft-quoted sentiment of Winston Churchill when talking about Russia often comes to mind in attempting to determine just what President Trump will finally decide: "Russia is a riddle wrapped in a mystery inside an enigma." So too is the Trump position on Cuba.

Caught in the middle are moderate Cuban Americans who travel back to Cuba to visit family and Americans who seek to take advantage of a slackening in U.S. restrictions to visit the island. Both groups overwhelmingly support a continuation of the reforms toward Cuba first introduced by the Obama administration (and outlined in the LeoGrande chapter), as do the majority of Americans and even Cuban Americans, according to all recent polls. In 2016 the numbers for these two categories of visitors to Cuba were 447,000 and 282,000, respectively, while the first three months of 2017 also saw a significant increase, with visits by over 159,000 Americans (up from 72,000 for the same period in the previous year) and 120,000 Cuban Americans (compared with 88,000 during the January–March period in 2016). According to the Cuban Ministry of Foreign Relations, by the end of 2017 some 453,905 "Cubans resident in the United States" had visited Cuba.[28] Despite many years of tension between the United States and Cuba, the renewal of diplomatic relations between both countries has been widely accepted by Americans.

Given the enormous importance of U.S.-Cuban relations and the psychological and historical baggage that accompany them, it would not be surprising for the Cuban government to feel confused and puzzled about how Washington intends to deal with the future of bilateral relations. Thus far Cuban policymakers have largely kept their concerns to themselves, looking askance at some of President Trump's foreign policy statements but refraining from any remarks that could be considered inflammatory. At the same time, they cannot help but be concerned by the lack of clarity, and especially the inconsistency, of Trump's remarks.

Some historical context is appropriate here. In the rush to support a full "normalization" of bilateral relations, many often forget the complicated historical relations between the two countries. "Es complicado," Cubans will note. In particular it is important not to forget that Cuba has survived over five decades of U.S. hostility. In fact the "Trading with the Enemy" Act remains legally in effect with relation to Cuba, still seen officially as the "enemy."

These decades of hostility emanating from U.S. shores have resulted in dozens of assassination attempts against Fidel Castro, scores of acts of sabotage and terrorism emanating from the United States (with the deaths of thirty-four hundred Cubans), an attempted invasion in April 1961 (at the Bay of Pigs), an embargo (still in place, despite the fact that it was condemned by 191 countries at the United Nations General Assembly in October 2017), and lobbying by some U.S. allies to break relations with Cuba. And Cuba, it must be remembered, is just ninety miles from the United States, a country with the most powerful military machine in the world. Given this track record of hostility, the Obama-Castro negotiations resulting in the renewal of diplomatic relations are all the more remarkable.

In many ways the survival of the Cuban revolutionary process defies logic, given these decades of enmity, the huge disparity in size, wealth, and military power between the two countries, and their geographical proximity. From January 1961, when Washington broke diplomatic relations with Cuba, until December 17, 2014, when both presidents simultaneously announced their intention to restore them, the relationship had been decidedly frosty, with various U.S. administrations vowing—unsuccessfully—to overthrow the Castro government. Indeed one wonders why it took so long before Obama finally realized that following decades of seeking to overthrow the revolutionary system, this was not going to happen and a different strategy was called for. He is therefore to be commended for his initiative in supporting the renewal of diplomatic relations with Havana.

While the United States–Cuba dynamic is clearly the most significant bilateral relationship in play after Raúl Castro leaves the presidency, there are many other factors to be considered. Often lost in any analysis of Cuban foreign policy is the effective role played by policymakers on the island and the commitment to basic socialist principles held by the revolutionary government (occasionally, but not always, tempered by pragmatism). Cuban diplomats as a body are well trained and extremely professional, and they support their government's positions firmly. They are rarely political appointees and instead have come through rigorous training in diplomacy and international relations. Many, including the current ambassador to the United States, José Ramón Cabañas (who has a PhD), hold graduate degrees and have studied at the University of Havana and the Instituto Superior de Relaciones Internacionales. There is also close contact with a number of think tanks (such as the Centro de Estudios Hemisféricos y sobre Estados Unidos and the Centro de Investigaciones de Política Internacional), where many former diplomats are employed as analysts and policymakers.

The question of Cuba's adhering to basic diplomatic principles is referred to in the introductory chapter and should not be ignored. Since the early days of the revolution, and with little subtlety, the government has consistently promulgated the principles of noninterference in the domestic affairs of other countries, of respect for national sovereignty, and of the right of nations to develop their own political systems and directions. This is a basic, fundamental, and nonnegotiable tenet in Havana's approach to its relations with all other countries. It has been held firmly for the over fifty years that Cuba has resisted pressure from Washington to bring about regime change. Indeed, as recently as October 2017, First Vice President Miguel Díaz-Canel stated this position unequivocally: "Cuba will not make concessions to its sovereignty and independence, nor negotiate its principles or accept the imposition of conditions. . . . The changes needed in Cuba will solely be carried out by the Cuban people."[29]

The Cuban Revolution has succeeded in part because of its successful foreign policy, since it has been able to knit together firm alliances with other nations that have contributed largely to its survival—despite major challenges. Since the implosion of the Soviet Union in 1989–1990 (a process with disastrous effect upon the economy and society of Cuba), the Cuban Revolution has made a number of strategic alliances with numerous developing countries and has diversified its trading relationships. Undoubtedly the most significant bilateral relationship, in economic and political matters, in the past decade has been that with Venezuela, dealt with by Carlos Romero in this volume. But Cuba has learned from the error of its dependence upon the United States and the Soviet Union in previous eras, as the chapter by Michael Erisman illustrates, and as a result has radically shifted its trading relationships.

Under Raúl Castro the traditional revolutionary principles of solidarity and cooperation with developing countries remain firm. The difference now is that they are moderated by a large dose of pragmatism, since countries with the capacity to pay for services rendered are expected to do so. The end result is an effective foreign policy that provides international cooperation to developing countries throughout the world but also generates funding from Cuba's rich human capital (mainly in expertise in health care, but also in education, engineering, construction, and agronomy). At the same time the principles of solidarity can be noted in the fact that poorer nations, without the ability to pay the going rate for Cuban services, pay only a symbolic contribution toward the actual costs.

In particular Cuba's role in Latin America, analyzed by Andrés Serbin, deserves to be considered. While the "pink tide" of some dozen leftist countries from the region has clearly retreated from its high point under the Chávez-Castro alliance, there is still a significant degree of Latin American and Caribbean unity, which Washington ignores at its peril. Indeed Cuba maintains solid diplomatic relations with countries that are led by conservative governments, such as Mexico, Costa Rica, and Peru. This unified approach by countries of the region was seen several years ago most clearly in the demand to Washington that Cuba be included in all regional summit meetings; otherwise the countries of the region threatened to boycott future Summits of the Americas.

The founding of the Community of Latin American and Caribbean States, the regional opposition to the wall that the Trump administration has threatened to build in order to keep Mexican (and by extension Central American) migrants out of the United States, and Trump's arrogant treatment of Mexico and the NAFTA agreement have all hardened regional opposition to Washington, despite the many differing ideological positions held by countries in the region. Moreover Cuba's position as the conscience of the region has been strengthened by a number of social and political contributions, ranging from its medical internationalism to its major role in helping to bring the Colombian civil war to a close in 2016. In 2013 Julia Sweig provided some useful advice for President Obama, a suggestion that remains pertinent for his successor: "The geopolitical context in Latin America provides another reason the U.S. government should make a serious shift on Cuba. For five years now, Obama has ignored Latin America's unanimous disapproval of Washington's position on Cuba. Rather than perpetuate Havana's diplomatic isolation, U.S. policy embodies the imperial pretensions of a bygone era, contributing to Washington's own marginalization."[30]

Sweig's argument is valid. She could have also added that Cuba's role in the Global South is highly respected and that decades of cooperation and assistance have resulted in significant political influence. Its long-standing anticolonial philosophy and its outspoken stance on both the right of self-determination for all countries and support for liberation struggles have been remarkably consistent for almost six decades. Likewise its role as the elected leader of the Non-Aligned Movement (1979–1983 and 2006–2009) has strengthened its influence in the Global South. It was therefore no surprise that in December 2013 Raúl Castro was one of the few world leaders invited to speak at the memorial service for Nelson Mandela.

Cubans are rightfully proud of their foreign policy successes, and for decades this small country (population of 11.2 million) has played a role in international politics that far outstrips its size. In boxing terms, it fights far above its weight class—and consistently wins. Havana has positioned itself well in international circles, in no small part because of its skilled diplomats and foreign policy makers who possess long-term political and diplomatic goals. It is unlikely that this ideological and strategic approach will change in the post-Raúl political world.

Common (albeit understandable) errors are made as people look to the future of Cuba and talk of the country becoming "another Vietnam" or "another China," with a centralized one-party political structure and significant free enterprise. While there is some accuracy in this very basic reference, it is much too simplistic and fails to take into account a number of historical, cultural, and geographic elements.[31] Instead Cuba will pursue its own path, borrowing elements where they are deemed to be useful, inventing and adapting the political and developmental model *a la cubana*. In terms of foreign policy, it will continue to trade with countries throughout the world and diversify its dependence, looking askance at the Trump approach(es) to the island and ensuring that it never becomes too dependent on its neighbor—while always having an alternative plan in trade diversification if Washington turns hostile.

Cuba's international relations continue to evolve successfully, and the country remains as respected on the world diplomatic stage as it has for many years. Yet the future of the country depends largely upon economic growth, an area in which Cuba's performance is disappointing. This is not just because of the slow economic growth (GDP declined 0.96 percent in 2016 and grew only 1.69 percent in 2017, illustrating a severe downturn in the economy, and foreign investment levels remain disappointingly low) but also because of the top-heavy bureaucratic structure, which is largely loath to follow the exhortations of Raúl Castro. This of course raises the question as to how this complex situation will evolve in the post-Castro reality and, among other questions, what impact it will have upon Cuban foreign policy.

While less dramatic than the intention to update the Cuban economy, seen clearly in the 2011 *Lineamientos* (guidelines) and subsequently in the updating of these goals presented in 2016 at the Seventh Congress of the Communist Party of Cuba, there is an ongoing and multifaceted revision of Cuban foreign policy taking place. Its goal is basically twofold: to reduce economic dependency upon one or two trading partners (and, in tandem with this, to broaden the base of investors in Cuba) and also to obtain maximum benefit from its decades of international cooperation. In these challenges Cuba "can count upon important allies in Latin America and the Caribbean, China and Russia, which are major powers with significant influence, and key developing groups. Another important priority is maintaining, and developing, economic and political relations with major allies of the United States such as the European Union and Canada, especially because of their significant role in the Cuban economy."[32]

So, will Cuba change much after Raúl Castro departs the presidency? Will there be any major changes in the island's diplomatic relations? While it is foolish to speculate too much about a future where many key elements are still in play, it is clear that, based upon the track record of Cuban foreign policy since 1959, the island will continue to develop and strengthen diplomatic relations around the globe. An emphasis will continue to be placed upon South-South relations. Increasingly, too, Cuba is strengthening relations with the Middle East. At the same time it faces severe economic challenges and needs to provide greater incentives, both in the domestic market and for foreign investment.

The principled pragmatism that has been developed under Raúl Castro will be continued, with the clear intent of maintaining and developing solid diplomatic relations, regardless of ideological affinity. But revolutionary principles die hard, and for the foreseeable future Cuba will continue the trajectory established for over fifty years by the revolutionary government—while at the same diversifying its trade relationships and searching for new markets. It promises to be an extremely interesting period, as with so many matters related to Cuba—complex, contradictory, but never boring.

NOTES

1. For a general introduction to the broad sweep of changes in Cuba during the government of Raúl Castro, see Philip Brenner et al., eds., *A Contemporary Cuba Reader: The Revolution under Raúl Castro* (Lanham, MD: Rowman & Littlefield, 2015).

2. These rankings can be found at "Historical Rankings of Presidents of the United States," Wikipedia, https://en.wikipedia.org/wiki/Historical_rankings_of_presidents_of_the_United_States.

3. For an excellent biography of Raúl, see Hal Klepak, *Raúl Castro and Cuba: A Military Story* (London: Palgrave Macmillan, 2012).

4. The only other country to be so honored was Yugoslavia (1961 and 1989)

5. For an overview of ALBA, see H. Michael Erisman, "Cuba, Venezuela, and ALBA: The NeoBolivarian Challenge," in *Cuban-Latin American Relations in the Context of a Changing Hemisphere*, ed. Gary Prevost and Carlos Oliva Campos (Amherst, NY: Cambria Press, 2011), 101–48.

6. See, for example, the chapters by Andrés Serbin and Carlos A. Romero in this volume, where ALBA is frequently mentioned, but there is little to indicate that Raúl has evidenced any great interest in playing a leadership role in it. With respect to the Non-Aligned Movement, it is never mentioned in the chapters in this volume by Isaac Saney (Africa) and Pedro Monzón and Eduardo Regalado Florido (Asia/Oceana).

7. These concepts and their relevance to Raúl's approach to managing Cuba's foreign relations are developed more fully in H. Michael Erisman, "Raúlista Foreign Policy: A Macroperspective," in Brenner et al., *A Contemporary Cuba Reader*, 221–29.

8. See Figure 3.1, which shows that Cuba's total trade with Venezuela had dropped 74.02 percent by 2016 from its high point in 2012.

9. William LeoGrande, "Cuba Diversifies Its Risk," Yahoo! Groups, October 12, 2016, https://groups.yahoo.com/neo/groups/CubaNews/conversations/topics/158825. See also Mervyn Bain's chapter in this volume.

10. This information comes from "Russia Resumes Oil Shipments to Cuba, Helps Fill Venezuelan Breach," *Reuters*, May 3, 2017, http://www.reuters.com/article/us-cuba-energy-russia-idUSKBN17Z2B8.

11. For an overview of Russian initiatives in Latin America, see Vladimir Rouvinski, "Understanding Russian Priorities in Latin America," *Kennan Institute/Wilson Center*, February 3, 2017, https://www.wilsoncenter.org/publication/kennan-cable-no20-understanding-russian-priorities-latin-america.

12. Nora Gámez Torres, "Amidst Growing Tensions with the U.S., Cuba Gets Cozier with Russia," *Miami Herald*, October 13, 2017.

13. This data comes from Abel González Alayon, "Travel from the U.S. to Cuba Grew 34 percent in 2016," January 13, 2017, Yahoo! Groups, https://groups.yahoo.com/neo/groups/CubaNews/conversations/topics/159632.

14. Andrea Rodríguez, "Tourism Booming in Cuba despite Tougher New Trump Policy," *ABC News*, January 19, 2018, abcnews.go.com/International/wirestory/tourism-booming -cuba-tougher-trump-policy-52454200.

15. Sarah Zhang, "Cuba's Innovative Cancer Vaccine Is Finally Coming to America: The Country Has a Whole Arsenal of Unique Drugs Locked behind the U.S. Embargo," *Atlantic*, November 7, 2016.

16. Cited in William LeoGrande, "Trump Has Set U.S.-Cuban Relations Back Decades," *Foreign Policy*, June 22, 2017, http://www.foreignpolicy.com2017/06/22/trump-has-set-u-s -cuba-relations-back-decades.

17. Among those riding this pink tide who adopted strongly pro-Cuban foreign policies were leaders in Argentina, Brazil, Chile, Ecuador, Nicaragua, and Venezuela.

18. Joseph S. Nye, "Think Again: Soft Power," *Foreign Policy*, February 23, 2006, http:// foreignpolicy.com/2006/02/23/think-again-soft-power.

19. Quoted from a transcript of his April 19, 2009, press conference, Barack Obama, "The President's News Conference in Port of Spain, April 19, 2009," American Presidency Project, http://www.presidency.ucsb.edu/ws/index.php?pid=86033.

20. These figures, as well as additional supporting data, can be found in John M. Kirk, *Healthcare without Borders: Understanding Cuban Medical Internationalism* (Gainesville: University Press of Florida, 2015).

21. William Demas, *Consolidating Our Independence: The Major Challenge for the West Indies* (Distinguished Lecture Series, Institute of International Relations, University of the West Indies, Saint Augustine, Republic of Trinidad and Tobago, 1986), 12.

22. Manuel E. Yepe, "Washington's Unserious Response to Cuba's Offer," Yahoo! Groups, January 4, 2014, http://groups.yahoo.com/neo/groups/CubaNews/conversations/ topics/144875.

23. A contrary view can be found in Peter Kornbluh, "Normalization of Relations with Cuba Is All but Irreversible Now," *Nation*, October 19, 2016.

24. In his concluding chapter, titled "Requiem for a Revolution," Oppenheimer notes, "Cuba's tragedy in the aftermath of the Fourth Congress was that the longer Castro stuck to his 'Socialism or Death,' the more difficult a peaceful transition to democracy would be, and the less inconceivable it was that a right-wing *caudillo* would take office with the backing of the Cuban people in a not-too-distant future." Andrés Oppenheimer, *Castro's Final Hour: The Secret Story behind the Coming Downfall of Communist Cuba* (New York: Simon and Schuster, 1992), 423. To date this has not occurred, while it can be argued that "Socialism or Death," albeit in a diluted format, remains significant in Cuba today.

25. "Well, I was going to terminate NAFTA as of two or three days from now. The President of Mexico, who I have a very, very good relationship, called me, and also the Prime Minister of Canada, who I have a very good relationship with, and I like both of these gentlemen very much, and they said: 'Rather than terminating NAFTA, could you please renegotiate' . . . and I said 'I will hold on the termination. Let's see if we can make it a fair deal.'" Adrian Morrow, Steven Chase, and Greg Keenan, "Trump Ready to Renegotiate after Calls from Peña Nieto, Trudeau," *Globe and Mail*, April 27, 2017.

26. "All of the concessions Barack Obama has granted the Castro regime were done through executive order, which means the next president can reverse them, and that I will do unless the Castro regime meets our demands." Cited in Frances Robles, "Business or Politics? What Trump Means for Cuba," *New York Times*, November 15, 2016. In the same article

Trump suggested that he might also break off diplomatic relations with Havana and probably would not appoint a US ambassador to Cuba.

27. Katherine Faulders, "Trump Threatens to Reverse Obama's Cuba Policy unless Cuba Makes a 'Better Deal,'" *ABC News*, November 28, 2016, abcnews.go.com/Politics/trump-threatens-reverse-obamas-cuba-policy-makes/story?id=43820479.

28. "Más de un millón cien mil visitantes desde EE UU. Llegaron a Cuba en 2017," *Cubadebate*, January 9, 2018, www.cubadebate.cu/noticias/2018/01/09/mas-de-un-millon-cien-mil-visitantes-desde-ee-uu-llegaron-a-cuba-en-2017/#.Wmgl.

29. Cited in Marc Frank, "Likely Successor to Cuba's Castro Rejects U.S. Demands for Change," *Reuters*, October 8, 2017.

30. See Julia Sweig, "Cuba after Communism," *Council on Foreign Relations*, July/August 2013, http://www.cfr.org/cuba/cuba-after-communism/p30991.

31. "Still, Cuba does not appear poised to adopt the Chinese or Vietnamese blueprint for market liberalization anytime soon. Cuba's unique demographic, geographic and economic realities—particularly the island's aging population of 11 million, its proximity to the United States, and its combination of advanced human capital and dilapidated physical infrastructure—set Cuba apart from other countries that have moved away from communism." Ibid.

32. Carlos Alzugaray, "La actualización de la política exterior cubana," *Política Exterior*, no. 161 (September–October 2014): 82.

Index

ACS. *See* Association of Caribbean States
Africa: "Black Atlantic" connection with, 95, 108; Brazil and Cuba with vaccine for, 102–3; Castro, F., on Latin people from, 99, 107; Ebola assistance in, 71, 96, 103; FAR in, 99; medical education and, 96, 99, 102, 104; medical internationalism for, 96–97, 100–101, 106; medical internationalism statistics in, 100–101, 106; military assistance to, 97–99, 108; slave statistics and, 95
African Diaspora, 96, 107
African Union (AU), 95–96
ALADI. *See* Latin American Integration Association (Asociación Latinoamericana de Integración)
ALBA. *See* Bolivarian Alliance for the Peoples of Our America (Alianza Bolivariana para los Pueblos de Nuestra América)
ALBA-TCP. *See* Bolivarian Alternative for the Peoples of Our America–Treaty of Commerce between Peoples (Alianza Bolivariana para los Pueblos de Nuestra América–Tratado de Comercio de los Pueblos)
Algeria, 100
Alianza Bolivariana para los Pueblos de Nuestra América. *See* Bolivarian Alliance for the Peoples of Our America
Alianza Bolivariana para los Pueblos de Nuestra América–Tratado de Comercio de los Pueblos. *See* Bolivarian Alternative for the Peoples of Our America–Treaty of Commerce between Peoples
alliances: Castro, R., as low profile in, 131; China and, 129; Cuba goals for, 286; Harper and U.S., 185, 188; Latin America as, 93n12, 284–85; Pacific Alliance, Latin America as, 82, 93n12; Russia and, 129; U.S. balanced with, 78, 79, 81, 83, 90, 176, 210, 284; Venezuela and, 88, 129
Angola: apartheid struggle in, 97–98; medical education with, 105–6; oil exploration and, 106
Anti-Air Defense and Revolutionary Air Force, 31
antiapartheid efforts, 97–98, 103–4, 106
Araujo, Rui, 155n32
Argentina: Brazil primary trading partner as, 93n18; Cuba relationship with, 84; Latin America region rifts and, 93n12; "pink tide" and Cuba by, 288n17;

political shifts in, 204; support from Cámpora in and, 92n4
Asamblea Nacional, 20n20
Asia: finance and, 115; investment and tourism increases by, 122; statistics on, 115; trade and Vietnam in, 118; trade with, 115, 121–22
Asia-Oceania: objectives in, 116–17; Russia, China, India in, 115–16; socialism and, 115, 122; trade with, 121–22; training doctors for, 145–46, *148*
Asociación Latinoamericana de Integración. *See* Latin American Integration Association
Association of Caribbean States (ACS), 14, 79
AU. *See* African Union
Australia: cooperation efforts by, 151–52; Cuba literacy for Aboriginal, 121, 141, *152*, 152–53; medical competition from, 150–51; resistance in, 152; trade potentials with, 121

balance of trade, *44*, 44–45, 50, *50*
Batista regime, 26–27, 40n3, 41n9
BioCubaFarma, 68
biotechnology: BioCubaFarma overseeing, 68; China and, 117–18; LABIOFAM for exports of, 69; Polo Científico producing, 67; Russia links with Cuba, 240
Bolivarian Alliance for the Peoples of Our America (Alianza Bolivariana para los Pueblos de Nuestra América, or ALBA): challenges for, 221; Chávez rhetoric on, 37; Cuba focus on, 165; as FAR allies, 36–38; FTAA alternative as, 9–10; limited military cooperation with, 37; post-U.S. hegemony as, 80; for South-South cooperation, 82; Venezuelan oil for influence in, 88
Bolivarian Alternative for the Peoples of Our America–Treaty of Commerce between Peoples (Alianza Bolivariana para los Pueblos de Nuestra América–Tratado de Comercio de los Pueblos, or ALBA-TCP): commerce and trade promoted by, 212; Cuba and Latin America region after, 83; decline of, 221; Venezuela and Nicaragua in, 212
Bolivia, 204, 212
Botello, Emilia, 157n69
Brazil: Africa vaccine from, 102–3; Argentina as trading partner of, 93n18; BRICS leader as, 85; China as primary trade partner of, 85; Cuba activity reduced by, 86; Cuba airports by Odebrecht of, 230; Cuba and bank of, 225, 229–30; Cuba critic Sánchez visiting, 226; Cuba ethanol by, 233; Cuba oil help from, 85; export, import statistics with, 52–53, *53*, 226, 230, *231*, *232*; FTZ with help from, 85–86, 225–26; investments and companies of, 86, 91, 226–27, 229–33; Latin America leader as, 84; Latin America rifts and, 93n12; Lula da Silva during relationship with, 225, 233; Mais Médicos with, 52, 62–63, 86, 91, 226–29; Mariel port as investment of, 229–30, 259; medical internationalism and, 52–53, 62–63, *65*; OAS leader as, 85; "pink tide" and Cuba by, 288n17; political shifts in, 204; during Rousseff and, 84, 85, 225–27; Rousseff impeachment in, 16, 52–53, 62–63, 84–85, 226; Sandinistas and Cuba with, 93n19; South America policies of, 93n16; Temer as Rousseff successor in, 226; trade with, 52–53, *53*, 79, 86, 226, 230–32, *231*, *232*; U.S. not challenged by, 85
BRICS (Brazil, Russia, India, China and South Africa) bloc, 85
Bush, George W.: Cuba relations under, 4, 177; medical internationalism rejected by, 60; not open to cooperation, 161–62

Calderón Reynoso, Irene, 156n55
Cámpora, Héctor José, 92n4
Canada: Castro, F., on, 194; conservative views from, 183; Cuba and education from, 186, 191; on Cuba as dictatorship, 185; with FEMA blocking U.S. laws, 194n6; Harper on Cuba and democracy,

195n9; largest tourism from, 55, 186; liberal views from, 184; music exchange with, 191; naval ship visit to Cuba, 190; Quebec and Cuba book fair, 190–91; "sonic attacks" and no reprisal by, 193; sports exchange with, 191; trade and, 185, 188, 192, 247; Trudeau, J., on Cuba and, 183–94; uninterrupted relations with, 12, 79, 127, 136, 194; UN Security Council seat lost by, 188; U.S.-Cuba secret negotiations in, 189; U.S. pressure on banks of, 194n7

Caribbean Community (CARICOM), 79, 90, 129, 160; acquiring status in, 80, 92n5; slavery reparations lawsuit by, 107

Caribbean nations, 41n14

CARICOM. *See* Caribbean Community

Castro, Fidel: adaptive foreign policy of, 128; on Canada, 194; on Chávez death, 215; on Chernobyl Program costs, 66; death of, 2, 125; dissident crackdowns by, 11, 129, 130, 134, 203, 226; EU restrictions on, 130; FAR under, 27–28; great man theory and, 244, 252n50; internationalism and, 104; on Latin African people, 99, 107; on Mao, 260; medical internationalism begun by, 59; pharmaceutical industry started by, 67; rapprochement and defiance from, 171; Russia and Soviet oil for, 274; São Paulo Forum and, 92n6; South-South activism of, 273; Spain disparaged by, 198; Trudeau, J., on death of, 194

Castro, Raúl: authoritarian single-party of, 129; CARICOM lawsuit supported by, 107; China and, 261, 262; Colombia peace role of, 21n22, 273; Cuba changed by, 12; economic reforms of, 127, 129, 144; on effective sovereignty and U.S., 280; FAR headed by, 25–27, 99; foreign leaders visiting, 13–14; foreign policy after, 248–49; foreign policy of, 1–19, 27, 40, 128, 129, 131; foreign relations goals under, 5, 18–19; GDP during administration of, 44, *44*; internationalism and socialism under, 114, 122, 131; international recognition under, 129, 131; international relations under, 271; Internet access under, 2, 164; Latin America emphasis by, 277; Maduro supported by, 217–18; Mandela funeral and, 285; medical internationalism under, 60–63, 66–73, 278–79; military inherited by, 272–73; Moncada Barracks and, 26–27, 40n3; pragmatism of, 3, 15–16, 272; Putin and, 165, 237, 239–40, 242, 274; as reliable and less charismatic, 129; retirement of, 1, 16, 17; Russia visited by, 237, 249n1; on slave history duty, 99, 100; soft power of, 277–78; South-South organizations and, 273, 286, 287n6; Spain relations and, 205–7; state-to-state relations by, 277; successes of, 18; on Trump, 174, 175; 2006 government and, 28–29; United Kingdom and Norway softened by, 206; U.S. dialogue under, 130; U.S. policy of, 161–64, 177–78; Venezuela and, 215, 217–19, 274. *See also* trade

CELAC. *See* Community of Latin American and Caribbean States (Comunidad de Estados Latinoamericanos y Caribeños)

Center for Molecular Immunology (Centro de Inmunología Molecular, or CIM), 67–68, 276

Centro de Inmunología Molecular. *See* Center for Molecular Immunology

Chávez, Hugo: ALBA rhetoric of, 37; Castro, F., on death of, 215; Cuba medical treatment of, 215; Cuba relations with, 3, 9–10; no direct early Cuba connection by, 211; Venezuela as Cuba revolution via, 209

Chernobyl Program, 65–66, 74n5

Chile, 82; Latin America region rifts and, 93n12; "pink tide" and Cuba by, 288n17; support from Allende in, 92n4

China: after Soviet Union collapse, 263, 266; alliance with, 129; Asia-Oceania with, 115–16; automotive investment of, 260; bilateral connections with, 117; biotechnology and, 117–18; Brazil primary trade partner as, 85; business development of, 255; Castro, R., and, 261–62; Cuba inspiring people of, 265; Cuba on Tiananmen Square and, 260–61; Cuba socialism and, 262, 266; debt repayment to, 261–62; economic suggestions from, 263–66; economy statistics of, 264; human rights and Cuba with, 117; investment and, 165, 260; lack of equality in, 265, 266; Latin America emphasizing, 81–82; Latin America learning socialism from, 261; Mariel port utilized by, 258, 259; market socialist model of, 167; no small business interaction with, 262–63; oil and, 117–18; pragmatism of, 255; as priority, 122–23, 165; rapprochement after Soviet collapse, 263, 266; recognition of single, 117; Russia split with, 260; socialism and, 255–56, 261–64, 266; socialism and lack of equality in, 265, 266; Special Period assistance from, 260, 261; strained relations with, 260; telecom, construction, renewable energy and, 117–18; tourism and, 117; trade statistics with, 257, *258*; trade with, 17, 50–51, *51*, 79, 256–60, *258*; U.S. and economy lessons for, 261; U.S. cooperation and mistrust by, 263; U.S. remittances and consumer goods of, 258; U.S. survey of students in, 263–66

China survey: China and economy balance in, 264; concerns voiced in, 265–66; Latin America and socialism principles in, 264; lessons from China successes and mistakes, 266; socialist ideologies as similar, 263–64

Cienfuegos, Camilo, 41n9

CIM. *See* Center for Molecular Immunology (Centro de Inmunología Molecular)

Clinton, Bill, 134, 202

Clinton, Hillary, 163–64, 172, 257

Colombia, 82; Castro, R., role with, 21n22, 273; Cuba and peace in, 15, 94n36, 273

Commission for Assistance to a Free Cuba, 6, 19n6

Common Market of South America (Mercosur), 93n12

Common Position, 10–12; EU and Spain on, 202–3; to Political Dialogue and Cooperation Agreement, 127–28

Communist Party of Cuba: internationalism reaffirmed by, 101, 114; *Lineamientos* passed by, 61, 144, 167–68; Obama talks criticized by, 15

Community of Latin American and Caribbean States (Comunidad de Estados Latinoamericanos y Caribeños, or CELAC): ambitions not realized by, 227; Cuba and founding of, 80–83, 214; Cuba as president of, 144; Cuba focus on, 165; post-U.S. hegemony as, 80; U.S. embargo discussed at, 227

counternarcotics activity: Caribbean nations cooperation on, 41n14; Cuba coasts and *bombardeo*, 41n15; FAR involved in, 30, 35–36; France cooperation on, 39; Mexico and Cuba on, 88; MININT involved in, 30, 35–36; MININT officials punished in, 36; Revolutionary Navy and, 31; United Kingdom cooperation on, 38–39; with U.S., 35–36

Cuba: effective sovereignty of, 279; foreign policy personnel of, 283–84; international interest in, 114; nonnegotiable tenets of, 5, 17–19, 136, 161–63, 174–75, 217, 284; population of, 43, 210; regime continuity in, 128–31; from "revolutionary" to "broker" as, 77. *See also specific subjects*

Cuba citizens, 2; coffee export refusal by, 170

Cuban Americans: Cuba diplomats expulsion and, 176; family visits by, 4, 6, 7; future with, 282; property rights of, 8, 26, 168; remittances and, 2, 4, 8, 51–52, *52*, 163; Trump speech to, 175; U.S. normalization opposed by, 91, 138, 161–62

Cuban Five, 7, 164–67, 241

Cuban Medical Brigade, 147

Cuban Revolutionary Forces (Fuerzas Armadas Revolucionarias de Cuba, or FAR): in Africa, 99; ALBA as allies with, 36–38; budget cut influences on, 29; Castro, R., heading, 25–27, 99; under Castro, F., 27–28; Cienfuegos as namesake for, 41n9; control of economy as unknown, 41n10; corruption countered by, 33–34; counternarcotics activity for, 30, 35–36; current status of, 29–33; Eastern, Central, and Western Armies of, 31; export of revolution abandoned by, 34, 78, 89–90; general population as not active in, 32; government support by, 26; international rebel groups trained by, 27–28; NATO countries and, 38–40; new technology lacking for, 33; not firing on citizens as, 25–26; serving numbers of, 30–31; 60% of economy run by, 28–30; social actions of, 26, 31–32; Soviet armament of, 28; Special Period slashing budgets of, 28–30; U.S. military cooperation with, 36, 40; Venezuela military differences to, 37–38. *See also* Anti-Air Defense and Revolutionary Air Force; Revolutionary Navy

da Conceição, Ercia, 156n52
da Costa Nunes, Ildefonso, 157n56
da Silva, Colombianus, 157n58
debt: China support for repayment of, 261–62; in economy, 44, *44*, *45*; Japan cancelling, 118; nations renegotiating, 17–18; potential U.S. influence on, *44*, 44–45, *45*; Putin forgiving, 256; to Russia, 240, 248, 251n26; Spain holding unpaid, 201
defense, 25–40
democracy promotion: EU softening of, 131–32; Harper on Cuba and, 195n9; Western decline of, 127
developing nations: Cuba relations with, 4–5; pharmaceuticals expertise to, 68–69
dissidents: Castro, F., crackdowns on, 11, 129, 130, 134, 203, 226; U.S. supporting, 6, 8, 162, 171

Ebola: assistance for, 71, 96, 103; Henry Reeve Brigade for, 70; recognition on, 60, 103
economy: ALADI for legitimacy of, 79; balance of trade in, 44, *44*; capitalist usefulness for, 117; Castro, R., reforms of, 127, 129, 144; China and U.S. cooperating in, 263; China suggestions on, 263–66; China teaching balance in, 264; Cuba as anti-market, 80; Cuba goals for, 286; Cuba pursuing path on, 285–86; EU relationship and, 125–26; external debt in, 44, *44*, *45*; FAR control of, 30, 41n10; FAR officers and, 28–30, 41n10; forces of change on, 142; foreign policy as choice on, 18–19; foreign policy as diversification of, 5; future dependent on, 286; GDP and Castro, R., administration, 44, *44*; goal for global integration of, 167–68; medical services benefit to, 142, *143*, 144; modifying structure of, 114; reforms for, 88; scenarios of future, 91–92; slowing of, 90–91; socialism and development of, 79–80; South Africa forgiving loans for, 104–5; Soviets for survival of, 128; Spain relationship and, 201; Special Period as challenging, 28, 142, 167; successes for, 54; threats to, 131; tourism benefit to, *143*, 144; 2016 strength in, 144–45; U.S. and potential for Cuba, 167; U.S. embargo deterring globalization of, 168; U.S. normalization and strategy for, 168, 172, 174; Venezuela and collapsing, 56–57, 88–89; Venezuela and slow Cuba growth of, 220–21; Venezuela cooperation dependent on, 219
Ecuador, 204, 288n17
Ejército Juvenil de Trabajo. *See* Youth Labor Army
EJT. *See* Youth Labor Army (Ejército Juvenil de Trabajo)
Escuela Latinoamericana de Medicina. *See* Latin American Medical School
EU. *See* European Union
EU normalization: development of, 127–28, 130; progress toward, 135–37

European Union (EU): Castro, F., evoking restrictions from, 130; Common Position and, 10–12; Common Position prompted by U.S., 202; Cuba focus on, 165; on Cuba human rights, 4, 11–12, 132; Cuba integrated by, 130, 133; Cuba interactions with U.S. and, 127; Cuba reinforcing focus on, 204; Cuba relations with, 10–12, 135–37; Cuba socialism and, 127; economic relationship with, 125–26; foreign policy of, 132–33; investments and, 134, 138; Latin America connected via Spain to, 202; nationalism, protectionism, self-interest and, 127; Obama link de-emphasizing, 204–5; Political Dialogue and Cooperation Agreement and, 10–11, 12, 127–28, 137; political reform urged by, 126; pragmatism and external factors of, 126–28, 132–33; softening on democracy promotion, 131–32; trade statistics with, 137; on Trump, 133, 135; U.S. embargo opposed by, 134; U.S. influencing relations with, 134, 135, 137, 138, 139; U.S. link and de-emphasizing, 204–5; Venezuela influencing relations with, 134, 137, 138–39

exports: to Brazil, 52–53, *53*, 231–32; Brazil statistics on, 226, 230, *231*, *232*; Cuban, 46–47, *47*, *48*, 49; to developed trading partners, *49*, 50; *Lineamientos* emphasizing, 61; medical internationalism as, 46–47, *47*; partners and statistics, 89; pharmaceuticals expertise as, 68–69; sugar as, 46, *47*; tourism in, 47, *48*; to Venezuela, 50, *50*

FAR. *See* Cuban Revolutionary Forces (Fuerzas Armadas Revolucionarias de Cuba)

FEMA. *See* Foreign Extraterritorial Measures Act

finance: Asia and, 115; Brazil bank as, 225, 229–30; United Kingdom and, 257

Foreign Extraterritorial Measures Act (FEMA), 194n6

foreign investment law: FTZ from, 53, 259–60; holdover problems from prior, 55; new, 54–55, 105, 142, 167–68

foreign policy: of EU, 132–33; goals of, 5, 18–19; realism theories of, 244–45; of Russia in 1990s, 245. *See also specific subjects*

France, 39, 107

Free Trade Area of the Americas (FTAA): ALBA alternative as, 9–10

free trade zone (FTZ): Brazil helping build Cuba, 85–86, 225–26; foreign investment law for, 53, 259–60; port of Mariel with, 52–53, 259

FTAA. *See* Free Trade Area of the Americas

FTZ. *See* free trade zone

Fuerzas Armadas Revolucionarias de Cuba. *See* Cuban Revolutionary Forces

GDP. *See* gross domestic product

Grenada, 79

Gross, Alan, 7, 164–66

gross domestic product (GDP), 44, *44*

Guantánamo naval base, 8, 9, 36, 185

Haiti, 70–71

hard currencies: Cuban American remittances for, 51–52, *52*, 167; income missed in, 47, *48*, 49; medical internationalism as source of, 62; tourism producing, 47, *48*

Harper, Stephen: Canada conservative as, 183, 184–89; Canada view of, 195n8; on Cuba and democracy, 195n9; Cuba non-acceptance by, 187, 189; trade as emphasis of, 195n13; U.S. alliance and, 185, 188

Helms-Burton Act, 202

Henry Reeve Brigade, 60, 69–70, 121. *See also* Cuban Medical Brigade

Hickey, John, 156n42

Historical Memory Law, 207n3

Hitler, Adolf, 252n50

human rights: China and Cuba on, 117; Cuba position on, 113–14, 119; EU on Cuba, 4, 11–12, 132; Harper on Cuba, 185; Harper refusing on U.S., 185; Latin America on Cuba and, 89; Mexico on Cuba and, 87; political prisoner release as, 136, 163–64; Rousseff avoiding Cuba, 226; Sánchez as critic on Cuba, 226; Spain measures on Cuba, 203; Western relaxation on, 127

Ibero-American Summits, 79, 89
illegal migration: Mexico and Cuba on, 88; MININT suppression of, 30; Revolutionary Navy and, 31; United Kingdom cooperation on, 39
India, 115–16, 121
internationalism: call for revolution abandoned in, 34, 78; Castro, F., and, 104; Castro, R., and socialist, 114, 122, 131; Communist Party of Cuba reaffirming, 101, 114; maintenance of, 117; in medicine, sports, education, arts, 34; supporting socialism, 97, 113–14. *See also* socialism
international relations, 3–5; under Castro, R., 129, 131, 271; of Cuba, 12–16; Cuba context in, 19n1; Cuban leader visits as, 20n21; FAR training rebel groups as, 27–28; foreign leader visits as, 13; medical internationalism for, 13; Special Period as broadening, 16–17
investments: Asia increasing, 122; Brazil and, 86, 91, 226–27, 229–33; China and, 165; China and automotive, 260; EU and, 134, 138; Mexico and, 79, 87–88; NAFTA sapping U.S., 55; new law for, 54–55, 105, 142, 167–68; Russia plans for, 239, 240; Spain and, 201, 206; in 2002-2013, 53; as of 2016, 144–45; before U.S. companies, 17, 44; U.S. companies and, 15, 170–71; U.S. embargo and, 114, 186; Venezuela and, 219–20
Islamic Republic of Iran, 81, 146, 257

Japan, 118
Jiménez, Yiliam, 156n42

LABIOFAM, 69
Latin American Integration Association (Asociación Latinoamericana de Integración, or ALADI), 79
Latin American Medical School (Escuela Latinoamericana de Medicina, or ELAM), 59, 106, 119; praise for, 72; sliding payment scale for, 63, 65, 70, 74n2, 101, 120, 142, 153, 284
Latin America region: ALBA as regionalism in, 82; ALBA-TCP and Cuba integration in, 83; alliances with, 93n12, 284–85; Argentina, Brazil, Mexico and rifts in, 93n12; Asia interest in, 115; assisting Russia in, 246–47, 250n19; autonomy in 1960s-80s for, 81; Brazil, Mexico, Venezuela as leaders in, 84; Castro, R., emphasis on, 277; with challenged revolution, 221; challenges for socialism in, 16; China instead of U.S. for, 81–82; China teaching socialism to, 261; Cold War end influencing, 89; country differences influencing, 83–84; on Cuba and human rights, 89; Cuba as anti-market economy in, 80; Cuba influencing agendas of, 83–84; Cuba role in, 77–92; Cuba supported in, 214; Cuba suspended in 1962 by, 79; diplomacy in, 89–90; focus on, 165; "honest broker" in, 80; medical internationalism in, 278–79; Mexico efforts in, 86–87; not exporting revolution to, 34, 78, 89–90; "pink tide" of socialism in, 16, 37, 79, 266, 277, 278, 284, 288n17; political cooperation in 2005 for, 81; Putin interest in, 275; role in Cuba as unlikely, 92; socialism principles lacking for, 264; Spain benefited by de-emphasis on, 204; Spain for EU connection to, 202; Special Period and involvement, 78; Third World support as capital in, 78; trade barrier reduction in 1980s-90s for, 81; U.S. and, 204–5; U.S. as ignoring, 81; U.S. de-emphasized by, 211; U.S. influenced by, 89; Venezuela and, 88–89; Venezuela and trade in, 46, *46*, 79
Lineamientos. *See* Resolution on the Guidelines of the Economic and Social Policy of the Party and the Revolution

literacy: for Australia Aboriginal population, 121, 141, *152*, 152–53; as "Yes, I Can," 152
Llero, Maité, 156n54
Lula da Silva, Luiz Inacio, 92n6, 225, 233

Maduro, Nicolás, 88–89, 215–18
Mais Médicos: with Brazil, 226–29; Brazil doctors program as, 52, 62–63; Brazil reducing, 86, 91; statistics of, 228
Malaysia, 118–19
Mandela, Nelson, 28, 74n12, 99, 285
Mao, Zedong, 260
Mariel port: Brazil investment in, 229–30, 259; China use of, 258, 259; FTZ in, 52–53, 259
Martín Díaz, Geidi, 156n53
Marx, Karl, 97, 109n14
medical education: Africa benefitting from, 96, 99, 102; Angola and, 105–6; for Asia-Oceania, 145–46, *148*; as medical internationalism, 55, 62–63; Namibia and, 106; Pacific Islands with, 147–49, *148*; Pakistan and, 121; private practice doctors and, 148–49, 152; South Africa receiving, 104; Timor-Leste with, 141, 146–47. *See also* Latin American Medical School
medical internationalism: Africa and, 96–97, 100–101, 106; Algeria as first, 100; Australia competition on, 150–51; "battle of ideas" in, 146; Brazil and, 52–53, 62–63, *65*; Bush rejecting offer of, 60; Castro, F., inaugurating, 59; Castro, R., changes in, 60–63, 66–73, 278–79; countries paying for, 73; countries served in, 5, 63, *64–65*; Cuba providing assistance with, 5; doctors defecting via, 217; economic benefit from, 142, *143*, 144; as exports, 46–47, *47*; geopolitics changed by, 145–46, 153; Haiti and doctors from, 70–71; hard currency source as, 62; Henry Reeve Brigade as, 60, 69–70, 121; human health before profit in, 68; international experience from, 62; international relations via, 13; *Lineamientos* and costs of, 61–62; medical education as, 55, 62–63; moral authority of, 278; Obama on, 278; Operación Milagro as, 59, 101–2; reliance on, 54–55; sliding payment scale in, 63, 65, 70, 74n2, 101, 120, 142, 153, 284; South Africa receiving, 104; statistics of, 59; with Timor-Leste, 120–21, 141, 146–47; unique institutional ethic of, 74n2; Venezuela and, 49, *49*, *50*, 56, 57n5, 142, 212, 217; WHO and support for, 70–71, 145
medical tourism, 71–72
Medina, Francisco, 155n31
Mercosur. *See* Common Market of South America
Mexico: counternarcotics and migration with, 88; on Cuba and human rights, 87; Cuba rapprochement with, 79; Cuba supported by, 92n4; investments and, 79, 87–88; Latin America and, 84, 86–87, 93n12; NAFTA and Latin America challenges for, 86, 88, 91; in Pacific Alliance, 82; U.S. and, 86, 91; U.S.-Cuba diplomacy enabling, 87; WTO on Cuba and, 87
military assistance: Africa countries receiving, 97–98, 108; ALBA and limited cooperation in, 37; Castro, R., and, 272–73; Russia and upkeep of, 176, 240–41, 248; U.S. and FAR cooperation in, 36, 40; Venezuela and, 37–38, 212, 214
MINFAR. *See* Ministry of Revolutionary Forces
MININT. *See* Ministry of the Interior
Ministry of Revolutionary Forces (MINFAR), 25, 35
Ministry of the Interior (MININT), 25; corruption countered by, 33–34; counternarcotics and migration with, 30, 35–36; United Kingdom connections with, 38–39
Mogherini, Federica, 10, 12–13, 125, 133, 137
Moncada Barracks, 26–27, 40n3
Monzón, Pedro, 157n70
Mozambique, 97–98

NAFTA. *See* North American Free Trade Agreement
NAM. *See* Non-Aligned Movement
Namibia, 97–99, 104, 106
National Office of Statistics (Oficina Nacional de Estadísticas, or ONE), 43, 57n1
NATO. *See* North Atlantic Treaty Organization
Netherlands, 39–40, 107
New Zealand, 121, 152
Nicaragua: ALBA-TCP commerce and trade and, 212; "pink tide" and Cuba by, 288n17; Sandinistas taking power in, 93n19; shifting from Cuba, 204
Nobel Peace Prize, 70
Non-Aligned Movement (NAM): Cuba and, 273, 287n6; Cuba leading, 4–5; Yugoslavia and, 287n4
North American Free Trade Agreement (NAFTA): Mexico and challenges from, 86, 88, 91; Trump policy flip-flops on, 288n25; U.S. investments sapped by, 55
North Atlantic Treaty Organization (NATO): EU on Trump and, 133, 135; FAR and countries of, 38–40; Trudeau, P. and visit as, 185–86
Norway, 206
nuclear arms, 119

OAS. *See* Organization of American States
Obama, Barack: Communist Party of Cuba on talks with, 15; Cubans not trusting, 171; Cuba policy by, 162–64; Cuba visit by, 7, 14–15, 130; EU and Spain link de-emphasized by, 204–5; "honest broker" role pressuring, 80; on medical internationalism, 278; rapprochement by, 177; restrictions reduced by, 7–8; Summit of the Americas confronting, 166; U.S.-Cuba dialogue under, 6–7, 130, 135, 166; U.S.-Cuba normalization and, 257
Oficina Nacional de Estadísticas. *See* National Office of Statistics
oil: Angola and exploration for, 106; Brazil helping with Cuba, 85; Castro, R., and Venezuela, 274; China and, 117–18; import of Venezuelan, 220; imports dependence, 54; medical assistance for, 142; potential deposits of, 54; Russia sending, 275; U.S. interests in Cuba, 256–57; Venezuela and, 210–12; Venezuela cutting supplies of, 89, 91; Venezuela expansion and contraction on, 49, *49*, *50*, 56–57, 220; Venezuela influenced by, 88
ONE. *See* National Office of Statistics (Oficina Nacional de Estadísticas)
Operación Milagro, 59, 101–2, 217
Organization of American States (OAS), 79, 83, 85

Pacific Alliance, 82, 93n12
Pacific Islands: medical education for, 147–49, *148*; private doctor resistance in, 148–49, 152; relations and health care with, 119–20
Pakistan, 60, 69–70, 121
Panama, 89
Papua New Guinea (PNG), 148–49, 151
Patriarch Kirill, 14, 242
People's Republic of Korea (PRK), 119
Peru, 82
pharmaceuticals: BioCubaFarma for biotechnology and, 68; Brazil and Cuba with vaccine as, 102–3; Brazil importing Cuba, 232; cancer vaccines as, 67–68, 276; Castro, F., starting in 1980s, 67; Cuba exporting to U.S., 170; expertise as exported, 68–69; Heberprot-P treatment for diabetes, 67–68; influenza vaccine as, 68; meningococcal meningitis vaccine as, 102–3; Polo Científico producing, 67; for southern countries, 102; statistics, 67–68; U.S. joint ventures in, 67, 276
Philippines, 118
"pink tide" of socialism: Latin America countries in, 288n17; Latin America with, 16, 37, 79, 266, 277, 278, 284; trade reversal and, 278
PNG. *See* Papua New Guinea
Political Dialogue and Cooperation Agreement, 203; EU and Cuba

under, 10–11, 12, 130, 137; EU from Common Position to, 127–28
political prisoners: Cuban Five as, 7, 164–67, 241; Gross as, 7, 164–66; human rights as release of, 136, 163–64; Sarraff Trujillo as, 166; Villar as, 226
Polo Científico, 67
Pope Francis, 7, 14–15
PRK. *See* People's Republic of Korea
property rights, 8, 26, 168
Putin, Vladimir, 20; Castro, R., and, 165, 237, 239–40, 242, 274; on Cuba relationship, 238; debt forgiven by, 256; Latin America interest by, 275; "Putin Doctrine" of, 245, 246, 249

Quebec, 190–93

Ramón Balaguer, José, 156n42
regime change: Cuba protecting against, 128–31; U.S. dropping goal of, 170; U.S. still funding, 171
remittances: Chinese consumer goods and U.S., 258; Cuban Americans sending, 2, 8, 163; hard currencies and increasing, 51–52, *52*, 167; limits on, 4; U.S. normalization and, 52, 169, 210, 258
Republic of Korea, 119
Resolution on the Guidelines of the Economic and Social Policy of the Party and the Revolution (*Lineamientos*), 62; Communist Party of Cuba passing, 61, 144, 167–68; exports emphasized in, 61
revolution: abandoning export of, 34, 78, 89–90; foreign policy and survival of, 245; Latin America with challenged, 221; Venezuela and, 209–10, 219
Revolutionary Navy, 31
Rice, Condoleezza, 6, 19n6
Rigñak, Alberto, 155n29
Rousseff, Dilma: Brazil relationship during, 225–26; Brazil role changing after, 84, 85; Cuba experiences with, 226–27; Cuba human rights avoided by, 226; impeachment of, 16, 52–53, 62–63, 84–85, 226
Russia: alliance with, 129; Asia-Oceania with, 115–16; backing in UN by, 246; biotechnology links with, 240; Castro, R., visiting, 237, 249n1; China split with, 260; Crimea and, 238; Cuba as U.S. irritant by, 246; Cuba military bases and, 176; cultural performances by, 241; debt held by, 240, 248, 251n26; dependence on, 275; diversification and influence of, 243–44; investment plans of, 239, 240; Latin America and, 246–47, 250n19; military and upkeep by, 240–41, 248; 1990s foreign policy of, 245; normalization with, 253n77; oil statistics, 275; Orthodox Christian cathedral, 241–42; Putin Doctrine of, 245, 246, 249; rapprochement with, 274–75; relationship with, 165, 237–38, 242, 244–49; tourism statistics with, 242–43; trade statistics with, 239; trade with, 16, 212, 240, 247; on U.S. embargo, 238; on U.S. normalization with Cuba, 238, 241, 248
Russian Orthodox Church, 14, 15, 241–42

Sánchez, Yoani, 226
São Paulo Forum, 92n6
Sarraff Trujillo, Rolando, 166
Servicios Médicos Cubanos S.A., 71–72
slaves: Africa statistics of, 95; Castro, R., on history of, 99, 100; Cuba and history with, 95, 97, 99; United Kingdom, Netherlands, France and lawsuit on, 107
Smith, Wayne, 6
socialism: Asia-Oceania and, 115, 122; capitalism with, 264; China and Cuba retaining, 167, 262–63; China and Latin America learning, 261; China and modified, 255–56; China students and Cuba affinity on, 263–64; China view on Cuba, 266; Cuba and future of, 283, 289n31; Cuba and modified, 255–56; Cuba goals for, 286–87; Cuba purer than China in, 262; Cuba retaining, 288n24; economic development and, 79–80; EU and Cuba, 127; internationalism supporting, 97, 113–

14; lack of equality in Chinese, 265, 266; Latin America lacking principles for, 264; São Paulo Forum meeting and, 92n6; Venezuela and, 211; Vietnam model of market, 167. *See also* "pink tide" of socialism
Solomon Islands, 146
Somare, Michael, 156n42
South Africa: apartheid clashes with, 97–98, 103–4, 106; forgiving loans, 104–5; wartime statistics on, 98. *See also* Mandela, Nelson
South-South organizations: ALBA for cooperation in, 82; ALBA-TCP for cooperation in, 221; Castro, R., on, 273, 286, 287n6; medical internationalism and, 72; pharmaceuticals for countries in, 102
Soviet Union: Castro, F., enjoying oil of, 274; China rapprochement after collapse of, 263, 266; dependence on, 210; economic survival with, 128; effective sovereignty counterbalance as, 280; FAR and, 28; Stalin of, 252n50; thanks to, 241; U.S. embargo balanced with, 128
Spain: Castro, F., disparaging, 198; Castro, R., relations and, 205–7; Common Position initiated by, 202–3; companies and tourism, 201; continuous diplomatic relations with, 198; Cuba and Galicia region of, 200; Cuba and political parties in, 126; Cuba history with, 197–201; democratic approach of, 200–201; economic relationship with, 201; EU and Latin America via, 202; as "ever-faithful" to, 198–99; with "foreign policy of substitution," 199–200; Historical Memory Law of, 207n3; human rights measures on Cuba, 203; importance of, 197, 207; independence accepted by, 199; internal politics of, 198; investments and, 201, 206; Latin America de-emphasis benefiting, 204; Obama link de-emphasizing, 204–5; political change and Cuba softening, 203; reinforcing focus on, 204; Special Period connections to, 202; unpaid debts to, 201
Special Period: air force influenced by, 31; Chernobyl Program during, 66; China assistance through, 260, 261; economy challenged by, 28, 142, 167; FAR budgets slashed during, 28–29; international relations after, 16–17; Latin America involvement during, 78; Revolutionary Navy hurt by, 31; Spain connections during, 202; Venezuela decline and potential, 57
Stalin, Joseph, 252n50
Summit of the Americas: Cuba invited to Seventh, 89, 165; gradual inclusion in, 90; Obama confronted at, 166
Syria, 238

Taiwan, 117
telecommunications, 117–18, 169–70
Temer, Michel, 226, 234
terrorism, 7
Timor-Leste: healthcare as social support in, 150; medical education with, 141, 146–47; medical internationalism with, 120–21, 141, 146–47; private doctor resistance in, 148–49, 152
tourism: Asia increasing, 122; Canada as largest in, 55, 186; China and, 117; Cuba citizens and services for, 2; economic benefit from, *143*, 144; exports as, 47, *48*; hard currencies from, 47, *48*; income missed as leakage in, 47, *48*, 49, 55–56; Russia and statistics of, 242–43; Spanish companies in Cuba, 201; Trump and prospects for, 56, 276–77; U.S. and statistics on, 276; U.S. citizens and, 7, 58n13; U.S. potential for, 55–56. *See also* medical tourism
trade: Asia and Asia-Oceania, 121–22; Australia and potential for, 121; Brazil and, 52–53, *53*, 79, 86; Brazil statistics on, 230–32, *231*, *232*; Canada and, 185, 188, 192, 247; Castro, R., and expansion of, 52–53, *53*; with China, 17, 50–51, *51*, 79, 256–60, *258*; China and statistics of, 257, *258*; Cuba goals for, 287; diversification of regional, 45–46, *46*; EU statistics on, 137;

evolution of, 49, *49*; foreign investment law for, 53, 259–60; Harper emphasis on Canada, 195n13; Latin America reducing barriers for, 81; Mexico-Cuba, 87–88; partners in, *49*, 49–51, *50*, *51*; partners in retreat, 91; "pink tide" reversal and, 278; Russia and, 16, 239, 240, 247; Russia statistics in, 239; with South Africa, 105; U.S. embargo continuing, 114, 116; U.S. with goods and services in, 275, *275*; Venezuela and, 46, *46*, 212, *213*; Venezuela dependence in, 220, 247, 253n72; Venezuela expansion and contraction in, 10, *49*, 49–50, *50*, 56–57, 79, 287n8; Venezuela statistics on, 247; Vietnam as partner in, 118

Trudeau, Justin: Canada as liberal with, 183–84; on Castro, F., death, 194; proactive diplomacy of, 189–93

Trudeau, Pierre, 185–86

Trump, Donald: Castro, R., on, 174, 175; Cuba policy flip-flops of, 172–76, 281, 283; on Cuba relations, 288n26; EU reaction to, 133, 135; future interactions with, 281–82; NAFTA policy flip-flops of, 288n25; as opportunistic, 257; policy regression by, 177; potential policies of, 9, 138–39; tourism prospects under, 56, 276–77

Ukraine, 66

United Kingdom: CARICOM slavery lawsuit against, 107; Castro, R., softening stance of, 206; counternarcotics and migration with, 38–39; Cuba and financial services of, 257

United Nations: Canada losing Security Council seat in, 188; Russia backing Cuba in, 246; U.S. abstaining on embargo vote at, 8, 127; U.S. embargo condemned at, 4, 119, 165–66

United States (U.S.), 2; authorized activities by, 168–70; balance of trade influence by, *44*, 44–45; Brazil not challenging, 85; businesses and Cuba bureaucracy, 170–71; Canada and, 194n6, 194n7; Castro, R., on, 130, 161–64, 177–78, 280; China and, 258, 261, 263–66; counternarcotics activity with, 35–36, 41n15; Cuba and U.S. dollar transactions, 170; Cuba diplomats expelled by, 176; Cuba economy potential and, 167; Cuban Five jailed by, 7, 164–67, 241; Cuba oil and interest of, 256–57; Cuba weakening by, 169; dissidents supported by, 6, 8, 162, 171; diversification and influence of, 243; doctors defecting to, 217; effective sovereignty and, 279–80; EU-Cuba relations influenced by, 134, 135, 137, 138, 139; EU on Cuba and, 127, 204–5; external debt and trade influence from, *44*, 44–45, *45*; FAR military cooperation with, 36, 40; future influence of, 281–82; goods and services with, 275, *275*; Grenada invasion as warning from, 79; Gross release demanded by, 7, 164–66; Guantánamo naval base and, 8, 9; Harper and alliance with, 185, 188; Helms-Burton Act of, 202; importance of, 34–36; investments before entry of, 17, 44; investments by companies of, 15, 170–71; Latin America and, 81–82, 89, 204–5, 211; laws against Cuba, 5–6; as marginalized, 285; Mexico and, 86, 91; mistrust of, 177–78; NAFTA sapping investments of, 55; pharmaceuticals and, 67, 170, 276; policy change on Cuba, 167; regime change goal and, 170, 171; rejected by, 164–65, 283; Russia and Cuba as irritant for, 246; "sonic attacks" reprisal of, 1, 175–77, 277; sports exchange with, 191; Syria action of, 238; telecommunications investments of, 169–70; tourism and, 55–56, 276; trade with, 275, *275*; 2016 elections in, 172–74; Venezuela emphasizing Cuba and not, 88, 211

U.S. *See* United States

U.S. Chamber of Commerce, 15

U.S. citizens, 1; Cuba and tourism by, 7, 58n13

U.S.-Cuba: citizens approval of, 172; cooperation on Guantánamo, 36; diplomatic negotiations, 168, 189; Japan and, 118; Mexico enabled by diplomacy of, 87; Obama and normalization of, 6–7, 130, 135, 166, 257; regulations incompatibility of, 169; U.S. embargo slowing negotiations of, 168
U.S. embargo, 5; allies for counterbalancing, 78, 79, 81, 83, 90, 176, 210, 284; AU condemning, 95–96; CELAC discussions on, 227; condemned at UN, 4, 119, 165–66; as continuing, 114, 116; economic globalization deterred by, 168; EU opposing, 134; foreign investments and, 114, 186; introduction of, 130; normalization as tenuous, 56, 135, 139, 177, 205, 257, 276, 280; redress for influence of, 8; Russia on, 238; Soviets for balancing, 128; Timor-Leste support and U.S., 120; U.S. abstaining and UN vote on, 8, 127; U.S. Chamber of Commerce against, 15; U.S.-Cuba negotiations slowed by, 168
U.S. normalization: with Cuba, 5–9; Cuban Americans opposing, 91, 138, 161–62; without dependence, 5, 18, 248; economic strategy of, 168, 172, 174; hindrances to, 8; political prisoner talks and, 166; remittance inflows and, 52, 169, 210, 258; as restricting, 91; Russia on Cuba and, 238, 241, 248; U.S. embargo perpetuating tenuous, 56, 135, 139, 177, 205, 257, 276, 280

Venezuela: ALBA-TCP commerce and trade and, 212; balanced exports to, 50, *50*; bourgeois of the Bolivarian model in, 214; Castro, R., mistake as, 274; Castro, R., supporting, 215, 217–19; chaos in, 271–72; Chávez and Cuba revolution in, 209; crisis in, 204, *213*, 220; Cuba emphasis by, 211; Cuba slow economic growth and, 220–21; economic collapse of, 56–57; economic reforms and exiting, 88; economy determining cooperation with, 219; EU-Cuba relations influenced by, 134, 137, 138–39; FAR differences to military of, 37–38; investments and, 219–20; Latin America leader as, 84; as major trading partner, 212, *213*; medical internationalism for, 49, *49*, *50*, 56, 57n5, 142, 217; military assistance to, 212, 214; oil and Cuba connections, 89, 91, 210–12; oil imported from, 49, *49*, *50*, 56–57, 220; "one revolution" with, 219; Operación Milagro for, 217; opposition politics and Cuba, 216; "pink tide" and Cuba by, 288n17; private enterprise continuing in, 209; privatization and executive branch of, 214; problems for Cuba, 10; regional trade influence from, 46, *46*, 79; relations with, 9–10, 19n11, 128–29; revolution differences and similarities with, 209–10; socialist politics of, 211; Special Period and, 57; trade dropping with, 10, *49*, 49–50, *50*, 56–57, 79, 287n8; trade statistics with, 247; trade with, 46, *46*, 220, 247, 253n72
Vietnam, 118, 122–23, 167
Villar, Wilman, 226

World Health Organization (WHO), 59, 70–71, 142
World Trade Organization (WTO), 87

Youth Labor Army (Ejército Juvenil de Trabajo, or EJT), 30
Yugoslavia, 287n4

About the Contributors

H. Michael Erisman is professor of international affairs at Indiana State University. He has published eight books. Among those focusing on Cuban affairs are *Cuba's International Relations: The Anatomy of a Nationalistic Foreign Policy* (1985), *Cuba's Foreign Relations in a Post-Soviet World* (2000), and *Cuban Medical Internationalism: Origins, Evolution and Goals* (2010, with John Kirk). With Kirk he has also coedited *Cuban Foreign Policy Confronts a New International Order* (1991) and *Redefining Cuban Foreign Policy: The Impact of the "Special Period"* (2006).

John M. Kirk is professor of Latin American studies at Dalhousie University. He has published several books on Cuba, of which the most pertinent are *Healthcare without Borders: Understanding Cuban Medical Internationalism* (2015), *Cuban Medical Internationalism: Origins, Evolution and Goals* (2010, with Michael Erisman), and *Cuba in the International System: Normalization and Integration* (1995, with Archibald Ritter).

Tim Anderson is senior lecturer in political economy at the University of Sydney. He is author of *Land and Livelihoods in Papua New Guinea* (2015), *Aid: Is It Worth It?* (2012), and *In Defence of Melanesian Customary Land* (2010). He also wrote *Latin America, the Caribbean and the South West Pacific: Opportunities for South-South Cooperation* (United Nations Development Program report, 2012). He has written extensively about Cuban medical cooperation in Timor-Leste and the South Pacific.

Mervyn Bain is senior lecturer at the University of Aberdeen and has published widely on the relationship between Moscow and Havana. He is author of three books on bilateral ties: *Soviet-Cuban Relations 1985 to 1991: Changing Perceptions in Moscow and Havana* (2006), *Russian-Cuban Relations since 1992: Continuing*

Camaraderie in a Post-Soviet World (2008), and *From Lenin to Castro, 1917–1959: Early Encounters between Moscow and Havana* (2013).

Regiane Nitsch Bressan is professor of international relations at the University of São Paulo. Her research focuses on issues of Latin American integration. She has published widely on political developments in South America, was a visiting professor at the University of Salamanca in Spain, and is a frequent commentator on Latin American affairs in the Brazilian media.

Susanne Gratius is professor of international relations at the Autonomous University of Madrid and a former researcher for the think tank FRIDE (2005–2013). Before that she worked at the German Institute for International and Security Affairs in Berlin and the Ibero-American Studies Institute in Hamburg. Her research focuses on EU–Latin American relations, Cuba, Venezuela, Brazil, and emerging powers.

Adrian H. Hearn is associate professor at the University of Melbourne. His research focuses on social challenges and opportunities arising from Asia-Pacific integration. He is author of *Diaspora and Trust: Cuba, Mexico and the Rise of China* (2016) and coeditor of *China and the New Triangular Relationships in the Americas: China and the Future of U.S.-Mexican Relations* (2013) and *China Engages Latin America: Tracing the Trajectory* (2011).

Rafael Hernández is chief editor of *Temas*, Cuba's leading magazine in the social sciences. He has been professor at the University of Havana, director of U.S. studies at the Centro de Estudios sobre América (a think tank of the Cuban Communist Party Central Committee), and a senior fellow at El Instituto Juan Marinello in Havana. He authored *Looking at Cuba: Essays on Culture and Civil Society* (2001), *The Other War: Studies on Strategy and International Security* (2001), and *Vietnam, China and Cuban Foreign Policies towards the United States* (2015); he coauthored *The History of Havana* (2006) and coedited *Play Ball! Debating US-Cuban Relations* (2015).

Hal Klepak is professor emeritus of history and strategy at the Royal Military College of Canada and special adviser on inter-American army affairs to the commander of the Canadian army. He is a frequent adviser to the Canadian foreign and defense ministries. His latest books are *Churchill Comes of Age: Cuba 1895* (2015), *Raúl Castro: A Military Story* (2012), and *Cuba's Military 1900–2005: Revolutionary Soldiers in Counter-revolutionary Times* (2006).

William M. LeoGrande is associate vice provost for academic affairs and professor of government at American University in Washington, DC. He has written widely on Latin American politics and U.S. policy toward Latin America. Most recently he is coauthor of *Back Channel to Cuba: The Hidden History of Negotiations between*

Washington and Havana (2014). He is also author of *Our Own Backyard: The United States in Central America, 1977–1992* (1998) and *Cuba's Policy in Africa* (1980).

Pedro Monzón is affiliated with the International Policy Research Center and previously served as Cuba's ambassador to Malaysia and to Australia and as its concurrent ambassador in Timor-Leste, Brunei, Solomon Islands, Vanuatu, Papua New Guinea, and Nauru.

Eduardo Regalado Florido has published widely on Asian affairs as the head of the Asia Section of the International Policy Research Center (Centro de Investigaciones de Política Internacional) in Havana.

Raúl Rodríguez is director of the Center for Hemispheric and United States Studies at the University of Havana. He has been a visiting scholar and guest lecturer at Canadian, UK, U.S., and Latin American universities on topics related to Cuban foreign policy and U.S.-Cuban/Canadian-Cuban relations. His most recent publications include "US Foreign Policy towards Cuba: Traditional Explanations and Levels of Analysis," *International Journal of Cuban Studies* (2014, with Harry Targ) and "US Economic Sanctions on Cuba: An International Ethics Perspective," *LASA Forum* (2016).

Carlos A. Romero is a retired professor/researcher at the Instituto de Estudios Políticos of the Universidad Central de Venezuela in Caracas. He has published seven books, coedited seventeen others, and published over 130 academic articles. He has also been a commentator on many occasions, analyzing international developments in various forms of social communication, both in Venezuela and throughout Latin America.

Joaquín Roy is Jean Monnet Professor and director of the University of Miami European Union Center of Excellence. He is author or editor of forty books, among them *Cuba, the U.S. and the Helms-Burton Doctrine: International Reactions* (2000), *The European Union and Regional Integration* (2005), and *The Cuban Revolution (1959–2009): Its Relationship with Spain, the European Union and the United States* (2009). He was awarded the Encomienda of the Order of Merit by King Juan Carlos of Spain.

Isaac Saney is director of the Transition Programme at Dalhousie University and adjunct professor of history at Saint Mary's University. He is cochair and national spokesman of the Canadian Network on Cuba. He is author of *Cuba: A Revolution in Motion* and is currently working on a new book, *Africa's Children: Cuba, the War in Angola and the End of Apartheid.*

Andrés Serbin is president of the Coordinadora Regional de Investigaciones Económicas y Sociales (CRIES), a network of over seventy research centers, think tanks, foundations, nongovernmental organizations, and professional associations, and former director of Caribbean affairs of the Sistema Económico Latinoamericano (SELA). A professor at the Universidad Central de Venezuela, he is author or editor of over thirty books.